❧ Divining History ❧

MAKING SENSE OF HISTORY
Studies in Historical Cultures
General Editor: Stefan Berger
Founding Editor: Jörn Rüsen

Bridging the gap between historical theory and the study of historical memory, this series crosses the boundaries between both academic disciplines and cultural, social, political and historical contexts. In an age of rapid globalization, which tends to manifest itself on an economic and political level, locating the cultural practices involved in generating its underlying historical sense is an increasingly urgent task.

For a full volume listing please see back matter

DIVINING HISTORY

Prophetism, Messianism and the Development of the Spirit

Jayne Svenungsson
Translated by Stephen Donovan

berghahn
NEW YORK • OXFORD
www.berghahnbooks.com

First published in 2016 by
Berghahn Books
www.berghahnbooks.com

English-language edition © 2016, 2021 Jayne Svenungsson
First paperback edition published in 2021

Originally published in Swedish in 2014 as *Den gudomliga historien: profetism, messianism och andens utveckling* by Glänta

All rights reserved. Except for the quotation of short passages for the purposes of criticism and review, no part of this book may be reproduced in any form or by any means, electronic or mechanical, including photocopying, recording, or any information storage and retrieval system now known or to be invented, without written permission of the publisher.

Library of Congress Cataloging-in-Publication Data

Names: Svenungsson, Jayne, author.
Title: Diving history : prophetism, messianism, and the development of the spirit / Jayne Svenungsson ; translated by Stephen Donovan.
Other Titles: Gudomliga historien. English
Description: First edition. | New York : Berghahn Books, 2016 | Series: Making sense of history ;Volume 26| Includes bibliographical references and index.
Identifiers: LCCN 2016025129 (print) | ISBN 9781785331732 (hardback : alk. paper) | ISBN 9781785331749 (ebook)
Subjects: LCSH: Jewish philosophy. | History--Religious aspects. | Christianity.
Classification: LCC B5802.U86 S9413 2016 | DDC 181/.06--dc23
LC record available at hnps://lccn.loc.gov/2016025129

British Library Cataloguing in Publication Data
A catalogue record for this book is available from the British Library

ISBN 978-1-78533-173-2 hardback
ISBN 978-1-80073-217-9 paperback
ISBN 978-1-78533-174-9 ebook

Contents

Preface	vii
Chapter 1. The God of History	1
Chapter 2. The Ages of History	35
Chapter 3. Romantic History	64
Chapter 4. History after God	105
Chapter 5. The Politics of History	151
Postscript. A Theopolitical Vision	203
Bibliography	207
Index	217

Preface

From the vantage point of the present, long swathes of the twentieth century today resemble a wasteland, in which grandiose political, scientific and architectural visions lie scattered about like toppled gravestones. Time and again, what began with a starry-eyed faith in humanity's boundless abilities was followed by withdrawal into a self-created world of horror. The twentieth century is often described as the godless century. But it might be closer to the mark to think of it as the century in which humanity itself took the place of God. Where history was previously thought of as lying within the shielding embrace of God, twentieth-century humanity took history into its own hands and established its own furthest goals for history. The century's grand utopian social projects stand as reckless and devastating attempts to realize those goals.

Such at least is how these projects were regarded in the aftermath of the Second World War. During these years Europe's intellectuals exerted themselves to put into perspective the atrocities of the past decades. Such analyses not infrequently had a political subtext. Doubtless the best known to posterity of these is the succession of liberal thinkers, from Karl Popper and Isaiah Berlin to the Swedish political scientist Herbert Tingsten, who sought to trace the origins of totalitarian ideology back to the grandiose philosophies of history of the nineteenth century. But liberals were not alone in shouldering this task. Theodor Adorno and Max Horkheimer's *Dialectic of Enlightenment*, perhaps the most famous response from the Marxist quarter, appeared as early as 1944, and a decade later Georg Lukács delivered a comprehensive indictment of the entire 'irrational' legacy of German thought, 'from Schelling to Hitler'.[1] Conservatives, too, offered analyses, of which the most famous is associated with the German political thinker Eric Voegelin.

Within a historico-philosophical context, the classic work is Karl Löwith's *Meaning in History* from 1949. In just over three hundred pages Löwith sketches the genealogy of a historical perspective that paved the way for the utopian

---

Notes for this section begin on page xiv.

ideologies of modernity. By revealing the mythological conceptions behind the notion of progress, he seeks to persuade us moderns to abandon the dream of creating a heaven on earth. With a view to further establishing the folly inherent in the idea of historical progression, Löwith chooses to present history in reverse. Taking his cue from Jacob Burckhardt, he presents a lineage running through Marx, Hegel, Proudhon, Comte, Condorcet, Voltaire, Vico, Bossuet, Joachim of Fiore, Augustine and Orosius, ending with the Bible. For Löwith, it is not enough to try to locate the roots of modern utopias in the Enlightenment and Romanticism. Rather, the problem lies in the biblical legacy as such. For it was there that humanity for the first time began to conceive of history as *divine*, as an eschatological drama of damnation and redemption governed by divine providence. This conception persisted and was refined during the entire medieval period, reaching its culmination in the millenarian dreams of Joachim of Fiore. With the eventual fading of the biblical worldview, humanity turned its faith in a suprahistorical object towards history itself. Thus was born the modern utopia of a definitively just society, an idea that generated successive totalitarian projects in which the ends justified the means.

The anti-utopian tradition which Löwith sets out has been further developed by a series of studies ranging from Norman Cohn's *The Pursuit of the Millennium* (1957) to John Gray's bestselling *Black Mass: Apocalyptic Religion and the Death of Utopia* (2007). Their shared thesis is that the supposedly secular ideologies which underpin Western modernity ultimately derive their inspiration from a Jewish and Christian messianic tradition. For his part, Gray laconically observes that 'modern revolutionary movements are a continuation of religion by other means'.[2]

The question is whether this is exclusively evil – that is to say, whether the history of Western theology is only ever a burden upon modern political thought. In the following study I propose to develop this line of enquiry. In parallel with the comprehensive critique of utopia that spread in the wake of the Second World War, a series of thinkers, primarily of Jewish heritage, have emerged to defend the prophetic tradition. Their number includes Ernst Bloch, Martin Buber, Abraham Heschel, Yehezkel Kaufmann, Gershom Scholem and Jacob Taubes, to name but a few. These thinkers differ from each other in several key respects. What they share, however, is a rejection of the idea that the biblical legacy has been discredited by the violent ideologies of modernity. While such a connection can undeniably be made, the same tradition contains quite different potentialities. It was the ancient Jewish prophets who first advanced the idea of a God for all of humanity. In their dream of all people returning to the God of Israel, these prophets extended what had initially been a national idea into a universal vision. History is where this vision will be realized, and it is humanity's vocation to realize in its everyday life the higher justice that is the ultimate goal of history. In this way, thinkers such as Bloch and Taubes, in sharp contrast to those who reflexively reject the biblical legacy, are able to argue that the prophetic promise of impending redemption has throughout history inspired people to revolt against unjust and oppressive orders.

The present analysis will situate itself theoretically between these two poles of twentieth-century debate over the theological underpinnings of history. Although I do not deny that this book has been inspired in part by Löwith's classic study, my intention is to show that the theology of history to which the biblical legacy gave rise is nowhere as one-dimensional as postwar anti-utopian writers often imply. In this respect I have been considerably inspired by those many writers who have identified the enduring theological, philosophical and political value of the biblical legacy.

Any critical discussion of the biblical legacy must concede that it, like all the great traditions of thought, contains numerous tensions and contradictions. In this case, the most fundamental tension stems from the fact that two different traditions – Jewish and Christian – lay claim to the same narratives. And yet throughout history the relationship between these two traditions has been anything but symmetrical, something that is reflected *inter alia* in the theological claims made by each party with regard to history. Christian theology of history, which has to a considerable degree defined Western views of history, can essentially be said to have arisen as part of the early church's efforts to differentiate itself from the majority of Jews, who did not acknowledge Jesus of Nazareth as the Messiah. From an early stage, Christian commentators developed an account of history in which Christians were presented as having assumed the role of God's chosen people. This line of reasoning rested upon a dialectic that associated Judaism with the past, closure and materiality, while Christianity for its part was identified with the future, openness and spirituality. With the dawning of the new era, Christian theologies of history were transformed into more or less secularized philosophies of history, which sublimated several of the inherited anti-Jewish tropes and carried them forward into a modern, secular Europe.

This problematic, something Jacques Derrida has characterized as a 'duel between Christian and Jew', forms a recurrent theme in my argument. In this respect this study has an entirely different starting point from the aforementioned critiques of utopianism, which almost exclusively consider the 'Judaeo-Christian' tradition as a unitary whole. What follows will not only map out the complex interrelationship of these two strands of the Western historico-theological tradition but also break with the stereotyping tendency to connect Judaism with the particular and Christianity with the universal. On the contrary, I assert that both these traditions are complex and include deeply heterogeneous elements, with the result that the line of demarcation rarely runs between the two traditions, more commonly being found, rather, within each of them. That such is the case will become readily apparent when, for example, the messianic motif in each tradition is addressed in order to highlight the resulting differences in their respective relations to history.

The argument presented here also differs methodologically from several of the classic accounts of the Western historico-theological legacy. The occasional tendency towards one-sidedness exhibited by such studies can largely be traced to their scope and the nature of their claims. Löwith's *Meaning in History* offers an illustrative example. The study outlines an intellectual trajectory reaching from antiquity to the last century, a chronological span that comes, not unexpectedly, at the price of analytical depth in its treatment of those thinkers represented in Löwith's argument. Furthermore, if Löwith's attempt to offer a panoramic overview of the Western notion of history were to be repeated, it would today be necessary to cover the complex historico-philosophical debates of the twentieth century (in which Löwith himself represents a central figure). Given this background, it is self-evidently neither desirable nor feasible to seek to achieve the kind of comprehensive chronicle that Löwith sets out for himself.

In an attempt to unite breadth with depth, I have chosen in the present study to combine a chronological disposition with a thematic one. Their connecting thread comprises three central historico-theological motifs, namely, *prophetism*, *messianism* and *the development of the spirit* (the latter will additionally be examined in terms of a *pneumatic* motif). The intention is thus not to make an exhaustive description of the historical development of these intellectual motifs. Instead, the following five chapters offer a series of strategic case studies from different periods, showing how a close reading of selected texts can enable identification of a revealing continuity of motifs across time.

A methodological approach of this kind nonetheless raises the question of selectivity. Given the virtual inexhaustibility of the Western intellectual tradition, why focus on these five case studies in particular? The rationale behind this selectivity is an already established history of theological and philosophical influence (*Wirkungsgeschichte*), which involves a number of interconnected thinkers and works. My aim, however, is not only to inscribe myself in this history of influence, but simultaneously to problematize it. Although this account follows a chronological axis, it resembles Löwith's structure insofar as it traces a history of influence that is extrapolated from later historical developments. It is, in other words, a genealogy of the contemporary politico-philosophical debate that leads back to particular interventions in late-twentieth-century debates, which in turn points backwards to a line running from German Romanticism, via medieval Christianity, to the Bible. A brief summary of the structure of the book will clarify this perspective.

Chapter One, 'The God of History', re-examines the ways in which the prophetic, messianic and pneumatic motifs were originally constituted in antiquity. The textual focus here is the prophetic literature in the Hebrew Bible – that is, the Old Testament of the Christian Bible. Engaging critically with these texts necessitates something of a detour through exegetical scholarship, for which reason the discussion is grounded as far as possible on current perspectives on the prophetic literature. Since my intention is to highlight the politico-philosophical potential of these texts that subsequent thinkers have drawn upon, I also take my lead from Martin Buber, Abraham Heschel and Yehezkel Kaufmann. In the middle of the last century these Jewish writers, as mentioned above, published a series of famous works that treated the ethical and political value of the prophetic literature. Drawing on the argument of these thinkers, the central thesis of this chapter is that biblical historico-theological motifs in a number of respects laid the basis for the understanding of history that would become dominant in the Western civilization.

Chapter Two, 'The Ages of History', describes how the prophetic tradition was taken up by the medieval theologian Joachim of Fiore. Joachim and the ancient prophets are separated not only by more than a thousand years but also by the birth and expansion of Christianity. The opening sub-section presents a concise overview of how Christian theology of history emerged partly as a way to control Christianity's relationship to the Judaic tradition from which it gradually distanced itself, and partly as an attempt to account for the deferral of the Second Coming. In the writings of Joachim, who was active in the twelfth century, Christian theology of history is given a new direction. In contrast to the definitions of history given by previous Christian commentators, in which the passage of time is considered primarily as an interim period of waiting for the eschatological fulfilment of history, Joachim turns his attention towards an impending, intrahistorical period of peace and reconciliation. This vision, which Joachim refers to as an 'age of the spirit', forms the basis *inter alia* for the charges levelled at him by anti-utopian critics in the twentieth century, of having established the intellectual premise for modern utopianism. A key goal of this part of the study is to problematize such simplifying accounts through reference of Joachim's own writings as well as the pioneering research into this author that has been carried out in the last fifty years.

Chapter Three, 'Romantic History', illustrates how central strands of Christian theology of history were secularized during the Romantic period, mutating into politically charged philosophies of history. Specifically, it highlights the way in which Joachim's conception of an age of the spirit finds an echo in the idea of a new, higher religion – a 'religion of the spirit' – that is articulated in broadly similar terms by Novalis, Friedrich Schleiermacher and F.W.J. Schelling. Now, it is axiomatic that Romanticism's visionary elements are made problematic by subsequent intellectual developments in Germany. Yet the prevailing critique of Romanticism tends to obscure the considerable dislocations between early and late Romanticism. Challenging this simplified paradigm, the key insight into the non-attainability of the Ideal that distinguishes early Romantic thought, as well as Schelling's later writings, is addressed. Against this background, the claim is made that early Romantic philosophy of history ought rather to be understood as suffused with *anti-utopian* elements.

The critique of Romanticism lives on nonetheless. As already noted, in the wake of the totalitarian projects of the 1930s and 1940s thinkers from both the

Right and the Left sought to identify the roots of the evils that had beset the West; not infrequently, they found the culprit in Romanticism. Chapter Four, 'History after God', builds on twentieth-century ideology critique to show how talk of 'the end of ideologies' not infrequently gives way to an illusory conviction as to the writer's own freedom from ideology. After a brief discussion of these mid-century debates, attention turns to the famous symposium on Capri in 1994 whose participants included Jacques Derrida, Gianni Vattimo, Eugenio Trías and Hans-Georg Gadamer. At this point the discussion returns to the topic of early Romanticism, including its concept of a religion of the spirit, with which several of the symposium's participants sought to restore a visionary impulse to philosophical thinking but without resorting to the grandiose utopias of the preceding one hundred years. In this effort to engage in a post-critical fashion with Western theology and philosophy of history, these philosophers made an interesting return to religion also in the wider sense of the term: above all to the critical potentialities that inhere in the prophetic strands of both Jewish and Christian traditions.

The final chapter, 'The Politics of History', draws together the various strands of the discussion in order to concentrate on the current politico-philosophical conversation. My principal interlocutors here are Giorgio Agamben, Alain Badiou and Slavoj Žižek, all central figures in the debate that has been revived in the twenty-first century over the political radicalism of the biblical legacy. At first sight, this intervention in an ongoing critical discussion might seem to run counter to the narrative thread of the intellectual trajectory traced out in previous chapters. Despite their substantial disagreements, Agamben, Badiou and Žižek in many respects herald a break with the deconstructive and hermeneutic philosophy associated with figures such as Derrida and Vattimo. On closer scrutiny, however, the nature of this relationship reveals itself as markedly more complex. Above all in their treatment of the historico-theological motifs examined in this study, these thinkers exhibit an important thematic continuity, albeit with important differences when it comes to the exact application of these motifs. To be more precise, the prophetic, messianic and pneumatic motifs recur in the philosophies of Agamben, Badiou and Žižek, but often for very different purposes than those found in the philosophies of Derrida and Vattimo. This critical contrast compellingly highlights the way in which tensions within the Western historico-theological tradition continue to inform politico-philosophical debate in the present moment.

The underlying premise throughout these chapters is a recognition of the complex and double-edged nature of the biblical legacy. Recognizing this complexity, however, is not tantamount to saying that any interpretation of its essential tropes and motifs is as reasonable or desirable as any other. What this study offers, therefore, is not simply a close reading of selected texts from five different historical periods. Rather, through my reading of these particular texts I develop an argument for a specific interpretation, a certain way of framing what I consider to be the enduring politico-philosophical value of the biblical legacy. Thus, for reasons that will become clear throughout the study, I argue for a 'theopolitical' interpretation of the prophetic motif, invoking of a form of justice that does not allow itself to be reduced to any existing political order, in contrast to what in the modern era has come to be known as 'political theology' – the tendency to use theological claims to support a specific political agenda. Similarly, I argue for the inclusion of the messianic motif in its 'restorative' interpretation rather than its 'apocalyptic' one, the former putting the emphasis on justice as an ongoing task whereas the latter tends to focus on justice as a sudden irruption of a new order. Finally, regarding the pneumatic motif, I argue for a 'spectral' reading of the concept of spirit – taking its inspiration from Derrida's 'hauntology' – in contrast to the often coercive dialectic schemas that have characterized idealist philosophies of history throughout European modernity.

This line of reasoning also has consequences for my critical assessment of the contemporary debate. While figures such as Agamben, Badiou and Žižek offer highly interesting analyses of the biblical legacy as a potential resource for political reflection, I am less convinced by the conclusions they draw from these analyses. Above all, I raise serious concerns about the way in which decisionist elements in a neo-Schmittian fashion are being combined with a select number of theological concepts – 'grace' rather than 'law', 'spirit rather than 'letter', etc. – in order to break what is conceived as the political deadlock of our liberal societies. This revitalization of the apocalyptic (or, in the case of Agamben, antinomian) strand of the biblical legacy not only tends to place politics above dialogue and negotiation; it also invites the potentially authoritarian quality that Löwith identified as the tragic culmination of the Western historico-philosophical tradition: a quasi-theologically legitimated worship of the present and the moment, which in its most extreme form regards the actual course of history as self-justifying.

Is the biblical legacy, then, only ever a burden upon modern political thought? Despite Löwith's incisive critique, I contend that it is not, although it remains a matter of debate as to what the enduring politico-philosophical value of this legacy is. While in this study I conclude that its single most important insight consists in the idea of justice as a never-completed mission, I would prefer this to be seen less as a conclusion than as an invitation to the continuous task of exploring, restoring and redefining the delicate notion of justice.

★

This book has a long prehistory and my thanks are due to a large number of colleagues, institutions and foundations that have played a role in its conception and development. A generous grant from the Swedish Research Council in 2007 first enabled me to embark on the project. Since 2010 I have been part of the research programme 'Time, Memory and Representation: A Multidisciplinary Programme on Transformations in Historical Consciousness', funded by

Riksbankens Jubileumsfond (The Swedish Foundation for Humanities and Social Sciences). I would like to express my gratitude to all the participants in the programme. My special thanks go to Hans Ruin, the director of the programme, for inviting me to join it in the first place, but also for encouraging me to have this book translated and published in English.

I am grateful for the support given by my colleagues and students at Stockholm School of Theology, my home faculty during the years that I developed this project. The book has also benefited from rehearsals at various seminars at Lund and Uppsala Universities. In 2008, I had the privilege to spend a term at Glasgow University. I would like to express my gratitude to Ward Blanton, Julie Clague, Mark Godin, Werner Jeanrond and Alana Vincent for engaging intellectual conversations during those months. Over the years I have also enjoyed long and short sojourns at the Centre Culturel Suédois (CCS) in Paris, The Swedish Institute in Rome and Villa San Michele on Capri. Many thanks to all the staff and fellow residents for making these sojourns such pleasant and stimulating experiences.

This book has also benefited greatly from the input, questions and criticisms of those who have read it in various states of completion: Jonna Bornemark, Andrus Ers, Carl-Henric Grenholm, Gösta Hallonsten, Mattias Martinson, Elena Namli, Anders Piltz, Johan Redin, Anna-Lena Renqvist, Göran Rosenberg, Hans Ruin, Blaženka Scheuer, Marcia Sá Cavalcante Schuback, Ola Sigurdson, Jesper Svartvik, Bengt Kristensson Uggla, Thomas Wagner, Sven-Olov Wallenstein and Susanne Wigorts Yngvesson.

I would also like to express my gratitude to St Benet's Hall in Oxford for offering a highly stimulating milieu during my work on the English edition of the book. Special thanks are due to Werner Jeanrond, the current Master of the Hall, for his inspiration as a colleague and friend over the years. My thanks also go to Brian Manning Delaney, Mark Godin and Alana Vincent for tweaking my English translations of French, German, Italian and Spanish quotes. Finally, I would like to thank my translator, Stephen Donovan, for his sensitive and skilful rendering of the original Swedish text.[3]

Oxford, December 2014

Notes

1. It should be clarified here that Lukács's *Die Zerstörung der Vernunft: Der Weg des Irrationalismus von Schelling zu Hitler* (Berlin: Aufbau Verlag, 1955), to which I am alluding, has an ideological slant that differs markedly from both *Dialectic of Enlightenment* and Lukács's own earlier works. I return to Lukács in more detail in Chapter Four.

2. J. Gray. 2008. *Black Mass: Apocalyptic Religion and the Death of Utopia*, London: Penguin Books, 3.

3. All italics in quoted matter are in the original source, unless otherwise stated by the author.

CHAPTER 1

The God of History

'Christianity is not one of the great things of history: it is history which is one of the great things of Christianity.'[1] This grand assertion appeared in a posthumously circulated aphorism by the French cardinal Henri de Lubac, an influential voice in twentieth-century debates over the relationship between the West's view of history and the Christian legacy. The assertion needs modification and nuancing, but de Lubac was onto something. When Christianity emerged during the first centuries of the first millennium, history writing played a central role. The early church relied to a significant degree upon theological readings of history in order to constitute itself as a tradition and to specify its relationship to the Jewish-rabbinical tradition from which it would successively distance itself.

These 'theologies of history' were supported by a series of components that regulated both the early church's rupture and its continuity with the Jewish tradition. One such was the prophetic promise of deliverance, whose theological roots go back to Exodus – the story of how God liberates his people from Egyptian captivity. The early Christian movement incorporated this central motif within Judaism into its own reading of history, which holds that the promised redemption was set in motion by Jesus's death and resurrection. Complete liberation, however, is yet to come. Only with the return of the resurrected Jesus, that is to say, at the end of history, will salvation be fully realized. Until then, humanity participates in a historical drama in which it is called upon to make a choice with respect to the offer of redemption manifested in Jesus of Nazareth.

This claim is nothing less than that the very goal and purpose of history have assumed new meaning because of Jesus's death and resurrection. According to this view, it is equally clear that Jesus cannot be considered as merely the latest in a line of prophets promising redemption. He *is* the redemption, God's

---

Notes for this section begin on page 32.

anointed servant as promised by the prophets. Here another essential component of the early Christian reading of history comes into view: the messianic event. And it is perhaps here that both the break and continuity with the Jewish tradition appear most clearly. Announcing that the messianic period had been ushered in by Jesus's resurrection, the fledgling Christian movement went on to successively distance itself from the majority of Jews, who did not acknowledge Jesus of Nazareth as their Messiah. At the same time, the very claim that Jesus was the promised Messiah clearly indicated that the movement saw itself as in a relation of continuity with the Jewish messianic tradition. For anyone wishing to grasp this issue properly, it is essential to understand that the embryo of what was eventually to develop into Christianity remained for a long time a movement within Judaism.[2]

In the texts of the New Testament this need to register continuity with the messianic tradition is everywhere in evidence. What is more, a third key component of the emergent theologies of history, the spirit, makes its appearance here. Particularly in Luke–Acts (the composite work of the Gospel of Luke and the Acts of the Apostles), the spirit appears as a guarantor of the continuity between the established tradition of spiritually anointed prophets and Jesus, who is accordingly seen as the fulfilment of that tradition. An illustrative example is offered by Luke's account of Jesus's visit to the Nazareth synagogue, in which the author has Jesus, speaking of himself, recite from the Book of Isaiah, 'The Spirit of the Lord is upon me, because he has anointed me to bring good news to the poor' (Luke 4:18; cf. Isa. 61:1).[3] The implication is that the spirit which inspired the prophets is now upon Jesus, and, moreover, that he is God's chosen Messiah.

However, the spirit is not invoked solely as a marker of continuity between Jesus's activities and the older messianic tradition but is also taken to guarantee continuity between Jesus himself and his followers – that is, what would become the Christian church. This notion receives its most forceful expression in the depiction of the descent of the spirit at Pentecost in the second chapter of the Acts of the Apostles. The author here makes clear that the spirit which descends upon the apostles is not merely that foretold by the prophet Joel (Joel 2:28), but also identical with that conferred upon Jesus by God at his baptism. The significance which this notion held for early Christian theologies of history – and, indirectly, for later philosophies of history – can hardly be overstated: the spirit as a marker of God's continuous presence and influence in human history.

With this in mind, let us return to de Lubac's aphorism. While there is an important grain of truth in de Lubac's yoking of Christianity and history – as the latter has been conceptualized in the West – the background outlined here clearly illustrates why his claim requires slight modification. The Christian concept of history did not appear from nowhere as a given part of Christianity's own development. On the contrary, a number of its constituent elements already existed in the prophetic traditions of Jewish antiquity, even if they underwent fundamental changes by being incorporated into a Christian theological framework. In order to find the roots of the three historico-theological motifs that are the focus of the present study I will therefore be relying primarily upon the prophetic literature in the Hebrew Bible.

An additional clarification with regard to de Lubac's aphorism is warranted. The statement that Christianity gave birth to the Western conception of history should not be equated with the claim that the narrating of history per se is, in the final instance, a Christian invention. Those familiar with the classics will be well aware that the culture of ancient Greece in particular could boast a distinguished tradition of historical narrative. Indeed, it is in ancient Greece that we find those figures customarily held up as the very first historians: Herodotus (c. 484–425 BC), 'the Father of History', and Thucydides (c. 460–400 BC). In other words, the Jewish and (by extension) Christian traditions gave birth not to history writing as such, but to the specific form of theology of history that has been of decisive importance for the West's conception of history.

God as the Lord of History

'Prophecy' is often associated with augury or prediction of the future. The term is also used in this sense within certain forms of Christianity, notably charismatic forms of modern Protestantism. While the prophecy of Jewish antiquity encompasses such variants, it is not in this sense that the notion is primarily of interest from a historico-theological perspective. Rather, it is a question of a specific understanding of history that emerges in the prophetic literature of the Hebrew Bible. Several distinctive features of this perspective on history have been examined in the modern era by an array of Jewish biblical scholars and philosophers, including the aforementioned Martin Buber, Abraham Heschel and Yehezkel Kaufmann. These twentieth-century thinkers made a substantial contribution towards revitalizing and opening up new perspectives on modern biblical scholarship (which to a large degree had been shaped by Christian theology).

The founding of historical-critical analysis as a textual methodology in the nineteenth century unquestionably resulted in a major shift in perceptions of the prophetic literature. Where previous generations of Christian theologians had primarily studied the prophets in light of Christ – considered as the realization of the prophets' promises – subsequent scholars were instead to turn their attention to the prophets themselves. Among nineteenth-century Protestant biblical scholars, the prophets came to be seen as the culmination of a religious-historical development. Briefly, this development described the displacement of a primitive Israelite tribal religion by an ethically superior monotheism, to which the prophetic literature bore witness. In the years following their Babylonian exile, the Israelites' divine worship relapsed into a narrowly legalistic and nationalistic religion in the form of rabbinic Judaism. In contrast to this 'late Judaism' (*Spätjudentum*), Christianity – particularly the morality-focused liberal Protestantism to which these biblical scholars generally belonged – was presented as the true heir of the universal and ethical religion founded by the prophets.[4]

During the twentieth century this more or less explicitly anti-Jewish interpretation has been successively dismantled. In particular, a deepened understanding of Second Temple Judaism (c. 515 BC–70 AD) has had the effect of undermining the dogmatizing efforts to counterpose the prophets to law and cultic life. Indeed, such efforts have often revealed more about the advocates of Protestantism than they do about the prophets themselves. A similar challenge has been mounted to the view that the prophets heralded a dramatically new era in Judaism. Several of the Jewish textual scholars already mentioned have played a central role here. Both Kaufmann and Heschel emphasize that the prophets rely to a great extent upon an ethics whose core features had already emerged by the time (eighth century BC) the earliest so-called literary prophets (i.e., the biblical figures who wrote down their prophecies and are represented by books in the Bible) made their appearance.[5]

Kaufmann perhaps goes furthest in emphasizing the continuity within the ancient Jewish religion. It is also in this context that he foregrounds those defining characteristics of the view of history to which prophetism gives expression. In his magisterial study *The Religion of Israel*, written over twenty years, Kaufmann argues that the religion of the Bible is, as such, based upon a claim to historical continuity.[6] This continuity goes beyond the fact that the prophets essentially share and presuppose the same conception of God held by the older religion with its popular roots. In the case of Judaism, the continuity also derives from the way in which the religion itself finds support in arguments taken from history. Accordingly, when the prophets make the case for God, they do so without the aid of sophisticated philosophical reasoning. Instead, they turn to historical legends from deep within the popular imaginary: the story of the Exodus, of God's revelation of the Tablets of Law on Mount Sinai, of the occupation of the land of Canaan, and so on.[7]

In the eyes of the prophets, it is these *historical* events that make the God of Israel worthy of faith and trust. In corresponding fashion, the divine prohibition against other gods articulated by the First Commandment rests upon a historical claim about God's role as deliverer of his people: 'I am the Lord your God, who brought you out of the land of Egypt, out of the house of slavery; you shall have no other gods before me' (Exod. 20:2–3). And this motif from Exodus is repeatedly invoked by the prophets as a basis for their pronouncement of judgement. Thus Amos declares:

> Thus says the Lord:
> For three transgressions of Israel,
> and for four, I will not revoke the punishment;
> because they sell the righteous for silver.
> and the needy for a pair of sandals –
> they who trample the head of the poor into the dust of the earth,
>   and push the afflicted out of the way;
> father and son go to the same girl,
>   so that my holy name is profaned;
> they lay themselves down beside every altar
>   on garments taken in pledge;
> and in the house of their God they drink
>   wine bought with fines they imposed.
>
> Yet I destroyed the Amorite before them,
>   whose height was like the height of cedars,
>   and who was as strong as oaks;
> I destroyed his fruit above,
>   and his roots beneath.
> Also I brought you up out of the land of Egypt,
>   and led you for forty years in the wilderness,
>   to possess the land of the Amorite.
> (Amos 2:6–10)

The very fact that God came to the rescue of his people at an earlier point in history is here presented as sufficient grounds for Israel to show its faith in God – in this instance, as manifested in justice – in the present moment also. Yet the prophets do not advance this historical claim solely in order to pronounce judgement. As frequently, Exodus and similar motifs are invoked by the prophets when announcing the promise of future liberation. Thus, for example, Isaiah's vigorous proclamation of the restoration of Israel concludes with the following words:

> so there shall be a highway from Assyria
>   for the remnant that is left of his people,
> as there was for Israel
>   when they came up from the land of Egypt.
> (Isa. 11:16)

The prophets evince a similar reliance upon history even when treating the future; that God has performed miracles for Israel during its wanderings throughout history is taken as grounds for its people to keep faith with God.

At this point we can begin to sketch an outline of the particular view of history that finds expression in the prophetic literature. History here takes the form of a drama in which the memory of previous divine acts not only lends meaning to the present but enables a forward-looking orientation within history – a kind of dialectic of memory and hope, as it were. This view rests upon the conviction that God is essentially situated in history rather than in nature. There is no shortage of references to nature by the prophets, to be sure, but it is clearly not what governs God's creation. Rather, nature is taken to be subordinate to God, with allusions to nature primarily serving the purpose of emphasizing God's historical power. The following verses, taken from a famous passage in Jeremiah announcing God's desire to form a new covenant with Israel, provide an illustrative example:

Thus says the Lord,
who gives the sun for light by day
   and the fixed order of the moon and the stars for light by night,
who stirs up the sea so that its waves roar –
   the Lord of hosts is his name:
If this fixed order were ever to cease
   from my presence, says the Lord,
then also the offspring of Israel would cease
   to be a nation before me forever.
(Jer. 31:35–36)

God appears here as the Lord of history. The attributes ascribed to God by the prophets are similarly based on God's historical actions: God frees from oppression, forms covenants, keeps faith with the covenant, condemns disloyalty to the covenant, forgives disloyalty and establishes his people anew.

It is also from this historical experience – from the experience of God's interaction with humanity in history – that knowledge of God is obtained. To use the somewhat anachronistic term 'theology' in this context, it may be noted that theology here takes the form of a kind of testimonial literature. The prophets' talk of God is almost entirely lacking in speculation as to the nature of God or arguments for his existence. The prophetic literature in this respect stands in stark contrast to the emergent philosophy of contemporary Greece and its imprint on later Jewish and Christian doctrine. Instead, knowledge of God is conveyed narratively in the form of stories – handed down and, eventually, written down – about how humanity has experienced God's presence in and through history. Something of this quality is well captured by Heschel when he stresses that a prophet never argues or proves but merely attests: 'There are no proofs for the existence of the God of Abraham. There are only witnesses. The greatness of the prophet lies not only in the ideas he expressed, but also in the moments he experienced. The prophet is a witness, and his words a testimony – to *His* power and judgment, to *His* justice and mercy.'[8]

In these words can be glimpsed a key aspect of the prophetic theology of history. What the prophets bear witness to is not God's power in general terms. In the prophetic literature the concept of God having intervened forcefully in history is interwoven with a pervading idea of *justice*. God's power is recurrently invoked in order to criticize a particular form of worldly power that runs contrary to the idea of justice associated with divine power. Several of the prophets level quite relentless criticism at kings and lawmakers for behaving unjustly or trampling the vulnerable. The verses from Amos cited above are illustrative. No less caustic are the words directed by Jeremiah at Jehoiakim, one of the last rulers of the Kingdom of Judah before the Babylonian exile of the sixth century BC. The impending fall of Jerusalem is understood by the prophet not only as a natural consequence of abandoning the way of God but also as a result of corruption and iniquity on the part of the country's rulers:

> Woe to him who builds his house by unrighteousness,
>   and his upper rooms by injustice;
> who makes his neighbours work for nothing,
>   and does not give them their wages;
> who says, 'I will build myself a spacious house
>   with large upper rooms',
> and who cuts out windows for it,
>   panelling with cedar,
>   and painting it with vermilion.
> Are you a king
>   because you compete in cedar?
> Did not your father eat and drink
>   and do justice and righteousness?
>   Then it was well with him.
> He judged the cause of the poor and needy;
>   then it was well.
> Is not this to know me?
>   says the Lord.
> But your eyes and heart
>   are only on your dishonest gain,
> for shedding innocent blood,
>   and for practising oppression and violence.
> (Jer. 22:13–17)

The decisive factor in this context is that the prophet regards himself as a mouthpiece for God. The claim being advanced here is nothing less than that God himself in his majesty and power condemns King Jehoiakim for abusing his earthly power. The prophetic tradition's habit of invoking divine power to condemn human power was unique for its time. As a religious-historical phenomenon prophetism is known to extend as far back as the third millennium BC. Archaeological finds indicate that prophetism, whether in the form of singly recorded oracles or of oracular collections, occurred in a range of different cultures of Middle Eastern antiquity, including the Sumerian and Assyrian. Yet these finds indicate that prophetic assertions were invariably made in support of royal power (for instance, in the form of counsel on political and military matters). In the Kingdom of Israel, both before and after its partition in the tenth century BC, prophets loyal to the royal court seem to have been evidence, possibly enjoying institutional ties to the Temple Cult. Beginning with the era of literary prophetism (c. eighth century BC), however, the image of the prophet as presenting a counterpoint to sovereign power became increasingly prominent, with several of the prophets adopting a stance of explicit opposition.

Theopolitics *versus* Political Theology

The notion that there is a divine power and a divine justice that does not necessarily endorse the prevailing earthly power entails a relativization of human power. This aspect perhaps finds its clearest expression in the work of the hypothetical author, usually referred to as 'Proto-Isaiah', of the first part of the Book of Isaiah (ch. 1–39). Although Isaiah, who was active in Judah during the eighth century BC, is thought to have been loyal at times to the royal court, he did not hesitate to challenge the king and his policies. In no uncertain terms he denounces the temptation to put one's hopes in military armaments and strategic alliances rather than in God's power.

It should be recalled that in this period vast empires were displacing each other and a tiny kingdom such as Judah stood to gain by playing its cards carefully. Even so, when King Ahaz in the 730s BC turns for help to the great power Assyria in order to save himself from enemies closer to hand, Isaiah firmly counsels him to put his faith instead in the God of Israel (Isa. 7:1–17). The king does not heed the prophet, however, with the consequence that he eventually finds himself in a ruinous state of vassalage to Assyria. Still more relentless is Isaiah's condemnation, a few decades later, of those in power under King Hezekiah, when Judah tries to shake off the Assyrian yoke by seeking the aid of Egypt:

> Alas for those who go down to Egypt for help
>   and who rely on horses,
> who trust in chariots because they are many
>   and in horsemen because they are very strong,

> but do not look to the Holy One of Israel
>   or consult the Lord!
>
> ...
>
> The Egyptians are human, and not God;
>   their horses are flesh, and not spirit.
> When the Lord stretches out his hand,
>   the helper will stumble, and the one helped will fall,
>   and they will all perish together.
> (Isa. 31:1,3)

What constitutes the basis for this vigorous censure of faith in military force and strategic political calculation? The answer is that for the prophets it represents a denial of God's power over history. For Isaiah, humanity's false belief in its own sovereignty – an idolatry of power – is quite simply the root of evil in history. It is true that this isolationist dimension of Proto-Isaiah is not shared by all of the biblical prophets. Nonetheless, the very relativizing of worldly power remains one of the most pervasive themes in the prophetic literature. Time and again, humanity's tendency to allow itself to be dazzled by power and success is laid bare; time and again, the inability of military violence to create enduring human prosperity is exposed. And herein lies perhaps the most striking aspect of the view of history to which the prophetic literature gives expression: that history is not primarily treated from the perspective of those in power – a litany of indestructible rulers, glorious conquests and epoch-defining victories. Rather, history is considered from a perspective of justice that draws its lifeblood from a quite peculiar conception of divinity. Contrary to the rules governing the world of classical mythology, in which the gods are generally allied with the powerful and the victorious, the prophets write history from the perspective of the weak and the vulnerable:

> Shall not Lebanon in a very little while
>   become a fruitful field,
>   and the fruitful field be regarded as a forest?
> On that day the deaf shall hear
>   the words of a scroll,
> and out of their gloom and darkness
>   the eyes of the blind shall see.
> The meek shall obtain fresh joy in the Lord,
>   and the neediest people shall exult in the Holy One of Israel.
> For the tyrant shall be no more,
>   and the scoffer shall cease to be;
>   all those alert to do evil shall be cut off –

> those who cause a person to lose a lawsuit,
>> who set a trap for the arbiter in the gate,
>> and without grounds deny justice to the one in the right.
> (Isa. 29:17–21)

One thinker of the modern era who has captured, with singular acuity, this biblical deviation from the conventions of classical mythology is Friedrich Nietzsche. Indeed, the contrast between the 'master morality' of Greek literature and the prophetic tradition's advocacy of the weak and vulnerable is a veritable leitmotiv of his celebrated genealogy of human morals. As is well known, Nietzsche's sympathies lie with the former, and his entire critical genealogy is ultimately directed against the glorification of weakness – at the expense of nobility and aristocracy – that was initiated by the Jewish 'slave revolt in morality'.[9]

Nietzsche, as one of his most energetic contemporary critics has observed, nonetheless remains one of the few to have pinpointed what is peculiar to the Bible's view of the vulnerable. I am alluding here to the work of René Girard, whose many studies of sacrifice and exclusionary mechanisms in human history return unfailingly to the distinctive aspects of the biblical legacy. Girard follows Nietzsche in taking as his starting point the transposition of sacrificial victim and executioner – in which God takes the side of the victim – that finds expression not only in the prophetic literature, but also in Exodus, the Psalms and the Book of Job. Unlike Nietzsche, however, Girard strongly endorses the biblical literature's concern with the weak and the vulnerable, and where Nietzsche sees a 'downward progression' of the concept of God – that is to say, in the Christian notion of God's identification with the crucified victim – Girard sees a 'triumph' of the truth.[10]

Although Girard has a tendency to end up with an almost idealizing conception of Christian 'truth', he captures in an unparalleled way the foregrounding of the victim that occurs within the frame of the prophetic tradition. Moreover, he brings attention to how this foregrounding also gives rise to a growing criticism of cultic sacrificial practices – which, according to Girard, in all cultures ultimately represents a sublimated form of what were once actually mechanisms of real social expulsion. Briefly, his theory holds that in its earliest phase humanity discovered the expiatory power of expelling an innocent person or group as a way to restore harmony in a community racked by conflict. A causal relation was quickly established between sacrifices to the gods and reconciliation within the social group, a pattern that over time was ritualized, thereby effectively masking its originary violence.

A number of questions may reasonably be asked of Girard's ambitious theory about the origins of expiatiory sacrifice. Notwithstanding, my own view is that he has identified something fundamental by asserting that the prophetic tradition gives rise to a mode of opposition to precisely this tendency of sacralizing violence and thereby glossing over the actual innocence and vulnerability of its victims. This emerging view of injustice as permeating all forms of theologically sanctioned violence is expressed most acutely in the criticism of the sacrificial cult that accompanies the social criticism of several prophets of the eighth century (primarily Amos, Micah and Proto-Isaiah). At this time there existed an advanced sacrificial system in which different forms of animal sacrifice were held to regulate the relationship between God and his people. In several of the prophets, perhaps most forcefully in Amos, attention is nonetheless focused elsewhere. If the proffered sacrifices were intended to form part of a relationship with the God who had redeemed the sins of the people, it is here implied that the entire lavish apparatus of sacrificial rituals and holy festivities in fact covered over a deeper sin – the injustices done to the poor and the defenceless. Having thrown accusation after accusation at those who 'trample on the poor and take from them levies of grain' (Amos 5:11), who 'afflict the righteous, who take a bribe, and push aside the needy in the gate' (Amos 5:12), Amos has the Lord ruthlessly declare:

> I hate, I despise your festivals,
>   and I take no delight in your solemn assemblies.
> Even though you offer me your burnt offerings and grain offerings,
>   I will not accept them;
> and the offerings of well-being of your fatted animals
>   I will not look upon.
> Take away from me the noise of your songs;
>   I will not listen to the melody of your harps.
> But let justice roll down like waters,
>   and righteousness like an ever-flowing stream.
> (Amos 5:21–24)

As Heschel remarks, when reading these verses one needs to bear in mind the extraordinariness of the way in which the prophets challenge the practices of cultic sacrifice.[11] To challenge the premises of the established cult was not merely to position oneself against a supreme political authority that, at least since the days of Solomon (in the tenth century BC), had enjoyed an intimate alliance with institutionalized religion, it was to seek to dislodge the very cornerstone of a religious practice for which sacrifice represented a means of establishing community with God. When human beings brought forth an animal sacrifice, they were quite simply offering a proxy for themselves.

Given the central role of cultic sacrifice in ancient Israelite culture it is nevertheless equally important to avoid over-interpreting the degree to which the prophets counterpose sacrificial offerings to justice. As I have already argued, this has been a tendency among a certain strand of Protestant readings of the prophets that seeks to portray an older, cult-based religion as finding itself opposed by a superior, ethical religion that (for these commentators) anticipates Christianity. To claim that eighth-century prophets rejected worship as such in favour of a 'higher' spiritualized religion is a fairly unreasonable assertion. It is therefore important to stress that their critique was directed not at cultic practices per se. What they were objecting to was the political abuse of cultism: the exploitation of the cult in order to legitimate and sustain an unjust social order.[12]

The perspective of several millennia of human history, in which the tendency to use theology to support politics has been the rule rather than the exception, confers extraordinary significance upon these testimonial records from Hebrew antiquity. In order to understand the defining characteristic of prophetic opposition to theologically sanctioned politics – what in the modern era has come to be known as 'political theology' – it is important to return to the idea of a justice that transcends the existing political order. In particular, it is necessary to see how closely connected this notion of justice is to the concept of a higher divine will. Justice, writes Heschel, 'is not an ancient custom, a human convention, a value, but a transcendent demand, freighted with divine concern. It is not only a relationship between man and man, it is an *act* involving God, a divine need'.[13]

To be sure, it may be asked what makes this theological notion of justice different from political theology. Does reference to a form of justice superior to actual politics not run the risk of creating yet more subtle varieties of theocratic rule? This risk is, of course, something that prophet-inspired thinking can never fully disavow. But one can also turn the question around in order to ask whether an institutionalized, divinely sanctioned form of political order does not mean that the prophetic call to justice has already been betrayed. Indeed it has, if prophetism is understood as the invoking of a form of justice that does not allow itself to be ossified into a fixed political, legal or cultic order, but rather transcends all such orders. The prophetic vocation, in other words, is not about exerting theological authority in order to unfairly appropriate a position superior to the prevailing political order, but rather to act as a critical voice from within the existing system.

Prophetism in this sense emerges at several points in the Hebrew Bible. The idea of justice that finds expression here should thus not be confused with the notion of a higher divine order which a chosen elite (kings, priests or even prophets) can claim to embody. Rather, the prophets indicate that justice is something that can never be taken as a given for all time. Justice, in other words, can never be reduced to the existing system of moral regulations, laws and norms.

This dynamic conception of justice is also reflected in the absence from the Bible of moral-philosophical reflections of a more principled nature. Allusions to justice and righteousness are made exclusively in relation to specific situations involving concrete figures: false prophets who prognosticate for money, estate owners who expropriate the poor from the land, judges who take bribes and merchants who manipulate their scales. Justice, to quote Heschel once again, in this biblical sense always exists 'in relation to a person, and is something done by a person. An act of injustice is condemned, not because the law is broken, but because a person has been hurt'.[14]

To claim that justice is something that emerges from the concrete is simultaneously to claim that every individual in every new situation is called upon to exercise his or her moral judgement. The use of justice quite simply requires more of human beings than passive reliance upon an abstract or cultic order.

> 'With what shall I come before the Lord,
>   and bow myself before God on high?
> Shall I come before him with burnt offerings,
>   with calves a year old?
> Will the Lord be pleased with thousands of rams,
>   with tens of thousands of rivers of oil?
> Shall I give my firstborn for my transgression,
>   the fruit of my body for the sins of my soul?'
> He has told you, O mortal, what is good;
>   and what does the Lord require of you
> but to do justice, and to love kindness,
>   and to walk humbly with your God?
> (Mic. 6:6–8)

The insight that justice requires independent moral judgement can also be applied at the macro-historical level, shedding further light upon the isolationist tendencies observable in some of the prophets. Their injunction to the sovereign to follow the path of God rather than that of great empires can quite simply be understood as expressing the view that serving justice requires more than merely allowing oneself to be swept along by the geopolitical forces of the moment. It is in this light that Martin Buber reads Isaiah's opposition to the trust placed by monarchs in military armaments and strategic political alliances. From a harshly political perspective such an attitude is certainly opportunistic. From a theological perspective, by contrast, it reflects the conviction that history's ultimate outcome is not determined by the extension of mighty empires. Beneath this conviction lies a faith in a superior historical loyalty that is tied to a notion of divine justice. This faith, which also includes the task of enacting justice and righteousness in an exemplary way among the nations, is what Buber calls 'theopolitics'.[15]

In the process, however, the question is once again raised as to what differentiates this theopolitics from political theology. The dividing line is, in fact, razor-thin – and an awareness that such is indeed the case runs throughout the biblical literature, being most clearly reflected in the Deuteronomistic History,[16] where a recurrent motif is the contrast between a Mosaic model of the true prophet and kings who unfailingly tend to confuse their own power with God's. The picture is additionally complicated by a historical contrast between the time when God led his people through the desert and that of the later kingdoms with their institutionalized temple cults. While the portrait of a time prior to accession to the Promised Land reveals a powerful God who communicates with his people through inspired leaders – judges and prophets – the period of monarchy is represented as one of decline in which God is increasingly overshadowed by leaders who make claim to divine authority. It is against such leaders that the prophets counterpose their 'theopolitical realism'. In place of corrupt leaders who typically seek divine sanction for the exercise of power, the prophets invoke a God whose power and justice never allow themselves to be circumscribed by the human order of the day.[17]

The defining characteristic of prophetic theopolitics can now be pinpointed: rather than lending theological endorsement to the existing order, the prophets identify its failings and thereby assert the possibility of changing that order. In this respect prophetism contains an obviously visionary component. Yet it is important at this point not to confuse prophetism with apocalypticism, which is a later phenomenon, represented in the Hebrew Bible primarily by the Book of Daniel. Although the boundary can at times be blurred – several of the younger prophetic books contain apocalyptic strains – this is in essence a question of two substantially different ways of relating to historical reality. Visionary elements feature in both, to be sure, but where those in the apocalyptic literature have a definite, often symbolically coded, content, such wealth of detail is generally absent from the prophetic literature.

A case in point is offered by Daniel's vision of a succession of ages associated with the great empires of antiquity (ch. 7–12). At no point does the author refer to the empires explicitly. Instead, he relates how a series of monstrous creatures rise from the sea and are defeated in turn. The vision has a palpably deterministic character, concluding with the prophesy that the fourth beast – a contemporary allusion to the Seleucid Empire and its ruthless king, Antiochus IV Epiphanes (175–164 BC) – would shortly be slain, to be followed by the restoration of God's people.

This apocalyptic text offers an illuminating point of contrast with parts of the Book of Isaiah, whose no less obviously visionary elements take the form of a promise that the Israelites will be restored from their Babylonian exile. Yet the latter gives no details as to when or how this restoration will come about. The reason is that the prophet neither knows nor claims to know the answer. And it is on this very point that it differs crucially from apocalyptic texts. Where the apocalyptic literature presupposes that the course of history has been laid down by God since before the dawn of time – and can be deciphered accordingly by the apocalyptic visionary – the prophetic literature bears hardly any trace of this kind of historical determinism.[18]

None of this is to deny that the prophets also portray God as the unchallenged master of history. Even so, the fact that God holds sway over history means that the future, far from being laid out in advance, is conditional upon choices made in the present moment by God's people. The prophets' preoccupation with the future must be understood in this context – not as the augury of an predetermined future but as an exhortation to the people to choose the path of God in the present and thereby create a different future. When proclaiming redemption the prophets have in mind repentance – in Hebrew, *teshuvah* – literally, a 'return' to the path marked out by God.[19]

Here, encountered in embryo, is a motif that recurs in many different forms in subsequent Jewish thought: the idea of humanity as the co-redeemer of creation. Far from the view that humanity is blindly subordinate to the course of history, what emerges here is a perspective on creation as the shared project of God and humanity. Humanity has quite simply been called upon to realize God's work. In this sense, prophetic theopolitics contains, if anything, an *anti-utopian* dimension: not a belief in another historical reality, let alone a reality other than the historical, but a belief, plain and simple, that historical reality can be different.

Another pronounced feature of prophetic literature can be discerned here: an unwillingness to assign transhistorical authority to a worldly institution or social order. It is difficult to overstate the historical value of this notion, which includes an awareness that existing social and cultural security, where such exists, should never be taken for granted, but as an incentive to criticize, protest and perhaps even overthrow a corrupt and unjust social order. Formulated at an early stage, this belief that oppression can be abolished and that opposition warrants the effort has a cogency that has manifested itself throughout history, not least in the Jewish people's self-understanding and capacity to endure a wide range of modes of historical oppression.[20]

It is worth pausing at this point in order to reflect upon the source of this oppositional force. From where do prophetic teachings derive their emancipatory impulse? A core part of the answer lies in this notion of a divine justice that transcends every fixed political, legal or cultic order. Perhaps, as Walter Brueggemann, extending the argument of George Mendenhall, has proposed, this is the 'social purpose' of a truly transcendent God: 'to have a court of appeal against the highest courts and orders of society around us'.[21] Belief in a transcendent God, Brueggemann reminds us, has in every age been a vital force for marginalized peoples, who have found in their faith a bastion against repressive structures of both a political and a religious kind.

Against the backdrop of this broader historical perspective, in which even secular liberation movements have drawn inspiration from the prophetic tradition, it may nonetheless be asked whether the key factor is belief in the possibility of transcendence rather than in any particular divine being. Does the notion of a critical corrective to the existing order in itself not presuppose an oppositional impulse? Conversely, it may be asked whether faith in a redemptive horizon would have come about in the first place had it not been for the specific concept of God that emerged from the Jewish prophetic tradition. Is it not the case that the prophetic understanding of God, closely tied as it is to the idea of unconditional justice, provides the actual basis for the notion that history contains a redemptive impulse which humanity itself can to some extent hasten?

Whatever the case, the key to the prophets' emancipatory teachings comprises more than just a vision of an alternative order. Of equal significance is the way in which this vision is conveyed. The prophets had a peculiar facility for using language as a means of supplying images that enabled their audience to imagine the world differently. Inspired by Heschel, Brueggemann and others have on several occasions highlighted this aspect of the prophetic literature.[22] Particularly striking is how the prophets grasp the importance of anchoring their message of redemption in concrete terms by drawing on popular stories and legends. It is worth recalling here Yehezkel Kaufmann's emphasis upon the role of historical argumentation within prophetism. By referring to normative occurrences from the past – delivery from Egypt being the example *par excellence* – they effectively relativize current socio-political and religious structures. Here, in what might almost be termed a practice of collective memorialization, once again the transformative power in prophetism is glimpsed.[23]

At the same time, it may be asked whether this is not also the weakest link in classical prophetism. Put differently, is there not a risk of becoming trapped in a negative critique which lacks the ability to offer an alternative to the current order that goes beyond nostalgia for an idealized past?[24] While this represents one tendency in part of the prophetic tradition, it is also challenged by a counter-tendency within the apocalyptic literature of announcing the imminence of an alternative reality. At the risk of simplification, it could be argued that in both cases the dialectic between memory and hope mentioned earlier risks imploding as a consequence of overemphasizing the poles of past and future, respectively. As will be seen, the tensions between these poles – as well as efforts to find a balance between them – are a recurrent theme in Jewish messianism.

The Messianic Event

In the late 1950s Gershom Scholem published an essay that was to become one of the most influential texts on Jewish messianism in the twentieth century. His goal was, among other things, to free the messianic idea from the notoriety in which it had become swathed as a result of the pseudo-apocalyptical activities of the 1930s and 1940s. This is not to say that he sought to deny the apocalyptic element in Jewish messianism. Quite the reverse. In contrast to many Jewish commentators – from Maimonides to Emmanuel Levinas – who throughout history have striven to suppress this element, Scholem partly adopts the role of its defender. What he defends in apocalyptic messianism is its emancipatory power, its courage and the hope it has given to the Jewish people during times when the pressure of history has become unendurable.[25]

Scholem even goes so far as to describe messianism as 'a theory of catastrophe'.[26] He uses this term as a way to focus attention on the connection that exists between the loss of a bearable historical reality and the desire for a radically different reality. As the degree of persecution and hardship increases, the messianic expectations become more intense. In this light it is perhaps not so strange that the origins of messianism are often traced back to the Babylonian exile and the accompanying experience of rootlessness. For this reason the prophetic literature – which for the most part appeared during and after the exile – also naturally presents itself as the place to find the first written traces of the messianic idea. Even so, a number of hurdles confront any attempt to inscribe messianism as a motif in the prophetic texts. The very term *ha-mashiach*, 'the anointed one', occurs at a number of points, it is true, but this need not denote anything more than the practice, widespread in antiquity, of anointing kings and priests for office. The prophetic texts simply fail to provide any more explicit representation of the Messiah as an eschatological saviour.[27]

One of the difficulties here has to do with the risk of retrospectively projecting onto the biblical texts conceptual frameworks that were only developed later in history. Theological readings from a Christian perspective offer a particularly clear illustration. During Christianity's entire history the Old Testament has been read in light of a belief that Jesus of Nazareth was the promised Messiah. Messianic passages in both the prophetic books and the Psalms have accordingly been treated as predictions of Jesus's impending arrival. That the majority of Christian believers today presumably also read the Bible in this way – that is, from a perspective of faith – is not particularly noteworthy. What is more problematic is when strictly historical approaches restore a fully fledged messianism to the prophetic literature. While messianic movements were indeed flourishing at the popular level during the period in which most prophetic books emerged, it is of critical significance that messianism as an elaborate theological notion only assumed definitive form after the emergence of these books.[28]

Another difficulty relates to the distinction between messianism and prophetism. For instance, how should we differentiate in the prophetic literature between characteristically 'messianic' expectations and more general hopes for an imminent redemption?[29] This question will be revisited in due course, but for now it may be observed that drawing a clear line of demarcation remains difficult so long as prophetic literature constitutes the object being discussed. In several respects messianism can be considered an offshoot of the prophetic tradition and thus a separate strand within the broader intellectual context of prophetism. In the post-biblical period, however, messianism was to evolve in an array of directions – not only the historic division between Judaism and Christianity – that both developed and deepened the prophetic tradition. This holds particularly true for its understanding of history.

What, then, can be said about the messianic motif in the prophetic literature? One succinct formulation would be to note that the motif is evident in embryonic form in several of the books and that these embryonic forms will play a role in the development of the messianic idea in Jewish as well as Christian theology. That a growing practice of messianic interpretation was already in existence by the time of the Second Temple, as William Horbury points out, has been confirmed by the discovery of the Qumran literature (Dead Sea Scrolls) in the mid-twentieth century. Various examples have been found of messianic interpretations of biblical passages – the eleventh chapter of the Book of Isaiah, for instance – that would later serve as classical messianic prophesies within both Judaism and Christianity.[30]

Indeed, several of the most influential embryonic forms of messianism are to be found in the Book of Isaiah, a work that incorporates texts from several different epochs. The book took shape over a period of almost five hundred years, spanning both the time before and the time after the Babylonian exile. This was a period during which entire civilizations rose and fell, kingdoms were subjugated and restored, and entire populations were deported and liberated. The Israelites were profoundly involved in these geopolitical upheavals. In 722, the Assyrians invaded the Northern Kingdom (Israel), carrying off a large portion of its population. The Southern Kingdom (Judah), in which Isaiah (Proto-Isaiah) was active, was spared on this occasion, in part because King Ahaz had refused to join the anti-Assyrian alliance formed between Israel and Syria (see above). But when the Assyrians were forced off the world stage by a rising star, the Neo-Babylonian Empire, Judah was next in line. In 597, a series of alliances formed and broken resulted in Nebuchadnezzar II entering Jerusalem and deporting the city's ruling class. The following decade was marked by recurrent turbulence. Finally the unthinkable happened. In early 587, another Babylonian army arrived; a year later, catastrophe. The Temple and much of the city were razed to the ground and yet more of the inhabitants deported to Babylon.

This chain of geopolitical events provides the background against which the Book of Isaiah's reiterated visions of imminent redemption took shape. Scholem's identification of a link between the loss of a secure existence and the hope of a radically different one has relevance here. Yet it is also important to see where such hope draws its strength: namely from the motif of Exodus mentioned earlier that during the exile period was to be accorded far greater significance.[31] It is easy to imagine the appeal made by this powerful epic of liberation to a people who for generations had suffered occupation, oppression and deportation. These exiles hoped that the Lord who had formerly brought

Israel out of Egypt and delivered them to the Promised Land would once again bring relief to his people. The motif is to be found in the very earliest of the prophetic texts. With the destruction of the Temple and the deportations of the sixth century, however, these visions of an imminent redemption assumed new dimensions. The object of hope is no longer merely that which once was. The new order at hand is conceived of as *surpassing* everything that has ever been:

> The wolf shall live with the lamb,
>   the leopard shall lie down with the kid,
> the calf and the lion and the fatling together,
>   and a little child shall lead them.
> The cow and the bear shall graze,
>   their young shall lie down together;
>   and the lion shall eat straw like the ox.
> The nursing child shall play over the hole of the asp,
>   and the weaned child shall put its hand on the adder's den.
> They will not hurt or destroy
>   on all my holy mountain;
> for the earth will be full of the knowledge of the Lord
>   as the waters cover the sea.
> On that day the root of Jesse shall stand as a signal to the peoples;
> the nations shall inquire of him, and his dwelling shall be glorious.
> (Isa. 11:6–10)[32]

This compelling vision of a paradise to come constitutes one of the most important sources of inspiration for later messianic notions. But if we recall the difficulty mentioned earlier in drawing a distinction in the prophetic literature between messianic visions and general visions of redemption, it may reasonably be asked what makes this passage identifiably messianic. Setting aside the fact that the passage is not messianic in the strict sense of the word, an answer is provided by the verses that almost immediately precede it:

> A shoot shall come out from the stock of Jesse,
>   and a branch shall grow out of his roots.
> The spirit of the Lord shall rest on him,
>   the spirit of wisdom and understanding,
>   the spirit of counsel and might,
>   the spirit of knowledge and the fear of the Lord.
> His delight shall be in the fear of the Lord.
> He shall not judge by what his eyes see,
>   or decide by what his ears hear;
> but with righteousness he shall judge the poor,
>   and decide with equity for the meek of the earth;

> he shall strike the earth with the rod of his mouth,
> and with the breath of his lips he shall kill the wicked.
> Righteousness shall be the belt around his waist,
> and faithfulness the belt around his loins.
> (Isa. 11:1–5)

The vision is here connected to a *figure* who is imagined as playing a key role in its realization (cf. Isa. 9:2–7). Although the epithet 'anointed one' is not conferred upon this figure, the two passages contain several essential elements of the messianic idea that was to be developed during the following centuries: first, the hope for deliverance from an existing situation by which the persecuted will be gathered and justice administered; second, the very idea of a figure to whom such hope can be attached – a figure who in turn can be linked to the line of David (Jesse was the father of King David) and thereby given royal traits; and third, a vision of a coming time of peace and justice that is associated with an originary paradisiacal state but that is nonetheless imagined as superseding the latter in its perfection.[33]

That said, it is also necessary to specify what these passages do not say. While this text – alongside an array of other passages from the Book of Isaiah – has during the course of history elicited eschatological interpretations from both Jewish and Christian commentators, such connotations are absent in the originary sense of the text. To be sure, the term 'eschatological' has a variety of applications. If the term is merely taken to mean general notions of a glorious existence to come, then the text can very well be said to have eschatological qualities. More commonly, however, eschatology is taken as denoting a conception of the end of time, of that which will come after the cessation of history as we know it. And it is on precisely this issue that a clarification is required. In Isaiah, as in the other literary prophets, visions of coming redemption are intrahistorical in character and intimately bound up with concrete political expectations.[34]

This is especially true of the prophets active during exile. To a greater extent than previously the promised redemption in these instances has the qualities of a *national* vision. Thus in both Jeremiah and Ezekiel the Temple's restoration and the people's return to Jerusalem occupy a central place (cf. Jer. 30; Ezek. 39:21–29). In this context it is also important to clarify that the figure with which redemption is on several occasions associated (particularly in Isaiah) is clearly not intended to be understood in eschatological or transhistorical terms. Rather, this is the portrait of a political leader. Significantly, reference is repeatedly made to David, an ideal king who was both an inspired man of God and a virtuous leader. Like David, the promised leader figure is expected to unite the tribes of Israel and found a kingdom of justice and enduring peace.[35]

Several of the prophetic books also contain passages in which messianic qualities, in the sense of being God's chosen agent, are attributed to specific historical figures. The most remarkable example is found in Deutero-Isaiah, i.e. the second part of the Book of Isaiah (ch. 40–55). The anonymous author of Deutero-Isaiah, who was active during the middle of the sixth century when the Neo-Babylonian Empire was being driven back by the Persians, presents no less a person than the Persian king Cyrus as God's chosen servant:

> Thus says the Lord to his anointed, to Cyrus,
>   whose right hand I have grasped
> to subdue nations before him
>   and strip kings of their robes,
> to open doors before him –
>   and the gates shall not be closed:
> I will go before you
>   and level the mountains,
> I will break in pieces the doors of bronze
>   and cut through the bars of iron,
> I will give you the treasures of darkness
>   and riches hidden in secret places,
> so that you may know that it is I, the Lord,
>   the God of Israel, who call you by your name.
> For the sake of my servant Jacob,
>   and Israel my chosen,
> I call you by your name,
>   I surname you, though you do not know me.
> (Isa. 45:1–4)

Here, in other words, is an example of how a straightforwardly political figure, despite not professing to be an adherent of the God of Israel, can be accorded the honorary title of 'the anointed one'. If one examines the broader historical context, it becomes clear that the Israelites had good grounds for honouring Cyrus II. In 539, he occupied Babylon, causing its mighty empire to collapse. Shortly thereafter, he gave its various deported populations permission to return to their homelands. Many, albeit far from all, of the exiled Israelites returned home. Judah became the Persian province of Yehud and the country was steadily restored. The temple cult was once again centred upon Jerusalem and in 515 the new temple consecrated.

While the vision of the exilic prophets seemed in this way to have been confirmed, the reality was in fact quite different. The country was consumed by internal tensions between returnees and those who had never left. Even though the social and economic conditions under Persian rule had been bad from the very start, the situation worsened further during the fifth century. In the following centuries, in which power over the region passed among various Hellenistic regimes and, finally, the Romans, the situation continued to be characterized by political oppression and social upheaval. It was during this time, usually termed the Second Temple period, that the embryonic forms found in several of the prophetic books were to develop into fully fledged messianic ideas. This process went hand in hand with a gradual spread of messianic expectations among the population at large.[36]

These ideas and expectations were far from being in mutual agreement. This period also saw the emergence of the contrast mentioned above between an older prophetism and a growing apocalypticism. As Benjamin Gross has argued, this contrast was reflected in the various messianic tendencies. At this early stage the foundations were laid for a tension between more restorative and more apocalyptic strands that was to permeate later Jewish messianism. Where the former emphasizes continuity with the past and connects messianic redemption with an ongoing transformation of creation through the practice of justice, the latter conceives of redemption as an external divine intervention that also involves a radical break with all previous history.[37]

Gross has a bone to pick with the apocalyptic strand. As he sees it, the apocalyptic literature gave rise to a conception of history characterized by fatalism and thus also by a deeply pessimistic view of the human condition. In a world in which the future is already laid out and in which only external intervention can bring about radical change, human acts are ultimately insignificant. To be sure, humanity can – like the apocalyptic visionary – calculate and predict the divine redemption. Beyond this, it can merely wait passively for the onset of the messianic era. In the process, humanity is defrauded of the very core of the prophetic legacy – humanity's vocation to join with God in bringing history to completion.[38]

A similarly polemical tone can be heard in Gross's account of emergent Christianity. The resurrection of Jesus, the basis for the 'good news' (*euangelion*), indicated to the apocalyptically inclined followers of the new movement that the messianic era had already begun and that redemption was at hand. Prophetic claims for an ongoing redemption in this world were thereby subordinated to a mirage of another, more perfect world thought to be humanity's real home. Redemption also ceased to be a shared concern for God's people. Instead, individual salvation moved centre stage, with the key issue being to ensure one's own place in the world to come.[39]

Drawing a contrast with Christianity's spiritualizing of messianism, Gross sketches the later development of the messianic idea within the Jewish tradition. While the messianic is loosely formulated as far back as the prophetic books and comes to the fore in the apocalyptic literature, it was Christianity that challenged the emerging rabbinic Judaism to clarify the messianic idea and give it the shape it would finally take in the Talmudic literature. Of the various factions that dominated Judaism during the Second Temple period – among them the early Jesus movement – it was primarily the Pharisees, Gross argues, who laid the foundations for rabbinic messianism. Not the least of their achievements was to reinterpret the Jewish covenant in light of new historical circumstances and thereby establish a continuity with the past. In sharp distinction to the caricature of hypocritical zealots that Christianity has bequeathed to posterity, Pharisees were distinguished by a faith in pragmatism and an emphasis upon right living rather than right convictions as the primary expression of loyalty to the covenant. Repentance (*teshuvah*) was to play a prominent role in this respect. As with earlier prophets, redemption would be considered primarily as an intrahistorical matter.[40]

Thus it was in this worldly variant that messianism primarily lived on in the rabbinic tradition. In contrast to what Gross describes as Christianity's tendency to suppress the messianic impulse by attaching it to a particular historical instant, the emphasis here is very much upon the redemptive process itself. Scepticism was from early on directed towards the desire to calculate the advent of the messianic era or to attempt to hasten the Messiah's arrival. Instead, redemption came to be considered as the fruit of a laborious process by which humanity *successively* realizes the messianic promise. This particular theology of history can at first glance seem somewhat harsh; God seems quite simply to have abandoned history to its own fate. In fact, it expresses a profound conviction of God's faith in humanity's capacity to confer meaning itself upon history. It is also significant, as Gross underscores, that the role of the redemptive figure was to be toned down in relation to the *demand* for redemption. And it is perhaps here that one sees most clearly the continuity with the prophetic tradition, namely in the link that is established between history and an unconditional demand for justice: 'Jewish messianism is more than anything a vibrant protest, an energetic refusal to accept the conditions of this world as definite'.[41]

There is much to be said for Gross's map of the differing fates of the messianic idea within emergent Christianity and rabbinic Judaism. There has long been a broad consensus among historians and biblical scholars about the apocalyptic character of both the original Jesus movement and the early church.[42] The shift that occurs in the view of the messianic figure is illustrative in this respect. Where the proto-messianic figure who emerges in the Book of Isaiah (and elsewhere in the prophetic literature) is in all respects an intrahistorical figure, the Messiah of the early church – interpreted in light of the belief in Jesus's resurrection – came to be understood as a transhistorical figure of divine nature.[43] In this regard it stands in undeniably stark contrast to the understanding of the messianic figure that came to assume definite form in the rabbinic tradition.

Even so, Gross's map is nowhere near as irrefutable as its author's polemical tone would suggest. In the first place, Judaism during the remainder of classical antiquity was anything but free of apocalyptic movements. The rabbinic tradition may have sought to suppress apocalyptic movements in favour of a more rationalistic and restorative position, but the Talmudic tradition contains elements of both strands. As regards the nature of the messianic event, in other words, one finds *both* the notion that it is a matter of a dramatic external intervention beyond the influence of humans *and* the notion that redemption is the fruit of humanity's patient preparations. At a concrete historical level, too, apocalyptic messianic movements have continued to play a role within Judaism during medieval as well as modern periods. Perhaps, as Scholem proposes in his celebrated essay, the fact is that this persistent tension between the two strands is what has given, and continues to give, Jewish messianism its particular dynamism.[44]

In corresponding fashion, it would be an oversimplification to pigeonhole emergent Christianity as unambiguously apocalyptic. True, the early Christian interpretation of Jesus as the Messiah (or *Christos*, to give the Greek term) was unmistakeably apocalyptic in nature. Thus the early Christian movement was driven by a strong hope in Jesus's imminent return (*parousia*) and the end of the present era. However, once it became clear that parousia was not in fact imminent, a theological explanation was called for. Soon a dynamic theology of history emerged, which, not unlike the restorative strand within rabbinic messianism, emphasized the positive significance of the postponed messianic event, treating incomplete redemption as a possibility rather than a failure. In these constructive new interpretations of history, the notion of God's continued presence via his spirit was to play a decisive role.

Spirit and Redemption

The term 'spirit of God' conceals one of the most enduring concepts in Jewish and Christian history, that is also one of the least amenable to definition. The temptation of projecting *post hoc* concepts onto older texts, as evinced in the case of the messianic motif, holds, if anything, doubly true for the idea of the spirit of God. Throughout history Christian theologians have interpreted the spirit concept in the Hebrew Bible in light of its meaning in the New Testament and the later Christian tradition in which 'the Holy Spirit' gradually evolves into part of the Christian creed.[45]

Before returning to the prophetic literature, it should be pointed out that the spirit's central role within Christian theology of history cannot be derived from the prophetic books in any simple way. Even so, the Hebrew Bible represents an important background text for any understanding of how the concept of the spirit is linked to history in the later Western tradition; above all, the connection between the spirit concept and the proclamation of impending justice that can be discerned at several points in the prophetic literature. The proposed connection between the spirit and imminent redemption not only forms the basis for early Christian notions of the spirit's role in the history of salvation, but also constitutes the germ of the very idea that history has a purpose and a meaning, and that this meaning is produced by the spirit of God.

Yet it is essential to retain an awareness of the complexity and the slippages in meaning that characterize the idea of the spirit within the frame of the Hebrew Bible. The Hebrew word that the New Revised Standard Version as often as not translates as 'spirit' is *ruach*. Unlike the English notion of 'spirit' (and comparable concepts in other modern European languages), this term encompasses a wider semantic field, even connoting such concepts as wind, storm, breath, or life force. This semantic breadth is also a hallmark of the Greek word *pneuma*, which in most cases corresponds to *ruach* in the Septuagint, the oldest Greek translation of the Hebrew Bible. The Latin word *spiritus* is considerably narrower in meaning, however, denoting among other things a clearer contrast with corporeal and material reality.[46]

Given all this, it is interesting to note how *ruach*, particularly in the older texts, is closely associated with what might be termed forces of nature. Unlike the later dualistic tendencies, *ruach* here appears as an integrated part of material reality. An instructive example is provided by the account of the Flood in Genesis, in which God, mindful of the righteous Noah and the other creatures in the Ark, decides to allow *ruach*, 'a wind', to blow across the earth so that the waters recede (Gen. 8:1). In similar fashion, God has 'a strong east wind' part the Red Sea in the middle when rescuing his people from Egyptian slavery in Exodus (Exod. 14:21).

In the Deuteronomistic History, *ruach* assumes a range of different meanings. In many contexts it refers quite simply to life force in a more general sense, describing the force or, rather, energy that imbues matter or individual bodies with life. Thus the Book of Judges relates how the warlike hero Samson, exhausted and near to death after fighting the Philistines, renews his 'spirit' when God causes water to gush forth from a crater in the ground (Judg. 15:19). Elsewhere, *ruach* seems instead to denote a kind of charisma that is temporarily bestowed upon courageous leaders, allowing them to perform great feats of arms. The third chapter relates how the Lord's spirit 'comes upon' the judge Othniel, prompting him to go to war and subjugate the enemies of Israel (Judg. 3:10). The brave warrior Gideon is similarly prepared for battle with the Midianites (Judg. 6:34), as, too, is the commander Jephthah, whom God tasks with bringing victory against the Ammonites (Judg. 11:29).

This connection between leadership and the spirit also characterizes the later historical literature of the Bible. When the prophet Samuel anoints Saul as the first king of the Israelites, the text relates how the spirit of the Lord descends upon the king and causes him to fall into an ecstasy and prophesy 'with the prophets' (1 Sam. 10:11). When Saul later strays from the path of God and is stripped of his royal powers, the spirit of the Lord abandons him and he is tormented by an 'evil spirit' (1 Sam. 16:14). Instead, it is the young shepherd boy David who now finds grace in God's sight and whom Samuel is enjoined to anoint as king: 'Then Samuel took the horn of oil, and anointed him in the presence of his brothers; and the spirit of the Lord came mightily upon David from that day forward' (1 Sam. 16:13). Interestingly, both episodes associate the spirit with anointing, something reflected in the later connecting of the spirit to the notion of a messianic redeemer. Of particular significance for the future development of the notion of the spirit is also how they show that in David's case the presence of the spirit – unlike the short-lived charismatic force that affected the leaders of olden times – is something permanent.[47]

Nevertheless, political and military leaders are not the only figures whom the historical books associate with the power of God's spirit. As the example of Saul's anointing indicates, power is also linked to the near-ecstatic expressions that are on a number of occasions attributed to prophetic figures (cf. 1 Sam. 19:20–24). But how do matters stand in the prophetic literature itself? Here, too, semantic slippages and shifting relations to the spirit concept may be noted among the various prophets. For instance, only in Ezekiel is there an explicit connection between God's spirit and ecstatic prophetic declarations. In Amos the spirit concept is essentially absent, while in Jeremiah it is used in a more subdued and often slightly pejorative fashion.

This should not prevent some general tendencies in the evolving concept of the spirit in the prophetic literature from being identified – tendencies that both deviate from the historical literature of the Bible and anticipate future developments of the concept. The most remarkable of these is how the spirit concept is steadily interwoven with the notion of justice that forms the very heart of the prophetic books. While *ruach* – in the form of the charisma with which prominent leaders are endowed – in the historical literature undeniably helps bring prosperity to the Israelites, there is no mention here of any more radical notion of justice. This will change in several respects in the prophetic literature.

One obvious example is how the concept of the spirit is incorporated into the pronouncement of judgement of several of the prophets. The first indication comes in Hosea. In a resounding denunciation of both the people and their priests, Hosea lets the Lord conclude with the words: 'A wind [*ruach*] has wrapped them in its wings, and they shall be ashamed because of their altars' (Hosea 4:19). In rather softer tones, Isaiah announces the impending restoration of Jerusalem, albeit only after God, in 'a spirit of judgement and by a spirit of burning', has 'washed away the filth of the daughters of Zion and cleansed the bloodstains of Jerusalem from its midst' (Isa. 4:4).[48] The motif is even more explicit in Micah, who tilts at the nation's corrupt leaders and deceitful prophets:

> Listen, you heads of Jacob
>   and rulers of the house of Israel!
> Should you not know justice? –
>   you who hate the good and love the evil,
> who tear the skin off my people,
>   and the flesh off their bones;

> who eat the flesh of my people,
>> flay their skin off them,
> break their bones in pieces,
>> and chop them up like meat in a kettle,
>> like flesh in a cauldron.
> Then they will cry out to the Lord,
>> but he will not answer them;
> he will hide his face from them at that time,
>> because they have acted wickedly.
> Thus says the Lord concerning the prophets
>> who lead my people astray,
> who cry 'Peace'
>> when they have something to eat,
> but declare war against those
>> who put nothing in their mouths.
> Therefore it shall be night to you, without vision,
>> and darkness to you, without revelation.
> The sun shall go down upon the prophets,
>> and the day shall be black over them;
> the seers shall be disgraced,
>> and the diviners put to shame;
> they shall all cover their lips,
>> for there is no answer from God.
> But as for me, I am filled with power,
>> with the spirit of the Lord,
>> and with justice and might,
> to declare to Jacob his transgression
>> and to Israel his sin.
>
> (Mic. 3:1–8)

This passage contains several curiosities. First, *ruach* is not connected to judgement and purification at a level of mere generality. Rather, the spirit of the Lord is presented as the force driving Micah to concretely show the unrighteous their sins. Where the spirit in olden times bestowed on political leaders the charisma to perform great feats of arms, the spirit in the prophet provides the inspiration needed to stand in judgement upon the moral lapses of the people's leaders. Interestingly, however, it is not only the nation's political leaders who are targets for criticism. Those prophets who lend their support to the unjust order by predicting peace and happiness – thereby persuading the people that all is as it should be – get their due. Being a prophet is thus in itself no guarantee of being endowed with the spirit. Rather, as Micah indicates, it is the *qualitative* content of the prophet's preaching that determines whether he is speaking with the force of God's spirit. As noted earlier, this content is inseparable from justice.

This may be why Heschel in his reading of the prophets can plausibly interpret the term *ruach* in terms of pathos. The experience of being filled by the power of the spirit would in this case correspond to the way in which the prophet is touched and moved by God's pathos, by God's indefatigable preoccupation with his people's recurrent betrayal of justice: 'In contrast to the Stoic sage who is a *homo apathetikos*, the prophet may be characterised as a *homo sympathetikos*. ... The pathos of God is upon him. It moves him. It breaks out in him like a storm in the soul, overwhelming his inner life, his thoughts, feelings, wishes, and hopes. It takes possession of his heart and mind, giving him the courage to act against the world.'[49]

Without disregarding the multifaceted uses of *ruach* in the prophetic literature, the passage from Micah quoted above indicates that one connotation of the term relates to the capacity to be moved – or roused – by unrighteous states of affairs: that is to say, by injustice. At the same time, it would be misleading to reduce the prophetic pathos to a generalized spirit of justice in the modern sense of the word. To do so would be to disregard the strongly theological aspect of the ancient Hebrew notion of justice. Returning to an earlier point, it should be recalled that justice in the biblical context is a concept that encompasses considerably more than practices and conventions between human beings. The concept also involves a transcendental order that is ultimately indistinguishable from God himself.[50]

Interpreting spirit in terms of pathos in this way also illuminates the proto-messianic passages quoted earlier from the eleventh chapter of Isaiah. The depicted figure, who is expected to 'decide with equity for the meek of the earth' (Isa. 11:4), is here said to have been filled with 'the spirit of wisdom and understanding, the spirit of counsel and might, the spirit of knowledge and the fear of the Lord' (Isa. 11:4). At this point we reencounter an important source not only for the messianic idea but also for how the spirit will later be associated with the messianic figure. The same tendency of connecting the spirit with the idea of a righteous leader recurs in a number of other places in the Book of Isaiah, as here in the first of the so-called Servant songs in Deutero-Isaiah:

> Here is my servant, whom I uphold,
>> my chosen, in whom my soul delights;
>
> I have put my spirit upon him;
>> he will bring justice to the nations.
>
> He will not cry or lift up his voice,
>> or make it heard in the street;
>
> a bruised reed he will not break,
>> and a dimly burning wick he will not quench;
>> he will faithfully bring forth justice.
>
> He will not grow faint or be crushed

> until he has established justice in the earth;
> and the coastlands wait for his teaching.
(Isa. 42:1–4)

In a formulation that seems to allude to how God in former times let his spirit descend upon military leaders, the chosen servant is here described as having been endowed with the power of the spirit for the purposes of bringing justice to the people. A corresponding parallel between God's actions in former times and God's dealings with the prophets can be found in the book's sixty-first chapter, in which the prophetic mission is for the first time associated with anointment:

> The spirit of the Lord God is upon me,
> because the Lord has anointed me;
> he has sent me to bring good news to the oppressed,
> to bind up the broken-hearted,
> to proclaim liberty to the captives,
> and release to the prisoners.
(Isa. 61:1)

The passage recalls both Saul's and David's anointments, but with one essential difference. Where the anointment ritual had long been primarily associated with the office of king, it would here – in the post-exilian period – be symbolically connected with the prophetic mission to proclaim liberation and restoration for the oppressed. At the very start of this chapter attention was drawn to how the author of the Gospel of Luke has Jesus recite this very passage from the Book of Isaiah in relation to himself (Luke 4:16–30). The author thereby situates Jesus within the tradition of anointed prophets, allowing the spirit to serve as a marker of the continuity between former times and the present.

There is yet another aspect that warrants mention in this regard. The spirit is here used not only to signal the continuity within God's dealings with humanity throughout history but also to represent the impulse to transcend current historical conditions. This notion of a kind of historical progression is hinted at in Luke (as in the other Gospels) when it portrays Jesus as the fulfilment of the prophetic tradition. This concept was to prove decisive for Christian understanding of the history of salvation but would quickly give rise to conflict between Judaism and Christianity, precisely as a consequence of Christian theologians' claims that their own tradition contained a more complete version of God's revelation. At the same time, it is important to note that the spirit in this 'progressive' sense is also present in the prophetic literature. In the passages cited above the spirit takes the form of a power or pathos that drives the prophet to challenge the current order of things and to draw attention to the fact that historical conditions could look very different: 'I have put my spirit upon him; / he will bring justice to the nations'.

Once again we are confronted by a motif with deep reverberations for religious as well as secular liberation movements throughout history. On the one hand, this is a pathos that drives the prophet to criticize and condemn unjust regulations, whether political or religious in nature. On the other hand, the same pathos drives the prophet to infuse the people with new hope and courage by proclaiming the possibility of another, more righteous order. Both instances attest to a certain shift in emphasis within the prophetic literature, most notably in the Book of Isaiah. Where Proto-Isaiah makes a connection to the spirit concept in order to condemn sin and pass judgement upon the wickedness of Jerusalem, Deutero- and Trito-Isaiah in particular present a link between the spirit and the promise of imminent redemption. This link is visible in the proto-messianic passages discussed previously, in which the spirit is depicted as a force that prepares God's chosen servant to bring about the redemption. The connection is clearer still in those later passages which associate imminent redemption with a more general outpouring of God's spirit:

> But now hear, O Jacob my servant,
>   Israel whom I have chosen!
> Thus says the Lord who made you,
>   who formed you in the womb and will help you:
> Do not fear, O Jacob my servant,
>   Jeshurun whom I have chosen.
> For I will pour water on the thirsty land,
>   and streams on the dry ground;
> I will pour my spirit upon your descendants,
>   and my blessing on your offspring.
> They shall spring up like a green tamarisk,
>   like willows by flowing streams.
> This one will say, 'I am the Lord's',
>   another will be called by the name of Jacob,
> yet another will write on the hand, 'The Lord's',
>   and adopt the name of Israel.
> (Isa. 44:1–5)

Although this powerful oracle of redemption is addressed to the Jewish people ('Jacob'), and more precisely to the exile population in Babylon, it is worth noting that the words are spoken by Deutero-Isaiah. The bulk of the Book of Isaiah, authored by this anonymous prophet, in fact contains what is usually considered the oldest documented evidence of monotheism known to history.[51] To be sure, an emphasis upon the Israelites' exclusive bond of faith to the God who had revealed himself on Sinai can be traced back as far as the older prophets, but it also presupposes as self-evident that other peoples follow other gods. In Deutero-Isaiah, by contrast, can be found a resolute denial of the existence of any other gods: 'Before me no god was formed, nor shall there be any after me. I, I am the Lord, and besides me there is no saviour' (Isa. 43:10–11). The God of Israel is the only God, in other words, by implication making him the God of all peoples.

Discernible here is the beginning of a universalizing tendency, a tendency reflected, not least, in the shift that took place at around this time in how the spirit was regarded. More precisely, it represents a spatial and temporal widening of the concept.[52] Where *ruach* had in the past primarily denoted a power that could be bestowed upon individual figures in the present, it is connected by several of the later prophets to the promise of a time when God's spirit will descend upon the entire Jewish people until that time when peace and justice will have established themselves. A few decades before Deutero-Isaiah, Ezekiel had also proclaimed that the exiled people would be restored following an outpouring of God's spirit: 'I will put my spirit within you, and you shall live, and I will place you on your own soil; then you shall know that I, the Lord, have spoken and will act, says the Lord' (Ezek. 37:14; see also 39:29). Prophetism's universalizing tendency finds its most famous expression in Joel's prophesy of the effusion of the spirit upon all flesh:

> Then afterwards
>   I will pour out my spirit on all flesh;
> your sons and your daughters shall prophesy,
>   your old men shall dream dreams,
>   and your young men shall see visions.
> Even on the male and female slaves,
>   in those days, I will pour out my spirit.
> I will show portents in the heavens and on the earth,
>   blood and fire and columns of smoke.
> The sun shall be turned to darkness, and the moon to blood,
>   before the great and terrible day of the Lord comes.
> (Joel 2:28–31)

Where Deutero-Isaiah and Ezekiel announce an outpouring of the spirit upon the people of Israel, Joel's apocalyptically freighted proclamation alludes to a still more comprehensive redemption. Read in its entirety, however, the book makes quite clear that even in Joel the reference is in the final instance to his own people. Notwithstanding, this passage has had a decisive influence upon later notions – Jewish and Christian – of universal redemption. As a result, it has also played a role in the evolution of the idea of a common goal for humanity in history, or, one might say, of the very idea of history itself.

Let me conclude this odyssey through the prophetic literature by returning to this chapter's opening words by Henri de Lubac on history as one of the great events of Christianity. As this study moves forward, it will become apparent that there is a great deal of truth in de Lubac's formulation. In a number of essential respects early Christian theology of history laid the basis for the understanding of history that would become dominant in Western civilization.

The problem with de Lubac's assertion is that it covers up what this rather fragmentary odyssey has shown, namely, that several of the constitutive elements of the Christian conception of history are to be found in the tradition from which Christianity primarily derives – the Judaism of classical antiquity. It was within this specific framework that the idea of one God as the Lord of history emerged – and also, eventually, the idea of history as such.

> [T]hus the concepts of Israel and its land, of Jerusalem, the temple, and the dynasty of David became religious symbols of supranational significance. When first conceived, these were national expressions of an essentially universal idea. ... The prophets, while accepting and employing national symbols (they are not 'cosmopolitan' or 'citizens of the world'), gave them universal significance by their new eschatological vision of the return of the nations to God. Israel, the elect of God, is the arena of God's self-disclosure to all the nations. The national symbols became supranational, eternal, beyond the power of any political collapse to destroy. Classical prophecy created the idea of universal history in its conception of the kingdom of God as ultimately destined to extend over all mankind.[53]

Kaufmann's words offer as sound a précis as any of the theology of history that emerges from the prophetic literature. One might follow Heschel in clarifying that this notion of God as the Lord of history should not be confused with the idea of God as intrinsic to history itself and thus of history as a necessary – organic or dialectical – process: 'The prophets never taught that God and history are one, or that whatever happens below reflects the will of God above'.[54] Rather, history is the place where humanity puts God's will to the test and where justice suffers a continual succession of defeats. But this is only one side of the coin. History is also the place where God puts humanity's will to the test and challenges it to rise up against worldly wickedness in the name of a higher justice. Perhaps this latter is the most important insight yielded by the literature bequeathed by a prophetic tradition reaching back more than two millennia: that actual historical processes should never be considered as self-justifying; that history at every moment stands ready to be put on trial by an authority which refuses to allow itself to be made subordinate to that history.

Notes

1. H. de Lubac. 1987. *Paradoxes of Faith*, trans. P. Simon and S. Kreilkamp, San Francisco: Ignatus Press, 145.

2. See also J.D.G. Dunn (ed.). 1999. *Jews and Christians: The Parting of the Ways AD 70 to 135*, Grand Rapids: Eerdmans.

3. All Bible quotes are taken from the New Revised Standard Version (NRSV).

4. For a critical overview of early Old Testament scholarship, see H.J. Kraus. 1982. *Geschichte der historisch-kritischen Erforschung des Alten Testaments*, 3rd edn, Neukirchen-Vluyn: Neukirchener Verlag.

5. See Y. Kaufmann. 1960. *The Religion of Israel: From Its Beginnings to the Babylonian Exile*, trans. M. Greenberg, Chicago: University of Chicago Press, 216–329; A.J. Heschel. 2001. *The Prophets*, vols 1–2, New York: Harper Perennial Classics, 278–280 (the work was originally published as *Das prophetische Bewusstsein* in Berlin in 1932).

6. Kaufmann, *Religion of Israel*. The English edition is an abridged version of the Hebrew original, which appeared in eight volumes between 1937 and 1956.

7. Kaufmann, *Religion of Israel*, 132–133.

8. Heschel, *The Prophets*, 27.

9. F. Nietzsche. 1989. *On the Genealogy of Morals; Ecce Homo*, trans. W. Kaufmann and R.J. Hollingdale, New York: Vintage, 33–36. Nietzsche's relationship to Judaism and Jewishness is, of course, more complex than this brief paragraph suggests; see e.g. Y. Yovel. 1998. *Dark Riddle: Hegel, Nietzsche and the Jews*, Cambridge: Polity Press.

10. R. Girard. 2001. *I See Satan Fall Like Lightning*, trans. J.G. Williams, Maryknoll: Orbis Books, 138.

11. Heschel, *The Prophets*, 250–252.

12. See also J. Blenkinsopp. 1983. *A History of Prophecy in Israel*, 2nd edn, Louisville and London: Westminster John Knox Press, 80–81.

13. Heschel, *The Prophets*, 253.

14. Ibid., 276.

15. M. Buber. 1949. *The Prophetic Faith*, trans. C. Witton-Davies, New York: Collier Books, 126–145. See also W. Dietrich. 2002. *"Theopolitik": Studien zur Theologie und Ethik des Alten Testaments*, Neukirchen-Vluyn: Neukirchener Verlag.

16. This refers to the Books of Deuteronomy, Joshua, Judges, Samuel and Kings, which form an integrated block of texts governed by a specific construct of history.

17. See Buber, *The Prophetic Faith*, 151–154.

18. See also N. Cohn. 1993. *Cosmos, Chaos and the World to Come: The Ancient Roots of Apocalyptic Faith*, New Haven and London: Yale University Press, 163–166; and J.J. Collins. 2003. 'From Prophecy to Apocalypticism: The Expectation of the End', in J.J. Collins, B. McGinn and S.J. Stein (eds), *The Continuum History of Apocalypticism*, New York and London: Continuum, 64–88.

19. See Buber, *The Prophetic Faith*, 2–3. See also B. Scheuer. 2008. *The Return of YHWH: The Tension between Deliverance and Repentance in Isaiah 40–55*, Berlin: Walter de Gruyter.

20. See also J. Asurmendi. 1985. *Le prophétisme. Des origines à l'époque moderne*, Paris: Nouvelle cité, 28–30.

21. W. Brueggemann. 2001. *The Prophetic Imagination*, 2nd edn, Minneapolis: Fortress Press, 23.

22. See, in addition to ibid., W. Brueggemann. 1986. *Hopeful Imagination: Prophetic Voices in Exile*, Minneapolis: Augsburg Fortress Publishers, and idem. 2000. *Texts that Linger, Words that Explode: Listening to Prophetic Voices*, Minneapolis: Augsburg Fortress Publishers.

23. See Kaufmann, *Religion of Israel*, 132–133.

24. See also Blenkinsopp, *History of Prophecy*, 89–90.

25. G. Scholem. 1971. 'Toward an Understanding of the Messianic Idea in Judaism', trans. M.A. Meyer, in idem, *The Messianic Idea in Judaism and Other Essays on Jewish Spirituality*, New York: Schocken Books, 1–36. The German original was published in 1959.

26. Ibid., 7.

27. See also Cohn, *Cosmos*, 159, and H. Strauß. 1992. 'Messias/Messianische Bewegungen: I. Altes Testament', in *Theologische Realenzyklopädie*, vol. 22, Berlin and New York: Walter de Gruyter, 617–621.

28. See also D. Banon. 1998. *Le messianisme*, Paris: PUF, 9–12; and W. Horbury. 2003. *Messianism among Jews and Christians: Biblical and Historical Studies*, London and New York: T&T Clark, 1–21.

29. See also Strauß, 'Messias/Messianische Bewegungen', 617.

30. Horbury, *Messianism*, 4–5; 125–155.

31. See also Cohn, *Cosmos*, 146–147.

32. Most biblical scholars today consider the paragraph to be a later, probably post-exilian addition to Proto-Isaiah. For an erudite discussion of the kingdom visions in Isaiah, see further T. Wagner. 2006. *Gottes Herrschaft: Eine Analyse der Denkschrift (Jes 6,1–9,6)*, Leiden and Boston: Brill.

33. See also Strauß, 'Messias/Messianische Bewegungen', 618.

34. See also Collins, 'From Prophecy to Apocalypticism', 64–88.

35. See also B. Gross. 1994. *Messianisme et histoire juive*, Paris: Berg International Éditeurs, 29–35; and Cohn, *Cosmos*, 157–162.

36. See also Blenkinsopp, *History of Prophecy*, 212–216.

37. Gross, *Messianisme*, 35–38. Cf. also Scholem, 'Messianic Idea', and J.C. VanderKam. 2003, 'Messianism and Apocalypticism', in Collins et al. (eds), *The Continuum History of Apocalypticism*, 112–138.

38. Gross, *Messianisme*, 35–38.

39. Ibid., 39–41.

40. Ibid., 35–41.

41. Ibid., 54.

42. See e.g. J.J. Collins. 1989. *The Apocalyptic Imagination: An Introduction to the Jewish Matrix of Christianity*, New York: Crossroad, and C. Rowland. 2002. *Christian Origins: The Setting and Character of the Most Important Messianic Sect of Judaism*, 2nd edn, London: SPCK. Whether Jesus's own assessment of his mission was apocalyptic in character is a matter of scholarly debate; for an overview of this debate, see e.g. D.C. Allison. 2003. 'The Eschatology of Jesus', in Collins et al. (eds), *The Continuum History of Apocalypticism*, 139–165.

43. See also Cohn, *Cosmos*, 194–211.

44. Scholem, 'Messianic Idea', 32–33.

45. An illustrative example would be Y. Congar. 1997. *I Believe in the Holy Spirit*, trans. D. Smith, New York: Crossroad. Congar's monumental work, originally published in 1979–1980, served for decades as a standard reference for Christian pneumatology.

46. See also W.H. Schmidt. 1984. 'Geist/Heiliger Geist/Geistesgaben: I. Altes Testament', in *Theologische Realenzyklopädie*, vol. 12, Berlin and New York: Walter de Gruyter, 170–173.

47. See also G.T. Montague. 2006. *The Holy Spirit: The Growth of a Biblical Tradition*, Eugene: Wipf and Stock, 18–23.

48. The paragraph is generally assumed to be a relatively late – i.e. post-exilian – addition to Proto-Isaiah.

49. Heschel, *The Prophets*, 395.

50. Ibid., 252–254.

51. See also Cohn, *Cosmos*, 151–157.

52. See also J. McIntyre. 1979. *The Shape of Pneumatology: Studies in the Doctrine of the Holy Spirit*, Edinburgh: T&T Clark, 42–43.

53. Kaufmann, *Religion of Israel*, 346. See also Buber, *The Prophetic Faith*, 208–215.

54. Heschel, *The Prophets*, 214.

CHAPTER 2

The Ages of History

On Whitsun morning of 1183, Joachim of Fiore was seized by a powerful vision.[1] The Calabrian abbot had withdrawn some time previously to the abbey of Casamari in order to find peace in which to write and reflect. But on that very morning he had been troubled by doubts. The more he considered the matter, the more incomprehensible Joachim found the idea that God should be three distinct persons and yet one single being. Appalled by his inability to believe in the Holy Trinity of God, Joachim threw himself into intensive prayer. He invoked the Holy Spirit whose special feast day it happened to be. It was then that the vision occurred. In his mind's eye Joachim saw a ten-stringed instrument, a psalter through which the whole mystery of the Trinity shone forth so brightly and clearly that his doubts were instantly transformed into adoration. Inspired by the vision, he shortly thereafter began his *Psalterium Decem Chordarum*, a theological disquisition on the Trinity that had no precedent in earlier Christian tradition.[2]

What made Joachim's trinitarian theology so innovative was that he integrated the three divine persons into history, the stage upon which the drama of the world's redemption takes place. The earliest Christian theologians had already differentiated between the era of the Father, associated with the covenant between God and the Jewish people, and the era of the Son, instituted by Christ's resurrection and expected to continue until the Last Judgement. Joachim went a step further by identifying a third era of spiritual perfection associated with the Holy Spirit, and contended that this era still awaited its fulfilment in an earthly future.

Did Joachim, in the wake of his vision, invent the most important idea in Western history, an idea both ghastly and seductive, the catalyst of a boom in civilization but also the root of its darkest manifestations? It is as the inventor of the idea of progress that Joachim has often been portrayed, this often-overlooked

---

Notes for this section begin on page 61.

twelfth-century thinker whose influence is nonetheless difficult to overestimate. On the one hand, he has been celebrated as a proto-socialist figure whose vision of a new era of peace and concord lent force to religious as well as secular reform movements in the modern period. On the other, he has been singled out as the brains behind that vein of utopianism which received its most extreme expression in the totalitarian political projects of the twentieth century.[3]

But was Joachim really so unique and groundbreaking as his posthumous reputation would have us believe? The answer is both yes and no, and it is perhaps indicative in this context that when lists of saints and heretics began to proliferate in the late medieval period, his name figured prominently in both categories.[4] Even so, it cannot be denied that in *one* key respect Joachim parted company with the dominant interpretation of Christian tradition, namely that he introduced an element of inner-worldly progression into the course of events that comprise the salvation history. In Joachim's case, as will become clear in the following survey, there is no sense in which this is a simple, linear progression. Nor should the relative development identified by Joachim in the course of events that constitute the salvation history be regarded as the result of human exertions. In this regard he lies at a very considerable remove from modern secular ideologies of progress.

Joachim was nonetheless a pioneer in his theological thinking. By imagining a future intrahistorical era of spiritual perfection, he not only broke with the strain of apocalypticism that is a defining feature of early Christianity. He also broke with the pessimistic view of history that had dominated the Western church during the early medieval period. While the theologians of the first centuries had reconciled themselves to Christ's deferred return by gradually adopting a more affirmative attitude towards the worldly order of things, this stance had undergone a dramatic change with the fall of the Western Roman Empire. Henceforth the dominant image of the church would be as a pilgrim, a rootless traveller, in this world. The idea that the kingdom of God had already partly arrived faded away, taking with it any hopes for a new, blessed era for the church on earth.

In this light it is clear that Joachim, with his feeling for progression and renewal *within* history, departed from key aspects of previous Christian tradition. It is also in this sense that he can be described as unique and pioneering as a thinker. With a broader perspective, however, considering Joachim in light of classical Jewish prophetism, a different picture emerges. As described in Chapter One, the prophetic literature presents a theology of history that locates the redemptive process in the present moment, rather than at the end of time. Even when the messianic idea of a redemptive figure did emerge, it was originally an intrahistorical figure associated with concrete social and political expectations. Indeed, it was only with the spread of apocalypticism that the pattern changed and that redemption came to be defined in suprahistorical terms. In this respect it thus evinces a striking similarity with Joachim's theology of history. Like the prophets of antiquity before him, Joachim was less interested in the fate of the individual in a world to come than he was in the spiritual perfection of this world. Given this fact, it can be a source of puzzlement that Joachim is nonetheless usually characterized as an apocalyptic thinker.

How can these two aspects be reconciled? Reading Joachim's works, one finds significant similarities with earlier Christian apocalypticism, both stylistically and temperamentally. His tone is often dramatic and the end seems to be nigh; but Joachim does not announce the end of history but its impending transformation into a new era on earth whose hallmark will be a flourishing of contemplative life. What can be found in Joachim is, in other words, a non-eschatological apocalypticism. This should not, as some have argued, be understood as an abandoning of eschatology in favour of some dream of realizing heaven on earth. Joachim was convinced that the Last Judgement and the end of history would one day come, but only after the third person of the triune godhead had been allowed to perform its role in the historical salvation drama and thereby enable humanity to enjoy a protracted earthly Sabbath.

The distinction made above between prophetism and apocalypticism takes on a new aspect here. Where thinkers such as Benjamin Gross tend to counterpose prophetism's intrahistorical view of redemption to apocalypticism's striving for a world to come, Joachim attests to the limitations of this dichotomy. Joachim's mode of thought is at once radically apocalyptic and profoundly rooted in history.

Joachim's ingenious theology of history reunites prophetism's more restorative features with apocalypticism's forward-looking qualities. In this sense Joachim provides a solution to what was identified above as the weakest link in classical prophetism: the temptation to locate the ideal state in a vanished golden era, thereby failing to offer any alternative to the current order beyond nostalgia for an idealized past. By depicting the imminent ideal era as both temporary and essentially connected with earlier eras (tied to the Father and the Son, respectively), however, Joachim also avoids the reverse temptation: a contempt for the world that is latent in eschatological apocalypticism's projection of redemption onto a world to come.

In what follows I will show how Joachim integrates prophetic, pneumatic and messianic motifs in a way that was to leave a deep impression upon later European philosophy of history. In order to appreciate the subtlety of Joachim's trinitarian interpretation of history, however, it will be necessary to go back one step and say something about the development of the historico-theological tradition which Joachim simultaneously identifies with and breaks from. In very general terms, I will indicate how the Christian view of history evolved from the New Testament texts to Augustine in the fifth century. I have chosen to stop at Augustine because his position in several respects can be seen as paradigmatic of the view of history that would become predominant in the Western

Christian tradition. Augustine is also one of the few authorities in relation to whom Joachim explicitly situates himself, although this does not prevent the latter from taking a substantially different path.

Parousia Postponed

Both Judaism and Christianity are seen as messianic religions in most people's eyes. But is this really true? Is it not actually the case that both traditions emerged as counter-movements to the often riotous proliferation of messianic movements in antiquity? Going back to the period in which both Christianity and rabbinic Judaism emerged, there are ample reasons for posing this question. As already noted, Judaism early on took measures to defend itself against apocalyptic messianic movements. Its suspicion of unchecked messianic antics was fuelled by the apocalyptically inclined Jesus movement. Such suspicions were definitively confirmed by the bloody conclusion to the Bar Kokhba revolt (initiated by the messianic preacher Simon bar Kokhba) in Judea in 135. Rabbinic Judaism increasingly concentrated its faith upon the observance of the Torah, with the anarchic potential of messianism being forced to the margin. Naturally, this did not prevent such potential from making itself felt on repeated occasions in Jewish history. Nor did it prevent the messianic motif from playing an ongoing role in the rabbinic tradition.[5]

The situation is more intricate in the case of Christianity's relation to messianism. That the early Jesus movement was both apocalyptic and messianic in nature is beyond question. When the earthly Jesus was suddenly removed by execution at the hands of the Roman authorities, the course of events was interpreted in eschatological terms. The messianic era had begun and the heavenly Son of Man would return very shortly to judge the living and the dead. The problem that soon presented itself was that this return, called *parousia* in Greek, never took place. Was it a mistake? Was Jesus of Nazareth not the promised Messiah?

This was the dilemma that gave rise to the earliest Christian theologies of history. Rather than renounce the claim that Jesus of Nazareth was the Messiah, they solved the dilemma with a series of theological and historical reinterpretations. The connecting thread in these reinterpretations, precisely as in Judaism, was a steady modulating of their apocalyptic qualities. This also meant that the messianic motif, in the strict sense of the word, was abandoned. The development is already discernible within the framework of the New Testament texts. The Pauline epistles and the Gospel of Mark evince an expectation of Jesus's imminent return, whereas the later Gospel of John bears the hallmarks of a considerable theological sublimation of the original messianic faith. Paul's salvatory figure who is expected to come dramatically 'like a thief in the night' (1 Thess. 5:2) has been transformed into the timeless divine Word: 'In the beginning was the Word, and the Word was with God, and the Word was God' (John 1:1).

Yet the most remarkable example comes from Luke–Acts. 'Luke', the anonymous author of the Gospel of Luke and the Acts of the Apostles, has sometimes been identified as the first Christian historian.[6] The claim has a strong basis insofar as the narrative structure of his works draw considerably upon Greek historiography. However, as Daniel Marguerat has insisted, Luke is no Christian Thucydides. Content-wise, his writings lack the Greek historian's level-headed recording gaze. Luke is pursuing *theology* with the help of historiography. The tools of classical historiography enable him to develop a history that begins with Jesus's birth (albeit anchored firmly in the Jewish prophetic tradition), culminates with the crucifixion and resurrection, and then proceeds to the activities of the apostles. The theological yield is optimal. With one stroke of the pen, Luke manages to draw attention away from the postponed parousia while simultaneously directing it upon how the project of divine salvation lives on in history.[7]

Luke represents a first important step towards the modulating of Christian theology's apocalyptic elements. And yet this is only part of the picture. Although it is possible to discern a development away from apocalyptic interpretations of Jesus's fate within the frame of the New Testament texts, this does not mean that apocalyptic movements ceased to proliferate. It must be recalled that the most thoroughgoing example of apocalyptic literature in the New Testament, the Revelation of John, was also one of the latest books to be included in the collection.

The fact that apocalyptic ideas continued to leave their mark on emergent Christian theology is also evinced by the theological literature of subsequent centuries. Tertullian, who was active during the early third century, offers a rather dark view of history: the spread of heresy and the suffering of the righteous were auguries as good as any that time was running out and history nearing its end. At the same time, in his famous apologia for Christian faith, *Apology*, Tertullian maintains that Christians should prey for the continued existence of the Roman Empire and for the postponement of the dawn of the end of days.[8]

Tertullian's apologetic writings can be seen as one of the earliest attempts to solve what Jaroslav Pelikan has described as the apparent contradiction in Christianity between finality and universality. On the one hand, Christianity contends that in the coming of Christ history has attained its climatic end (*finis*) and that, as a consequence, its eschatological fulfilment ought reasonably to be near. On the other, it contends – as part of the legacy of Jewish prophetism – that God is the Lord of all nations, a belief that gives rise to the hope that all history will be encompassed by the redemption made possible by Christ.[9]

How can these ostensibly contradictory claims be reconciled? The question was of central importance for third-century theologians. Tertullian resolves the dilemma by redefining the very meaning of the statement that history reaches fulfilment in Christ. In order to cope with the numerous assertions in the gospels that have seemingly remained unfulfilled, he distances these assertions from their original, eschatology-tinged context. For example, Jesus's foretelling of the persecution that will afflict his disciples is applied to the hardships endured by Christians in Tertullian's own day. By relocating in this way the content of central biblical claims, Tertullian provides an implicit explanation for why history continues as it does, despite its promised fulfilment. At several points, however, he also gives an explicit theological explanation for why parousia has yet to occur: the reason for God's temporizing is quite simply that he wishes to give more people the chance to convert. For this reason, too, Christians should pray for the continued existence of Rome and its emperor.[10]

What is expressed in Tertullian, then, is how Christianity's fundamentally apocalyptic – and locally grounded – message is expanded into a universal theology of world history. This development at the theological level reflects a similar tendency at the popular level. Although apocalyptic movements continued to appear, not least during times of persecution, the Christian church slowly began to reconcile itself with its place in the world. The image of Rome as a new Babylon faded away, with many Christians seeming to have been fairly content to be peaceful Roman citizens.

This process culminated in the fourth century. In 313, Constantine the Great issued the Edict of Milan that gave Christianity equal status with other religions in the empire. Barely seventy years later, following the Edict of Thessalonica in 380, Nicene Trinitarian Christianity became the Roman Empire's official religion. This extraordinary development, from persecuted church of martyrs to official state religion, necessitated a number of theological adjustments. Once again help was provided by a rewriting of history. Thus, the writings of Eusebius of Caesarea present a theology whose apocalyptic elements have been entirely eliminated; indeed, more than eliminated. Eusebius invents a new genre of historiography, intended to demonstrate how God's providential plan for the world coincides with the actual course of historical events.

Eusebius's task, like Tertullian's, was apologetic in nature, and it is in this light that one must understand his ambition of describing the history of the Christian church from its earliest beginnings to Constantine's spectacular accession to power. Rebutting the common accusation that the Christian faith was lacking in historical pedigree, Eusebius referred to its roots in ancient Israel. The problem was that, in parallel with the Christian church, there existed another group which claimed to be the true inheritors of the Bible's prophetic tradition – the Jews. In his magisterial *Ecclesiastical History*, Eusebius therefore seeks to show not only how the prophets' words were fulfilled in Jesus Christ but also how the prophetic tradition has been misappropriated by the same Jews who never acknowledged Jesus as Christ. Just as the Jews of the past, in their blindness to the warnings of the prophets, brought God's wrath upon themselves, so, too, he claims, are present-day Jews unable to see that the promises of the prophets have been fulfilled by Jesus's death and resurrection.[11]

Ecclesiastical History is famous as the first substantial attempt to describe the history of the Christian church. However, it can also be considered as an expression of a rhetorical and literary genre variously designated *contra* or *adversus Iudaeos* ('against the Jews'). The genre can be traced as far back as the second century, growing in importance in the centuries that followed, something that mirrored a political development in which Christianity quickly moved towards a monopolistic position even as Judaism was increasingly regarded as a stumbling block for the expanding church (thus, for example, Jewish proselytizing was banned a mere two years after the Edict of Milan). Where the boundaries between Judaism and Christianity had until this point been far from fixed, Christian theologians now began to contrast the synagogue and the church; the children of flesh and those of the spirit; the Old Covenant and the New. Their arguments rested theologically upon the claim that the church was the New Israel, and literarily upon turning the rhetoric of the Jewish Scriptures against the Jews themselves.[12] In Eusebius's writings, such arguments were even given the support of history. The loss of Jerusalem and the hardships that afflicted the Jewish people following the destruction of the Temple in AD 70 were quite simply an expression of the fact that the Jews had lost their role as chosen people to the Christians.[13]

Yet, Eusebius was not merely writing a triumphalist history of Christianity. This is, rather, a history of the faithful and the lost; a history in which those who follow the path of God get their reward while those who stray from the path of God get their punishment. Discussing the Diocletianic Persecution (during the years 303–311), Eusebius can only interpret it as evidence that even the new Chosen People have sinned and brought God's wrath upon themselves.[14] But God's wrath is never permanent. Even during the direst persecution there were those who stood up for the Christian message, and these faithful witnesses paved the way for the magnificent reward conferred by God in the form of Constantine's accession to power: 'To him, accordingly, from heaven above as the worthy fruit of piety did He grant the trophies of victory over the impious ones, but the guilty one with all his counselors and friends He threw down prone under the feet of Constantine.'[15]

Eusebius's history of the church concludes with an almost lyrical portrait of Constantine. Later on he would also pen a biography of the emperor, *Life of Constantine*, a laudatory panegyric that portrayed Constantine as a holy leader modelled after the great prophet Moses. When read alongside each other, these works leave no doubt that Eusebius was writing not merely a theology of history, but also, as Bernard McGinn has noted, one of the earliest and most influential examples of 'political theology'.[16] McGinn's statement needs, however, to be nuanced. Recent scholarship has strongly contested the image of Eusebius as a 'court theologian' whose writings were representative of an official imperial platform. Eusebius does see God's providential will at work in the fall of Licinius (the last persecuting emperor) and in the victorious rise to power of Constantine. But this need not necessarily mean that he purported a pro-imperial theology. As Aaron Johnson remarks, '[r]ather than being an attempt to legitimize an emperor within a Christian framework (though this could no doubt be an effect of his narrative), the final book of the *History* provided proof of God's favour upon the Christian nation'.[17] The emphasis of Eusebius's historical narrative is not on the empire but rather on God's sovereign Logos, and compared to traditional panegyrical ways of representing military might and influence, it can even be argued that Eusebius diminished the emperor's role in great events of his time.[18]

Yet it may be asked whether Eusebius's writings do not in several respects represent a shift away from most of the Christian theology of history that preceded him. While Christianity's adoption of a more accommodating attitude towards state power occurred gradually, Eusebius nonetheless represents a crucial stage in this process. The reasons for this are partly connected with wider historical developments. During Eusebius's lifetime the Christian church went from being a provocative subculture of the Roman Empire to one of its core institutions. Where the early church saw in Rome a new Babylon, Eusebius saw in its empire the kingdom of peace promised by the prophets. Where the Christians of the first centuries, on the grounds of their faith in the One God, refused to take part in the imperial cult of ancient Rome, Eusebius portrayed Caesar as the image of God. Thus, while Eusebius may not have advocated a political theology in the sense of providing the empire with theological legitimacy, he certainly provided it with theological meaning.

Eusebius's providential theology was not the final word, however. Just a century later his theology of history would be challenged by a thinker whose influence on the Western Christian tradition was to be even more radical. Little of the optimism that permeates Eusebius's relation to history can be found in Augustine's writings. Augustine does not see Christian Rome as the fulfilment of the promised kingdom of peace; God's kingdom is not at all of this world. In *City of God* Augustine instead describes history as a struggle between the city of God (*civitas dei*) and the city of man (*civitas terrena*). He contends that this struggle will continue for as long as history lasts, which precludes any eventuality that the city of God might ever be realized on earth. Augustine thereby undermines the confident perspective which sustains Eusebius's theology of history. Nor does he allow for any possibility of discerning the hand of providence in the course of historical events. In fairness to both Eusebius and Augustine, however, it should be clarified that the actual course taken by history in the early fifth century had been in a direction that inevitably affected their theological prism. Whereas Eusebius wrote at a time when the course of events in the Roman Empire seemed to work in the church's favour, Augustine was active during a period when the empire was inexorably moving towards dissolution. As if this were not enough, Augustine was additionally called upon to defend the empire against the accusation that Christianity itself was the ultimate cause of imperial collapse.

From a present-day perspective it is almost impossible to imagine what the prospect of the collapse of the Roman Empire represented for contemporaries. Rome was thought to be for all time. Imagining the fall of Rome was therefore as impossible as imagining the end of history. When Rome seemed effectively to have reached its last breath, in other words, no interpretation was possible but that history itself had *de facto* run its course. In this context it should come as no surprise that apocalyptic ideas enjoyed a renaissance in the fifth century.[19] What is more strange, perhaps, is that Augustine should have presented a substantially anti-apocalyptic interpretation of history. In this regard he followed Eusebius closely. Even though historical conditions worsened considerably during the century that separates these two thinkers, Augustine dismissed all attempts to interpret contemporary upheavals as auguring the beginning of the last days. He similarly distanced himself from all forms of chiliasm or millenarianism. For Augustine, there were no grounds for a literal reading of the Book of Revelation's reference to a thousand-year reign (Rev. 20:1–6). Instead, he interpreted the passage allegorically, seeing the one thousand years as an allusion to present time – that is to say, the time between Christ's first and second coming. In the same way, he takes its allusion to a first resurrection for the righteous on earth (Rev. 20:1–5) to be referring to the spiritual resurrection granted to Christians by baptism.[20]

In a number of respects, then, Augustine represents the final stage of Christian theology's readjustment to the postponing of parousia. *City of God* evinces a theology that has found its place in history as it awaits the end of days. At the same time, Augustine avoids the mistake made by Eusebius in equating divine providence with the actual course of history. Not only did Eusebius thereby make himself vulnerable to criticism in the event that historical events did not turn out to benefit the Christian church; he ran up against a deeper problem in his inability to preserve a critical tension between the temporal order and God's eternal order. In other words, his theology of history runs the risk of being reduced to political theology. For Augustine, the temporal order, including the church, is never identical with God's order. True history, God's deepest intention with creation, is hidden within secular history. It may be divined – from the revelation of Christ as attested by Holy Scripture and from the lives of the righteous. Ultimately, however, the church is a stranger in the world, a pilgrim journeying towards its true home. As such, it must live in expectation and bide its time.

Even though various forms of providential theology would continue to appear during the medieval period, Augustine's somewhat melancholic yet level-headed theology of history would come to dominate the Western Christian tradition. It was also this Augustinian tradition that Joachim of Fiore to an essential degree would rely on – yet also break with in several key regards. Having surveyed the most important coordinates for early Christian theology of history, it is now time to look more closely at Joachim's own texts.

Joachim of Fiore and the Spirit of Prophecy

Joachim of Fiore was by far one of the most important apocalyptic figures of the medieval era, something that is perhaps not surprising given the connection between historical upheaval and expectations of imminent redemption. Joachim lived in a time of comprehensive political and cultural revolution that included an interminable conflict between the Pope and the Emperor, which had culminated in the previous century in a showdown between Gregory VII and Henry IV (the so-called Investiture Controversy). The rise of Islam under Saladin was for many contemporaries a sign of the times.

Joachim lived and wrote in a place where these upheavals were immediately present. Celico, the small town where he was born in around 1135, lies in Calabria, at that time part of the Kingdom of Sicily. Until the end of the eleventh century the area had been under Muslim control, but by Joachim's time a vigorous Norman dynasty had long occupied the throne. Of relevance here is the fact that the Norman kings showed their strength by repeatedly allying themselves with the papacy against the Holy Roman Emperor. The Normans thereby helped to undermine the Emperor's dominance and, by extension, the political balance of all Europe.

Calabria and Sicily were also a cultural melting pot. Besides the fact that the area had long been dominated by Arabic culture, the region had a relatively large Jewish population. What is more, the narrow Strait of Messina was a key waterway for the Mediterranean, making the city of Messina a hub for pilgrims, crusaders and merchants. This political and cultural mosaic needs to be borne in mind in order to understand Joachim's rich and complex intellectual world. It is also important to note the extent to which Joachim himself formed part of this mosaic. In his youth he had worked at the Sicilian court in Palermo, where he gained a good insight into the political life of the era. Early in life he undertook a pilgrimage to Jerusalem, a journey that marked the end of his political career and the beginning of his life as a theologian and monk. In 1171, he entered the Benedictine house at Corazzo, of which he became abbot around 1176–1177. Later in life he was granted permission by the Pope to found a monastery of his own, the house of San Giovanni in Fiore, and even his own order, the Florensian Order, which continued until 1570, when it was incorporated into the Cistercian Order.

Moving from politics to theology, however, did not mean that Joachim withdrew from the political concerns of the day. As a celebrated theologian and founder of an order, Joachim not only had close contact with several popes during his lifetime but was also consulted by temporal leaders. The most notable of these meetings took place in Messina in 1191, when Richard the Lionheart, then engaged upon the Third Crusade, sought out the famous abbot for prophetic counsel. A contemporary chronicler relates that Joachim gave the English king an interpretation of the seven-headed dragon in the Book of Revelation (Rev. 12). Following one of his famous illustrations or *figurae* (which his disciples published after his death in the book *Liber Figurarum*), he identified the dragon's various heads with the great persecutors of the Christian church down the ages. It was now the turn of the seventh head, which could be no other than the very Saladin whom Richard the Lionheart had set out to defeat.[21]

The episode confirms the extent to which Joachim was an apocalyptic thinker. Like the author of the Book of Revelation – the most famous work of Christian apocalypticism – he saw the present moment as a historic turning point and interpreted political events as signs of the imminent arrival of the Anti-Christ. However, some concepts must be clarified here. As argued in the opening section of this chapter, the apocalypse found in Joachim is not of the eschatological variety. The new times that he sees as imminent, in other words, are not the course of events that will follow upon the end of history. Instead, this is a matter of an imminent earthly state of affairs that will take the form of concrete changes to the material conditions of existence.[22]

Despite its markedly apocalyptic qualities, Joachim's theology of history in this respect lies closer to the prophetism of Jewish antiquity than does most of the older Christian apocalypticism. Here, again, it must be clarified that Joachim's vision of a coming time of earthly harmony and prosperity does not preclude belief in an eschatological fulfilment of history. However, like the Jewish prophets of antiquity, Joachim is primarily concerned with revealing God's redemptive actions towards humanity *in* the course of history.

Would it therefore be more accurate to characterize Joachim as a prophet? Roger Howden, the aforementioned chronicler who accompanied Richard the Lionheart, refers to the Calabrian abbot as a man who had the 'spirit of prophesy' (*spiritum propheticum*).[23] But how did Joachim view himself? One answer is provided by another contemporary chronicler, Ralph of Coggeshall, who describes a meeting that took place between Joachim and Adam of Perseigne at the papal residence in the late 1190s. To Adam's enquiry as to the source of his prophetic insights, Joachim is said to have first replied that he possessed neither the gift of prophesy nor a special ability to predict future events. 'But', he continued, 'the God who once gave the spirit of prophecy to the prophets has given me the spirit of understanding, so that in God's Spirit I very clearly understand all the mysteries of the Holy Scripture, just as the holy prophets understood who once wrote it down in God's Spirit'.[24]

The anecdote suggests that Joachim did not regard himself as a prophetic figure who had come to impart a new revelation, but rather as someone versed in the Scriptures who possessed a special gift, 'the spirit of understanding', for interpreting the mysteries already revealed by God in the Bible. In other words, Joachim was first and foremost an exegete who shared the established view of the Bible as the fulfilment of God's revelation. But did this mean that all that could be said about the divine revelation had already been said? It did not, and it is here that the truly daring element of Joachim's thinking comes into view. For Joachim, the text of the Bible was, figuratively speaking, the tip of an iceberg. Beyond the level of the written word lay an inexhaustible fund of meaning. Admittedly, this was not a new way of thinking. As is well known, as far back as classical antiquity there existed an advanced tradition of spiritual or allegorical readings of sacred texts. This tradition was taken over by the early Christian theologians and came to be developed and refined throughout the medieval period. And yet Joachim very much left his own mark on this tradition.

In his most famous work, *Liber de Concordia Novi ac Veteris Testamenti*, Joachim expounds a complex hermeneutical theory based upon both concordance and allegory. He understands 'concordance' as denoting an inner connectedness that can be found between the Old and New Testaments (between individuals, peoples, cities and, above all, numerical patterns). 'Allegory', meanwhile, denotes the deeper, spiritual content that lies hidden beneath the outer shell of the letters themselves. In a passage in the second book, he depicts what can almost be described as the very matrix of this deeper, spiritual reading: 'Therefore, because there are two divine Persons of whom one is ungenerated, the other generated, two Testaments have been set up, the first of which … pertains especially to the Father, the second to the Son, because the latter is from the former. In addition, the spiritual understanding, proceeding from both Testaments, is one that pertains especially to the Holy Spirit.'[25]

Joachim thus situates his hermeneutic within a trinitarian framework in which each of the three divine persons has its specific function. Where the Father is associated with the revelation granted by the Old Testament, and the Son with that granted by the New, the Holy Spirit is associated with a deeper, spiritual understanding of both Testaments. What Joachim thereby indicates is not that there exists some third revelation capable of superseding the two earlier – an interpretation that would be ascribed to his texts by later commentators – but that it is possible to acquire a deeper understanding of existing revelation.[26]

Joachim's hermeneutic is radical in two respects. First, he introduces a temporal dimension into the hermeneutic process: spiritual understanding (*intellectus spiritualis*), he insists, is deepened over time. Second, he sees the Bible as the source not merely of eternal truths but also of humanity's historical conditions. The Bible, in other words, is nothing less than a divine script for world history.[27]

Brought together, these two aspects provide a glimpse of the extraordinary potential of Joachim's ideas. If a spiritual understanding of the Scriptures is deepened over time, and the Scriptures also contain the key to God's ingenious plan for history, then it necessarily follows that humanity's grasp of the mysteries of world history is in a state of constant growth. It should be mentioned in passing at this point, however, that Joachim's view of this progression towards deeper knowledge was fairly elitist in nature. In other words, not just any reader could look up the biblical texts and behold in them an atlas of world history. Admittedly, Joachim imagined that a more profound spiritual vision would also take hold at the collective level. But only long practice of prayer, meditation and recitation of the psalms could ultimately confer spiritual understanding upon a believer.[28]

Joachim's encounter with Richard the Lionheart bears witness to the fact that he regarded himself as possessing the ability to decipher the mysteries of history. At the same time, what Joachim primarily understood by this concept of deepened spiritual vision was not an ability to foresee coming events. This much is evident from the account of his conversation with Adam of Perseigne, in which Joachim explicitly disavowed having such an ability. Rather, it was a matter of achieving a deeper understanding of history's essence, which is also the essence of the God who is Lord of history. Notwithstanding their substantial differences, there is a parallel here with the Jewish prophetism of classical antiquity, which was a matter less of predicting coming events than of surveying the passage of history and thereby uncovering the great world drama that weaves together God and humanity into a single destiny. The following section will elucidate how Joachim imagined this drama, including his famous notion of a coming age of the Holy Spirit. In order to express the complexity of this notion, however, I shall first return briefly to the concept of the spirit in Jewish and Christian antiquity.

The *Status* of the Holy Spirit

The writings of the prophets reveal how the ability to discern God's intentions through history was early on connected with spiritual inspiration. In the prophetic literature the spirit is also associated with the announcement of imminent justice – discerning God's intentions through history ultimately becomes indistinguishable from approaching history from the perspective of justice. Likewise, for several of the later literary prophets the redemptive course of events itself becomes fused with the notion of a more general outpouring of the spirit. This notion is expressed most forcefully in the prophesy from the Book of Joel cited above:

> Then afterwards
>   I will pour out my spirit on all flesh;
> your sons and your daughters shall prophesy,
>   your old men shall dream dreams,
>   and your young men shall see visions.

> Even on the male and female slaves,
>   in those days, I will pour out my spirit.
> (Joel 2:28–29)

This short passage has played a key role throughout history within both the Jewish and Christian traditions, albeit with significant differences. According to a prevalent Jewish tradition, the spirit of prophecy ceased with Malachi, held to be the last of the biblical prophets. The passage thus became linked to hopes for a new outpouring of the spirit that was expected to initiate the messianic age.[29] Conversely, the Christian tradition from its earliest beginnings was to claim that the promised outpouring of the spirit had already taken place. The event is described in the second chapter of the Acts of the Apostles and, according to tradition, constituted the birth of the Christian church:

> When the day of Pentecost had come, they were all together in one place. And suddenly from heaven there came a sound like the rush of a violent wind, and it filled the entire house where they were sitting. Divided tongues, as of fire, appeared among them, and a tongue rested on each of them. All of them were filled with the Holy Spirit and began to speak in other languages, as the Spirit gave them ability.
> (Acts 2:1–4)

After the Holy Spirit descends upon the gathered assembly, there follows a description of how, despite having utterly different native languages, each person present miraculously hears the others speaking in his or her own tongue. The apostle Peter then begins speaking and proclaims to the assembled multitude that the prophesy of Joel has now been fulfilled (Acts 2:14–21). It is not coincidence that the author has Peter interpret the event in light of these crucial prophetic words from the Jewish Scriptures. The specific theology of history that forms the basis for the Gospel of Luke and the Acts of the Apostles has been discussed above. Already, in his Gospel, Luke inscribes Jesus within the established tradition of spiritually anointed prophets, thereby allowing the spirit to serve as a marker of continuity with the tradition of the elders. In the Acts of the Apostles, the line of succession is extended even further, with the spirit also being portrayed as a marker of continuity between Jesus himself and his followers – what was to become the Christian church.

The fundamental idea is thus that the spirit, by virtue of its presence in the church, continues that redemption which was begun with the resurrected Christ. The intimate connection of spiritual outpouring and the redemption in progress can also be discerned in the inverted allusion to the Tower of Babel. Just as a proliferation of different languages had been the result of this lapse into sin early in human history, the Pentecostal transcending of linguistic difference served to indicate that redemption was at hand.

This scene affords a first glimpse of the dynamism inherent in the idea of the spirit as it was established in the early Christian tradition. Even so, the role of the spirit would be steadily toned down in a manner not wholly unlike its development within rabbinic Judaism. This is perhaps not so strange, given that charismatic movements have often posed a challenge to the established order and the authorities in their respective traditions. An example from the Jewish tradition that has already been mentioned is the messianic movement that led to the disastrous Bar Kokhba revolt in the second century. A comparable example in the Christian tradition is the movement that emerged just a few decades later in the wake of the Phrygian preacher Montanus. Admittedly, Montanism did not evolve as dramatically as the Bar Kokhba movement. But it can reasonably be argued that Montanism played a similar role in engendering suspicion of charismatic expressions within the emerging orthodox strand of Christianity. Above all, what made Montanism threatening to orthodoxy was that it challenged the finality of Christian revelation in that Montanus claimed to have been empowered by the Holy Spirit to proclaim a revelation which superseded that granted by Christ.[30] The church's stifling of Montanism attests to the potential for disorder in the notion that the spirit continues to be present in history. Quite simply, the idea of the spirit raises questions about the scope of the divine revelation and, above all, about who has the right to appoint themselves the interpreter of that revelation. The unruly potential of the idea also explains why the church, when in the fourth century it consolidated the doctrine of the Holy Spirit, was careful to insert the spirit into a trinitarian framework; God remained active in the salvation history through the agency of the Holy Spirit, but only in concert with the two other divine persons and within the frame of the Christian church.

This brief survey of early Christianity's ambivalent relation to the notion of the spirit is important for an understanding of Joachim's theology of history. Not unlike Montanus, Joachim was to test the limits of orthodox doctrine, something that goes some way towards explaining his controversial status in later Christian tradition. At the same time, he differed from Montanus in one crucial respect. Joachim was writing after the dogmatic concretion of Christian faith had taken place, which made it unthinkable for him to approach the spirit within anything other than a strictly trinitarian framework. Returning for a moment to the vision granted to Joachim on that Whitsun morning in 1183, it will also be recalled that his idea of a historical age connected to the Holy Spirit sprang from a deep conviction of God's triune being.

Although his writings would later be cited by movements deemed heretical, it may therefore be asked whether Joachim was really doing anything more than merely pursuing the doctrine of the Trinity to its ultimate conclusion. In a nutshell, Joachim's train of thought was precisely about strengthening the role of the Holy Spirit in the salvation history. If there is a historical age in which the Father is the principal figure, and another in which the Son is the principal figure, should there not reasonably also be an age in which the Holy Spirit plays the central role?

> [J]ust as there are three persons and one God, so frequently in those things that are common to all three distinct significations are found that show the respective likeness of the persons. For example, Abraham signifies the Father because he has primarily been called father. Isaac signifies the Son and Jacob the Holy Spirit. The first *status*, therefore, ought to be assigned to the Father, the second to the Son and to the Holy Spirit (although the works assigned to the Son may be noteworthy in it as is fitting), the third *status*, to the Holy Spirit. For this reason the Holy Spirit will reveal his glory in the third *status*, as the Son revealed his in the second, the Father his in the first.[31]

Joachim accordingly views history as a drama in three acts corresponding to the three persons of the godhead. Yet he does not content himself with noting this underlying trinitarian structure; on repeated occasions he also makes concrete historical references to their respective acts. For instance, each act is ascribed a historical personage who signals its beginning. The first act is initiated by Adam and continues to Christ. The second act begins with the righteous king Josiah (king of Judah 639–609 BC) and gets into its stride with Christ before continuing on into Joachim's own era. In corresponding fashion, the third act is set in motion by Saint Benedict in the sixth century and continues in Joachim's own era and on until the end of days.[32]

Joachim assigns different spiritual institutions to the various acts, connecting the first with the synagogue, the second with the church and the third with the monastic system (which, according to tradition, was founded by Benedict of Nursia). He additionally imagines the different acts as corresponding to three various 'orders' (*ordines*) or states of life: marital, clerical and monastic. The first of these is modelled upon the patriarchs, the second upon the apostles and the third upon the holy lives of the monks.[33]

Although the three 'orders' have complex inner relations and exist in parallel throughout the various ages, it is impossible to miss the progressive aspect of the course of events in the salvation history that Joachim describes. All the same, it is evident from Joachim's terminology alone that this is not a simple progression of stages. As the long quotation given earlier indicates, he mostly uses the word *status*, not *tempus*, when describing the three historical phases. While the precise connotation of the Latin *status* is debated (for which reason the original Latin word is usually retained by modern scholars of Joachim), the term indicates that this is a matter less of different ages, following chronologically upon each other, than of different 'conditions' or 'state of things' whose respective degree of dominance changes during the various phases of salvation history.[34]

Above all, it should be noted that history's three acts are intricately bound up with each other, as evinced by the quotation referenced earlier in which Joachim connects history's second *status* to both the Son and the Holy Spirit. In order to understand the intellectual underpinnings of this position, it is important to once again recall the extent to which Joachim was a trinitarian thinker. Like Augustine and other prominent theologians in the Western Christian tradition, Joachim regards the Holy Spirit as proceeding from both Father and Son (*filioque*). He likewise clarifies that the *status* of the Spirit was not only initiated by Benedict during the *status* of the Son, but in fact had already begun with the prophet Elisha during the *status* of the Father.

What Joachim presents, therefore, is not a strictly tripartite schema but rather an image of a complex fabric whose inner meaning in every age is tied to events in the two other ages. It should also be noted that Joachim – like rabbinic Judaism – regards Joel's prophesy of a complete outpouring of the spirit as still awaiting its fulfilment. This does not mean that he tones down the significance of the first Pentecost; but in the same way as Christ's life and deeds were anticipated by the righteous king Josiah, so, too, is the descent of the spirit upon the early church merely a foretaste of the more perfect outpouring to come.[35]

This train of thought attests to the general shift from 'flesh' to 'spirit' (cf. Gal. 5:16–26) that underpins Joachim's theology of history. Like many theologians before him, Joachim considers 'spiritual', i.e. allegorical, readings of the Scriptures to be superior to literal ones, and asserts the monastic vocation as a more developed form of life than marriage. Yet he is not seeking to distance himself from material reality. On the contrary, Joachim's theology in many regards implies a rehistoricization of the biblical text.

All of this recalls Joachim's dual relationship to Augustine. In his efforts to reconnect Scripture with the actual course of history, Joachim makes a radical break with Augustine. To be sure, Augustine was driven by particular historical motifs: the collapse of the Christian empire had exposed the weaknesses in Eusebius's providential theology and made Augustine sceptical of any attempt to correlate the scriptural message with actual historical events. Although it is a strength of Augustine's theology that it offers resistance to various kinds of political misuse of biblical claims, it is nonetheless weakened by a tendency to distance itself from the concrete level of history. In his doctrine of the two cities, Augustine quite simply tends to spiritualize and interiorize the scriptural message.

As has been described above, Joachim, too, was in many regards influenced by the historical circumstances of his time. But narrowing down the key difference between both theologians ultimately turns less on these historical conditions than on the fact that Joachim, unlike Augustine, was an apocalyptic thinker. This difference is expressed particularly forcefully in their differing relationships with the Book of Revelation. Augustine's relationship to this blazingly apocalyptic text is, as previously noted, consistently suprahistorical. In his reading, the mighty historical struggle described as taking place between angels and various apocalyptic beasts becomes the symbolic expression of an eternal struggle between good and evil within the souls of human beings, the thousand-year reign becomes a metaphor for the church's time on earth and the reference to the beast that is kept bound is interpreted as the trials to which the ungodly have subjected God's people.[36]

The contrast to Joachim could hardly be greater. To be sure, Joachim was not resistant to allegorical interpretations. Unlike Augustine, however, he used these allegorical explanations in order to reconnect the Scriptures with events in the salvation history. This approach can be observed with particular clarity in another of his major works, *Expositio in Apocalypsim*, which comprises a detailed exegetical commentary on the Book of Revelation.[37] The biblical text is here interpreted as a continuous prophesy of the history of the church, which becomes increasingly accessible as humanity's *intellectus spiritualis* deepens. Thus, for example, Joachim associates the six seals referred to in the text with specific events in the history of the church, allowing the opening of the seventh seal to correspond to the dawn of history's third *status*.

Joachim's break with established tradition is particularly striking here. In keeping with Augustine, the phase associated with the opening of the seventh seal was generally interpreted as the eternal peace that was expected to follow after the end of history.[38] Joachim departs from this seven-hundred-year tradition by instead identifying the seventh phase as an intrahistorical period synonymous with the thousand-year reign: 'Having described six parts of the Apocalypse in which six wearisome *tempora* are noted, we must then come to the seventh part which treats of the great Sabbath to come at the end of the world which can be called the third *status*'.[39]

While it must be borne in mind that Joachim's historico-theological schema is never strictly chronological, it is nonetheless obvious that he here imagines an actual time when the spirit will be poured out anew in order to bring about peace and prosperity on earth. We can begin to see here what is arguably the most important consequence of Joachim's connecting of revelation with concrete historical events: whereas Augustine's interiorization of the scriptural message tends to reduce the revelation to a spiritual matter for each individual, Joachim offers a collective vision of a brighter future for God's people on this side of eternity, that is, within the course of history.

This focus on the actual course of history notwithstanding, Joachim was not reviving some version of Eusebius's providential theology. On this crucial issue, he remained true to Augustine. Joachim tied his prophetic interpretations of the Scriptures to historical events, but he did not prophesy future political orders and definitely did not believe in salvation by means of political intervention.[40] Several texts, notably his early work *Expositio de prophetia ignota*, also attest to Joachim's adherence to a faction in the Roman *curia* that sought compromise rather than confrontation with the Holy Roman Empire. This is not to say that Joachim sympathized with the empire; for him, the German emperor was and remained *rex Babiloniae*, the church's eternal persecutor. Yet he was profoundly convinced that the church's role was not to be a rival political power to this worldly empire, but rather to be a long-suffering servant of God, patiently bearing witness to a higher truth and justice.[41]

Is the vision offered by Joachim's writings thus completely apolitical? The question is warranted, not least in view of the explosive effect his theology was to have during the later medieval period. In one sense it can be claimed, as does Mattias Riedl, that his vision was deeply political in nature. Like the political philosophers of classical antiquity, Joachim was concerned to find the perfect form of human coexistence on earth. For him, however, this was a profoundly theological vision. As the perfect worldly order was that which most reflected the heavenly, it is not very surprising that Joachim found this order in the holy community of the monastery. At stake here, then, is effectively a monastic vision – a vision in which growing numbers of people are nearing spiritual enlightenment and leaving the conflicts of the world behind them.[42]

Joachim can thus hardly be accused of championing a political theology. In fact, he imagined that worldly empires would wither away and be replaced by a universal church of the spirit (*Ecclesia spiritualis*) as growing numbers of people adopted the ideals of humility and purity that were hallmarks of the monastic life. Considering this, it makes more sense to associate Joachim's visionary theology with Martin Buber's concept of theopolitics, introduced in Chapter One of this volume. What Buber understands by theopolitics is the notion of a kind of prophetically inspired resistance, based on the idea of a higher, divine justice. What distinguishes this idea from political theology is that it never entirely allows itself to be equated with an actual political order, but remains transcendent in relation to the powers of this world. Notwithstanding such transcendence, it includes the task of enacting – in the form of a kind of counter-politics – this higher justice in an exemplary way among the nations.[43]

Joachim believed himself able to discern in the Scriptures something of this higher, divine order, and his vision of history's third *status* is primarily a vision of a form of life that reflects this order. Yet to understand his prophetic qualities properly, it must be remembered that this was a vision not merely of the future but of an order that had, at least partially, come into being with Benedict (and, further back still, with Elisha). In this light, his notion of the *status* of the Spirit more closely resembles a contrasting vision to the current order: humanity has been called upon to live a perfected spiritual life not merely in some future state but right here and now.

While the strength of the prophetic legacy lies in its unwillingness to ascribe permanent authority to any human institution or order, it should be made clear that Joachim never turned against the existing clerical orders. Just as the *status* of the Holy Spirit had been active during the ages of the Father and the Son, so, too, would the orders appertaining to the Father and the Son endure until the end of time. Having noted this, we return directly to the progressive qualities of Joachim, who, even while emphasizing the continued existence of the church as an institution, articulates his conviction that during the *status* of the Spirit the clerical order will be eclipsed in importance by the monastic. Although Joachim himself can hardly be accused of having devised a theology subversive of the established order, it is therefore not particularly surprising that his texts were to serve as an inspiration for critical movements within the church, above all during the high and late medieval periods when any resemblance between the real church and his vision of an *Ecclesia spiritualis* became increasingly faint.

A Messianic Vision

The preceding sections have outlined the continuity that exists between the prophetic literature of Jewish antiquity and the writings of Joachim: first, how the prophetic motif permeates the notion of history as a space for God's ongoing project of redeeming humanity; second, how Joachim envisions a series of redemptive events within history as connected with the activities of the spirit. But how does this relate to the messianic motif? The answer to this question depends on what one understands by messianism. As already suggested above, neither Judaism nor Christianity are messianic religions in the strict sense of being continually marked by acute expectations of an imminent redemption connected with a divine figure. While both traditions in their early phases were characterized by apocalyptic messianic qualities, these were steadily toned down, as has been described.

However, it would be a simplification to claim that these early developments were merely a matter of messianic qualities being toned down. In essence, this was a question of constructively reinterpreting the messianic motif so that it could continue to play a role even after having been stripped of its apocalyptic aspects. In the case of rabbinic Judaism, focus early on shifted away from the idea of a redemptive figure and towards the redemptive process, more precisely towards the observance of the Torah (*halakha*). Yet the Talmudic literature accommodates a certain ambivalence with regard to the issue of redemption: on the one hand, it depicts redemption as precisely the result of an ongoing sanctification of Israel through the Torah; on the other hand, it evinces a tendency to portray redemption as a miraculous intervention by God, irrespective of his people's way of life. This ambivalence may reflect an attempt from rabbinic quarters to reach a compromise between apocalyptic movements that lived on at the popular level and their own determination to stifle the anarchic potential of these more plebeian forms of messianism.[44]

Nonetheless, the idea that redemption was closely connected with the everyday observance of the Torah continues to dominate the rabbinic literature's interpretations of messianism. It is also reflected in the distinction drawn by several Talmudic texts between the days of the Messiah and the end of days. A shift is observable here away from the apocalyptic interpretations of the messianic idea that flourished during the Second Temple period. Where the coming of the Messiah was associated by these older interpretations with the beginning of the last days, the messianic age discussed in the rabbinic literature refers exclusively to an earthly time that marks the end of exile and the fulfilment of the prophets' vision of justice.[45]

This shift in understanding of the messianic age filled several functions, including serving precisely to stifle apocalyptic interpretations, which tended to create turbulence when they were translated into political action (as, for example, with the Bar Kokhba revolt). By making the Messiah's coming dependent on observance of the Torah, the incentive for political and religious activism was weakened, even as the rabbis – in their capacity as interpreters of the Torah – buttressed their own authority. Likewise, the idea that it was the condition of the Jewish people which determined the coming of the Messiah helped explain why the Messiah, despite scriptural predictions, had not come.[46]

This pattern may be recognized in the Christian tradition's attempts to cope with the postponement of parousia; yet there is a significant difference between the two traditions insofar as the emergent Christian tradition persisted in its claim that the messianic promise had been fulfilled in Jesus of Nazareth. The dilemma which Christianity faced was thus the problem of defending the claim that the Messiah had in fact arrived while simultaneously insisting that the final redemption had quite clearly not taken place.

Where rabbinic Judaism elaborated the messianic idea by shifting attention away from the redemptive figure and onto the redemptive process, Christianity would instead develop the idea further by situating it within an eschatological framework. On the one hand, it was stressed that redemption had been actuated by Christ's resurrection; from an eschatological viewpoint humanity's sins were thereby forgiven. On the other hand, Christianity stressed that within the framework of history humanity remained subject to the domination of sin; only with the second coming of Christ at the end of time would full redemption take place. In contrast to rabbinic Judaism, Christianity thereby left little space for a course of redemptive events between these two historical poles. This is not to say that Christian theology did not include a powerful summons to humanity to live, there and then, in a manner that anticipated the final redemption; but the very notion that human beings, by the way they lived, could affect the coming redemption was to remain de-emphasized within Christianity. The redemptive act had, in all essentials, been fulfilled by Christ's substitutory death on the cross.

Against this background, how should Joachim's vision of an impending earthly Sabbath be understood? Given that the messianic motif in the Christian tradition would develop into the idea of the fulfilment of history through Christ's second coming, what Joachim offered his readers can hardly be described as a messianic vision. As has been made clear at several points in this chapter,

Joachim in no sense renounces the established Christian belief in an eschatological fulfilment of history. Yet what he refers to in his vision of history's third *status* is not this eschatological series of events but an intrahistorical development; one connected with a new outpouring of the Holy Spirit rather than with the return of the Son.

I wish to argue nonetheless that there is an obviously messianic aspect to Joachim's vision. For this to become apparent, however, we must look away from Christianity's eschatological interpretation of the messianic motif and instead consider Joachim's writings in light of contemporary developments within Jewish messianism. A number of experts on his work have already remarked upon the fact that Joachim's ideas bear a number of resemblances to movements within medieval Judaism. Thus, for example, Alfons Rosenberg has noted the parallels between Joachim's writings and the esoteric theosophy of Kabbalah that was emerging during his lifetime. Of particular relevance here is his fascination with sacred numbers as a key to scriptural mysteries and his predilection for organic emblems. For example, the tree is a recurrent symbol in Joachim's illustrations, a symbol which also appears as an illustration of the divine emanation in *Sefer ha-Bahir*, 'The Book of Illumination', an early Kabbalistic work that was disseminated throughout southern Europe during the twelfth century.[47]

This kind of parallel early on gave rise to speculation among modern scholars about whether Joachim himself was of Jewish extraction. The hypothesis was strengthened by the discovery in 1948 of a document in which Joachim was explicitly identified as Jewish. Dated 1195, the text in question is a sermon by a contemporary Cistercian abbot named Gottfried of Auxerre. Gottfried, who was vehemently antipathetic towards his one-time fellow Cistercian, accuses Joachim of spreading false doctrines and attributes his faulty learning to his Jewish extraction and the fact that he 'was trained in Judaism for many years'.[48]

It is not impossible that Joachim came from a Jewish family that early in his life converted to Christianity. As noted earlier, medieval Calabria had a substantial Jewish population, and conversions, in order to acquire more senior positions in society, for example, were not unusual. Nonetheless, a series of factors speaks against the likelihood that Joachim was of Jewish descent. One of these is his early authorship of an *adversus Iudaeos* pamphlet.[49] Admittedly, its text differs in key respects from other known texts within the genre (an issue that will be discussed later), but it essentially presents the traditional argument that Christians levelled at Judaism. The factor that argues most strongly against Joachim's possible Jewish ancestry, however, is that neither his own texts nor the two extant contemporary biographies make any allusion to it.[50]

It must therefore remain a matter of speculation as to whether the parallels between Joachim's theology and contemporary Jewish thought have their basis in his own Jewishness. The question is also of minor importance for the purposes of the present study. The challenge here is to identify in Joachim's writings a continuity with the messianic idea that was first established in the classical prophetic literature. Let me therefore come back to the question of the messianic aspect of Joachim's vision.

This aspect appears most conspicuously when Joachim is considered in tandem with the most famous Jewish thinker of the medieval period, Moshe ben Maimon, better known by his Latin name Maimonides. As will be shown shortly, there exists a series of fundamental parallels between Joachim's vision of the third *status* of the Spirit and Maimonides's notion of an imminent messianic age. Although the two thinkers were almost exact contemporaries – and despite the fact that they were both active in the same cultural and geographical milieu – there exist no explicit references to their familiarity with each other's work. As indicated earlier in this chapter, Calabria, and, for that matter, the entire Mediterranean, was a cultural melting pot during the twelfth century. In particular, there was an intensive exchange of ideas between Jewish, Christian and Muslim thinkers. While this exchange was often polemical in nature, it contributed substantially towards various cross-pollinations within the three traditions.[51] Regarding the parallels between Joachim and Maimonides, it may therefore be reasonably assumed that these were quite simply ideas and intellectual constructs which were in circulation at the time – not that this makes their similarities any less interesting.

Like Joachim, Maimonides was aware that he lived in a time of political and cultural transformation. Also like Joachim, he interpreted contemporary upheavals – not least the hardships that afflicted the Jewish people in both Christian and Muslim worlds – as auguries of an imminent new era. But what was the meaning of this new age, which Maimonides described as 'the days of the Messiah'? The answer lies in the final chapters of Maimonides's comprehensive commentary on Jewish law, *Mishneh Torah*. What they make immediately clear is that it is an entirely intrahistorical period. In this respect, Maimonides adheres to the distinction made by the established rabbinic tradition between the messianic age and the end of days. He argues soberly that, far from any eschatological scenario, the world will continue 'to follow its normal course' even after the coming of the Messiah; there will be no altering of the laws of nature, let alone a revoking of the sacred laws of the Torah.[52]

The parallel with Joachim's third *status* does not just consist of the fact that both instances concern an intrahistorical vision. It should also be noted that both thinkers remain faithful to the existing revelation. It was suggested above that Joachim, despite seeing himself as inspired by God's spirit, did not consider himself a prophet: what he had received was not some new, prophetic insight but the ability to *better* interpret what God had already revealed in the Holy Scriptures. In similar fashion, Maimonides emphasizes that God's law will endure for an eternity of eternities, and that he who adds to or takes away from it in any respect 'is an imposter, a wicked man, and a heretic'.[53] Both thinkers thus treat Scripture (which in Joachim's case naturally also includes the New

Testament) as God's complete revelation, and both view the study of the sacred texts as the key to deeper spiritual insights.

In Maimonides's case, this faith in the redemptive power of the law becomes even clearer when one examines more closely the content of his vision of the messianic age. Maimonides expects not only that the Jewish diaspora will be gathered together but also that the kingdom of David will be restored to its former glory. Yet this is not primarily a political vision.[54] Liberation from exile is in fact merely a means of attaining the real goal – to allow the Jewish people to devote themselves to the Torah without fear of oppression and reprisal: 'The Sages and the Prophets did not long for the days of the Messiah that Israel might exercise dominion over the world, or rule over the nations, or that it might eat and drink and rejoice. Their aspiration was that Israel be free to devote itself to the Law and its wisdom, with no one to oppress or disturb it, and thus be worthy of life in the world to come.'[55]

Ultimately, then, it is the possibility of being able to devote oneself to the law that will lead to the realization of the messianic age. Not unlike Joachim's concept of an *intellectus spiritualis* that will be bestowed upon ever greater numbers of people, Maimonides imagines that the fruit of deepened study of the sacred texts will be that the Jewish people increasingly attain prophetic insight. This greater knowledge of the ways of God is, in turn, a precondition for the fulfilment of the prophets' vision of peace and justice. Although Maimonides is primarily referring to the situation of the Jewish people, it is his firm conviction that establishing peace in Israel will also have consequences for other nations. Invoking Isaiah's words about a time when the wolf will dwell with the lamb, and the leopard lie down with the kid (Isa. 11:6), he directly indicates that even heathens will be included in the messianic redemption: 'The words of Isaiah ... are to be understood figuratively, meaning that Israel will live securely among the wicked of the heathens who are likened to wolves and leopards. ... They will all accept the true religion, and will neither plunder nor destroy, and together with Israel earn a comfortable living in a legitimate way, as it is written: *And the lion shall eat straw like the ox* (Isa. 11:7).'[56]

At the same time, the intriguing parallels, highlighted above, between Maimonides and Joachim must not obscure their real differences. This refers not only to the substantial differences which follow upon their respective religious affiliation but also to the more general qualities of their respective modes of thought. While Joachim is one of the medieval period's most consummately apocalyptic thinkers, Maimonides is famous as marking the apex of the antiapocalyptic strand within Judaism. Even so, this contrast need not be exaggerated. Joachim's writings, it might be recalled, signal a substantive shift within the very category of apocalypticism. Whereas the (Jewish and Christian) apocalypticism of antiquity in general proclaimed the advent of a suprahistorical era, Joachim – not unlike Maimonides – announces a qualitative change in historical reality itself.

Another difference is that Joachim's writings can be seen to have a deterministic quality, a quality that is typically identified as definitive of the apocalyptic character of his works. Thus, for example, he refers to a specific date, 1260, as the actual moment when history's third *status* will begin. This would seem to run contrary to Maimonides's desire to make the realization of the messianic age dependent upon the moral perfection of the Jewish people. Here, too, matters are not black and white. Joachim might have applied himself to calculating the different phases of history, but his view of the relationship between the various phases was complex and he regarded them as intricately bound up with each other. It should also be pointed out that Maimonides's profound scepticism about apocalyptic messianic movements did not stop him from providing his own date, 1216, as the moment when the prophetic spirit would return to the world.[57]

Although Joachim's vision of the *status* of the Holy Spirit is not messianic in the Christian eschatological sense, it is my contention that these parallels with Maimonides reveal important similarities to the rabbinic notion of a messianic age. This means that there is also a certain resemblance between Joachim's vision and the messianic idea as it was originally crystallized within the classical prophetic literature. At that embryonic stage, messianism was precisely an intrahistorical vision of redemption tied to concrete social and political expectations. What Joachim offered was not primarily a political vision but rather a theological or monastic conception of the ideal society. Even so, there is an essential continuity in that Joachim, like the prophets of antiquity, was interested less in the fate of the individual in the world to come than in a future period of spiritual flourishing in this world.

This affinity between Joachim and Jewish messianism in no way jeopardizes his inclusion within the Christian tradition; the Calabrian abbot never considered himself anything other than a Christian theologian. What matters is that Joachim, by virtue of this affinity, made a substantial contribution to enriching and developing Christian theology of history. As Mattias Riedl points out, Joachim departed radically from the pessimistic view of history that since Augustine had exerted particular influence upon the Western Christian view of history. Whereas Augustine saw history as primarily a waiting room, Joachim introduced an element of progression (*profectus*) and change (*mutatio*) within the framework of the course of history.[58] This also involved a considerable shift in emphasis from the past to the future. Christian tradition had hitherto tended to locate the ideal state in the time of the apostles; Joachim discerned an incentive for change in the notion of impending spiritual perfection.[59]

Joachim's break with pessimistic theologies of history does not mean, however, that he can straightforwardly be categorized within a utopian strand, at least not if utopianism is taken to mean a mode of thought that disregards the past in favour of some ideal future state. Although Joachim imagined that the *status* of the Holy Spirit would shortly commence, bringing with it a visible change, he did not foresee a revolutionary phase. On the contrary, he was convinced that the three phases were imbricated with each other and worked in parallel. The third *status* could therefore only mean a qualitative deepening of the two preceding.

The strength of Joachim's visionary theology thus lies in how he provides a horizon that offers hope and constitutes a critical corrective to the current order of things without losing its foothold in the past. This rootedness in the past sheds further light on the particular character of Joachim's vision. Joachim stands out among medieval theologians for the value he placed upon the Old Testament, the Bible of Judaism as well as the locus from which his own tradition derived. In contrast to most other Christian theologians throughout the medieval age, Joachim was not interested in events described in the Old Testament merely as they foreshadowed events in the New. On the contrary, his exegetical theory of concordance (*concordia*) between the two Testaments meant that he read the Old Testament in light of the New as much as vice versa.[60]

It therefore comes as little surprise to find that the prospect of the Holy Spirit being poured out on both Christians and Jews constitutes a central feature in Joachim's vision of the third *status* of history. This does not mean that the two peoples – *populus iudaicus* and *populus gentilis* – will be dissolved and reformed into a third, new people of God. Just as the Bible's two Testaments will remain yet be deepened by *intellectus spiritualis* during the *status* of the Holy Spirit, so, too, will both peoples undergo a historic apotheosis without thereby ceasing to exist as distinct peoples.[61]

This apotheosis of both peoples, it should at once be clarified, will be anything but symmetrical in nature. On the contrary, it will involve the Jews, during this new outpouring of the spirit, coming to realize the truth of the *Christian* revelation. Joachim had previously developed these themes in the pamphlet *Adversus Iudeos*, where, in paradigmatic fashion, he had associated the Jewish people with fleshliness and Christianity with spirituality. In this light, the notion of the conversion of the Jews takes on the aspect of a corollary to Joachim's general notion of the salvation history as a journey from literalness to spirituality.[62]

Nonetheless, it is impossible to escape the fact that Joachim's polemical pamphlet differs from other examples of this genre. In contrast to the vitriolic portraits of Judaism offered by most *Adversus Iudeos* pamphlets, Joachim exerts himself to understand and do justice to his opponents' positions. This tone also characterizes his view of the conversion of the Jews, something he imagines as a peaceful process entirely free of coercion or violence. What is most conspicuous, however, is how Joachim, when later developing his theory of history's three ages, locates the moment of the Jews' conversion in the near future. Whereas traditional Christian teachings situated the conversion of the Jews at the end of time, Joachim imagines, in other words, an earthly time when the two peoples, Jews and gentiles, will live in peace like two branches of a single tree.[63]

Interestingly, Joachim here comes close to Maimonides's vision of a messianic age, with this difference: that Maimonides, writing from a Jewish perspective, imagines the other peoples as converting to the 'true religion' – that is to say, Judaism. Of similar relevance is the fact that Joachim, despite the asymmetry of his vision, imagines that even Christianity will undergo a profound transformation following the onset of the *status* of the Holy Spirit. Both Jewish and gentile branches of the common tree will one day experience a new era of prosperity. This vision of a higher, more universal religion was to have a profound impact on the spiritual life of Europe and its reverberations are still detectable, six hundred years later, in Romanticism's concept of a 'religion of the spirit' to which this study will now turn.

Notes

1. There is, in fact, no consensus as to whether Joachim's vision occurred in 1183 or 1184; see B. McGinn. 1985. *The Calabrian Abbot: Joachim of Fiore in the History of Western Thought*, New York: Macmillan, 22.

2. Joachim relates this vision in his introduction to the work: Joachim of Fiore. 2009. *Psalterium Decem Chordarum*, Monumenta Germaniae Historica, vol. 20, ed. K.-V. Selge, Hannover: Hahnsche Buchhandlung, 9–10.

3. On the former, see e.g. E. Bloch. 1991. *Heritage of our Times*, trans. N. and S. Plaice, Oxford: Polity Press, 122–128, and J. Taubes. 2009. *Occidental Eschatology*, trans. D. Ratmoko, Stanford: Stanford University Press, 85–122. On the latter, see e.g. E. Voegelin. 1952. *The New Science of Politics*, Chicago: University of Chicago Press, 110–121, and M.J. Lasky. 1976. *Utopia and Revolution: On the Origins of a Metaphor*, Chicago: University of Chicago Press, 18–22. These varying readings of Joachim will be elaborated in Chapter Four.

4. See M. Reeves. 1999. *Joachim of Fiore and the Prophetic Future: A Medieval Study in Historical Thinking*, 2nd edn, Stroud: Sutton Publishing, 28.

5. For a good overview of these developments, see K. Zetterholm. 2007. 'Elijah and the Messiah as Spokesmen of Rabbinic Ideology', in M. Zetterholm (ed.), *The Messiah in Early Judaism and Christianity*, Minneapolis: Fortress Press, 57–78.

6. See e.g. M. Dibelius. 1968. *Aufsätze zur Apostelgeschichte*, 5th edn, Göttingen: Vandenhoeck and Ruprecht, 108–119.

7. See D. Marguerat. 1999. *La première histoire du Christianisme: Les Actes des apôtres*, Paris and Geneva: Cerf/Labor et Fides.

8. Tertullian. 1950. 'Apology', in *Apologetical Works and Minucius Felix Octavius*, trans. R. Arbersmann, E.J. Daly and E.A. Quain, Washington: Catholic University of America Press, chapters 32 and 39.

9. J. Pelikan. 1966. *The Finality of Jesus Christ in an Age of Universal History: A Dilemma of the Third Century*, Richmond: John Knox Press, 5.

10. Ibid., 7–18. See also Tertullian, 'Apology', chapters 39 and 40.

11. Eusebius. 1953. *Ecclesiastical History (Books I–V)*, trans. R.J. Deferrari, Washington: Catholic University of America Press, books 1.1–4 and 3.5–8.

12. See also J. Carroll. 2001. *Constantine's Sword: The Church and the Jews*, Boston and New York: Houghton Mifflin Company, 165–194, and P. Fredriksen. 2002. 'The Birth of Christianity and the Origins of Christian Anti-Judaism', in P. Fredriksen and A. Reinhartz (eds), *Jesus, Judaism*

and Christian Anti-Judaism: Reading the New Testament after the Holocaust, Louisville: Westminster John Knox Press, 8–30.

13. See also R. Williams. 2005. *Why Study the Past: The Quest for the Historical Church*, London: Darton, Longman and Todd Ltd, 12–15; A.P. Johnson. 2014. *Eusebius*, London and New York: I.B. Tauris, 96–103.

14. See Eusebius. 1955. *Ecclesiastical History (Books VI–X)*, trans. R.J. Deferrari, Washington: Catholic University of America Press, book VIII.I.

15. Ibid., book X.IX.

16. McGinn, *Calabrian Abbot*, 60–61.

17. Johnson, *Eusebius*, 110.

18. Ibid., 150.

19. See also B. McGinn. 1979. *Visions of the End: Apocalyptic Traditions in the Middle Ages*, New York: Columbia University Press, 39–41.

20. Augustine. 2013. *The Works of Saint Augustine: A Translation for the 21st Century*, vol. 7, *The City of God (Books XI–XXII)*, trans. W. Babcock, New York: New City Press, book XX.VII–IX.

21. See also McGinn, *Calabrian Abbot*, 26–30. The illustration (and an English translation of the accompanying text) is reproduced in B. McGinn (ed.). 1979. *Apocalyptic Spirituality: Treatises and Letters of Lactantius, Adso of Montier-en-Der, Joachim of Fiore, the Franciscan Spirituals, Savonarola*, New York: Paulist Press, 135–141.

22. See also M. Riedl. 2004. *Joachim von Fiore: Denker der vollendeten Menschheit*, Würzburg: Königshausen and Neumann, 264.

23. McGinn, *Calabrian Abbot*, 26.

24. Ralph of Coggeshall, *Cronicon Anglicanum*, quoted in McGinn, *Calabrian Abbot*, 29.

25. Joachim of Fiore. 1983. *Liber de Concordia Novi ac Veteris Testamenti*, in E.R. Daniel (ed.), *Transactions of the American Philosophical Society* 73:8, Philadelphia, book II.I.X (Eng. trans. by McGinn in *Calabrian Abbot*, 125).

26. See also McGinn's erudite discussion of this debated aspect of Joachim's view of revelation; *Calabrian Abbot*, 123–144.

27. See ibid., 124–125.

28. See e.g. Joachim, *Psalterium*, 103–104.

29. See e.g. Blenkinsopp, *History of Prophecy*, 229–230.

30. See also Pelikan, *Finality of Jesus Christ*, 38–47.

31. Joachim, *Concordia*, book II.I.IX (Eng. trans. by McGinn in *Apocalyptic Spirituality*, 130–131).

32. Ibid.

33. Ibid., book II.I.V.

34. See ibid., book II.I.IV.

35. See ibid., book II.I.VII–IX.

36. See Augustine, *City of God*, book XX.VII–IX.

37. The work is available only in a facsimile: Joachim of Fiore. 1964. *Expositio in Apocalypsim*, unaltered reproduction from 1527, Frankfurt am Main: Minerva, 1964. Shorter paragraphs are translated and edited by McGinn in *Visions of the End*, and (in German) by A. Rosenberg. 1977. *Joachim von Fiore: Das Reich des Heiligen Geistes*, Bietigheim: Turm Verlag.

38. See McGinn, *Calabrian Abbot*, 154–155.

39. Joachim, *Expositio in Apocalypsim*, f 209vb (Eng. trans. by McGinn in *Calabrian Abbot*, 153).

40. See also Reeves, *Joachim of Fiore*, 59.

41. See Joachim of Fiore. 1999. *Expositio de Prophetia Ignota*, in M. Kaup (ed.), *Gioacchino da Fiore: Commento a una profezia ignota*, Rome: Viella, 160–162. See also McGinn, *Calabrian Abbot*, 23–24.

42. Riedl, *Joachim von Fiore*, 9–16.

43. Buber, *Prophetic Faith*, 134–145.

44. See Zetterholm, 'Elijah and the Messiah as Spokesmen of Rabbinic Ideology', 67–69.

45. Ibid., 64. See also Banon, *Messianisme*, 12–28.
46. Zetterholm, 'Elijah and the Messiah as Spokesmen of Rabbinic Ideology', 76.
47. See e.g. Rosenberg, *Joachim von Fiore*, 32–33.
48. See also B. Hirsch-Reich. 1966. 'Joachim von Fiore und das Judentum', in P. Wilpert (ed.), *Judentum im Mittelalter: Beiträge zum christlich-jüdischen Gespräch*, Berlin: Walter de Gruyter & Co, 237.
49. Joachim of Fiore. 1957. *Adversus Iudeos*, The Latin Library. Source of the database: Arseneo Frugoni (ed.), *Fonti per la storia d'Italia* 95, Rome: Istituto Storico Italiano per il Medio Evo.
50. See Hirsch-Reich, 'Joachim von Fiore', 239–243 and R. Lerner. 2001. See also *The Feast of Saint Abraham: Medieval Millenarians and the Jews*, Philadelphia: University of Pennsylvania Press, 24–29.
51. See e.g. D.J. Lasker. 2007. *Jewish Philosophical Polemics against Christianity in the Middle Ages*, 2nd edn, Oxford and Portland: The Littman Library of Jewish Civilization.
52. Maimonides. 1949. *The Code of Maimonides. Book Fourteen: The Book of Judges*, trans. A.M. Hershman. New Haven: Yale University Press, 240.
53. Ibid., 240.
54. See also R. Lévy. 2005. 'Le messianisme de Maïmonide', *Cahiers d'études Lévinassiennes: Messianisme* 4, 151–176.
55. Maimonides, *The Code of Maimonides*, 242.
56. Ibid., 240.
57. See A.J. Heschel. 1982. *Maimonides: A Biography*, New York: Farrar, Strauss, Giroux, 25–32.
58. See Riedl, *Joachim von Fiore*, 259–270.
59. See McGinn, *Calabrian Abbot*, 236.
60. See Lerner, *Feast*, 29–31.
61. See Hirsch-Reich, 'Joachim von Fiore', 244–263.
62. Joachim, *Adversus Iudeos*.
63. See Hirsch-Reich, 'Joachim von Fiore', 244–249.

CHAPTER 3

Romantic History

Dresden, 1813. Napoleon's army has moved on, leaving behind thousands of corpses and maimed bodies on the battlefield. Sepsis sets in quickly in the late summer heat, and the stench spreads across the countryside. A few days later, the writer E.T.A. Hoffmann, carrying a glass of wine, enters the scene of slaughter. He records the gruesome impressions, which later provide material for his famous horror novels.[1]

The scene may seem macabre, but it was hardly more macabre than everyday life itself in Napoleonic Europe. It encapsulates nicely the way in which life, history and literature often blurred into each other in the early nineteenth century, an era that is now called, not coincidentally, Romanticism. History became literature and literature became life. The notion that literature can shape life – indeed, that life is a novel – fascinated people in a time when real life was dominated by suffering and poverty. The popularity of Hoffmann's horror novels and even the historical novel, which emerged at this time, is often accounted for in this way. In a Europe defined by war and social crises, literature provided an imaginary world that allowed readers to raise themselves above the brutality of everyday life.

This era's fascination with the past as well as with the inexplicable is also reflected in a fatigue for the Enlightenment's strong emphasis upon progress, reason and clarity. On the Continent, orders and secret societies – Jesuits, Freemasons, Illuminati and Rosicrucians – flourished. Cultural life was suffused with theosophical movements, fuelling a belief in hidden connections in the social sphere. Germany saw the emergence of an entirely new genre, *der Geheimbundroman*, dedicated to this fascination with secret conspiracies emanating from these associations. Its authors – whose number include Friedrich Schiller and even Hoffmann – became masters of the Romantic art of making the everyday seem unusual and enigmatic.

Notes for this section begin on page 100.

Such tales of hidden connections between different epochs gave a spur to the imagination of a generation that had only recently begun to think of history as an intellectual object in its own right. The transition from the eighteenth century to the nineteenth century was a period in which historical awareness emerged in a broad range of areas. As they glimpsed themselves for the first time as historical entities, Europeans enthusiastically plunged into the monuments of previous ages. Ancient mythology, medieval legends and popular folk tales all formed part of an expanding jigsaw. This meeting between the ideas and images of the past also spawned the idea that humanity and its works had been refined by history – in the words of a figure whose works will be revisited shortly, 'nothing captured by history is ephemeral, from countless transformations it comes forth renewed in ever richer forms'.[2]

The transition from eighteenth to nineteenth century was not only the time when the concept of history in its modern sense was born. It was also when the modern concept of literature was born. As Andrew Bowie has observed, both these developments can be considered in light of the fact that theology found itself on a defensive footing. In the case of the latter, it was not only that literature increasingly competed with religion as a source of existential meaning. More profoundly, how language itself was seen as a medium of truth and meaning also changed. To simplify somewhat, Romanticism signalled a break with an earlier conception of language as merely the names given by God to the various component elements of creation. Rather than locating truth and meaning beyond words – in the referent or 'bearer' of the name assigned by God – the early Romantics evinced a revolutionary awareness of the close connection between language and meaning. Meaning was no longer seen primarily as that to which words referred, but as something generated in and through language itself. This perceptual shift with regard to language was also reflected in the modern concept of literature. With Romanticism, literature revealed itself as a linguistic realm that existed for its own sake, irrespective of any reality beyond its narratives and thus also independent of God as a guarantor of the relationship between storytelling and reality.[3]

A similar pattern of secularization can be discerned in the concept of history that developed under Romanticism. Slowly but surely, the theological notion of history as directed by divine providence was replaced by a conviction that history is driven forward by the forces of nature or, indeed, humanity itself. This development had begun with the Enlightenment. In 1765, Voltaire published a long essay entitled *La philosophie de l'histoire*, which coined the term 'philosophy of history' as a modern rival to 'theology of history'. When he wrote the essay, the devastating Lisbon earthquake lay only a decade in the past. Just as in his satirical work of 1759, *Candide*, Voltaire directed his polemic at those who sought to exculpate God entirely from the horrors of history by means of intricate theodicies. As he saw it, history was no more and no less than what humanity made of it, and only after jettisoning its theological baggage could humanity gain a proper understanding of history.[4]

Interest in the driving forces of history was also growing among early Romantics, who, like Voltaire, were dissatisfied with the answers provided by traditional theology of history. In the preceding quotation about the renewal of historical material in ever richer forms can be discerned a view of history as a dynamic process that continues independently of divine providence. These words were penned by Friedrich von Hardenberg – better known by his pseudonym, Novalis – a thinker who was captivated not only by the forces of nature but also by the self-generative capacity of the human subject.

Novalis shared this fascination with nature as an animated process with another key figure of early Romanticism, F.W.J. Schelling. For Schelling, nature appears as a dynamic series of stages through which it advances towards an ever-greater degree of self-realization. Its dynamic points, in an analogous way, to history. In paradigmatically Romantic fashion, Schelling views history as a series of stages by which the spirit (*Geist*) struggles towards consciousness of itself.

However, the most famous interpretation of the Romantic view of history was undoubtedly that of G.W.F. Hegel. Hegel studied with Schelling in the early 1790s and essentially shared the other's view of history. At the same time, Hegel did not share Schelling's interest in natural-philosophical speculations and was eventually to take his philosophy of history in a markedly rationalistic direction. Spirit – the principle that realizes itself through the passage of world history – revealed itself in the final instance to be intrinsically linked to human mind, thereby making the historical process synonymous with humanity's journey towards an ever-greater degree of self-consciousness.

Hegel's rationalistic and increasingly secularized view of history finally left behind the Romantic concept of history. But staying with Romanticism for a moment, a more ambivalent relation between the religious and the secular will be discovered. Far from being a reductive account of religion, the Romantic view involved a refinement of religion by aesthetic means. In other words, its new perspective on literature and history should not be interpreted as an effort to distil the divine into the human. What the Romantics strove to achieve was precisely the reverse – to elevate the human to the divine by aesthetic means. Novalis formulated this striving in a fragment that is often presented as the quintessence of Romanticism: 'By endowing the commonplace with a higher meaning, the ordinary with mysterious respect, the known with the dignity of the unknown, the finite with the appearance of the infinite, I am making it Romantic'.[5]

This striving for what Novalis in the same fragment identified as 'a qualitative raising to a higher power' perhaps received its most forceful expression in the Romantic idea of a new, higher religion. As will be shown in the following sections, this was an idea that integrated several of the prophetic, messianic and pneumatic motifs that are now familiar from the classical prophetic literature and as a recurrent theme in the writings of Joachim of Fiore. Clearly, the Romantic idea of a higher religion posed a challenge to the boundaries of traditional religion. Equally clearly, however, it also flew in the face of the disparaging view of religion held by the philosophers of the French Enlightenment. Voltaire's dividing line between philosophy of history and theology of history ultimately revealed itself to be far from self-evident.

One of the more famous articulations of the idea of a new religion with aesthetic overtones occurred in Novalis's poetical essay *Christendom or Europe* from 1799. Novalis was only twenty-seven when he penned this visionary description of Europe's spiritual destiny. It will never be known how the concept might have been developed by Novalis if his life had not been cut short two years later. Several of the Romantic thinkers were to abandon the idea and instead take refuge in the safe haven of conventional religion. And yet one of these early Romantic thinkers not only continued to foster the idea of a higher religion, but refined it during his long philosophical career. In the late writings of Schelling can be found a philosophically reflected form of the same idea that is encountered in the passionate vision of the youthful Novalis. The idea is given its most concentrated form in the final lecture of Schelling's *Philosophy of Revelation* (1841/42), his comprehensive attempt to develop a philosophical interpretation of the history of the Christian religion.

However, there is also a third, as yet unmentioned, thinker, who must not be overlooked in order to properly understand Novalis's and Schelling's historico-theological reflections: the young theologian Friedrich Schleiermacher, who was the very first to offer a more systematic formulation of the idea of a refined religion. In his epochal work *On Religion*, published in spring 1799, Schleiermacher gave a theological interpretation of the Romantic conviction that an aestheticized form of religion would be capable of raising the human spirit to ever-higher levels of freedom. Although Schleiermacher himself was one of those who came to partially distance themselves from their youthful radicalism, his study exerted a lasting influence upon the entire early-Romantic generation. These three texts and their authors – Novalis, Schelling and Schleiermacher – will occupy a central position in the following analysis of the Romantic dream of a new religion. As will soon become evident, any discussion of historico-theological motifs in Romanticism must also consider, at least in passing, the role of three other key figures: Hegel, Hölderlin and Friedrich Schlegel.

The Poet as Prophet

'There once were beautiful, splendid times when Europe was a Christian land, when *one* Christendom dwelt in this continent, shaped by human hand.'[6] Thus begins Novalis's tract on the spiritual destiny of Europe, offering the reader a painterly description of the Middle Ages under Christianity. The epoch is portrayed as a superior culture, defined by harmony at every level of society. A time of hierarchy, to be sure, but one in which the powerful protected the weak, and the weak trusted in their protector. Somewhat unexpectedly, given his Protestant background, Novalis identifies the secret of this organic, ordered and integrated culture in the Roman church's 'mighty peace-making society'. The corruption and autocracy of the medieval papacy are not mentioned. Instead, he offers a picture of a sensuous religion deeply rooted in the soul of the people: 'With what serenity one left beautiful gatherings in mysterious churches decorated with inspiring pictures, filled with sweet scents and enlivened by uplifting sacred music'.[7]

The reader nonetheless has a creeping feeling that all is not as it should be. On closer inspection, the inhabitants of this tapestry-like medieval idyll seem like beatific children, and Novalis indeed makes reference to simple people's 'childlike trust' in the teachings of those in power. His double-edged description of the epoch which followed also suggests that this essay is not a naive appeal for a return to the medieval period. The Reformation, the Enlightenment and the French Revolution unquestionably led to a deplorable carving-up of the continent, but they also brought with them a critical awakening. People began to rise up against unjust authorities and assert their own right to be the judge in matters of faith and morality.

Even so, there can be no doubt that Novalis ultimately regarded the new era as a time of decadence with devastating consequences for the soul of Europe. The real damage was done by the Reformation, he asserts, when religion lost its 'great political influence as a peacemaker' and fell into the hands of local princes who used faith for their own sordid interests. The cosmopolitan spirit of the medieval era was thereby undermined, and 'in a most irreligious manner' religion became 'confined with national borders'. Yet Novalis's objections to Protestantism go beyond politics, taking aim at the very core of Lutheran theology, the principle of *Sola Scriptura*:

> Luther treated Christianity altogether as he pleased, mistook its spirit and introduced another letter and another religion, namely the holy universal validity of the Bible, whereby unfortunately another extremely alien aspect of secular learning was introduced into the matter of religion – philology – whose all-consuming influence becomes unmistakable from that moment onward. ... This choice was highly damaging to the religious sense, since nothing destroys its responsiveness so much as the letter itself.[8]

In order to understand Novalis's polemical tone the symbolic significance of the dichotomy between 'spirit' and 'letter' in the Christian tradition must be recalled. Novalis's objection is not to philology in the general sense; indeed, he had great respect for philology as a discipline. Still less is his objection to a preoccupation with the written word; as a poet, he was profoundly fascinated by the inexhaustibility of the written word. And yet it was precisely this poetic infinitude that was lost in the Lutheran tradition's heavy emphasis upon the historical or literal level of Scripture at the expense of its deeper, spiritual meaning. What Novalis deplores, in other words, is Protestantism's misappropriation of the medieval era's rich allegorical tradition.

Novalis's attack on Protestantism was not limited to hermeneutical questions, however. Later in the essay, he summarizes the new faith's devastating effects by describing how 'the holy sense is drying up'.[9] In Novalis's writings, the 'sense of the holy' (*der heilige Sinn*) is a recurring concept, which refers to a human being's capacity to behold, despite its finitude, something of the infinite. Beneath this concept can be discerned the Romantic conviction of the sacramental character of the world; that the world of the senses in fact comprehends a transcendental reality. At this point the deeper significance of Novalis's critique can be glimpsed. Protestant theology's insensitivity to the symbolic complexity of language quite simply further deprives humanity of its capacity for wonder at the world's mystery.

The process set in motion by the Reformation, Novalis continues, was fully realized in the Enlightenment. The only difference is that the original 'hatred of the Catholic faith' has been replaced by a hatred of religion as such – indeed, of everything that wakens our higher senses: imagination, feeling, love of art. In its place, a new faith has emerged, 'stuck together out of nothing but knowledge' and reaching its apex in the way in which the proponents of the French Enlightenment were 'tirelessly engaged in cleansing nature, the earth, human souls, and learning of poetry, rooting out every trace of the sacred, spoiling the memory of all uplifting incidents and people by sarcastic remarks, and stripping the world of all bright ornament'.[10]

Europe may for the present be characterized by this spiritually barren landscape, but Novalis is in no doubt that this is merely a passing phase. His essay culminates with a visionary announcement of a new era of prosperity for Europe, an era of harmony and reconciliation in which freedom will be united with order. Novalis sees signs that this new era is imminent. In Germany, in particular, he finds 'traces of a new world'. While other European countries concern themselves with war and political intrigue, 'the German is educating himself with all diligence to participate in a higher cultural epoch, and in the course of time this advance must give him much superiority over the others'.[11]

Setting aside for the moment the knotty question of Romanticism's legacy in subsequent German history, nonetheless Novalis's celebration of his own culture's superiority ought to be placed in context. As is suggested by his sardonic portrayal of Protestantism as a carving-up of religion into national units, Novalis is not animated by narrowly nationalistic sentiments. What he praises in contemporary German culture is, rather, its 'versatility', 'limitlessness', and 'vigorous imagination'. In short, Novalis sees a revival in his own day of the medieval cosmopolitan spirit. Yet this spirit will only flourish if it is accompanied by a renewed appreciation of the indispensable place of religion within the soul of Europe:

> Who knows if there has been enough of war, but it will never cease if we do not seize the palm which only a spiritual power can confer. Blood will flow across Europe until the nations become aware of the terrible madness which drives them around in circles and until, affected and soothed by holy music, all in a varied group they approach their former altars to undertake the work of peace, and as a festival of peace a great love feast will be celebrated with warm tears as smoke rises from the sacred places. Only religion can awaken Europe again and make the peoples secure, and with new splendor install Christendom visibly on earth once more in its old peace-bringing office.[12]

What should be made of this curious plea for a Christian Europe? Rereading the quotation above, it is perhaps unsurprising that *Christendom or Europe* has so often been invoked in support of conservative or even reactionary conceptions of Europe. Such was certainly the case when the text was published posthumously in 1826. A quarter of a century had passed since Novalis's death, and the radicalism of early Romanticism was a distant memory; several of its principal representatives had followed a conservative path, politically and spiritually. On the cultural level more broadly, the revolutionary movements of the eighteenth century had given way to the political reaction of the early nineteenth. In such a climate Novalis's essay would be celebrated as an appeal for Christianity as Europe's spiritual foundation, in contrast to the Enlightenment's more general humanism. In this way the ground was laid for the text's philosophical afterlife.[13]

In fact, the essay has one of the more problematic reception histories in modern European literature. To understand its radicalism, we therefore need to force our way past this history in order to reach the time, place and spirit in which Novalis the author was born: in the heyday of Jena Romanticism. Much has been written about why Jena of all places should for a while have played host to the late-eighteenth-century spirit of freedom. Barely a stone's throw from Weimar, this little town in the heart of Thüringen was in the 1790s part of Sachsen-Weimar, one of several minor dukedoms in the region. The town's university dates back to the sixteenth century and was at this time financially maintained by four different dukes. This shifting responsibility may have been an important factor in the relative freedom that existed among the university's teachers and students that made it possible for radical ideas to spread.[14]

Jena, as the German intellectual historian Rüdiger Safranski has remarked, gathered together 'all those with high aspirations for the I' (*alle, die mit ihrem Ich hoch hinauswollten*).[15] In 1794, Johann Gottlieb Fichte was installed as a professor. At that time Fichte was German philosophy's rising star and the most important representative of what would soon emerge as transcendental idealism; but important groundwork had already been carried out by Karl Leonard Reinhold, whose professorial chair Fichte inherited. Both thinkers wrestled with the potential dualism between consciousness and the world brought into being by Kant's critical philosophy, and both sought with varying degrees of consistency to find a solution in the human I (*das Ich*). Both also exerted great influence upon Novalis.[16]

Besides Fichte, Jena in the late 1790s gathered together an array of brilliant figures now considered the core of Jena Romanticism: the brothers August Wilhelm and Friedrich Schlegel, Friedrich Hölderlin, Franz Brentano, Ludwig Tieck, Schelling and Novalis. Though never a resident of Jena, Schleiermacher is usually considered as part of their circle. Narrowing down the epicentre of this grouping more precisely leads to the inauspicious building across a courtyard where August Wilhelm Schlegel lived for a while together with his new wife, Caroline. Their house played host to one of history's most famous salons, in which Caroline Schlegel was a driving force. Several of the aforementioned figures spent longer or shorter periods at the house, reading, discussing, playing music or taking long walks in the picturesque countryside around Jena.

It is against this backdrop of Jena Romanticism's lively and radical intellectual climate that Novalis's ideas must be understood. It was the intellectual exchange within this circle of friends – particularly with Friedrich Schlegel – that inspired his vision, and it was to this circle that he presented his essay on Europe, in the form of a lecture, for the first time in November 1799. Interestingly, its contemporary reception attests to the fact that its radical message is not immediately apparent. Among those in whom Novalis's paean to Christianity inspired mixed feelings was Dorothea Veit, the daughter of the Jewish Enlightenment philosopher Moses Mendelssohn and the companion of Friedrich Schlegel. 'Christianity is here à l'*ordre du jour*', complained Veit a few days after Novalis's presentation, in a letter to Schleiermacher, who was in Berlin at the time. Schelling was also doubtful, something that is worth noting given the fact that he later in his life would go on to develop a historico-theological schema with striking similarities to Novalis's essay. In a letter, also to Schleiermacher, Friedrich Schlegel related how Novalis's address had prompted 'a new attack' of Schelling's 'old enthusiasm for irreligion'.[17]

These mixed reactions also gave rise to differences of opinion as to whether the text should be allowed to appear in *Athenäum*, the Schlegel brothers' short-lived journal and also Jena Romanticism's most important organ. In order to solve the dispute, the group turned to Goethe, then living in Weimar, who occasionally acted as a kind of mentor for the younger Romantics. The eminent poet advised caution in view of the fact that the visionary text might easily give rise to misinterpretations that could harm the group's good name. The result, as already noted, was that the text did not appear publicly until 1826. One can only speculate about how it would have been received if it had been published at the zenith of radical Romanticism and not in the wake of the political reaction of the 1820s.

As indicated earlier, a precondition for understanding the radicalism of Novalis's text is that one is not misled by his quaint portrait of the medieval period. Or rather, that one remains aware that it is precisely that, a quaint portrait, and not a historical account in its modern sense. In other words, Novalis's conscious aim is to achieve a poetical aestheticizing of the past. Consider, for instance, the following vignette of the medieval priesthood and its teachings:

> Peace emanated from them. They preached nothing but love for the holy, wonderfully beautiful Lady of Christendom, who, endowed with divine powers, was ready to save every believer from the most terrible dangers. They told of those long dead in heaven, who, through devotion and fidelity to the Blessed Mother and her friendly divine Child, withstood the temptation of the earthly world, achieving honor in the sight of God, and who now have become protective, benevolent forces for their living brethren, willing helpers in need, intercessors on behalf of human failings and efficacious friends of mankind before the heavenly throne.[18]

Naturally, it is no coincidence that Novalis idealizes the medieval cult of the Virgin Mary and the saints, nor that he later speaks warmly of the miraculous power of relics for the devout. In the age of Enlightenment, hagiolatry and relic cults were the very symbols of a contemptible superstition. And yet Novalis emphasizes precisely these aspects that contemporaries so disdained as a means of embellishing his account of the past. It is possible to interpret this gesture as a desire on Novalis's part to poke fun at the Enlightenment's preoccupation with reason and progress. But the gesture can also be seen as expressing an aesthetic strategy. Recalling Novalis's reference to 'a qualitative raising to a higher power', it can quite simply be asked whether he is not in fact practising what he himself calls 'romanticizing'; that is, using the power of poetry to challenge a conventional image – in this case, of the past – in order to reveal as yet unrealized potentialities.[19]

This impression, that Novalis is intentionally producing a stylized, poetic image of the medieval era, is reinforced by the striking absence of any concrete dates in his survey. What emerges is, rather, the image of an ideal world, a timeless homeland in which humanity lives in complete harmony with both God and nature. In other words, Novalis's portrait of the Middle Ages serves a critical prophetic function. Its idyllic image of 'truly Christian times' in fact has very little to do with what medieval Europe was actually like. What Novalis is evoking are the as-yet-unrealized potentialities that lie hidden in humanity's past. This futural aspect can be discerned in the vignette that ends the essay's first part, in which Novalis claims that '[h]umanity was not mature enough, not cultivated enough for this splendid kingdom'.[20]

It may be asked, however, why this prophetic vision should need such rich narrative embellishment. And, above all, why go via an idealized past when the vision of an ideal order could equally well be elaborated from a contemporary viewpoint? Asking these kinds of questions, as will become clear, brings out the truly interesting dimensions of Novalis's Romantic poetics of history. It also throws up a series of interesting parallels with the classical prophetic tradition. A defining characteristic of this tradition, as Yehezkel Kaufmann and others have shown, is the powerful significance which historical legend held for the literary prophets.[21] By grounding their preaching in significant events from the past, such as the story of Exodus, the prophets succeeded in conjuring up images that enabled the adoption of a critical perspective towards the existing socio-political and religious order. A similar dialectic of memory and hope is familiar from the writings of Joachim of Fiore. In Joachim's prophetic interpretations, history appears as a drama in which the memory of God's actions in the past make it possible to orient oneself in the present, but also to catch a glimpse of what lies ahead.

Yet between Joachim and Novalis lies the beginning of secularization. Demonstrating the continuity between this older historico-theological tradition and Romantic poetics of history is thus a delicate matter. For example, Novalis's writings lack the firm assurance given by both the classical prophets and Joachim that history rests securely in God's hands. But this does not mean that the prophetic motif should be discounted in either Novalis or Romanticism at large. *Christendom or Europe* is very much a testimony to how deeply rooted the idea that history contains a redemptive impulse was in the intellectual world of early Romanticism.

Novalis's conviction that history contains the key to a greater understanding of both the present and the future also finds expression in his notes from the same period. In order to acquire any grasp of the contemporary moment and ourselves, writes Novalis, we must acquaint ourselves with the past – with 'the highest products' and 'the purest spirit of the age'. Only by means of such an arduous relation to the past can we recover 'the human prophetic glance' that will enable us to discern the higher potentialities of the present.[22] At the same time, Novalis indicates that the conventional historian is not always best suited to prophetic interpretation. A good historian must be good storyteller, a poet, indeed, even a prophet: 'In his discourse, the historian must often become an orator. Indeed he speaks *gospel*, for the whole of history is gospel.'[23]

What does it mean for history to be gospel and the historian a prophet? Before the question is considered any further, it should be recalled that Novalis's object here is not historiographical but poetical and visionary. In other words, his controversial assertion should not be understood as a contribution to a widening debate among historians. In this sense Novalis is rather situating himself within an older historico-theological tradition. Like the earlier thinkers discussed in previous chapters, Novalis is concerned to find a language for showing the redemptive potentialities of history; to produce images that make it possible to imagine the world differently.

However, there is a decisive difference between Novalis's poetics of history and the prophetic motif as it appears in the older tradition. In classical prophetism, and even its medieval echo in Joachim, the prophet is fundamentally a passive figure. In classical antiquity, the prophet acts as God's mouthpiece: a voice that conveys God's intentions with history ('Thus sayeth the Lord…'). Even Joachim, who was undeniably very active in interpreting the signs of his time, essentially saw himself as the receiver of a pre-existing revelation. Not so with Novalis. The Romantic poet is more than the passive receiver of an already complete gospel. In a fragment, Novalis notes that '[t]he sense for poetry is closely related to the sense of prophecy and the religious, the seer's sense itself'. The following sentence reads: 'The poet orders, combines, chooses, invents – and even to himself it is incomprehensible why it is just so and not otherwise'.[24] The prophet-like poet is an extremely active figure who orders, unites, chooses and invents. At the same time, Novalis indicates that the poet, in the midst of this creative act, becomes the object of an inspiration that does not originate within himself – why these words have come to him 'just so and not otherwise' is, for him, incomprehensible.

This subtle dialectic between activity and passivity also characterizes our relation to history. In his notes, Novalis describes the historian as an 'active, idealistic person who works with the data of history'.[25] Historical narrative becomes an act of poetical creation intended to reveal the redemptive potentialities of the present. At the same time, this redemptive power is not elicited by humanity itself. It is made visible by means of patient investigation into the passage of history, by analogies and patterns that help us to impose a trajectory upon history and to differentiate better visions from worse. The poetical historiographer reveals himself to be both a discoverer and an inventor.

Novalis's use of what he himself calls 'the magic wand of analogy' (*der Zauberstab der Analogie*) is most in evidence in his fascination with triadic structures in history. As Hans-Joachim Mähl has shown, several of his works rest upon a triadic pattern in which a golden but archaic era is succeeded by one of division and critical awakening, which paves the way in turn for a time of higher harmony in which unity is combined with multiplicity.[26] The question of the Joachite tradition's influence upon this very common philosophical trope in Romanticism will be revisited later in this chapter. For now it may only be noted that this triadic interpretation of history is also completely pervasive in *Christendom or Europe*. Novalis's naivist description of the medieval era thus corresponds to what Mähl terms *das goldene Zeitalter*, a myth of origins that is shown to hold the key to an ideal future state; the equivocal account of the Reformation, the Enlightenment and the French Revolution represents the critical phase, while the visionary image of Europe's coming heyday expresses the dream of a time when the 'holy sense' will join with critical reason to form a new, higher religion. It is now time to look more closely at this vision and, with it, how the pneumatic motif is actualized in Romantic philosophy.

A Religion of the Spirit

In October 1798, Friedrich Schlegel wrote a letter to Novalis that attested both to the growing intensity of their friendship and to the increasingly central place that religion now occupied in their thinking: 'It is not until now that I begin to understand you. In recent times, I have had numerous revelations and I would now understand you better, since I understand religion'.[27] During the following months, the two friends conducted a lively correspondence on the idea of creating a new Bible, a kind of universal lexicon that would schematize the underlying analogies between all human understanding. The exchange culminated in a famous passage in a letter written by Schlegel on 2 December, in which he explained to Novalis that he in fact had more in mind than a purely literary project:

> My biblical project is, however, not a literary project, but a biblical and an entirely religious project. I am thinking of founding a new religion, or rather, of helping to promulgate it, since it will come and prevail also without me. ... That this should be achieved through a book should not surprise us, since the great *authors* of religion – Moses, Christ, Mohammed, Luther – became progressively less and less politicians and more and more teachers and writers.

He ended the letter by remarking that '[p]robably *you* have a greater talent for being a new Christ, one who finds in me his gallant Paul'.[28]

By this point Schlegel and Novalis were far from being alone in nurturing a dream of a new religion inflected by aesthetics. In fact, the idea of a higher religion located beyond the reach of dogmatic and clerical interference was a common motif in late eighteenth- and early nineteenth-century European thought.[29] Confining ourselves for the moment to German Romanticism, we find the motif occurring prior to Schlegel's and Novalis's messianic correspondence. The idea is expressed in a concentrated form, for example, in a text fragment that was titled 'Oldest Programme for a System of German Idealism' when it was rediscovered in the 1910s. Composed sometime between 1796 and 1797, the fragment has since been variously attributed to Hegel, Schelling and Hölderlin (all fellow students in Tübingen in the early 1790s who continued to maintain a lively exchange of ideas during the following years).[30]

The text is written in the spirit of Enlightenment and opens with a radicalized declaration of Kant's concept of freedom: 'The first idea is, of course, the representation *of myself as* an absolutely free being'.[31] Unsurprisingly, this heady declaration of freedom lies on a collision course with the traditional forms of state and religious authority. As absolutely free beings, we must take our leave of the 'completely wretched human production' represented by constitutions, governments, priesthoods and superstitions. All free spirits 'carry the intelligible world in themselves and may seek neither god nor immortality *outside of themselves*'.[32]

Yet this is not the expression of a one-dimensional fetishizing of reason. Reason's highest faculty lies not in abstract conceptualization but in its ability to value the beautiful; the highest philosophy, 'the philosophy of spirit', must therefore be an aesthetic philosophy. Using a rhetoric that is already familiar from Novalis's writings, the author declares that one cannot be rich in spirit, let alone argue cogently about history, without an aesthetic sense. Poetry thus moves centre stage, becoming once again 'what it was at its inception – *the teacher of humanity*; for there is no longer any philosophy, any history; the art of poetry alone will outlive all other sciences and arts'.[33]

It is as a consequence of this elevation of poetry to the highest standing that religion re-enters the picture. If the most elevated ideas are to become available to 'the great masses', the fragment goes on, they must be given some form of concrete embodiment. And yet it is not only ordinary people but also the abstraction-fixated 'philosophers of literalness' (*Buchstabenphilosophen*) who stand in need of such spiritualizing. Aestheticizing the most exalted ideas will thus necessarily require their transformation into myths – to create a 'new mythology'; a mythology 'in the service of ideas'; a 'mythology of reason'. Only by means of such a mythology can 'those who are enlightened and those who are not … make common cause'; philosophers need no longer be ashamed of religion, and people need no longer tremble before their wise men and priests. The fragment concludes with a messianic expectation that also contains a vague summons: 'A higher spirit, sent from heaven, must found this new religion among us, it will be the last, greatest task of humanity'.[34]

The fragment's rhetorical proximity to Schlegel's and Novalis's correspondence barely two years later is unmistakeable, and there is also a very clear intellectual affinity. Even so, it must be borne in mind that both fragment and correspondence came about at a time when German idealism began to part company with German Romantic philosophy, the key figures being Hegel and Schelling in the former camp, and Hölderlin, Schlegel and Novalis in the latter. This chapter will return to this watershed later but for now it may be asked whether the fragment does not substantially anticipate the idealistic systems that Hegel and Schelling were to develop, something that can be glimpsed in the concept of religion that emerges in the text: the new mythology called for by its author should be entirely at the service of reason and ideas. It is certainly germane that both 'reason' and 'ideas' are complex concepts in this context; as already noted, the author not only urges that mythology become reasonable but that reason, too, should become sensuous or even mythological. It is in any case difficult to disregard the fact that, when all is said and done, the dense argument of this text is wholly premised upon the postulation of an absolute I.[35]

In Hölderlin, Schlegel and, to an even greater extent, Novalis, a different relationship with religion emerged at this time. This is not to say that they were uncritical of traditional religion and its purportedly restraining influence upon the creative life; yet they adopted an increasingly sceptical posture towards the all-encompassing I that Fichte had paved the way for and that had now begun its triumphal progress through German philosophy. Convinced that the I could not be its own ultimate foundation, they shifted their focus towards the point at which the I reaches its own limits. In so doing, they also approached religion with more than just the goal of reinstating it within the absolute I. In its higher forms religion enables us to hover on the boundary between the finite and the infinite without ever eliding that boundary.

In Greek mythology Hölderlin sought – and found – these higher forms of religion, recording this vision of a Hellenic renaissance in his symbolic novel *Hyperion*, published in two parts in 1797 and 1799.[36] Schlegel turned his gaze eastwards instead, learning Sanskrit and acquiring an extensive knowledge of Indian mythology during the following decade. As early as 1800, however, he presented his own proposal for a new, universal mythology in his study *Rede über die Mythologie*.[37]

Novalis chose a third way, as has been described. Barely a year after his animated correspondence with Schlegel, he set about writing his own vision of a new, higher religion. But when he eventually came to write *Christendom or Europe*, it was not in himself that he saw 'a new Christ'; nor did he grant Schlegel the honour of being his 'gallant Paul'. It was in another figure that Novalis found his herald of the spirituality of a new age, and he made no secret of his admiration for this 'brother' who spoke to people in a way that made their 'hearts rejoice' and allowed them once again to feel all that this stale, earthly state had suppressed: 'This brother is the heartbeat of the new age; whoever has felt his presence does not doubt anymore that it will come, and he too steps out from the crowd with sweet pride in being a contemporary to join the new band of disciples. He has made a new veil for the Holy One which caresses her body, betraying the heavenly shape of her limbs, and yet covers her more chastely than any other.'[38] To whom was Novalis referring? Though never stated, his name would have been obvious to any sensitive reader: Schleiermacher, the 'veil-maker' who had made a new veil for the Holy One (*Er hat einen neuen Schleier für die Heilige gemacht*).

Friedrich Schleiermacher had become part of the Jena circle after becoming friendly with Friedrich Schlegel in the salons of Berlin towards the end of summer 1797. At that time he was working as a priest at La Charité, a hospital for invalids, although his path to priesthood had been anything but straight. During an earlier phase he had thrown off his strict Moravian upbringing in favour of Kant's critical philosophy. When he later began reading Montaigne and other sceptics, even Kant's inexorable faith in reason came to be viewed in a critical light. His meeting with Schlegel and the other Romantics supplied the remaining pieces of the puzzle.

In June 1799, Schleiermacher published *On Religion*, a work that would confer upon him the enduring title of 'father of modern theology'. Further, *On Religion* provided early Romanticism with one of its founding documents, a well-argued philosophical apologia for a concept of religion that spanned mysticism and aesthetics. In September Novalis ordered the book to be delivered to Jena by express courier. In his notes from this period he wrote enthusiastically that Schleiermacher had proclaimed an '*art*-religion – almost a religion like that of the *artist*, which venerates beauty and the ideal'.[39]

Novalis's characterization of Schleiermacher as a divinely sent herald ostensibly matches Schleiermacher's own self-image. From time to time, he writes in his introduction, the godhead sends figures who are particularly suited to serve as intermediaries between the finite and the infinite. While Schleiermacher admittedly does not say outright that he himself is such a figure, he nonetheless lets the reader know that his disquisition on religion has its origin in an inner necessity: 'it is a divine calling; it is that which determines my place in the universe and makes me the being I am'.[40]

Whether or not Schleiermacher was heeding a divine summons, a more immediate driving force behind the study lay in the early Romantics' frustration with the occasionally banal critique of religion that was taking root among contemporaries. Schleiermacher's text is nothing less than a series of speeches in the defence of religion, as the study's full title makes clear: *On Religion: Speeches to its Cultured Despisers*. Schleiermacher was thus addressing an educated body of scorners of religion with the goal of exculpating religion from what he saw as misdirected accusations.

Right from the opening speech, however, it is clear that Schleiermacher's aim is more sophisticated than merely offering a knee-jerk defence of religion in its current forms. On the contrary, Schleiermacher admits that on many points he shares the contempt in which the church and priesthood are held by educated contemporaries. However, what the most zealous detractors of religion are missing is that existing forms of religion in fact have precious little to do with its real essence. Schleiermacher wants, in effect, to inform the educated elite that religion is something else and considerably richer than what its critics are repudiating.[41]

To understand the audacity of Schleiermacher's argument, it is important to be clear as to how well rooted it is in contemporary philosophical debates on religion. Schleiermacher entirely shares Kant's critique of religion's claim to provide systematic knowledge about the nature of reality. Religion, he thus writes, is 'by its whole nature ... just as far removed from all that is systematic as philosophy is by its nature inclined toward it'.[42] Armed with this conviction, Schleiermacher is also able to dismiss those critics who treat theological doctrine as rational propositions which they can then easily confute; these critics are simply aiming to the side of their real target. What Schleiermacher does not share with Kant, however, is the latter's desire to preserve religion by creating a place for it in the area of morals. A ruse of this kind, he contends, is intended solely to increase contempt for religion further. No, there is nothing for religion in the area of morals, either: 'it must not use the universe in order to derive duties and is not permitted to contain any code of laws'.[43] Those who criticize religion for its lack of moral clarity have thus also failed to understand that, at the end of the day, they are criticizing, not religion, but a mere shadow of religion's real essence.

What, then, is the essence of religion? Schleiermacher's famous reply is that religion is a 'sensibility and taste for the infinite' (*Sinn und Geschmack fürs Unendliche*).⁴⁴ If thought falls within the domain of knowledge and action within that of morality, then humanity's capacity for religion lies nearer the domain of aesthetics. In effect, Schleiermacher compares a sensibility for religion with a sensibility for art, thereby also seeking to show that the issue is one of an innate disposition. As such, it can be either cultivated and developed, or malnourished and suppressed. Unfortunately, Schleiermacher argues, it is the latter which is occurring in the enlightened culture of the present time: 'With anguish I see daily how the rage of understanding does not allow this sense to arise at all and how everything unites to bind us to the finite and to a very small spot of it, so that the infinite is removed from our view as far as possible'.⁴⁵

To understand the essence of religion, Schleiermacher claims, we must set aside our eagerness to substantiate and prove, and instead turn our gaze towards the infinite. Schleiermacher is quick to clarify that, in seeking the essence of religion, it is not the infinite per se that we are studying but rather humanity's feeling for (*Gefühl*) and intuition of (*Anschauen*) the infinite. He thus situates the realm of religion within our inner being, linking it to the moment when our engagement with the world takes the form of an experience of the eternal and infinite: 'I entreat you to become familiar with this concept: intuition of the universe. It is the hinge of my whole speech; it is the highest and most universal formula of religion.'⁴⁶

Nevertheless, Schleiermacher's definition of religion in terms of a pre-theoretical experience of the infinite does not mean that he is oblivious to reason. On the contrary, and despite his raillery towards the 'cultured despisers' of his time, *On Religion* has a distinctly rationalistic voice. If not before, this becomes apparent when Schleiermacher examines more closely the issue of how a feeling for the infinite is awakened in the first place. Alluding to the words in the Sermon on the Mount about the lilies of the field that neither toil nor spin yet are arrayed in greater glory than Solomon, Schleiermacher proposes that the universe can be glimpsed by means of silent wonder at the world's sensory richness.⁴⁷ Those able to see how the 'world-spirit' (*der Weltgeist*) reveals itself equally in the greatest and the smallest things will find the eternal and infinite in their inner life. Yet it is not only, and perhaps not even primarily, from observation of the riches of the natural world that the religious predisposition derives. The religious feeling is awakened most strongly through meditation on the progress of the world-spirit through history: 'History, in the most proper sense, is the highest object of religion. Religion begins and ends with history – for in religion's eyes prophecy is also history, and the two are not to be distinguished from each other – and at all times all true history has first had a religious purpose and proceeded from religious ideas.'⁴⁸

Although Schleiermacher does not make use of the triadic patterns found in *Christendom or Europe*, the above begins to reveal how *On Religion* became a direct inspiration for Novalis. Both thinkers were driven by a prophetic conviction that history contained a redemptive potential, and both connected this potential to the essence of religion. To a greater degree than Novalis, however, Schleiermacher used the spirit concept as the very principle behind history's – and humanity's – redemption:

> If you then compare the isolated striving of the individual ... with the calm and uniform progress of the whole, you see how the lofty world spirit smilingly strides across all that tumultuously opposes it. ... The vulgar, the barbaric, the misshapen shall be engulfed and transformed in an organic development. Nothing shall be a dead mass that is moved only by dead impact and resists only by unconscious friction. Everything shall be its own assembled, much intertwined, and elevated life. Blind instinct, unthinking habit, dead obedience, everything indolent and passive – all these sad symptoms of the asphyxia of freedom and humanity shall be annihilated. The work of the moment and of centuries points in this direction; that is the great, ever-continuous redemptive work of eternal love.[49]

Regardless of the differences of nuance between Novalis and Schleiermacher, it is interesting to compare their visions with those of Joachim of Fiore and the historico-theological tradition to which his writings gave rise. Both Romantics not only share with the medieval abbot a conviction that history is being driven forward towards perfection; like Joachim, they assign the spirit a specific role in this process. What, then, is the relation between Joachim and these two Romantics? At a concrete level there is nothing to indicate that Novalis or Schleiermacher had any direct knowledge of Joachim's writings. Yet there is an indirect and highly complex intellectual genealogy that extends from Joachim via the radical Franciscans of the late medieval period and Protestant pietism, all the way up to German Romanticism. To date, by far the best account of this lineage is Henri de Lubac's classical study *La postérité de Joachim de Flore*, whose two volumes appeared in 1979 and 1981.[50] De Lubac emphasizes the paradox that Joachim, who was in key respects a conservative thinker, should have given rise to a largely radical tradition. But this radicalism lies less in his biography than in the idea that forms the core of his thinking – the idea of a new outpouring of the spirit and a subsequent age of human flourishing.[51]

From the very earliest history of the church, as discussed earlier, this notion has challenged the finality of the Christian revelation. Such was also the case in the late medieval period, when Joachim's vision of *Ecclesia spiritualis* became an inspiration for radical factions that regarded the existing church, in its worldly extravagance, as having betrayed the apostolic ideal. Well into the Reformation, Joachim's ideas were still being invoked by charismatic groups which sought to break away from the existing church framework. Joachite influences are visible in the writings of the radical reformer Thomas Müntzer as well as Protestantism's most important mystic, Jacob Böhme. In the eighteenth century, the chiliastic movements of the high medieval era could be found living on in pietism's social visions of an impending ideal society on earth. As Hans-Joachim

Mähl has argued, it is important to situate Novalis – who, like Schleiermacher, was brought up in a Moravian milieu – against this chiliastic-pietistic background.[52] One might add that the same goes for Schleiermacher.

But it was Gotthold Lessing who provided the most obvious link between the Joachite tradition and the early Romantics. In his influential study *The Education of the Human Race* from 1780, Lessing described the development of the human spirit towards a higher stage defined by freedom and moral fulfilment. Although Lessing never refers directly to Joachim's writings, instead making only a general allusion to the prophetic 'spiritualists' (*Schwärmer*) of the thirteenth century, he seems to have been well acquainted with the main features of Joachim's theology of history.[53] To the extent that Joachite elements may be identified in early Romanticism – such as Novalis's triadic interpretation of history or Schleiermacher's vision of a spiritualized religion – it is reasonable to assume that the greater part of this influence stems from Lessing rather than from any direct knowledge of Joachim's writings.[54]

There is nonetheless an important exception. When F.W.J. Schelling, many years after the heyday of Jena Romanticism, returned to the question of a higher religion, he discovered his opinions to be 'in *close affinity with the thoughts of the Abbot Joachim of Fiore*'.[55] Novalis was long dead by this time, and, as already noted, it will never be known how his vision of a new religion might have evolved had tuberculosis not ended his life prematurely. The same goes for Hölderlin, who by the early 1800s had been affected by severe mental illness. Together with Dorothea Veit (at that time called Schlegel), Friedrich Schlegel converted to Catholicism in 1808. Like Schleiermacher – who, by contrast, remained true to his Protestant faith – his relation to religion developed in a more conservative direction with the passage of time. Schelling's preoccupation with the history of the Christian church has often been interpreted in a comparative light – that is to say, as an expression of a growing religious conservatism. However, closer scrutiny of his idea of a 'religion of the spirit' and a 'truly universal church' makes it difficult to sustain such a reading.

It is in the last chapter of *Philosophy of Revelation* that Schelling develops his idea of a truly universal church and acknowledges his affinity with Joachim of Fiore. This posthumously published work consists of the famous lectures which Schelling gave in Berlin in 1841–1842, whither he had been summoned in order to stifle the purportedly 'anti-Christian' sentiments that had resulted from Hegel's protracted presence at the university. Although Hegel himself had then been dead for a decade, Schelling's audience contained an array of young radicals who would in various ways become famous to posterity – Mikhail Bakunin, Friedrich Engels and Søren Kierkegaard, to name but a few.[56]

Whether Schelling was successful in his task of stifling anti-Christian sentiments at the University of Berlin is too complex a question to consider here. What needs to be rectified, however, is the enduring misconception that Schelling's religious views became increasingly conservative. On the contrary,

Schelling is perhaps the only one of the early Romantics who remained faithful his entire life to the radical vision of a new, higher religion.

Schelling's Berlin lectures rest upon his conviction that Christ has merely laid the foundations for an ongoing process, one that necessarily challenges the current form of the church: 'As Christ through his life, suffering and death had sown *the seed* of a life bound to grow into eternity, he wanted ... [this seed] to successively develop in the midst of the storms of this world.'[57] More specifically, Schelling's goal is to describe three guiding ideas or principles in the history of the Christian church. Easily discernible here is a triadic pattern reminiscent of Joachim's writings and also of Novalis's essay on Europe (which Schelling, ironically enough, had mocked in his youth). The three principles, which define three distinct epochs in the history of the Christian church, are symbolized by the three main apostles: Peter, Paul and John. Peter symbolizes the church's bedrock principle, the 'strictly legalistic' element of Christian faith. Although Peter has been traditionally portrayed as the leading apostle and the founder of the church, Schelling sees here only the first stage of Christian history. In terms of historical epochs, the Petrine church symbolizes the Roman Catholic Church prior to the Reformation. Like Novalis, Schelling praises this church for its unifying power. Like Novalis, he is nonetheless aware that this unity has only been achieved at the price of absolute authority.[58]

In order for the seed planted by Christ to grow and flourish, Schelling argues, it was necessary that the principle symbolized by Paul should take centre stage. In terms of historical epochs, this coincided with the upheavals that resulted in the Reformation. Hence, the Pauline principle stands for development and movement but also for the freedom of the individual in relation to the whole. Just as Paul, at the very dawn of Christianity, departed from Peter in essential matters, so, too, did Luther break with a church that had ossified into its own forms; '*a church, free and independent of the exclusively Petrine church, was foreseen already by the vocation of Paul*'.[59] At the same time, there is a certain ambivalence in Schelling's position on the upheavals of the new era, an ambivalence that again recalls Novalis's essay. On the one hand, Schelling – who, like Novalis, had a Lutheran background – attributes great value to Protestantism for its acknowledgement of individual human freedom. On the other hand, he blames Protestantism for containing the principle of destruction. In other words, the price of individual freedom has been a tragic dismembering of the body of the church, for which reason even the Protestant Church should be seen as a transitional form that paves the way for the true church.

What, then, distinguishes the true church? Schelling's answer contains the entire philosophy of Romanticism in a nutshell: '*The Pauline principle* has liberated the church from blind unity. *The third period* is the period of deliberately chosen and hence eternally enduring unity.'[60] In this ideal church individual freedom will be united with a higher order. Schelling finds the principle of this higher order in John, traditionally called the Apostle of Love. Yet John is more than an apostle of love, and in order to understand the audacity of Schelling's vision the triadic – more precisely, trinitarian – underlying structure of his argument must be highlighted. That is to say, Schelling's three principles not only describe epochs in church history; they also possess a deeper theological significance that relates to the very essence of the Christian concept of God: 'Peter is the apostle of the Father[,] … Paul the apostle of the Son, and John the apostle of the Spirit'.[61]

Linking John to the spirit is not completely far-fetched. According to tradition, John is the author of the gospel that relates how Christ promised to send his spirit to the disciples (John 16:5–15). Again this implies the dynamic nature of the notion of the spirit; the account of how Christ sent his spirit indicates that God continues to reveal himself to humanity.

It is against this background – of John as symbolizing a dynamic principle – and not as the expression of a growing religious orthodoxy, therefore, that the later Schelling's idea of a higher religion should be understood. 'My goal', he declares towards the end of his lecture, is 'to build that first truly universal [*wahrhaft allgemeine*] church (if church is still the right word here) *only in the spirit, and only through the complete fusion of Christianity with general science and knowledge*'.[62] Despite the differences in genre between Novalis's prophetically freighted essayism and Schelling's mature philosophy, the vision offered by the latter is no less radical. In both cases, what is being discussed can hardly be considered a religion in the conventional sense. Rather, this is about a vision of an intellectually refined humanity, not unlike the one that Schleiermacher had outlined in *On Religion* but then partly abandoned for his mature theology.

The above has offered an insight into the content of the Romantic idea of a higher religion. A more profound question is how this ideal state was ever to be achieved – that is to say, the issue of the messianic strand within Romantic philosophy. To grasp this issue in all its complexity, it is necessary to understand the way in which it is interwoven with a larger philosophical debate over the ultimate aims and conditions of knowledge.

Messianism and Utopianism

The heyday of Jena Romanticism took place only a decade after the French Revolution. In addition to the extraordinary geopolitical reverberations of the Revolution, events in France lent an unparalleled impetus to Europe's cultural life. The Revolution had a decisive impact upon intellectuals across the continent. More than ever, it was clear that ideas not merely were capable of interpreting the world but had the potential to transform it. Critical thought had completed its historic journey from the writing table to the political battlefield.[63]

All of the key figures in early Romanticism paid tribute to the Revolution's radical fervour; but they were no less affected by its dark side, the Jacobin Terror and new forms of oppression in the name of freedom. This duality finds expression in *Christianity or Europe* when Novalis praises the Revolution as an inevitable 'second Reformation' even while rejecting, in a tone of admonishment, the excessive faith in humanity's power to shape history: 'O! that you were filled with the spirit of spirits and might desist from this foolish striving to mould history and humanity and give them your own direction'.[64]

While the French Revolution lent vital impetus to German Romanticism, it should not be forgotten that German intellectual life during this period was undergoing, albeit more quietly, a revolution of its own. With the publication of his *Critique of Pure Reason* in 1781, Immanuel Kant had initiated nothing less than what he himself called a 'Copernican revolution'. Kant asserted that it is not, as we so like to believe, our knowledge that adapts itself to the properties of the universe. On the contrary, the world, as we know it, is arranged according to the categories of human consciousness. Of *das Ding an sich*, that which is the condition of possibility for the empirical world of appearances, we can know nothing.

Kant's bold thesis may seem solipsistic. Yet contemporaries thought otherwise. Kant was regarded as having liberated philosophy from centuries of fruitless metaphysical speculation. The real question was whether his thesis was radical enough. To be sure, Kant had directed attention towards consciousness as the generative principle of all knowledge. At the same time, his argument nonetheless seemed to presuppose a reality independent of consciousness – a 'thing in itself' – which, for his critics, created a problematic tension. As if this were not enough, they also discerned a tension between Kant's *Critique of Pure Reason* and his *Critique of Practical Reason*, published seven years later. In short, there appeared to be a conflict between Kant's theory of knowledge and his moral philosophy, in that the former supposedly dealt with consciousness as tied to the laws of nature even as the latter postulated free will.

It was in many ways dissatisfaction with these purported dualisms – between consciousness and the world, between freedom and necessity – that generated one of the most significant debates in the history of Germany philosophy, a debate that was to give rise to, among other things, absolute idealism. That Kant did not see himself as having said the final word on the matter became clear in 1790 when he published his third critique, *Critique of Judgement*, something that has often been interpreted as an attempt to use aesthetics as a means of overcoming the purported dualism of the two previous critiques. But by the time Kant published his third critique, several of his students, including Karl Leonard Reinhold, had already drafted an outline intended precisely to overcome metaphysical dualism. Reinhold's solution was to establish a first principle (*Grundsatz*) that could integrate critical philosophy into a single system.

Opinion was divided over whether Reinhold succeeded in his ambition of creating such a first principle; he himself later abandoned this position. By contrast, there was no doubt about his capacity to inspire critical philosophical thinking. During the years he was resident in Jena (1787–1794), he attracted a lively circle of students (including Novalis) with interests in both theology and philosophy.[65]

As already mentioned, Fichte succeeded to Reinhold's professorial chair in 1794. Fichte also tried to resolve the potential dualism in Kant's work and presented what may have been an even more consistent solution to Kant's dilemma. In broad strokes, Fichte's solution involved sacrificing Kant's 'thing in itself' entirely and postulating in its place the 'absolute I' as the single, all-encompassing principle of all reality. A more nuanced way of putting it would be to say that he sought to intensify Kant's view of the indispensable role played by consciousness in constituting the object world. Ultimately, the activities of consciousness were the basis for the world's being at all knowable. Taken to its extreme, this notion unavoidably leads to the conclusion that the postulate of a 'thing in itself' is redundant. This conclusion also laid the foundation stone for absolute idealism.

Posterity long regarded Fichte as Romanticism's preeminent philosophical mouthpiece. Fichte's world-creating I (*das Ich*) was seen as a philosophically weighty concept that had subsequently been converted into aesthetic reflections by literary thinkers such as Hölderlin, Novalis and Friedrich Schlegel. This picture has been substantially challenged by the discovery and dissemination of new documents relating to early Romanticism.[66] It is quite true that several of the leading Romantics were influenced by Fichte and his strong conviction as to the role of the I in creating the world that we experience. Yet it has become increasingly untenable to treat their works as merely literary echoes of an already worked-through philosophical concept. On the contrary, they should be seen as robust interventions within the multifaceted philosophical debate that followed upon the publication of Kant's critical works and that for several years had its focal point in Jena. Above all, it is essential to note that their claims deviated from Fichte's in several key respects.

We here touch upon the historic divide, mentioned earlier, that began to open up in the mid-1790s between idealism and Romantic philosophy. Considered in the light of recent scholarship, it is thus clear that the positions taken by Hölderlin, Novalis and Schlegel on fundamental philosophical issues differed from those being developed by Fichte and, later, Hegel. These diverse perspectives have already been addressed in passing in relation to the notion of religion that was emerging from various attempts to create a 'new mythology'. As discussed, both Hölderlin and Novalis took a sceptical view towards the notion that the I might be the all-encompassing principle which Fichte argued for, looking instead within the realm of religion for a perspective on the absolute that did not equate it with the totality of human knowledge.

To understand this sceptical perspective, a hitherto unmentioned influence on Romantic philosophy, namely Friedrich Heinrich Jacobi, must be considered. Like Reinhold, Jacobi was one of those who early on identified tensions within Kant's philosophy. Like Reinhold, he also considered an idealist solution to the problem of dualism; indeed, as Manfred Frank has argued, he was the first to anticipate the possibility of an absolute idealism.[67] But Jacobi chose another path instead, adopting a sceptical view of the goal of establishing the foundation of thought in consciousness. Any such ambition was quite simply doomed to fall into an infinite regression, since the foundation being proposed raised in turn the question of what comprised its own foundation. In other words, Jacobi pointed out philosophy's failure to demonstrate the unconditional. At the same time, Jacobi did not choose the path of radical scepticism. Like Fichte, he proposed an absolute foundation but denied that this foundation could be established by consciousness itself. Jacobi used the term 'being' (*Seyn*) to denote this unconditional foundation, claiming that humanity could only perceive this unconditionality by means of a special sense (*Sinn*) that was linked to feeling (*Gefühl*).

That Hölderlin, like Novalis and Schlegel, was influenced by Jacobi is well documented, as is the fact that this influence coloured their reception of Fichte.[68] For Schlegel, it was a relatively late occurrence, coinciding with his move to Jena in 1796 and resumption of a more active philosophical dialogue with Novalis. Hölderlin's scepticism towards the aim of formulating an absolute foundation for philosophy can be traced back as far as spring 1795. In the text fragment *Urtheil und Seyn* ('On Judgement and Being'), he rebutted the idea that the I can conceive of the absolute, postulating instead the existence of a whole that superseded both the I and the not-I. Like Jacobi, he used the term *Seyn* to denote this inconceivable whole.[69]

Novalis's scepticism towards first principles can be traced back to the early 1790s when he mixed with the critical student grouping around Reinhold. A few years later, he began studying Fichte intensively, and it is in fragments written during this period that his critique of the search for an absolute foundation becomes explicit: 'Philosophy, the result of philosophy, arises … when the desire for knowledge of the foundation is aborted'.[70] Any philosophy that established an absolute foundation for all knowledge had *a priori* undermined the object of its own efforts. On the contrary, philosophizing must begin with indeterminacy and strive for the absolute. But Novalis rejected the claim that the absolute could ever be attained by thought. The absolute or infinite was, quite simply, that which drove philosophical inquiry forward at the same time as it kept human beings mindful of their finitude. This powerful commitment to the open-ended nature of philosophical inquiry found its most concise expression in the famous first fragment in his collection *Blüthenstaub* ('Pollen'), which Novalis published in *Athenäum* in 1798: 'We *seek* the absolute everywhere and only ever *find* things'.[71]

Turning now to Schleiermacher, it is at first glance less obvious where he should be situated in relation to the aforementioned historic divide. Earlier accounts often put Schleiermacher within the idealist tradition. Yet this has been questioned in recent years, not least by Manfred Frank.[72] What Frank and others have shown is that by the early 1790s Schleiermacher, quite independently of the other Romantics, had already begun studying Jacobi's works. Indeed, it may be asked whether Jacobi had a greater influence on Schleiermacher than on any of the other thinkers. For example, consider the following passage from *On Religion*: 'I ask you, therefore, What does ... your transcendental philosophy [do]? It ... deduces the necessity of what is real while spinning the reality of the world and its laws out of itself.'[73] The reproach is directed towards the emerging idealism's tendency of reducing reality to laws within its own system — that is to say, precisely the tendency that Schleiermacher had contested in his outline of the essence of religion. Like Jacobi, he assumed that the absolute lay beyond the reach of human consciousness and could only be experienced through the feeling that is elicited by the encounter with one's own finitude. At the same time, it must be clarified that neither Jacobi nor Schleiermacher were interested in a return to traditional theological metaphysics. Both denied the possibility of attaining systematic knowledge about the absolute foundations of existence; all that can be reflected upon is the I's experience of the *absence* of any absolute foundation within itself.

It is even less apparent where to situate Schelling in relation to the other thinkers. To continue with the metaphor of a watershed, it is very clear that Schelling ends up on the idealistic side. However, it is important not to over-interpret the image of a watershed between Romantic and idealist philosophy. Above all, it should be pointed out that this is not a case of counterposing a realist (and, implicitly, dualist) perspective to a monist view of reality in which thought and being coincide. On the contrary, as Manfred Frank maintains, all of these philosophers take a fundamentally monist position. Thus the fact that the absolute supersedes the subject, for Novalis and Schleiermacher, does not mean that it is thought of as existing in a reality separate from that subject. The real difference between these Romantic thinkers and idealist philosophers such as Fichte and Hegel therefore lies not in whether there exists a reality beyond that given to us, but whether the absolute foundation for all reality allows itself to be grasped by thought and integrated into a philosophical system.[74]

Reconstructing this historic divide along these lines quickly makes it clear that Schelling, in the last of these respects, is nearer to the Romantics. That this is indeed the case becomes particularly evident from his later writings, in which the essential line of demarcation from Hegel relates to the question of whether the absolute allows itself to be represented philosophically or not. Looking back to his early philosophy, the picture is less clear. On the one hand, from the very beginnings of Romanticism his writings were driven by a strongly idealistic impulse in which the influence of Fichte is unmistakeable. On the other hand, it is possible from an early stage to discern his incipient dissatisfaction with Fichte's tendency to reduce the entire natural world to the human I.[75] Schelling's growing distance from Fichte can be traced back to Hölderlin's critique, but also to his own lifelong fascination with nature and the natural-philosophical speculations of previous epochs.[76] Both influences become apparent in Schelling's works towards the end of the 1790s when he developed a natural philosophy that situated human consciousness within a larger whole that in itself resisted being made the object of conceptual knowledge. At this point parallels may be noted, not only to Hölderlin but also to Novalis's and Schleiermacher's explicit critique of the tendency to reduce the world to a reflection of one's own reason. And yet it is also possible to see in this early natural-philosophical phase an anticipation of the central idea in Schelling's late philosophy. In both cases, it is a matter of formulating the limits of philosophical thought, or, as Marcia Sá Cavalcante Schuback has put it, of admitting that the true precondition of philosophical thought is a work of *experience* rather than conceptual comprehension.[77]

Having completed this excursus, let me return once again to the question of the messianic strain in Romantic philosophy. The reason for spending so long on the philosophical debate prompted by Kant's critical philosophy is that it actualizes a problematic of transcendence that has been touched upon in different ways in previous chapters. At issue here is not transcendence in the sense of belief in another reality than the one we experience. Even in classical prophetism a marked distance can be seen towards such a notion of transcendence, as evinced by the critical tension that emerged in tandem with the growth of apocalypticism. The aim of the prophetic vision – in contrast to the apocalyptic – was not to abolish history in favour of another reality but to supersede the current historical order in the name of a justice that would never permit itself to be constrained by any particular historical order.

The concept of transcendence was foregrounded similarly in the debate within Romanticism over the basis for philosophical thinking. The matter at stake was thus not the relationship of thought to transcendence in a metaphysical or spatial sense – all of the aforementioned thinkers shared Kant's critique of metaphysics. Rather, it was the issue of the limits to human thought, of what allows itself to be incorporated into a rational system and what remains transcendent of any such system. This is expressed in the various ways in which Novalis, Schleiermacher and Schelling refer to the unattainability of the infinite and to a being that never accedes to thought but that nonetheless forms the condition of possibility for rational thought.

This insight into the finite character of consciousness is closely bound up with a deepened appreciation of the constitutive role of time in thought. Anticipating twentieth-century phenomenological debates in several respects, Romanticism evinces an intensive preoccupation with the temporal character of consciousness. Temporality makes itself visible precisely in our reflections upon our own thinking; the more we seek to cling to what is present in an act of consciousness, the more we realize how this presence has already disappeared into the flow of time. The present moment refuses to be fixed because it is already intersected by what has been and what is to come. It is therefore as an extension of this insight into the impossibility of rationalizing away time that we should understand the critique levelled by several Romantics towards the ambition of formulating a static first principle for philosophy: because there is no fixed point outside of time, it is impossible to catch more than a fleeting glimpse of the absolute, as a fragment in the eternal flow of time.[78]

In light of this the concept of transcendence that is at stake in the debate over first principles can also be narrowed down: what emerges here is an understanding of transcendence that is not spatial or metaphysical but temporal. This is reflected not only in the analyses of individual consciousness but also in Romantic philosophy of history more broadly. Coming back to the idea of a new, higher religion, it is clear that the question foregrounded here is whether the promised ideal state was ever meant to be fulfilled. In an essay on the central place of the concept of the fragment in Romantic philosophy, Daniel Birnbaum has formulated the question as follows: 'Is the dividedness of the fragment final, or does it contain the promise of some future reconciliation, some new harmony?'[79] The question is posed in relation to the opposing interpretations advanced during the twentieth century by Paul de Man and Peter Szondi, with de Man defending the insurmountability of the divide and Szondi writing the Romantic fragment into a dialectical philosophy of history.[80] Birnbaum rightly observes that both readings are somewhat tendentious, and he himself avoids siding with either position. And yet it could also be said that the question itself is misleading insofar as the alternatives were, in the case of Romantic philosophy, hardly mutually exclusive: the promise of a future reconciliation is absolute, but so, too, is the divide.

At this point we uncover a vein of paradox that runs through the messianic idea and that leads back to the theological sublimation which took place during early Judaism and Christianity. In both cases, as has been discussed, it concerns a reaction to the apocalyptic waves of the first centuries, during which ideas of imminent redemption were toned down in favour of a pragmatic theology of history that saw in the passing of time a possibility rather than a failure. Indeed, parts of rabbinic Judaism would come to see incomplete redemption as having value in its own right; in the continual postponement of its objective, humanity was being given the opportunity to make its own contribution towards history's gradual change for the better. The messianic promise remained, not as a promise to achieve an ideal state on earth but rather as the formulation of an ideal which humanity would always be called upon to realize.

Significant parallels with the Romantic ideal of a higher religion emerge at this point, recalling Schleiermacher's words on 'the great, ever-continuous redemptive work of eternal love', indicating that redemption is an ongoing process rather than some completed state in the future. When, towards the end of *On Religion*, Schleiermacher offers an image of the realization of this ideal religion – a time when God will be 'all in all' – he also makes a revealing answer to the question of when this time will commence: 'I fear it lies beyond all time'.[81] Schleiermacher's words have been interpreted as a reference to an eschatological series of events.[82] In context, however, his answer is more plausibly interpreted as alluding to the unattainability of the ideal: the question comes after a long disquisition on the merits of Christianity, which Schleiermacher concludes by noting that the latter constitutes the most ideal form of religion precisely because of its powerful insight into humanity's inability to reach the ideal.

> Nowhere is religion so completely idealized as it is in Christianity. ... Just because the irreligious principle is everywhere present and operative, and because everything real appears at the same time to be unholy, an infinite holiness is the goal of Christianity. Never satisfied with its attainment, it seeks, even in the purest intuitions, even in its holiest feelings, traces of the irreligious and the tendency of everything finite to be turned away from and opposed to the universe.[83]

The same dynamic understanding of redemption runs through both Novalis's essay on an impending golden age for Europe and Schelling's lecture on the religion of the spirit. Novalis even rounds off his survey by asking the question, 'When and how soon?', before replying immediately: 'That cannot be asked. Patience, only patience, it will come, it must come, the holy time of eternal peace.'[84] His answer should be seen in the context of the larger message of his essay – not least its critique, mentioned earlier, of the utopian vein within the French Revolution – but also in light of his general distrust of the goal of grasping the absolute. Even during the years prior to *Christendom or Europe* Novalis was already exploring the idea of a coming golden age, while firmly maintaining that '[t]he goal of man is not the golden age'.[85] However, another fragment from this period reveals that this was not a matter of simply denying the advent of an ideal state: 'The principle of fulfilment – humanity would not be humanity if a thousand-year kingdom did not have to come [*kommen müßte*]'.[86] The messianic paradox once again reveals itself: what is essential about the ideal is not its realization but its relentlessly futural quality. Were the golden era to commence, history would quite simply lose its forward impetus, thereby depriving humanity of its vocation continually to supersede itself.[87]

If the notion of a higher religion sometimes takes on the qualities of a prophetic invocation in Novalis's writings, it is no less the case with Schelling's references to a higher church in which the principle of freedom will be combined with that of unity. The church founded by John was a church solely of the future (*nur Kirche der Zukunft*), by which Schelling implied that it was an ideal to strive for, rather than an actually existing state.[88] The idea of an endlessly deferred church corresponded with the dynamic concept of tradition to which the start of his lecture alluded; at this point, the words about Christ merely sowing a seed that will continue to grow and develop during the passage of history may be recalled. Yet this idea can also be considered in light of Schelling's broader philosophical claims, particularly the way in which his later thinking rested upon the conviction that a philosophy which contained its own absolute goal necessarily excludes actual historical change.[89] The alternative path staked out by Schelling instead ascribed a central role to beginning; not in the sense of a static point of departure, but as an anarchic principle that preceded all philosophical reflection and that could only be apprehended by consciousness by virtue of its own implication in life's continual incipience. The absolute – or God – could thus never be apprehended as the goal of philosophy; God is the eternal beginning of life and, as such, was permanently in the making.[90] Similarly, Schelling's idea of a higher church seemed less like an object to be realized and more like the principle of an unattainable perfection. In other words, the church of the future would be a church of continual beginning.

The Romantic notion of a new, higher religion has sometimes been characterized as a utopia, or at least as a utopian idea. However, at this point I should like to paraphrase the Novalis scholar Johan Redin, who writes in connection of the futural quality of Romantic poetics: 'That Romantic poetry can only be described as a thing of the future does not at all mean that it is a *utopian* idea. It is about the conditions under which it can come into existence.'[91] What I want to argue, namely, is that the same holds for the Romantic idea of a higher religion as evinced in the writings of Novalis, Schleiermacher and Schelling. These thinkers offer a vision that is fundamentally critical of utopianism – an attempt to create a horizon for history in the crucial knowledge that, even as we move towards the horizon, it necessarily recedes.

A Truly Universal Church?

Romanticism is sometimes caricatured as an era of naive sentimentalism. This caricature is typically evoked by means of a contrast in which the Enlightenment's radical political fervour is counterposed to a culture of dreamy youths seeking to compensate for their lack of political engagement by means of religious enthusiasm. Admittedly, the early 1800s witnessed a political reaction in which religion played an important role (that will be discussed in the next chapter); but this development must be separated from the intellectual climate of 1790s Jena. The early Romantics unquestionably turned against aspects of the French Enlightenment, not least the dehistoricized Reason that ran amok during the later phases of the Revolution. Even so, this was not a reaction in the simple sense of the word. On the contrary, several of the key figures of Jena Romanticism would remain essentially true to the revolutionary ideals.[92]

In one respect, however, the Romantics did break with the ideals of the French Revolution. Where the Revolution had deeply anti-clerical roots, Romanticism from an early phase took a considerably more favourable view of religion. But it is on this very point that one must not muddy the picture by allowing the later reaction to obscure the radicalism which was a defining feature of the Jena Romantics' attitude towards religion. It has already been noted above that the idea of a new, higher religion was essentially an attempt to use aesthetics as a way to refine existing religion. Nevertheless, it is also important to see the radical *political* aspects which were attached to these ambitions and which were reflected in the messianic qualities of the Romantic concept of religion.

It is useful here to recall the distinction between 'political theology' and 'theopolitics': the first term designates a symbiosis between religion and political power, and the second an unwillingness to ascribe perpetual authority to any temporal authority. It is symptomatic that several leading Romantics were strongly critical of the state church as an institution and of the post-Reformation principle of *cuius regio, eius religio*. The idea of a state church found its most implacable enemy in Schleiermacher. In the fourth speech of *On Religion*, Schleiermacher, having clarified the nature of the true religion, identifies the root of every religion's decadence: 'As often as a prince declared a church to be a corporation, a community with its own privileges, a notable personage of the civil world, … the ruin of this church was irrevocably decided and commenced. Such constitutional charter of political existence affects the religious society like the terrible head of Medusa: Everything turns to stone as soon as it appears.'[93]

In Novalis's case the picture is slightly more complicated, something that may be owing to the tension between his aristocratic extraction and the low-church ideal of piety in which he was raised. In both *Christendom or Europe* and other, more political texts, Novalis seems to take for granted that the church should be a core institution of the state, or at least of civilization. At the same time, his texts are permeated by a sharply critical attitude towards the tendency to divide Christianity up into national churches. This duality is expressed near the end of his lecture on Europe, in which Novalis both predicted the end of Protestantism and called for a new 'visible' church: 'Will not Protestantism come to an end at last and make way for a new, more enduring church? … Christendom must again become lively and effective, and again form a visible Church without regard to national borders, one which will take up into its bosom all those souls who thirst for the supernatural, and gladly become the mediator between the old world and the new.'[94]

Although Novalis distanced himself from national churches, it may be asked whether this also entailed a disavowal of the symbiosis between religion and political power. Was his vision of a renewed and unified Christian culture not precisely a call for a political theology? To avoid misinterpreting Novalis, it is vital to foreground the symbolic nature of his flattering depiction of the medieval church: the romanticized Catholicism evoked by the Protestant Novalis fulfilled the function of a critical corrective to existing Protestantism – its division into national churches, its hierarchical structure, its fixation with biblical text – rather than a means of raising expectations of a revived papal church. It is also worth noting that Novalis, when discussing the congregation of the ideal church, uses the term *Verein* ('society', 'association'), a term that was widely used within radical Protestant circles and which referred to the ideal of an autonomous community of equals. Despite his sourness towards the Reformation's downsides, it is therefore fair to characterize Novalis as a radical reformist thinker, driven by the principle of *ecclesia semper reformanda* – a church that never ceases to be reformed.[95]

This pattern also recurs in Schelling's writings. By the time Schleiermacher had completed *On Religion* and Novalis *Christendom or Europe*, Schelling was already developing a corresponding critique of (Lutheran) Protestantism's tendency to produce churches that merely acted as an arm of the state. In his *Lectures on the Method of Academic Study*, delivered in Jena in 1802, he reproached Protestantism for reducing theology to a shallow moral doctrine and its priests for preaching domestic economy from the pulpit.[96] Despite the conventional image of Schelling as an increasingly conservative Lutheran thinker, this critical denunciation of Protestantism was to inform his mature philosophy, particularly the radical notion of the church that he developed in the last lecture in his *Philosophy of Revelation*.

Given this stereotyped image of Schelling, it is an interesting thought experiment to consider him alongside Hegel, who is usually considered the more radical of the two men as regards their relationship to the Christian tradition. This description holds true to the extent that Hegel saw the Christian religion as having been fulfilled by the growing realization of God's death, which is to say the insight that there exists no divine transcendence beyond the human spirit and, ultimately, that the human spirit *is* the absolute spirit. However, if Hegel is compared to Schelling with regard to political theology, it makes far more sense to describe Schelling as the truly radical thinker. As Mark Lilla notes, Hegel learned an important lesson from the French Revolution, namely that freedom is not attained by establishing a political authority in complete opposition to a religion with popular roots.[97] Hegel's solution was instead to conserve the morality of religion while making the church entirely subordinate to the state. The contrast with Schelling's 'truly universal church' that can be built 'only in the spirit' is striking here. That the ideal church would be built in the spirit did not mean that Schelling thought it would be absorbed into an absolute knowledge, let alone be made subordinate to state power. The church was 'truly universal' precisely by virtue of the fact that it did not allow itself to be made subordinate to any external authority, something that also required 'the complete fusion of Christianity with general science and knowledge'.[98] Custodianship of the Christian legacy was *res publica*, a matter for the general public, and as such was not answerable to any political power.

How, then, might the radicalism of not only Schelling's but also Novalis's and Schleiermacher's concepts of religion be defined? With a view to throwing into sharper relief the theopolitical and anti-authoritarian component of the Romantic idea of a higher religion, I will conclude this chapter by setting out three of its principal features. Interestingly, all of these features can be traced back to Joachim of Fiore (without needing to assert the claim that he was in any simple sense their author).

The first feature is *progression*. Despite their lively interest in history, the Romantics never indulged in any dewy-eyed nostalgia for a bygone era. Their interest in the past was always in the service of the future, a conviction that found clearest expression in Novalis's depiction of the historiographer as a prophetic figure. At first glance, *Christendom or Europe* might seem to express a yearning for the 'truly Christian times', but one need not delve very deeply into the text to appreciate that Novalis's underlying impulse is more aptly captured by his remark that '[p]rogressive, ever-expanding evolutions are the stuff of history'.[99] The same sentiment also informs not only Schleiermacher's words on 'the great, ever-continuous redemptive work of eternal love',[100] but also Schelling's metaphor of the seed that is sown by Christ and that grows and develops even as history marches onward.[101] In the same way as Joachim imagined that the Christian revelation evolved over time according to the pattern of the Trinity, so, too, did these Romantics think that religion had been cleansed by the passage of time in order to assume ever richer forms.[102]

The second characteristic feature is *universalism*; the Romantic idea of a new religion was a cosmopolitan vision that crossed national borders. We can recall once again Novalis's critique of Protestantism's narrow-minded state-church ideal. In contrast, he proposes a new, unified church whose hallmark is a freedom from both 'Christian and secular constraint'; a church that refuses to be contained within the boundaries of Europe, but that is likely to rouse a desire in the rest of the world to 'become citizens of the kingdom of heaven'.[103] In Schelling's writings, too, this universalizing feature finds expression in a notion of the church's steadily widening scope. While enumerating the characteristics of the three apostles, Schelling portrays Peter as a protector of Jewish Christians, the apostle who sought to defend the unity of the Jewish community. It was this ethnically demarcated unity that Paul, the apostle of the heathens, sought to disrupt and enlarge through his mission. Yet the foundations alone had been laid for the attainment of the real aim, a truly catholic church. And it is in John that Schelling finds 'the apostle for this non-excluding city of God, in which both Jews and Pagans are included in the highest sense, … and to which each and every person belongs through his own conviction'.[104]

Schleiermacher deserves a special mention in this context as one of the first prominent theologians to articulate a pluralistic view of religion, denying that any one tradition can be the repository of the whole truth. Such a notion quite simply runs contrary to the essence of religion, since religious traditions are finite while 'religion is infinite'.[105] However, this fundamental conviction does not mean that Schleiermacher rejected the various religious traditions in favour of some abstract moral essence – a widespread tendency among contemporary philosophers when considering religion in the wake of Kant. In fact, Schleiermacher had little time for such 'natural religion'. Ever faithful to the Romantic ideal, he instead remained convinced that the eternal essence of religion was to be found solely in its historical, concrete and continually changing forms – without ever allowing itself to be reduced to those forms.[106]

Despite this sensitivity to religion's concrete forms, the Romantic vision also includes a markedly anti-institutional quality. This tension is especially visible in Schleiermacher's own writings. In his fourth speech, which treated the Christian community, he explicitly took the side of the existing church against the adversaries of religion, yet also contrasted it with the 'true church'. The latter denoted the invisible or at least non-institutional community of those who had reached true spiritual maturity. The message was simple – once humanity has become spiritually mature, it will no longer need the visible church: 'Thus, in fact, people become all the more indifferent to the church the more they increase in religion, and the most pious sever themselves from it proudly and coldly. Nothing can in fact be clearer than that the seekers of religion are in this association only because they have no religion; they persevere in it only so long as they have none.'[107]

Behind this lukewarm stance on the institutional church can be detected the Moravian ideals with which Schleiermacher was raised; the lecture concludes with a celebration of the intimate domestic community as the most authentic form of Christian community. Yet the question is whether these words should in fact be understood as containing an even more radical vision. In his fifth and final speech, Schleiermacher rounds off a long and painstaking appeal for religion with the ambiguous declaration: 'I would gladly stand on the ruins of the religion I honor'.[108]

The writings of Novalis and Schelling evince a similar distance from the church as an institution. Novalis, it is true, sought a new 'visible' church, but by the end of his essay it is clear that this had less to do with a church in the institutional sense than with a larger vision of a culture:

> Christianity has three forms. One is the generative element of religion, namely joy in all religion. One is the notion of mediation itself, namely faith in the omnipotence of all earthly things to be the bread and wine of eternal life. One is the faith in Christ, his mother and the saints. Choose whichever you will, choose all three,

it is all the same[:] you will become Christians thereby and members of one single, eternal, inexpressibly happy community.[109]

The contours are hardly less blurred in the case of Schelling's church, which could be built 'only in the spirit'. Revealingly, Schelling includes the parenthetical insertion 'if church is still the right word here'.[110] The Romantic dream of a higher religion, it would seem, ultimately had very little to do with a concrete religious practice. At stake, rather, is a philosophical vision of a spiritually and intellectually elevated humanity.

This leads to the third and final characteristic feature of the Romantic concept of religion, which can be summarized by the term *spiritualization*. This feature is not only reflected in the polarization between the church as an empirical entity and a more idealistic notion of the essence of the true religion. It is also visible in the recurrent polarization between 'letter' and 'spirit'; between a rigidly dogmatic religion and a poeticized religion of free spirits. Here, again, Schelling's and Novalis's satirical tirades against Protestantism are revealing. In addition to its divisive and temporalizing effects, Novalis writes, the Lutheran theology introduced an unhealthy fixation with the written word, which 'made it infinitely difficult for the Holy Spirit to bring about free vivification, penetration, and revelation'.[111] Interestingly, however, it is Schleiermacher, the theologian, who goes furthest in his attack on a religion that he saw as fixated with the written word:

> Every holy writing is merely a mausoleum of religion, a monument that a great spirit was there that no longer exists; for if it still lived and were active, why would it attach such great importance to the dead letter that can only be a weak reproduction of it? It is not the person who believes in a holy writing who has a religion, but the one who needs none and probably could make one for himself.[112]

Despite the enduring image of Romanticism as an unworldly and religiously conservative epoch, there are therefore good grounds for claiming that precisely the opposite was the case. In the Romantic idea of a new religion, as in the writings of Joachim of Fiore, can be found a bold vision that continues a theopolitical tradition that first took shape during Jewish antiquity. At the same time, there is an ambivalence among the Romantics regarding precisely the Jewish element of this tradition, an ambivalence that recalls the latent anti-Jewish aspects of Joachim's attempt to present the Christian revelation as a higher and more complete stage of the process of divine creation.

This ambivalence becomes visible upon closer inspection of the three features that have been identified here – progression, universalism and spiritualization – in the Romantic idea of a new religion. Although these three features attest to the concept's politico-philosophical audaciousness, a problematic darker side reveals itself when they are considered in the larger context of the history of ideas. In fact, all three of the features are constitutive elements of the polemical genre of *adversus Iudaeos*, mentioned earlier, which at an early stage emerged as part of the Christian church's effort to distance itself from its Jewish origins. An illustrative example would be Eusebius's notion of the church as a 'New Israel' that assumed the role of God's chosen people and thereby inaugurated a higher stage of history. But the Jewish tradition was not merely represented as an earlier stage on a chronological scale. An equally pervasive motif in the *adversus Iudaeos* tradition is the claim that Judaism is exclusive and separatist, in contrast to a Christianity whose message is of universal salvation. In the writings of Eusebius and other theologians, this exclusivity is connected to the Jews' supposedly obstinate attachment to their ritual practices and regulations. A third rhetorical device thereby emerged in such anti-Jewish polemics, namely of presenting the Christian faith in terms of spiritual high-mindedness while describing Judaism and Jews as hopelessly bound to the literal, the material and the fleshly (blind obedience to the law, rituals of purification and circumcision).

Established as early as the Patristic period, anti-Jewish rhetoric has been a pervasive feature of the history of Christian theology. Joachim was no exception, even if his vision of an intrahistorical reconciliation between Jews and Christians broke with the prevalent habit of condemning the Jews until the End of Days. Nor did this pattern change with the Reformation. On the contrary, the reformist theology in a number of regards reinforced the contrast between Judaism and Christianity, associating the former with legalistic zeal and the latter with a generous offer of grace. As the new era advanced, several of these inherited anti-Jewish tropes underwent a process of secularization and politicization. These shifts, as Micha Brumlik has argued, were particularly evident in German Enlightenment philosophy which in many respects was steeped in the Protestant tradition. In this way the theological stereotype of the Jew as bound to the law found an echo in the philosophical stereotype of the Jew as the embodiment of heteronomy (as opposed to autonomy). And in the same way as Christian theological imagery, with few exceptions, had excluded the Jews from divine redemption, so, too, did modern philosophical imagery, with few exceptions, exclude Jews *qua* Jews from the Enlightenment's emancipatory ideals.[113]

It is illuminative in this context to read Kant's later work *The Conflict of the Faculties*, written during the heyday of Jena Romanticism. In it Kant addresses a topic close to his heart – humanity's autonomy from the realm of natural necessity. Yet when he comes to the question of the Jewish people's capacity to attain autonomy, his tone is ambivalent. Kant is in no doubt that Jews, by virtue of being individual human beings, are included in the emancipation that will follow upon the establishment of the universal order of reason. But this specifically presupposes that they distance themselves from their 'Jewishness' – their various rituals, regulations and traditions. Instead, Kant proposes, Jews should embrace 'the religion of Jesus' and adopt the Enlightenment's critical perspective on the Bible. Only after this has occurred can the Jews be fully assimilated into European culture and free themselves of their archaic religion. Kant summarizes this process with the infamous phrase *Euthanasie des Judentums*.[114]

Another illuminating example is to be found in Hegel's work *The Spirit of Christianity and its Fate*, also from this period (1797). In order to foreground the emancipatory potential of Christianity, Hegel began by offering a contrasting image of Judaism as a cult-fixated religion, doomed to extinction as part of humanity's ongoing development. The essence of Judaism was given paradigmatic form in the patriarch Abraham, 'a stranger on earth, a stranger to the soil and to man alike'.[115] Abraham appears here as the prototype of what Hegel would later call 'alienation', a necessary part of the estrangement process that characterized all movements towards real freedom. But the Jewish people would never abandon their state of heteronomy, and the Jewish religion would remain a cul-de-sac, at most a stage on the road towards freedom and enlightenment.[116]

Considered in the light of these prevalent contemporary conceptions, the Romantic idea of a new religion reveals an ambivalence that was to resonate throughout the concept's reception in the history of ideas. As already indicated, the concept sublimated several received anti-Jewish tropes from the Christian tradition, which it reformulated for a modern, secular Europe. To be sure, this process was rarely as explicit as in the case of Kant or Hegel. For instance, in *Christendom or Europe* Novalis, in contrast to Hegel, does not construct his idealizing image of Christianity upon a denigratory image of Judaism. Nevertheless, the fact remains that the new, higher religion which he describes is ultimately an idealized form of the *Christian* religion. That this putatively universal vision leaves practically no space for Jews *qua* Jews is suggested by Novalis's study notes from this period, in which he staunchly maintains that 'Judaism is the exact opposite of Christianity'.[117]

In this respect Schleiermacher appears as a more complex figure. Unlike most of the leading Romantics, Schleiermacher had close Jewish friends throughout his life. He was also a steadfast defender of the rights of Jewish citizens at a time when the external regulation of Jewish life in Europe was characterized by arbitrary vacillation between paternalistic benevolence and outright persecution. Somewhat unexpectedly, given this background, Schleiermacher was also critical of Jewish assimilation and strongly opposed Kant's proposal that the Jews should convert to Christianity. And yet it is precisely here that the ambivalence in his position reveals itself. On the one hand, his criticism of the policy of assimilation can be interpreted as a call for Jews to be acknowledged as having rights by virtue of being Jews, not just human beings. On the other hand, the conviction underpinning Schleiermacher's stance was anything but political. Rather, his argument was theological in nature, having to do with a principled antipathy towards conversion: to abandon one religion for another on political grounds was, quite simply, to violate the very essence of religion.[118]

This line of argument chimed closely with Schleiermacher's high regard for the special nature of each tradition as well as his conviction that the essence of religion could only be discovered in the concrete history of religion. The more problematic aspect of Schleiermacher's argument only becomes apparent when his specific account of the Jewish religion is studied more closely. For this reveals itself as running directly contrary to the rosy image that he elsewhere conjures up of religion in general and of Christianity in particular: 'Judaism is long since a dead religion, and those who at present still bear its colors are actually sitting and mourning beside the undecaying mummy and weeping over its demise and its sad legacy'.[119] The phrase occurs in the fifth speech, in which Schleiermacher develops his pluralistic theory of religion. Curiously, the text at this point also displays all of the stereotypical hallmarks of the *adversus Iudaeos* rhetoric, including the conclusion that Judaism is incompatible with the 'higher' forms of religion. What is striking is that Schleiermacher at no point gave a reason for why he nonetheless believed that Jews should persist in a religion that in his eyes was already long dead. It is an open question as to whether Schleiermacher intentionally relegated Jews to spiritual exclusion. What is not in question, however, is that the rhetoric of *On Religion* lent impetus to later anti-Jewish tendencies within Protestant theology, culminating in the pro-Nazi factions within the German church in the 1930s.[120]

Turning finally to Schelling, we encounter a similarly complex situation. As already noted, even Schelling's philosophy of history led into a sublimated form of Christianity, but, just as with Novalis, this speculative Christian philosophy was not grounded in an antagonistic relationship with Judaism. This did not mean that his account was free from stereotyping. Discussing the Jewish revelation in the twenty-seventh lecture of his *Philosophy of Revelation*, Schelling described it as wrapped in a casing of mythology that was only dispelled by the advent of Christianity. Schelling additionally maintained that the Jewish religion was typified by exclusive ritual practices. This defining feature, he said, went hand in hand with the Jews' tendency to set themselves apart from world history and to live their own lives faithful to their God.[121]

In the case of Kant and Hegel, it was precisely this feature that roused their contempt for the Jewish people and prompted their profound doubts as to whether Jews could or should be assimilated. But where Kant and Hegel saw a failing, Schelling saw instead a strength. If anything meant that the Jewish people deserved to be treated as God's chosen people, it was their very inability '*to found states in the name of the world spirit*. They were carriers of the divine history. For this people turned out to be so spineless [*schlaff*], that they could not even conquer their own land save under divine command'.[122] Notwithstanding his condescending tone, Schelling thus saw a virtue in this inability to conform to state authorities down the ages. As Micha Brumlik has argued, it is possible to discern here a direct polemic against Hegel's statist philosophy, something that once again highlights the tension between Hegel's political theology and Schelling's radical, theopolitical stance.[123] It is also notable that Schelling, in the same lecture, emphasized that the Jews, because of their adherence to the religion of their forefathers, 'are reserved the kingdom of God'.[124] The phrase finds an echo in the final lecture, in which Schelling, in a passage that has already been cited, announced a 'non-excluding city of God, in which both Jews and Pagans are included in the highest sense, ... and to which each and every person belongs through his own conviction'.[125]

Interestingly, there is an echo here of Joachim's vision of an intrahistorical reconciliation between the two peoples. But where Joachim's vision presupposed that the Jews would ultimately realize the truth of Christianity, Schelling depicts a community to which each party belongs by virtue of their own conviction. Even so, it may be asked to what extent his vision is, in the final instance, 'truly universal'. Is it not the case that even Schelling tends to reinforce a model in which Christians are associated with the universal and Jews with the particular?

At this point we touch once again upon the ambivalence that accompanied the Romantic notion of a higher religion, for all its radicalism and theological audacity. However much the Romantic philosophers sought to tear themselves free from the dogmatic legacy of religion in favour of a larger ethical and aesthetic vision, their vision would always be formulated within the framework of Christian theology. In itself, this was unremarkable, of course. What made it problematic was the subtle equating of 'Christian' with 'universal', something that paved the way for a universalism which tended to close its eyes to its own particular conditions of possibility. As European culture became increasingly secular, these hidden conditions of possibility receded even further from view, at the same time as its claims to universalism lived on. Two centuries later (as discussed in the next chapter), this invisible tension between the universal and the particular persisted on an even more subtle level. Not least, this tension is reflected in the difficulty encountered by European philosophy in formulating a horizon – a universal, emancipatory vision – that did not come at the expense of the Other.

Notes

1. R. Safranski. 2014. *Romanticism: A German Affair*, trans. R.E. Goodwin, Evanston: Northwestern University Press, 148.
2. Novalis. 1997. *Philosophical Writings*, ed. and trans. M.M. Stoljar, Albany: State University of New York Press, 140.
3. A. Bowie. 1997. *From Romanticism to Critical Theory: The Philosophy of German Literary Theory*, London and New York: Routledge, 1–16, 53–89.
4. Voltaire. 2010. *La philosophie de l'histoire*, Paris: Nabu Press.
5. Novalis, *Philosophical Writings*, 60.
6. Ibid., 137.
7. Ibid., 138.
8. Ibid., 141.
9. Ibid., 142 (translation modified by the author).
10. Ibid., 144.

11. Ibid., 147.
12. Ibid., 150.
13. See also W.A. O'Brien. 1995. *Novalis: Signs of Revolution*, Durham and London: Duke University Press, 1–73.
14. For a historical overview, see e.g. G. Müller, K. Ries and P. Ziche (eds). 2001. *Die Universität Jena: Tradition und Innovation um 1800*, Stuttgart: Franz Steiner Verlag.
15. Safranski, *Romanticism*, 49.
16. See also M. Frank. 1997. *"Unendliche Annäherung": Die Anfänge der philosophischen Frühromantik*, Frankfurt am Main: Suhrkamp, 26–66.
17. Both letters are included in Novalis. 1975. *Schriften*, vol. 4, *Tagebücher, Briefwechsel, Zeitgenössische Zeugnisse*, ed. R. Samuel, H.-J. Mähl and G. Schulz, Stuttgart: Kohlhammer, 646–647.
18. Novalis, *Philosophical Writings*, 137–138.
19. See also H.-J. Mähl. 1965. *Die Idee des goldenen Zeitalters im Werk des Novalis: Studien zur Wesensbestimmung der Frühromantischen Utopie und zu ihren ideengeschichtlichen Voraussetzungen*, Heidelberg: Carl Winter Universitätsverlag, 372–385.
20. Novalis, *Philosophical Writings*, 139.
21. See Kaufmann, *Religion of Israel*, 132–133.
22. Novalis, *Philosophical Writings*, 156 (translation modified by the author).
23. Ibid.
24. Ibid., 162.
25. Ibid., 156.
26. Mähl, *Die Idee des goldenen Zeitalters*, 305–314.
27. F. Schlegel in Novalis, *Schriften*, vol. 4, 501 (Eng. trans. by the author).
28. Ibid., 507–508 (Eng. trans. by the author).
29. See also W. Gould and M. Reeves. 2001. *Joachim of Fiore and the Myth of the Eternal Evangel in the Nineteenth and Twentieth Centuries*, 2nd edn, Oxford: Clarendon Press, 59–74.
30. F. Hölderlin [and/or G.W.F. Hegel and/or F.W.J. Schelling]. 2003. 'Oldest Programme for a System of German Idealism', in J.M. Bernstein (ed.), *Classic and Romantic German Aesthetics*, Cambridge: Cambridge University Press, 185–187. Although admitting that the fragment is most likely the result of an exchange of ideas between the three friends, the editor of the English translation primarily ascribes it to Hölderlin. As this is much debated – and as my argument below rather rests on the thesis that Hegel is its main author – I will in the following indicate all three names when referring to the text.
31. Ibid., 185.
32. Ibid., 186. For an elaboration of the radical political aspects of the fragment, see also M. Frank. 1982. *Der kommende Gott. Vorlesungen über die Neue Mythologie*, vol. 1, Frankfurt am Main: Suhrkamp, 153–216.
33. Hegel/Hölderlin/Schelling, 'Oldest Programme', 186.
34. Ibid., 187.
35. Such a reading presupposes, for reasons that will become clear below, a scepticism towards Hölderlin's role in the writing of the fragment. See also Safranski, *Romanticism*, 98–100.
36. F. Hölderlin. 2008. *Hyperion, Or, The Hermit in Greece*, trans. R. Benjamin, Brooklyn: Archipelago Books. For a discussion of Hölderlin's, Schlegel's and Novalis' growing distance to Fichte's notion of the self – and how this is mirrored in their various views of religion – see A. Bowie. 2009. 'Romantic Philosophy and Religion', in N. Saul (ed.), *The Cambridge Companion to German Romanticism*, Cambridge and New York: Cambridge University Press, 175–190.
37. F. Schlegel. 1967. *Kritische Ausgabe*, vol. 2: *Charakteristiken und Kritiken I (1796–1801)*, ed. H. Eichner, Paderborn: Verlag Ferdinand Schöningh, 311–338.
38. Novalis, *Philosophical Writings*, 149 (translation modified by the author).
39. Novalis. 1983. *Schriften*, vol. 3, *Das philosophische Werk II*, ed. R. Samuel, H.-J. Mähl and G. Schulz, Stuttgart: Kohlhammer, 562 (Eng. trans. by the author).
40. F. Schleiermacher. 1996. *On Religion: Speeches to its Cultured Despisers*, 2nd edn, ed. and trans. R. Crouter, Cambridge: Cambridge University Press, 5.

41. Ibid., 3–17.
42. Ibid., 14.
43. Ibid., 20.
44. Ibid., 23.
45. Ibid., 59.
46. Ibid., 24.
47. Ibid., 36–37.
48. Ibid., 42 (translation modified by the author).
49. Ibid., 43.
50. H. de Lubac. 1979/1980. *La postérité de Joachim de Flore*, vols 1–2, Paris: Lethielleux. For a discussion of the influence of Joachite thought in the immediately following centuries, see also Reeves, *Joachim of Fiore and the Prophetic Future*, and, in the nineteenth and twentieth centuries, Gould and Reeves, *Joachim of Fiore and the Myth of the Eternal Evangel*.
51. De Lubac, *La postérité*, 16–18.
52. Mähl, *Die Idee des goldenen Zeitalters*, 243–245.
53. As de Lubac points out, the most probable source of Lessing's knowledge of Joachim was the *Institutionum Historiae Ecclesiasticae*, an influential work by the contemporary church historian J.L. Mosheim; see de Lubac, *La postérité*, 270.
54. See Mähl, *Die Idee des goldenen Zeitalters*, 245–252, and Frank, *Kommende Gott*, 189–190.
55. F.W.J. Schelling. 1977. *Philosophie der Offenbarung 1841/42*, ed. M. Frank, Frankfurt am Main: Suhrkamp, 315 (Eng. trans. by the author).
56. For a more thorough discussion of the circumstances surrounding Schelling's legendary Berlin lectures, see Frank's introducing essay in ibid., 7–84.
57. Ibid., 314 (Eng. trans. by the author).
58. Ibid., 316–319.
59. Ibid., 319 (Eng. trans. by the author).
60. Ibid., 322 (Eng. trans. by the author).
61. Ibid. (Eng. trans. by the author).
62. Ibid., 321 (Eng. trans. by the author).
63. See Safranski, *Romanticism*, 12–14.
64. Novalis, *Philosophical Writings*, 146.
65. For a detailed discussion of Reinhold's critique of Kant, and of how this critique was elaborated by his students, see Frank, *"Unendliche Annäherung"*, 152–662.
66. See e.g. Frank, *"Unendliche Annäherung"*; D. Henrich. 1991. *Konstellationen: Probleme und Debatten am Ursprung der idealistischen Philosophie (1789–1795)*, Stuttgart: Klett-Cotta; idem. 2004. *Grundlegung aus dem Ich: Untersuchungen zur Vorgeschichte des Idealismus: Tübingen – Jena (1790–1794)*, Frankfurt am Main: Suhrkamp.
67. Frank, *"Unendliche Annäherung"*, 43.
68. See ibid., 662–689, and (with particular focus on Novalis) J. Redin. 2003. *Ars inventrix: En studie av Friedrich von Hardenbergs (Novalis) paraestetiska projekt*, Uppsala: Uppsala universitet, 23–36.
69. F. Hölderlin. 1961. *Sämtliche Werke: Große Stuttgarter Ausgabe*, vol. 4, ed. F. Beißner, Stuttgart: Kohlhammer, 216–217. See also D. Henrich. 1965/1966. 'Hölderlin über Urteil und Sein. Eine Studie zur Entstehungsgeschichte des Idealismus', *Hölderlin-Jahrbuch* 14, 73–96.
70. Novalis. 1981. *Schriften*, vol. 2, *Das philosophische Werk I*, ed. R. Samuel, H.-J. Mähl and G. Schulz, Stuttgart: Kohlhammer, 270 (Eng. trans. by the author).
71. Novalis, *Philosophical Writings*, 23.
72. M. Frank in F. Schleiermacher. 2001. *Dialektik*, ed. M. Frank, Frankfurt am Main: Suhrkamp, 15.
73. Schleiermacher, *On Religion*, 19–20.
74. See Frank, *"Unendliche Annäherung"*, 663.
75. See also A. Bowie. 1993. *Schelling and Modern European Philosophy: An Introduction*, London and New York: Routledge, 15–29.

76. On Hölderlin's importance for Schelling's growing criticism of Fichte, see M. Frank. 1985. *Eine Einführung in Schellings Philosophie*, Frankfurt am Main: Suhrkamp, 61–70; for a discussion of Schelling's relation to older philosophies of nature, see W. Schmidt-Biggemann. 1998. *Philosophia perennis: Historische Umrisse abendländischer Spiritualität in Antike, Mittelalter und Früher Neuzeit*, Frankfurt am Main: Suhrkamp, 702–733.

77. M. Sá Cavalcante Schuback. 2005. 'The Work of Experience: Schelling on Thinking beyond Image and Concept', in J.M. Wirth (ed.), *Schelling Now: Contemporary Readings*, Bloomington and Indianapolis: Indiana University Press, 66–83.

78. See also M. Frank. 1972. *Das Problem der "Zeit" in der deutschen Romantik: Zeitbewußtsein und Bewußtsein von Zeitlichkeit in der frühromantischen Philosophie und in Tiecks Dichtung*, Munich: Winkler Verlag.

79. D. Birnbaum. 1990. 'Det romantiska fragmentet', in Novalis, *Fragment*, Lund: Propexus, 146 (Eng. trans. by S. Donovan).

80. See P. de Man. 1983. *Blindness and Insight*, London: Methuen & Co.; P. Szondi. 1976. *Satz und Gegensatz*, Frankfurt am Main: Suhrkamp.

81. Schleiermacher, *On Religion*, 122.

82. See e.g. Mähl, *Die Idee des goldenen Zeitalters*, 383.

83. Schleiermacher, *On Religion*, 117–118.

84. Novalis, *Philosophical Writings*, 152 (translation modified by the author).

85. Novalis, *Schriften*, vol. 2, 269 (Eng. trans. by the author).

86. Ibid., 291 (Eng. trans. by the author).

87. See also Mähl, *Die Idee des goldenen Zeitalters*, 287–297.

88. Schelling, *Offenbarung*, 323.

89. See Bowie, *Schelling*, 148.

90. See also Schuback, 'Work of Experience', 68–69.

91. Redin, *Ars inventrix*, 24 (Eng. trans. by S. Donovan).

92. See O'Brien, *Novalis*, 121–130.

93. Schleiermacher, *On Religion*, 85–86.

94. Novalis, *Philosophical Writings*, 151.

95. See also A. Kubik. 2011. 'Restauration oder Liberalisierung? Christentumsteoretische Aspekte in Novalis' "Die Christenheit oder Europa"', in M. Pirholt (ed.), *Constructions of German Romanticism: Six Studies*, Uppsala: Historia litterarum, 45–77.

96. F.W.J. Schelling. 2008. *Vorlesungen über die Methode des akademischen Studiums*, Norderstedt: Books on Demand, 90–95.

97. M. Lilla. 2007. *The Stillborn God: Religion, Politics, and the Modern West*, New York: Alfred A. Knopf, 202–203.

98. Schelling, *Offenbarung*, 321 (Eng. trans. by the author).

99. Novalis, *Philosophical Writings*, 140.

100. Schleiermacher, *On Religion*, 43.

101. Schelling, *Offenbarung*, 314.

102. See also Mähl, *Die Idee des goldenen Zeitalters*, 314–319.

103. Novalis, *Philosophical Writings*, 151.

104. Schelling, *Offenbarung*, 323 (Eng. trans. by the author).

105. Schleiermacher, *On Religion*, 95.

106. Ibid., 95–113.

107. Ibid., 275–276.

108. Ibid., 324.

109. Novalis, *Philosophical Writings*, 151.

110. Schelling, *Offenbarung*, 321 (Eng. trans. by the author).

111. Novalis, *Philosophical Writings*, 141.

112. Schleiermacher, *On Religion*, 50.

113. M. Brumlik. 2000. *Deutscher Geist und Judenhass: Das Verhältnis des philosophischen Idealismus zum Judentum*, Munich: Luchterhand, 9–25. See also M. Mack. 2003. *German Idealism*

and the Jew: The Inner Anti-Semitism of Philosophy and German Jewish Responses, Chicago and London: University of Chicago Press.

114. I. Kant. 1992. *The Conflict of the Faculties*, trans. M.J. Gregor, Lincoln and London: University of Nebraska Press, 95.

115. G.F.W. Hegel. 1971. *Early Theological Writings*, trans. T.M. Knox, Philadelphia: University of Pennsylvania Press, 186.

116. For a more thorough discussion of Hegel's complex and evolving relation to the Jewish religion, see Yovel, *Dark Riddle*.

117. Novalis, *Schriften*, vol. 3, 567 (Eng. trans. by the author).

118. See F. Schleiermacher. 1984. *Briefe bei Gelegenheit der politisch theologischen Aufgabe und des Sendschreibens jüdischer Hausväter, KGA*, vol. 1.2, *Schriften aus der Berliner Zeit 1796–1799*, ed. G. Meckenstock, Berlin and New York: Walter de Gruyter, 327–361.

119. Schleiermacher, *On Religion*, 113–114.

120. See also Brumlik, *Deutscher Geist*, 132–195, and M. Blum. 2010. *"Ich wäre ein Judenfeind?": Zum Antijudaismus in Friedrich Schleiermachers Theologie und Pädagogik*, Cologne: Böhlau Verlag.

121. Schelling, *Offenbarung*, 278–285.

122. Ibid., 284 (Eng. trans. by the author).

123. Brumlik, *Deutscher Geist*, 270–271.

124. Schelling, *Offenbarung*, 285 (Eng. trans. by the author).

125. Ibid., 323 (Eng. trans. by the author).

CHAPTER 4

History after God

A feeling for the sacred goes hand in hand with a feeling for the beautiful, and only those with a profound understanding of the essence of art can understand the essence of religion. Perhaps it was this Romantic conviction that resulted in the choice of Capri, a mythologized place of natural beauty, for a gathering of several famous philosophers, who decided in 1994 to come together for a conversation about religion. The moment, not unlike the late 1790s, was one of sweeping geopolitical upheaval. The early 1990s had not only witnessed the passing of an entire worldview. In the heart of a Europe which had sworn 'never again', an armed conflict was taking place that within a short space of time allowed the very darkest aspects of the continent's history to come to the surface.

Around the table were seated Jacques Derrida, Eugenio Trías and Gianni Vattimo as well as three other Italian philosophers. Also sitting there, albeit mostly as a spectator, was the elderly Hans-Georg Gadamer. Born in 1900, Gadamer had been present from the very start of a turbulent century in which ideologies and utopias had emerged and flourished only to end in disaster. Suggestively, 1900 was also the year in which Friedrich Nietzsche had died, having formulated his prophetic words on the death of God – prophetic because for a summary of the historical predicament of the twentieth century, there is perhaps no more central factor than this one: the death of God. The twentieth century was when humanity took history into its own hands and established its own ultimate goals for history – goals that were put into practice by the totalitarian social projects of the 1930s. A decade later, after those projects had transformed Europe (and other parts of the world) into an all-out inferno, there began a period of critical reflection during which thinkers from Right to Left sought to decipher the lunacy of these depraved ideologies. But only for a while. Behind the scenes of the Cold War an ideological contest was also taking

Notes for this section begin on page 147.

place and by the end of the 1960s grandiose social visions were once again in evidence. Only after another twenty years did the collapse of the Eastern bloc put an end to the last of the century's grand utopias.

The 1994 Capri symposium bore obvious traces of the post-1989 mood. In the afterword to a landmark publication issued after the symposium, Gadamer offered an acute but gloomy sketch of the current moment: to be sure, the collapse of the Eastern bloc had spelled the end of the 'dogmatic atheism' and its totalitarian ambitions, yet this had not brought with it a release of vital new political and cultural visions. In the wake of Communism's active suppression of religion, Gadamer stated, former Eastern bloc countries had seen the spread of 'a new type of atheism which is based on indifference'. This grim verdict did not, however, lead Gadamer to join the chorus of contemporary commentators who were loudly announcing capitalist Western democracy as history's victor. On the contrary, in present-day developments in the industrialized nations he saw quiet confirmation of Max Weber's thesis about the fate of Protestantism, in which a formerly Christian religion had evolved into 'a religion of the world economy'. By this formulation Gadamer indicated that humanity in both West and East had been reduced to passive objects of a technological and economic process that even the grandest political visions could no longer encompass. The only question was whether humanity could indeed live without visions – whether it could even exist without having some kind of horizon towards which it was capable of striving. Gadamer was unwilling to let resignation have the final word: 'It seems almost unavoidable that our consciousness of our own existence should not only open up new horizons of memory and remembrance – an awareness of where we come from and how we came to be – but that it should also open up a horizon of futurity in which, even towards the end of one's life, expectation or hope strives to win out over faintheartedness'.[1]

In light of these pithy words it is perhaps not very surprising that the philosophical company which gathered on Capri in 1994 chose to return to religion, practically a taboo subject in large swathes of twentieth-century philosophy. If 1789 was the year that gave birth to a faith that politics, not religion, would make humanity good and the world better, then 1989 in many regards marked the end of the line for that faith. It thereby raised the question of whether religion, despite everything, might turn out to possess resources capable of giving inspiration to political philosophy and sustaining it beyond this morass of shattered social visions. The gathered philosophers seemed to be in agreement that such was indeed the case, and also that it was high time that humanity freed itself from 'that dogmatism which refuses to see in religion anything other than the deception or self-deception of human beings'.[2]

Although the symposium's delegates were in agreement that the harsh judgements pronounced by parts of the Enlightenment tradition had not exhausted the resources of religion, they were equally agreed on the undesirability of a return to religion in its traditional forms. In this respect they presented a striking similarity to the Romantic thinkers of the 1790s. As emblematically expressed by Novalis's lecture on Europe, the young Romantics were convinced that religion possessed riches which the French Enlightenment had rejected far too categorically. Yet this did not mean that they saw a future for religion in its current incarnation. Only a higher religion, untrammelled by dogmatism and institutional constraints, could restore to humanity a horizon that would allow it to unite freedom with order.

While the young Romantics had entertained such a radical vision, it cannot be denied that by the early 1800s such radicalism had already turned to reaction. In the wake of the Napoleonic wars and Germany's defeat, Romanticism's starting precepts had become entangled in grandiose, nationalist ideas. The delicate balance between freedom and order was abandoned at the expense of the former, and early Romanticism's messianic sense of an unattainable, ideal order increasingly took the form of utopian notions as to how that ideal order should be realized. In these circumstances it is not particularly surprising that philosophers in the mid-twentieth century, as they strove to comprehend the madness of previous decades, should have looked to elements of German intellectual life at the beginning of the nineteenth century for the roots of such evil.

In this light it was more surprising still that the philosophers gathered at Capri at the end of the twentieth century should have evinced so strong an affinity with the ideas of Romanticism. Yet it is important at this point to differentiate early Romanticism (but also the late Schelling), not only from its later politicization, but also from absolute idealism. To the extent that a kinship can be discerned between Romanticism and the hermeneutically oriented philosophy represented by several of the Capri symposium delegates, it should be stressed that this related strictly to Romanticism in its early phase. As discussed in previous chapters, the philosophies of Novalis, Schleiermacher and Schelling developed in opposition to attempts to establish an absolute foundation for thought. In a similar fashion, the philosophies of Derrida, Trías and Vattimo have a distinctly anti-metaphysical quality. Their renewed interest in religion, in other words, should not be interpreted as a desire to restore to philosophy the metaphysical underpinning of which it had been deprived by modernity; investment in religion, if anything, involved the opposite – finding intellectual figures capable of articulating the flaws in all human thinking. In this regard, as Gadamer noted, the late philosophy of Martin Heidegger exerted an unmistakeable influence on the discussions at Capri.[3]

This chapter will focus on the Capri symposium in order to show how prophetic, messianic and pneumatic motifs found expression in late-twentieth-century attempts to formulate an overarching political-philosophical vision without repeating the violent utopias of the preceding hundred years. However, the effort to balance utopian hubris and aimless resignation should not be seen solely against the background of a century of totalitarian ideologies. As importantly, it must be situated in relation to a broader critique of utopia and ideology that ebbed and flowed during the postwar era. Although this critique was justified in its historical context, it is a well-known fact that it often rested upon an illusory notion of its own lack of ideology. The discussions at Capri should therefore be considered in light of both these factors. While philosophers such as Derrida and Vattimo have often been portrayed as sceptics defined by their settling of accounts with twentieth-century totalitarianism, their scepticism was applied equally to those claiming to be free of ideology. Before examining the Capri symposium in more detail, I wish therefore to take a step back and say a few words about the pervasive talk of 'the end of ideologies' during the postwar period and the resurgence of such talk after 1989.

The Secularization of *Eschaton*

When Isaiah Berlin delivered his prestigious A.W. Mellon Lectures in 1965, he gave an account of the roots of German Romanticism that was acute and passionate but also typical of his day. Berlin traced Romanticism's origins to the specific plight of German culture in the seventeenth and early eighteenth centuries. During a period in which France, England and Holland were building strong nation-states, the territory of Germany was characterized by political divisions and a lack of urban centres. A clear discrepancy was noticeable at the philosophical and scientific level, too. While the rising Atlantic states were producing figures such as Descartes, Pascal, Spinoza, Locke and Newton, German culture – with the luminous exception of Leibniz – was shackled between the sterile scholasticism of Lutheran orthodoxy and the mawkish religiosity of pietism. Berlin's thesis was quite simply that German Romanticism had originated in a wounded national pride that generated a growing need to compensate for its own pettiness with grandiose poetic and philosophical visions.[4]

Although Berlin's analysis, which will be discussed further below, was marked by a certain postwar spirit, it is not without its merits. It is true that early Romanticism was characterized by an intoxication with freedom that at times verged on megalomania. It is also true that the young Romantics' euphoria at humanity's godlike creative powers always risked turning into a distaste and contempt for life. Thus the Swedish literary scholar Anders Olsson, for example, has traced the nihilistic strain in modern European literature back to the early Romantic's passion for truth. Given paradigmatic expression in Fichte's celebration of sovereignty, the world-creating I represented a mental hubris permanently teetering on the edge of its own abyss: 'Philosophical idealism is the springboard and catalyst of nihilism, since it is founded upon the newly self-important I that is its own insubstantial foundation and makes everything into its own creation'.[5]

As was described in Chapter Three, religion was also made into one of humanity's own creations. Friedrich Schlegel's lyrical announcement of his intention to 'found a new religion' in a letter to Novalis in 1798 might be recalled here; or, for that matter, the 'new mythology' that was called for in 'The Oldest Programme for a System of German Idealism', with its characteristic opening words: 'The first idea is, of course, the representation *of myself as* an absolutely free being'.[6] At issue in both cases was a desire to overthrow traditional religion in order to raise a new, poetical religion under the aegis of the poeticizing I. At the same time, it is important not to lose sight of the historic division, discussed earlier, that emerged between Romantic philosophers and systematizing idealists. In tandem with Fichte's philosophical breakthrough, a growing scepticism towards the idea that the I constitutes its own foundation can be noted in philosophers such as Jacobi, Novalis, Schleiermacher and, somewhat later, Schlegel. This shift was reflected in their relationship to religion. Religion was no longer represented as a product of the I, but rather as a window upon the infinite. Yet, this does not refer to religion in its traditional forms: as has been discussed, the higher religion that was in different ways to be a hallmark of the writings of Novalis, Schleiermacher and even the later Schelling referred to a state that was permanently in the making and thus never fully attainable. In other words, early Romantic visionary philosophy had a strongly messianic or anti-utopian quality.

Even so, this anti-utopian quality was largely lost during late Romanticism, a development lucidly evoked by Rüdiger Safranski in his study *Romanticism: A German Affair*. Like Anders Olsson, Safranski argues that the Romantic subject was pursued by a ghostly presentiment of futility and that its rising euphoria about its own I was also accompanied by a rising sense of *Weltschmerz* or world-weariness. Although early Romanticism may itself have rested upon a combination of extreme I-centredness and intemperate universalism, Safranski is careful to underscore that in this early phase the universal had an unfixed, 'transcendent' character. Some way into the nineteenth century, however, the transcendent began to be fixed and to assume an increasingly obvious political character, either in the form of a mania for Habsburg and the Catholic Church or in the form of patriotic Prussian nationalism. Alluding to Fichte's *Addresses to the German Nation* of 1807/1808, Safranski explains:

> [The] German *Volk* as an aggregate is now explained as the *Urvolk* of the 'German' (*germanisch*) desire for freedom. With this the cosmopolitan, universalistic characteristic of Early Romanticism disappears. The horizon narrows. The free playful spirit which with its passion for the infinite had passed beyond all boundaries now begins to draw transcendence into the political sphere. It is cautious first in Novalis, who seeks a combined superterrestrial and terrestrial protection in the church; then it grows more robust and determined in others who, like Fichte, become fixated on *Volk*, fatherland, and state. ... The Romantic metaphysics of the infinite turns into a metaphysics of history and society, *Volksgeist*, and nation, and it becomes ever more difficult for the individual to resist the suggestion of the We. A kind of intermediate transcendence in the form of history and society thrusts itself in between the individual and the great transcendence (God, the infinite). Previously there had been a God of history; now history itself becomes God.[7]

Behind these changes can be detected a series of key political developments in the early nineteenth century. The first years of the new century coincided with the zenith of Napoleon's power, which culminated in 1806 with the shattering of the Holy Roman Empire. That year Napoleon also crushed the renowned Prussian army. As a result, Prussia lost half its territory and was burdened with huge war reparations, which bred a profound sense of humiliation and degradation. From this fertile soil emerged a political and patriotic Romanticism centred on Heidelberg. In the wake of Germany's defeat, this beautiful city on the banks of the Neckar attracted such luminaries as Clemens Brentano, Achim von Arnim and Joseph Görres whose fascination with fables, myths and folk songs paved the way for a Romanticism with quite different qualities from those of its incarnation in Jena a decade earlier. In so doing, they also laid the foundation for making Romanticism in every sense what Safranski calls 'a German affair'.

This entire image must be borne in mind when reading Isaiah Berlin's account of Germany's fate. For Berlin's aim was not only to identify the historical conditions that made Romanticism possible in the first place. Like Safranski, he was also interested in the larger fate of German culture, tracing a direct line from the 'restrained' Romanticism of Kant and Schiller to the more 'unbridled' Romanticism of Fichte, Schelling and Novalis. Where the older philosophers held freedom and will in check by reason, the latter chose to dethrone reason. Into its place stepped the world-creating I: 'The most central aspect of this view is that your universe is as you chose to make it, to some degree at any rate; that is the philosophy of Fichte, [and] that is to some extent the philosophy of Schelling'.[8] Thus we find ourselves, albeit with a crucial detour via Schopenhauer and Nietzsche, a mere stone's throw from the follies of the twentieth century:

> Fascism ... is an inheritor of romanticism, not because it is irrational – plenty of movements have been that – nor because of a belief in élites – plenty of movements have held that belief. The reason why Fascism owes something to romanticism is, again, because of the notion of the unpredictable will either of a man or of a group, which forges forward in some fashion that is impossible to organise, impossible to predict, impossible to rationalise. That is the whole heart of Fascism: what the leader will say tomorrow, how the spirit will move us, where we shall go, what we shall do – that cannot be foretold.[9]

Berlin's observation contained a not insignificant grain of truth. Even so, his account was lacking in the nuance that characterizes Safranski's more recent attempt to make sense of the complex ties between the Romantic intellectual tradition and subsequent German history. While Berlin conceded the existence of internal differences, he lumped together Fichte, Schelling and Novalis, allowing them to stand as harbingers of unbridled will. More problematic still was the fact that he ignored the crucial difference between Romanticism's early and late phases. The upshot was that Romanticism constituted an enormous, irrational violation of the very core of Western thinking: what Berlin summarized as 'the old proposition that knowledge is virtue', that reality possessed 'some kind of form which could be studied, written down, learnt, communicated to others, and in other respects treated in a scientific manner'.[10] Consequently, Romanticism had also paved the way for the philosophical disarray that led to the ideological degeneration of the following century.

With a half-century's hindsight, Berlin's lectures on Romanticism and the fate of Germany seem on several counts to belong very much to their historical moment. In the aftermath of the previous decades of German arrogance, even the most clear-sighted philosophers appear to have found it difficult to formulate a nuanced account of German culture and its past. It seems to have been particularly difficult to resist the temptation to identify the belatedness of German civilization as the key to its self-assertiveness in the modern era. Berlin, for his part, was not content to emphasize the late development of its urban centres, but also underscored how Germans had in fact developed a 'huge national inferiority complex' in relation to the progressive states of Western Europe, particularly France, a 'brilliant glittering State which had managed to crush and humiliate them'. Nor did Berlin refrain from additionally reinforcing the image of Germany as a country bumpkin by noting the relatively modest origins of Romanticism's principal exponents (with the exception of Novalis). French philosophers from the same period came from a 'very, very different world'; Montesquieu was a baron, Condorcet a marquis and Buffon a count. Small wonder that their 'mere existence irritated, humiliated and infuriated the Germans'.[11]

Widening the purview slightly, Berlin's account appears to have been emblematic of an entire genre of critical studies, published during the decades after the Second World War. Examination of this genre reveals that liberal thinkers such as Berlin were not its only contributors. On the contrary, it reflected a widespread and almost frantic effort among European intellectuals, in their own ways and using the analytic tools of their various traditions, to put into perspective the traumas of the twentieth century. In 1954, Georg Lukács published *The Destruction of Reason*, a work of almost seven hundred pages that was reissued the following year with the explanatory subtitle *The Trajectory of Irrationalism from Schelling to Hitler*. Like Berlin, Lukács was interested in understanding the philosophical tradition that had made Nazism possible, and, like his liberal British colleague, he ended up with Romanticism. Like Berlin, too, Lukács identified the root of evil as the 'irrationalism' that ran from Schelling, via Schopenhauer, Kierkegaard and Nietzsche, up to the early-twentieth-century German concept of *Lebensphilosophie* and, finally, National Socialism. At this point, however, their analyses parted company. For the Marxist Lukács, the emergence and spread of modern irrationalism was in fact a reflection of the modern class struggle. More specifically, it was the expression of feudal and subsequently bourgeois reaction to the rise of socialism and its defence of the dialectical development of reason in society:

> If, therefore, we are seeking a proper understanding of the development of German irrationalist philosophy, we must always bear in mind the following related factors: the dependence of irrationalism's development on the crucial class struggles in Germany and throughout the world. ... Only [against this background] can we understand how Hitler contrived a demagogic popularization of all the intellectual motives of entrenched philosophical reaction, the ideological and political 'crowning' of the development of irrationalism.[12]

If there appears at first glance to be a striking consonance between the analyses of Germany's fate by the liberal Berlin and the Marxist Lukács, the picture is hardly less striking in the case of the conservative political philosopher Eric Voegelin. In 1964, the year before Berlin's Mellon lectures, Voegelin gave a series of lectures in Munich under the heading *Hitler and the Germans*. By this point Voegelin had returned to Germany after many years of exile in the United States, a consequence of his early and outspoken criticism of Nazi racial policies. In these lectures, Voegelin sought an answer to the riddle of the Germans and Nazism. When he came to offer a compact explanation as to where and when this peculiarly German form of political hubris had originated, he, like Berlin and Lukács, settled on Romanticism, more precisely a quotation from Novalis: '"The world shall be as I wish it!" There you already have in a nutshell the whole problem of Hitler, the central problem of dedivinizing and dehumanizing'.[13]

But at this point their analyses once again took different directions. Voegelin did not contrast the ideas of Romanticism, as Berlin had, with a tradition of common sense; nor, as Lukács had, with dialectical materialism. The locus of reason was instead to be found in the classical biblical and Greek traditions. Here Voegelin for the first time retrieved the notion of human beings as rational and able to aspire to and even become part of a higher, divine reality. Humanity was thus assigned a unique value and elevated to the status of a godlike being, *imago dei*. The Christian worldview rests upon this minute distinction between 'godlike' and 'divine' — a scheme that allows humanity to be the crown of God's creation without losing sight of its own finitude. It was precisely this balance that had been upset by the Enlightenment and then destroyed completely by Romanticism. Instead of being treated as an image of God, humanity itself had been made into God. Voegelin described the process in terms of a fall (*Abfall*) and a loss of dignity (*Würdeverlust*). In the very moment of denying God and closing itself off to the divine reality, humanity had lost an indispensable part of what it meant to be human. Humanity had not only lost its dignity, however. It had also lost that vital insight into its own finitude and the world's imperfection.[14]

Behind Voegelin's analysis of Germany's fate in 1964 can be discerned a number of intellectual motifs that had already appeared in his philosophical writings. In 1938, he had authored a book (*Political Religions*) that further developed a line of argument famously expounded by Carl Schmitt in his 1922 study *Political Theology* — that modern political ideologies were built upon secularized or even deformed theological concepts. At this stage Voegelin shared Schmitt's critique of liberal democracy's failings, and two years before *Anschluss* he wrote a defence of Austria's authoritarian constitution (*The Authoritarian State: An Essay on the Problem of the Austrian State*). The similarities with Schmitt ended, however, in Voegelin's later works. In 1952, he published his most famous work, *The New Science of Politics*, in which he offered a radical challenge to all forms of totalitarian thinking. At the same time, he retained the core of his thesis that modern ideologies were deformed religions. Specifically, he argued that the eschatological aspect of traditional Jewish and Christian faith had been channelled into the progressive political movements of modernity. This secularization of *eschaton* was reflected in the totalitarian direction in which several of these movements had developed. Rather than accept the world's imperfection while awaiting a redemption beyond history, humanity should seek to establish the kingdom of heaven here on earth – in the form of the racially cleansed nation or the classless society.[15]

As is clear from the argument developed in *The New Science of Politics*, Voegelin's critical judgement hence applied not only to Nazism but also to communism. It was also clear that, for him, the utopian aspects of modern ideologies had their roots not only in Romanticism but also in the larger theological tradition from which Romanticism sprang. Indeed, the fatal turning point did not lie with Novalis – it was *Joachim of Fiore* who had done the real damage. It was true, Voegelin argued, that the 'gnostic' temptation to seek divine perfection here on earth had existed already during antiquity. But these forces had been checked by an emergent orthodox theology which culminated in Augustine's powerful challenge to all forms of 'chiliastic phantasies'. By the high medieval period, however, as the relative calm of the medieval era gave way to a cultural proliferation, Augustine's defeatist view of history revealed itself as unsatisfactory. History had to be more than just a waiting room for divine fulfilment. It was Joachim who finally broke down Augustine's nice distinction between the City of God and the City of Man. Joachim wanted the City of God – the divine fulfilment – here and now.[16]

Voegelin highlighted four elements of Joachim's millenarian theology that had substantially influenced later political ideologies. The first was Joachim's notion of the three ages of history and its implied concept of an impending 'Third Realm' that would signal the advent of the ideal state. The second element was the ideal of a coming leader who would emerge at the appointed hour – an ideal whose sinister results ranged from Machiavelli's prince to the 'supermen' of Condorcet, Comte and Marx, and thence to the totalitarian leadership cults of the twentieth century. The third characteristic feature was the notion of a prophetic figure who would precede the coming leader, a figure who was presumed to possess unique insight into the course of events and someone whom Voegelin claimed to see in the intellectual standard-bearers of modern mass movements. Finally, and most fatally, Voegelin regarded Joachim as having laid the foundations for the ideal of a human community that believed itself capable of living without higher orders and authorities: 'In the third age the church will cease to exist because the charismatic gifts that are necessary for the perfect life will reach men without administration of sacraments'.[17] This anarchistic fantasy had been a recurrent feature of the sectarian groupings that had revolted against established institutions and authorities – from the radical Reformation's puritanical zeal to the dreams of 'Marxian mysticism' about the withering-away of the state.[18]

More than one objection might be levelled against this reading of Joachim. In polemically linking the Nazi Third Reich to communism's classless society and Joachim's *tertius status*, Voegelin overlooked an array of crucial aspects (quite apart from his problematic conflation of Nazism and communism). As already emphasized, Joachim did not proclaim a new era but the spiritual intensification of one that had already begun. In light of this fact, it is also deeply misleading to depict Joachim as an early anarchist who overturned the existing order. On the contrary, Joachim was obsessed with order and continuity. The main thread of all his thought was precisely a search for the most spiritually complete order for human community, an order that Joachim famously found in the contemplative life of the monastic world.

If Voegelin's representation of Joachim leaves much to be desired, the readiest explanation is that in all likelihood he had never read any of Joachim's works. Like a succession of other philosophers at around this time who tried to trace the origins of utopianism back to Joachim of Fiore, Voegelin based his claims on a received image that had been passed down from writer to writer.[19] Most immediately, Voegelin seems to have got his information from Karl Löwith, the philosopher responsible for perhaps the most famous challenge to Western theology of history and its secular varieties. When Löwith published *Meaning in History* in 1949, he found himself, like Voegelin, in exile in the United States. Europe lay in ruins, and Löwith, like so many others in the postwar period, sought an explanation as to how the Western political and philosophical tradition could have degenerated into the totalitarian movements of the 1930s, but also as to how a succession of prominent intellectuals – including Carl Schmitt and his own mentor Martin Heidegger – could have so lost their political judgement as to align themselves with these movements.[20]

In the introductory chapter to this book I emphasized Löwith's central role in twentieth-century anti-utopian debates. Let me expand somewhat on this claim. In *Meaning in History*, Löwith presented a genealogy of the historical perspective that had paved the way for the political illusion of a kingdom of heaven here on earth. Both Romanticism and Joachim of Fiore clearly belonged in this genealogy. But unlike Voegelin – who took pains to defend an authentic Christian theology from its later offshoots – Löwith did not stop there. The true root of evil in the West lay quite simply in the biblical tradition as such.

It was there that humanity for the first time began to conceive of history as salvation history, an eschatological drama of damnation and redemption governed by divine providence. All history was thereby to be seen in the light of a higher goal that conferred meaning on every historical event. The ancient Greeks, Löwith stressed, had a more balanced view on this matter; they 'did not presume to make sense of the world or to discover its ultimate meaning. They were impressed by the visible order and beauty of the cosmos, and the cosmic law of growth and decay was also the pattern for their understanding of history'.[21]

Unfortunately, it was not the Greek but the biblical perspective that had lived on and become a constitutive element in the West's relation to history. The same held true for the secularization of traditional Christian theology of history and its absorption into the historico-philosophical speculations of the new era. To be sure, the modern philosophers – with Voltaire at their head – had challenged the Christian doctrine of providence and the idea that history had a transcendent goal. Yet the world remained oriented towards the future. Although God had been replaced by humanity as the motive force of history and heaven reinterpreted as the ideal society on earth, there nonetheless remained a belief that history had a meaning – one that derived from an objective not yet achieved.[22]

Notwithstanding fundamental differences in other regards, Löwith therefore endorsed the thesis articulated by both Schmitt and Voegelin, that modern political ideologies essentially rested upon secularized theological patterns of thought. Even if Löwith traced this pattern all the way back to classical Jewish prophetism, he, like Voegelin, also assigned Joachim a key role in this development. To be fair, it should be stressed that Löwith's reading of Joachim was nowhere as tendentious as Voegelin's; above all, he differentiated between Joachim's own intentions and the subsequent reception history of his ideas. Nonetheless, Löwith ended up by offering a fairly unnuanced account of precisely this reception history. With a few rapid strokes of the pen, he drew a line from Joachim to Lessing, Fichte, Schelling, Hegel and on to Comte and Marx. He completed this sketch with the statement that the Joachite idea of a third world order had ultimately made its appearance as 'a third International and a third *Reich*, inaugurated by a *dux* or a *Führer* who was acclaimed as a savior and greeted by millions with *Heil!*'[23]

Admittedly, Löwith's simplificatory version of the Joachite reception history is perhaps not the most problematic part of his account. The real problem lies in the very thesis that undergirds his work, that the West's view of history as such is built upon illusory premises in the form of a belief that history has a direction, meaning or goal. A famous objection was raised early on by Hans Blumenberg, who above all questioned Löwith's tendency to reduce the entire modern project to a secularized – and thus in some sense illegitimate – extension of a Jewish-Christian theology of history that had already been debunked.

In so doing, Löwith had glossed over the fact that the new era's efforts to change society for the better had in significant respects entailed a break with an older, often suffocating faith in divine providence (as an example Blumenberg pointed to how the church's condemnation of *curiositas*, humanity's hunger for knowledge, had served to constrain the progress of modern science).[24] Yet Blumenberg's objection can also be formulated on a more principled level. It can quite simply be asked whether Löwith, in vehemently condemning the desire to give history a direction, paved the way for a fatalistic position that closes its eyes to the fact that even more benevolent efforts – modern as well as premodern – to change the world for the better presuppose to some extent a belief in historical progress.

Raising the gaze slightly, it may be asked whether this is not a problematic that has accompanied the entire wave of critical challenges to utopian and visionary thinking that swept the West in the postwar era. Such critiques seemed warranted in light of recent events, often providing a compelling reflection of the sympathies of a generation which had experienced the defencelessness of democratic humanity when faced by totalitarian visions. At the same time, these critical challenges almost invariably tended to lead into an exaggerated distrust of any form of overarching social vision.

This point is illustrated particularly well by the array of mostly liberal thinkers who during the 1950s and early 1960s proclaimed the end of ideologies. For these thinkers, 'ideologies' were synonymous with the grandiose social visions that had emerged in the nineteenth century and brought Europe to disaster during the 1930s, but that lived on in the rising dictatorships of the Eastern bloc.[25] However, the problem with these thinkers was perhaps not primarily their lack of vision; authors such as Raymond Aron and Daniel Bell were firm adherents of the liberal welfare state and had in that sense a fairly clear vision of what constituted a good society. Rather, their failing lay in the misleading conviction that they stood outside any form of ideological thinking. This tendency was perhaps most specious in West Germany, where, as Safranski notes, the 'no-ideology ideology' effectively helped the ideological remnants of the Nazi era to remain legitimate under the banner of anti-communism.[26] But even in the West this putative lack of ideology revealed itself, again and again, to be a false façade, as when it was revealed in the late 1960s that the Congress for Cultural Freedom – an international organization founded in the previous decade with the aim of defending the transatlantic democratic ideal of cultural freedom – had been a CIA project from start to finish, its real mission being to suppress the Soviet propaganda ideal of culture in the service of the revolution, people or party.[27]

Disappointment at the covert agendas of such supposed freedom from ideology was an important ingredient in the rise of the New Left in the 1960s, when talk of the end of ideologies ceased for a while. But only for a while. The steady distortion of an entirely legitimate critique of the defects of democratic society – colonial violence, class inequality, the subordination of women – into a variety of anti-democratic elitism only provided more grist to the mill of the self-styled opponents of all ideology.[28] The notoriety of the romantic-revolutionary Left was further accentuated by the revelation in the 1970s of the truth behind Mao's Cultural Revolution, and the last of the great social utopias finally came to the end of the road with the fall of the Soviet empire just over a decade later. Such, at least, was the chorus of commentary that greeted it. To be sure, there was a range of attitudes towards this ostensibly irrevocable fact – from triumphant elation to critical resignation – but on the whole a relatively striking degree of agreement prevailed: the end of the Cold War meant that there now remained but one world order and that the era of overarching social visions had ended. Under these circumstances, it is even more remarkable that the philosophers gathered at Capri in 1994 should have been so preoccupied with the emancipatory legacy of the Enlightenment, and also – seemingly contradictorily – with the visionary potential of religion.

The Philosopher as Prophet

Before examining the period after 1989 in greater depth, the period after 1789 must briefly be considered. In writing *Christendom or Europe*, Novalis was driven by a conviction that the densely symbolic language of religion was uniquely capable of giving poetic form to the human spirit's journey towards a higher freedom. 'Where there are no gods, ghosts reign' is perhaps the most cited phrase in his text and one which Novalis also intended as a reference to the origins of humanity's unfreedom: no sooner than it had abolished the thought of some higher entity, some reminder of its own finitude, than the shadows of its lesser self began gathering – self-interest, nationalism, fantasies of political power and a hubristic faith in the power of its own rationality. As is well known, Novalis saw these cultural vices as a rising force among his contemporaries. In order to check this development, the philosopher – who thereby assumed the role of poet or even prophet – would have to use the full power of his imagination in order to create images that challenged and provoked the barren self-sufficiency of the present time. It is in this light that the idealizing image Novalis painted of the Christian Middle Ages should be understood – not as a nostalgic longing for a vanished era, but as a poetically significant point of contrast to latter-day cultural and political impoverishment.[29]

Allowing oneself to use the 'magic wand of analogy' that Novalis himself offered, it can be tempting to claim that the philosophers gathered at Capri in the wake of the Eastern bloc's collapse saw early on the spectres which threatened to sweep in and take the place of those shattered social visions. In this sense it might also be said that they were prophetic; despite triumphalist declarations to the contrary, the world less than a decade later would be defined more than ever by ethnic, religious and economic conflicts – the only difference being that such conflicts then formed part of a considerably more intricate pattern than during the days of the Cold War. Even so, it could also be said that they were prophetic in the deeper sense indicated by Novalis, which is also the sense found in the Bible, where the prophet is not primarily a figure who predicts future events but rather a voice warning people of impending catastrophes and urging them to act before it is too late.

The most remarkable expression of this prophetic spirit was *Specters of Marx*, a deeply complex work that Jacques Derrida published a year before the Capri symposium. It should immediately be added that what made it remarkable was not merely the somewhat curious choice of this particular moment for writing a book on Karl Marx; on the face of it, it was equally remarkable that its author should have been Derrida. As everyone familiar with Derrida's work knows, his ideas emerged in part from a critical stance towards the Marxist-influenced climate of philosophical debate in the 1960s. Why Marx, then, and why in 1993? Why this untimeliness and why this apparently self-contradictory turn within Derrida's own body of work?

One clue lies in the famous line of Hamlet's that serves as a leitmotif throughout the entire book: 'The time is out of joint'. In modern times Hamlet's despairing reply to his father's ghost has sometimes been used as a prophetic cry, a protest against prevailing social conditions that are regarded as disjointed or, more precisely, out of joint. The prophetic cry here becomes an exhortation to twist time back on course, to restore a just social order. The only question is whether justice will allow itself to be restored quite so simply. Derrida is doubtful. Is it not the case that justice requires a constant respect for that which does not accord with the present moment – for the past and for what is yet to come, for those who are no longer with us and for those who are not yet with us? If so, as Derrida indicates from the very start, should justice not actually *presuppose* that the time is out of joint, in the sense that its full presence in the now is continually being disturbed by all that is absent?

This question will be considered further in due course. For the moment, I wish instead to focus on the figure who causes Hamlet to say that the time is out of joint: his father's ghost. Here is the second leitmotif of Derrida's argument. For his book is not merely a book about Marx, nor about Shakespeare (whom Marx admired deeply); as its title indicates, it is also, and perhaps primarily, a book about ghosts. These are not, however, 'ghosts' in the bluntly pejorative sense used by Novalis. The ghosts referred to by Derrida are there for better or for worse, and we must learn to live with them: 'To live otherwise, and better. No, not better, but more justly'.[30] Ghosts are here associated with the ancestors who visit us, the victims of history's violence. Yet there is also a deeper level of association that relates to a core theme of Derrida's entire oeuvre. Like the famous neologism, *la différance*, of his early writings, the 'ghost', *le spectre*, here stands as a trope for the indefinite, fugitive and elusive. It is the essence of a ghost that it has no essence; ghosts are neither alive nor dead, neither purely bodily nor purely spiritual, neither present nor absent. And yet they are sufficiently present to disturb our dreams of a pure and complete presence.

Euphoria at the collapse of Communist totalitarianism in the early 1990s was precisely the kind of dream of a fully harmonious world order that Derrida saw as taking hold. And this provides the answer to the question of why Marx and why in 1993. Where Marx and Engels had opened their 1848 *Communist Manifesto* with the famous declaration, 'A spectre is haunting Europe – the spectre of communism', Derrida was interested in how communism once again manifested itself as a mental phantasm, not for the 'old Europe' of Marx's day, but for the 'new', 'post-communist' Europe:

> Today, almost a century and a half later, there are many who, throughout the world, seem just as worried by the specter of communism, just as convinced that what one is dealing with there is only a specter without body, without present reality, without actuality or effectivity, but this time it is supposed to be a past specter. It was only a specter, an illusion, a phantasm, or a ghost: that is what one hears everywhere today ('Horatio saies, "tis but our Fantasie", And will not let beleefe take hold of him').[31]

Yet Derrida is not trying to lament the fall of the Communist regimes of Eastern Europe here; what gives him no peace is the unrestrained victory cries of political and economic liberalism. Although Francis Fukuyama's widely discussed study *The End of History and the Last Man* – which came out in 1992 – was an obvious point of reference in his argument, Derrida's polemic was directed towards the general cultural movements of the early 1990s, the 'dominating discourse' of the anti-Marxist jeremiads. There is, Derrida notes, something about the manic, jubilatory tone of these jeremiads ('Marx is dead! Long live the Market!') that leads the thoughts to what Freud identified as the triumphant phase of the work of mourning: a rhythmical, almost compulsive repetition of phrases by which the subject seeks to convince itself that a process which is far from finished has indeed finished: 'If this hegemony is attempting to install its dogmatic orchestration in suspect and paradoxical conditions, it is first of all because this triumphant conjuration is striving in truth to disavow, and therefore to hide from, the fact that never, never in history, has the horizon of the thing whose survival is being celebrated (namely, all the old models of the capitalist and liberal world) been as dark, threatening, and threatened'.[32]

What was happening in the new Europe was that people were blaming Marx himself for the historical sins of Marxism, in order to avoid acknowledging the troublingly urgent voice in his writings, a voice capable of sowing doubt in their own victory narrative. The question was, could we escape Marx quite so easily? For his part, Derrida was less certain that we were finished with Marx – at least, the Marx who refused to accommodate himself to the inherent injustices of the capitalist world order. Derrida was no more convinced than Marx that the 'new' – that is to say, neo-capitalist – world order was a victory narrative only, and he was similarly reluctant to gloss over what this supposed victory narrative was hiding: 'Let us name with a single trait that which could risk making the euphoria of liberal-democrat capitalism resemble the blindest and most delirious of hallucinations, or even an increasingly glaring hypocrisy in its formal or juridicist rhetoric of human rights'.[33]

In a 'ten-word telegram' Derrida offered a sampler of the 'plagues' of the new world order: (1) the global unemployment created by systematic deregulation; (2) the expulsion of people (homeless citizens, refugees, stateless persons); (3) economic war within the EU and between the EU and the rest of the world; (4) an escalating inability to manage the contradictions within free-market concepts; (5) growing economic debt between the nations of the world; (6) a continually expanding arms industry and arms trade; (7) a proliferation of nuclear weapons supported by the very countries that claimed to be trying to prevent it; (8) ethnic conflicts fuelled by modern concepts of nation and sovereignty as well as by archaic notions of borders, blood and soil; (9) the global power of mafias and drug cartels; and (10) the state of international law and its institutions, in which the activities of a supposedly universal law are largely dominated by a handful of economic and militarily powerful nation-states.[34] With the hindsight of a little more than twenty years, it is tempting to interject that these afflictions have, if anything, become more acute.

While *Specters of Marx* was a prophetic document in the sense of being a searing critique of the flaws of the 'new world order', the aim of the book extended much further. There was more to say about Marx and more to say about ghosts, particularly about the spectres of Marx. As so often in Derrida's writings, the title contained an ambiguity, in this case a double genitive. Derrida was thus not only interested in the spectres of Marx that were pursuing the new Europe, but also the spectres by which Marx himself had been haunted. In fact, the same Marx who had warned his contemporaries to exorcise 'the spectre of communism' was himself far from enamoured of ghosts. Derrida alluded here to Marx's fondness for 'spectral' categories in his analysis of the fetishism of the commodity. Marx had painstakingly shown how something, at the very moment when it became a commodity, acquired the aura of something not in the thing itself: an idealization of the thing occurred. But Marx opposed precisely such idealization or 'phantasmagoria'. On the contrary, the shift from use value to exchange value formed the hub of the deceptive set of appearances into which capitalism pulled people – and which Marx wanted to expose.[35]

Marx thus wanted to force the spectres of capitalism into the light and dispel them by juxtaposing its deceptive set of appearances with the real world of pure, uncorrupted materiality. But could we really be so sure of this distinction between things ideologically infected and things described objectively? It was here that Derrida's doubts returned. In directing his exorcism of the spectral forces of the world, was Marx not exhibiting a dangerous overconfidence in the stability and finality of his own account of reality as it truly was? And did he not thereby reinstate the treacherous dream of a world without ghosts, a world in which the Communist Party or the International marked the spectre's final incarnation and, with it, the end of any ambiguity – the end of the visitations of the past?[36]

Unsurprisingly, Derrida was as sceptical of this utopian victory narrative as he was of economic liberalism's narrative of the redemptive powers of the market. This touches upon another central theme of the book. While *Specters of Marx* made an unsparing anatomy of 1990s neo-capitalist euphoria, it was, as Michael Sprinker has stressed, equally an urgent invitation to Marxism to settle accounts with its own past – with the crimes which had been committed in its name, the terror in which it had been complicit and the massively undemocratic social forms which it had tolerated.[37] And while Derrida warned of the trick of blithely turning the sins of Marxism upon Marx himself, he left readers in no doubt that one particular Marx – the Marx who thought that ideologies could be abolished by means of the science of historical materialism – had paved the way for the utopian and totalitarian aspects of Marxism's history. Its unwavering conviction that its own perspective lay beyond ideological perversions had also given birth to a vision of the ultimate good society, that vision in whose name so many violations had been committed and so many injustices whitewashed.

Perhaps Marx's greatest mistake had been quite simply his eagerness to disavow those spectral forces. Not only because it is an illusion to believe that such a thing is possible, but also because spectral powers – ideologies, visions – are not only always evil. Here Derrida alluded to the kind of ideology which, for Marx, occupied a special position and constituted the very form of those spectral powers: religion. Marx had criticized religion as an illusory source of happiness – 'the opium of the people' – something that emancipated humanity would leave behind. But it was precisely this that Marx himself proved unable to do. On the contrary, religion remained a spectre for Marx, an unyielding spectre with which he continually struggled but never succeeded in vanquishing. What Derrida subtly implied here was that all of Marx's critical philosophy, despite its unreasonable contempt for religion, was built upon an emancipatory structure that ultimately drew its force from a specifically religious, prophetic or even messianic tradition.[38]

Derrida was not the first to make this connection, of course. Returning for a moment to Löwith, it can be noted that his *Meaning in History* included the slightly acerbic observation that Marx, 'though an emancipated Jew of the nineteenth century who felt strongly antireligious and even anti-Semitic', was also 'a Jew of Old Testament stature'. The true basis of Marx's historical materialism, Löwith pointedly added, was Jewish prophetism and its stern proclamation of a coming era of justice. Similarly, he argued that *The Communist Manifesto* was best characterized as a 'prophetic document', a call to action rather than an objective treatment; terms such as 'class struggle' and 'exploitation' were, when it came down to it, moralistic judgements, not the product of disinterested observation of the course of history. Löwith's final conclusion was that historical materialism was 'a history of fulfilment and salvation in terms of social economy', a secular version of the classical salvation drama with a definite goal in the future – in Marx's case, a heavenly kingdom without God.[39]

If Löwith adopted a somewhat sarcastic tone when emphasizing Marx's theological baggage, it was, as already noted, because he himself had little time for the theological tradition and its influence on Western views of history. On this issue he differed significantly from Derrida. If Marx's writings contained occasional echoes of Amos's and Isaiah's passionate invectives against the reduction of human beings to economic values and the worship of money, it was precisely this spirit in Marx that Derrida wished to affirm: 'Now, if there is a spirit of Marxism which I will never be ready to renounce, it is … a certain emancipatory and messianic affirmation, a certain experience of the promise that one can try to liberate from any dogmatics and even from any metaphysico-religious determination, from any messianism'.[40]

Of all the ghosts with which Marx struggled, it was thus the spectre of religion, in the form of a particular messianic spirit, that Derrida wanted to embrace and to let disrupt the new world order. It was also this spectre that he upbraided Marx in the book's final chapter for having been too eager to dispel: 'perhaps [Marx] should not have chased away so many ghosts too quickly. Not all of them at once or not so simply on the pretext that they did not exist (of course they do not exist, so what?) – or that all this was or ought to remain past'.[41]

Let me now return to the Capri symposium. At around the time that Derrida was working on his manuscript on Marx, a number of Italian philosophers, who were preparing a yearbook of European philosophy, decided to entrust the project to Gianni Vattimo and his French colleague Derrida. This became the prelude to the symposium at Capri which took place between 28 February and 1 March 1994. When the idea was first raised, the theme of the yearbook – and of the symposium – was anything but settled. This decision was also entrusted to Vattimo and Derrida, who, independently of each other, both proposed 'religion'.[42]

In the context, it was hardly a coincidence that both philosophers happened to think of religion as a suitable theme for philosophy. By the early 1990s, talk of 'the return of religion' was already widespread within sociology and was also making steady inroads into philosophy. A number of factors lay behind this reawakened interest in religion, perhaps the most urgent of which was the renewed visibility of religion in contemporary geopolitical conflicts. The *fatwa* issued against Salman Rushdie in 1989 revealed to a shocked world the explosive power of modern Islamic fundamentalism, and by the time war broke out in the Balkans two years later it had become abundantly clear that religion was very much alive as a culturally formative power, even in supposedly secular Europe.

Not wholly unexpectedly, the return of religion in the form of violence and extremism was a recurrent motif among the speeches at Capri. It is in this light, at least in part, that the symposium's repeated efforts to formulate a new universalism should be understood. This effort was articulated most explicitly by Eugenio Trías, who, somewhat surprisingly given the symposium's emphasis upon religion as a contributing factor to contemporary geopolitical conflicts, called for a new religion:

> Perhaps it is a matter of preparing for the emergence of a new religion. ... Perhaps the only way to counteract the wars of religion breaking out everywhere is to lay the basis for a new foundation. ... For the shards of religion that survive, in their diversity, clearly seem to be incapable of giving unity and solidity to an ever more regional and fragmented world. On the contrary, they heighten feelings of mutual suspicion, mistrust and hatred. The world that is emerging with the end of the Cold War and the Eastern/Western blocs is plainly polycentric. *Ideological* differences have made way for *cultural substrata* and these, in turn, are always rooted in the enduring ground of *religious* traditions.[43]

Recalling the parallels already noted between the period after 1789 and that after 1989, it is tempting to hear in these words an echo of Novalis's tract on Europe, in which he invoked religion as the guarantor of a higher, unifying spirit that would lead Europe beyond the divisions created by the Reformation and the Enlightenment: 'Who knows if there has been enough of war, but it will never cease if we do not seize the palm which only a spiritual power can confer'.[44] Yet the parallels ran even deeper. While Novalis and the other Romantics were enamoured of religion, their enthusiasm did not extend to any old religion. Trías and the other philosophers gathered at Capri were no less discriminating. Just as the early Romantics had to a large degree extended the Enlightenment's radical critique, the discussions at Capri fell within the framework of a very specific critical tradition – as indicated most clearly by Derrida's stated goal of approaching religion 'within the limits of reason alone'.[45]

Although Derrida thereby inscribed himself and his colleagues within a particular Enlightenment tradition, it was nonetheless with a number of reservations. Above all, there was one strand of Enlightenment thinking with which he felt less inclined to reconcile himself – that characterized by an impatience to banish excessive numbers of ghosts. As was well known, the Enlightenment had given birth not only to critical reason but also to a hubristic faith in that reason. From this derived the failings of so many of modernity's social utopias, which relied upon the notion of humanity as utterly rational. But humanity was precisely not utterly rational, and any social system which ignored the fact that individuals are capricious and unpredictable was ultimately doomed to political degeneracy. To backtrack for a moment to the middle of the last century, this utopian element in modern politics was precisely what thinkers from Right to Left had sought to disassociate themselves from by means of occasionally desperate proclamations of the end of ideology. Perhaps 1989 marked the definitive end of the utopian vision of a thoroughly good society. The real question was what would come after this end; what was left after all the euphoria about economic liberalism's global victory had subsided.

Alongside the return of religion in the form of violence and extremism, it was this question that continually hung over the discussions at Capri. On the one hand, the gathered philosophers were returning to religion in order to turn it upon itself; to find *in* religion a more overarching vision to *counterpose to* religion when it was used as a means of asserting national, religious or ethnic identities. On the other hand, they were returning to religion in order to turn religion against an Enlightenment tradition that regarded itself as having relegated religion forever to the past. In this latter sense, the visionary aspects of religion were presented as a riposte to the spirit of disillusion which was looming now that the Enlightenment political tradition had petered out. Not unlike the early Romantics, they could be said to be creating a kind of modified Enlightenment tradition, in which that tradition's critical strain was made more acute by means of its cross-fertilization with a modified form of religion.

What exactly did this cross-fertilization consist of? The answer was perhaps formulated most effectively by Derrida in *Specters of Marx* when he described an emancipatory spirit that drew its strength from a particular prophetic tradition. Attempts to pin down more closely the nature of this spirit, as it emerged during the discussions at Capri, will reveal, not unexpectedly, that it bears the hallmarks of several of the attributes identified earlier within the prophetic tradition. This holds especially true for its central idea, that history itself contains a redemptive impulse, which is another way of saying – with a nod to Abraham Heschel – that history should be considered from the perspective of justice rather than that of power. The vocation of the prophet (to use the terminology of Scripture), the exegete (to use that of Joachim), the poet (to use that of Novalis) or the philosopher thus becomes to challenge the prevailing conception of history by means of poetical images, theological patterns and historical analogies.

At this point, however, another warning is in order against drawing too many parallels. While the prophet's task, as Joachim saw it, may have been to reveal a divine course of events within history, there was a crucial shift in the writings of the Romantics, manifested most clearly in Novalis, whereby the task of the historian or poet became both to reveal and to invent divine patterns. Among the late-twentieth-century philosophers at Capri, by contrast, there was no question of conferring divine authority upon this critical-emancipatory task; in a fundamental sense history was history *after* the death of God. This did not mean, as one might think, that the human subject was elevated to the status of master of history. It should be remembered here that all of the philosophers in question worked primarily within the anti-metaphysical tradition established by Martin Heidegger. The discussions at Capri, as Gadamer argued, must therefore be seen in light of Heidegger's settling of accounts with Western philosophy's blind faith in the subject's ability to grasp reality in its entirety.[46] Translated into historico-philosophical terms, this meant calling into question both the theologies of history of an earlier age and the secular philosophies of history of the new era, both of which had in some measure claimed to represent history in its entirety.

As has been described above, the existence of so panoptical a view of history had already been cast in doubt by the Romantics – from Novalis's insight into the temporal and thus fragmentary character of our consciousness to the late Schelling's emphasis upon philosophical reflection as an activity in a state of continual evolution. This Romantic doubt was picked up in several ways by Nietzsche and further developed by Heidegger. There was a growing realization that human consciousness is always already a part of the passage of historical events and that history can therefore only be approached from *within* history itself – to use Heidegger's terminology, by attending critically to how being sends itself. As will be seen in the next section, this attentive, hermeneutic stance was to suffuse Vattimo's, Trías's and Derrida's critical reflections on history. Interestingly, it was also this stance that led them back to the historico-theological tradition to which modern critical philosophy had partly bidden farewell.

A Romantic Spirit

Although the twentieth century marked the end and, indeed, even the death of God, the question was simultaneously raised as to *which* God had died. The ambiguity could already be found in Nietzsche and was given explicit formulation by Heidegger in a famous text in which he offered an interpretation of Nietzsche's pronouncement of the death of God. Without in any way taking the sting out of Nietzsche's forceful critique of Christianity, Heidegger emphasized that 'the death of God' denoted a series of philosophical and cultural events whose significance went beyond the demise of the Christian God. The target of Nietzsche's critique had in fact been metaphysics as such – Western philosophy's stubborn tendency to devalue the world of the senses in order to fix its gaze instead upon a higher, divine or supernatural reality.[47]

Even so, it was clear that in Heidegger's eyes the death of God – that is, the dissolution of metaphysics – was no tragic or regrettable occurrence. On the contrary, it signalled the end of a philosophy that was fundamentally an act of power. At the same time, it is important to clarify that, for Heidegger, talk of the death of God was not a normative philosophical announcement in the form of an appeal to humanity to abandon the traditional theological worldview. Rather, it represented a hermeneutic interpretation of history as it *de facto* presented itself in the technological age: growing specialization of the sciences had been accompanied by the emergence of several mutually competing conceptions of reality, making it increasingly difficult to assert a single, overarching or inexhaustible conception of the world (theological or otherwise). In a seeming paradox, this development, in which the coercive structures of metaphysics were beginning to unravel, also presented an opportunity to approach the holy or sacred in a new way – at least if such terms were taken to refer to a dimension that did not allow itself to be apprehended by human thought.[48]

Could this be a key for understanding the return of religion during the last decades of the twentieth century? Judging from the often violent forms taken by religion in its new incarnations at that time, the answer would seem to be no. In its fundamentalist manifestations, religion seemed rather to be a desperate attempt to escape the fragmentizing effects of modernity by harking back to absolute metaphysical truths. On closer inspection, however, the answer is not quite as self-evident. Does the very fact that we experience religion's new visibility as a *return* not precisely mean that we are here dealing with a considerably more intricate process than initially seemed to be the case?

This suspicion provided the starting point for Gianni Vattimo's contribution to the discussion at Capri. More specifically, his essay 'The Trace of the Trace' focuses upon the bewildering discrepancy that exists between the return of religion at the concretely cultural level and the renewed interest in religion within philosophy. While the former represents an effort to recover a solid foundation in an increasingly transitory world, philosophical interest in religion seems to him rather to be a consequence of the break-up of metaphysics: 'It is (only) because metaphysical meta-narratives have been discarded that philosophy has rediscovered the plausibility of religion and can consequently approach the religious need of common consciousness independently of the framework of Enlightenment critique'.[49] On the level of philosophical reflection, in other words, renewed investment in religion can be seen as part of the 'postmodern' weakening of the notion of a firm or absolute foundation for thought – that is to say, the very foundation that adherents of religious fundamentalism seem to be striving for in their return to religion.

The question is whether, beneath this seeming contradiction, there lies a deeper connection between these different kinds of 'return'. Vattimo argues that such is indeed the case: 'The common root of the religious need that runs through our society and of the return of (the plausibility of) religion in philosophy today lies in the reference to modernity as an epoch of technoscience, or in Heidegger's words, as the epoch of the world-picture'.[50] Both instances, then, represent attempts to respond to a growing experience of fragmentation, a sense that our conception of the world is disintegrating into an array of different – often competing – conceptions. In the case of religious fundamentalism, a reactive answer is provided by trying to recycle an ideal authenticity for a society degraded by technoscience. This effort is, however, doomed to failure since this ideality will always find itself in competition with other claims to give an ideal representation of reality. In the spirit of Heidegger, Vattimo claims that the crisis in metaphysics should rather be responded to in non-reactive fashion by attending to being as it actually gives itself in the technoscientific age. This non-reactive way of relating to the dissolution of metaphysical structures could, according to Vattimo, likewise be seen in contemporary philosophical reflections on religion.

Behind this argument can be discerned something that Vattimo from an early stage in his philosophical career had termed 'weak thought' (*il pensiero debole*) – in fact, a rewriting of Heidegger's idea that being continually withdraws from the grasp of human thought during an epoch in which metaphysics nears its end. Put in more general terms, this concept alludes to a wider philosophical development by which the concept of objectivity – of the object's immediate presence in the subject – has been steadily replaced by a more hermeneutic kind of relationship. Both intraphilosophical developments and socio-political factors are responsible for this shift. Vattimo cites the decolonization wave of the 1960s and the oil crisis of the 1970s as examples of historical events that have served to help undermine the concept that one particular representation of reality – the Western – is necessarily superior to all others. In a similar fashion, he argues, philosophy has become increasingly suspicious of the attempt to establish absolute principles and fundamental underpinnings. In light of this development, the task of philosophy more properly consists of attending to and interpreting an ongoing historical process.[51]

Paying attention in the late twentieth century involves, among other things, being sensitive about the so-called return of religion. As a philosopher, how should one interpret this unforeseen turn? One possible interpretation has already been indicated: that the dissolution of modern philosophy's narrow ideals of truth and rationality has paved the way for a more open attitude towards religion. Yet Vattimo's thesis is that there exists an even deeper connection between 'weak thought' and religion. By this he has in mind not only the fact that modern hermeneutic thinking in many respects presupposes the interpretative practices which first emerged within the Western religious tradition. Moreover, there is an underlying structure to this religious tradition that has determined the growth of sophisticated hermeneutic practices in the first place: 'Beginning with St. Augustine and his reflection on the Trinity, Christian theology is in its deepest foundations a hermeneutic theology: the interpretative structure, transmission, mediation and, perhaps, the fallenness do not concern only the enunciation, the communication of God with man; they characterize the intimate life of God itself, which therefore cannot be conceived in terms of an immutable metaphysical plenitude.'[52]

Vattimo's thesis is that the ultimate core of Christian theology – that is to say, its concept of God – contains an anti-metaphysical impulse, which, after following the winding paths of the history of ideas, finally breaks through on a wider philosophical and cultural front. By constructing divinity as internally divided into three persons, the Christian doctrine of God erases from the very start any notion of an ultimate, stable principle for reality. The basis of Christian faith becomes instead a kind of anti-foundation – a dynamic and relational process that invariably defeats the efforts of human thought to grasp the ultimate principles of its existence. This pattern is also reflected in the notion of God's incarnation in Christ – where the Father empties himself in the Son (*kenosis*) – as well as in the doctrine of the Holy Spirit as marking the dynamic character of the divine revelation. While these ostensibly abstract speculations as to the nature of God can seem like a rather arbitrary source for the hermeneutic tradition, Vattimo reminds his audience that they have an extremely concrete origin. The theological notions of God's incarnation and the Trinity, in other words, have emerged from attempts to interpret the reality revealed in the person of Jesus of Nazareth – in his life, but perhaps especially in his death.[53]

What, then, was revealed on the Cross? The answer, which goes hand in glove with Vattimo's idea of weak thought, is that Jesus's fate in paradigmatic fashion exposed the illusion of the necessity of violence: 'Jesus, most especially, comes to be put to death not because he is the perfect victim, as has always been understood, but because he is the bearer of a message too radically in contrast with the deepest (sacral and victim-based) convictions of all the "natural" religions'.[54] Behind this argument can be discerned René Girard's theory of the scapegoat and how the biblical tradition represented a break with 'mythological violence', a theory that Vattimo has described as eye-opening and the key to his renewed interest in religion.[55]

It is not only Girard who paved the way for Vattimo's renewed interest in religion, or in the biblical tradition, to be precise. Two years after the Capri symposium, Vattimo published *Belief*, a rather more personal work in which he related his rediscovered fascination with the Christian faith. Although he had distanced himself early in his career from his youthful Catholicism, throwing himself, almost in protest, into the arms of Nietzsche and Heidegger, he discovered that protracted study of these anti-metaphysical philosophers had, paradoxically, brought him back to the Christian tradition. Or was it in fact the reverse? Was it possible that he had been attracted early in life by the critical strain in these two philosophers precisely because he had already been shaped by a particular, socially radical Catholic tradition? Vattimo left the question unanswered but gestured towards a deeper affinity between these seemingly incompatible sources of inspiration. Like few other philosophers, Nietzsche and Heidegger had spelled out the hermeneutic implications of Christian theology, thereby laying the basis for what Vattimo in turn would spell out as weak thought.[56]

How, then, should the Christianity to which Vattimo has returned under the sign of 'weakness' be understood? In order to track down the answer, it is worth looking at his other sources of inspiration. While Nietzsche, Heidegger and Girard are important influences, Vattimo's notion of weak thought is also obviously inspired by the ideas of Romanticism. In specifying more precisely the roots of weak thought, he refers repeatedly to an intellectual genealogy running from Joachim of Fiore to Novalis, Schleiermacher and Schelling. The tradition deriving from Joachim is particularly important for Vattimo in order to be able to defend himself against the objection that the Christian tradition in its concrete manifestations has not quite so often displayed 'weak' thought, but rather confined itself to dogmatic truths and the application of disciplinary violence to those who deviated from church teaching.

> But alongside this dogmatic-disciplinarian view of the revelation, ... the history of Christianity is traversed by another wholly different thread that one might well call Joachimist: for it was Joachim of Fiore who spoke of a third age in the histories of humanity and of salvation, namely, the reign of the spirit (following after that of the Father in the Old Testament, and that of the Son), in which the 'spiritual' sense of the scriptures is increasingly in evidence, with charity taking the place of discipline.[57]

According to Vattimo, Joachim in a unique way wove together revelation and salvation into a single, dynamic process. In other words, salvation was not simply guaranteed, once and for all, by Christ's death and resurrection. On the contrary, the sending of the spirit shows that the Christian church has been called upon to manage, shape and enrich the message of salvation by continuing to respond to divine revelation throughout history. In so doing, the revelation assumes a progressive quality: the interpretative community are not merely passive recipients of an inherited message, but actively contribute to realizing the Scriptures' spiritual significance by foregrounding ever-richer dimensions of meaning.[58]

Although Vattimo captures something of the general shift from letter to spirit that permeates Joachim's writings, it bears stating that his reading nonetheless has less to do with Joachim himself (who was antithetical towards the idea of a progressive revelation) and more to do with how the Romantic philosophers managed the Joachite legacy. Nor does Vattimo hide the fact that this is indeed the case, but openly admits his affinity with Novalis and Schleiermacher, primarily, and also with Schelling.[59] Early Romanticism's dream of a religion of the spirit that would explode dogmatic and institutional obstacles (another notion which Joachim strongly opposed) also finds a strong echo in Vattimo's own concept of weak thought. Indeed, to follow religion as it 'recurred' in Vattimo's thought during the first years of the 1990s, one can quite simply hold it up against a checklist of the three qualities identified earlier as significant for Romanticism's religion.

Hence, Vattimo's notion of the history of Christian revelation as a successive realization of the ontology of weakness foregrounds the *progressive* aspect of Romantic philosophy. In philosophical terms, this means that the notion of an unquestioned ultimate foundation has to make way for a weak thought that admits itself to being only one of several possible interpretations of reality. This process is reflected, in turn, in the political development towards democracy, tolerance and diversity. It should also be noted that Vattimo, at least in his contribution to the Capri symposium, expresses largely unqualified optimism that history truly possesses a 'redemptive revelation' that discloses itself as a slow but steady subversion of coercive structures within the domains of both knowledge and politics.[60]

The other obviously Romantic quality is the *universalist* character of the religion which Vattimo embraces. Just as the Romantics imagined a church whose scope continually grew until it finally exploded the confines of the Christian church, so, too, does Vattimo imagine that the dynamic interpretative practices begun by the church will lead ultimately to a genuinely universal religion which will continually grow as it incorporates new dimensions of the message: 'Salvation history is not only about those who receive the announcement. Rather, it is above all the history of an announcement whose reception is its constitutive, rather than accidental, moment. Perhaps this is the essence of the Judeo-Christian message, which makes it a unique case in the history of religions and a reasonable candidate to be a universal religion – above and beyond imperialist or Eurocentric claims.'[61]

Vattimo suggests that the Christian faith, by virtue of its inner impulse towards hermeneutic pluralism (and hence towards the weakening of authoritarian structures and claims) quite simply possesses a unique capacity for continually superseding itself. It is also in this light that the ambivalence accompanying Christian universalism should be understood: on the one hand, it has expressed itself in colonialism and the violent subjugation of non-Christian civilizations; on the other, colonized peoples have often eventually turned against their 'Christian' overlords in the name of a more authentic interpretation of the Bible's prophetic message.[62]

According to Vattimo, the subversive tendency of the Christian tradition is a consequence not only of its increasing diversity of interpretations but also of the quality of those interpretations. More precisely, there has been a continual shift from literal interpretations of the message towards a more spiritual or symbolic reading, which typically involves a shift from inflexible and exclusive claims to a more tolerant viewpoint. As is well known, this shift from letter to spirit captured the interest of the Romantics, and this touches on the third quality of Romanticism's religion: a striving for gradual *spiritualization*. It is worth recalling here not only Novalis's counterposing of a narrow-mindedly dogmatic religion with a poeticized religion for free spirits, but also the Romantics' coolness more generally towards institutionalized forms of religion. Each of these aspects is echoed by Vattimo, which explains why his rediscovered 'Catholicism' should under no circumstances be mistaken for an uncritical return to the church. On the contrary, Vattimo accuses the (Catholic) church of being stuck in a rigidly metaphysical conception of reality that very often entails absurd consequences at the moral and cultural levels. It is also in light of this critical attitude towards how the church has actually shaped the message of Christianity that Vattimo explicitly defines weak thought in terms of secularization:

> Secularization as a 'positive' fact signifying the dissolution of the sacral structures of Christian society, the transition to an ethics of autonomy, to a lay state, to a more flexible literalism in the interpretation of dogmas and precepts, should be understood not as the failure of or departure from Christianity, but as a fuller realization of its truth, which is, as we can recall, the kenosis, the abasement of God, which undermines the 'natural' features of divinity.[63]

With his strong emphasis upon concepts such as weakening (*indebolimento*) and secularization, Vattimo at first glance seems to be interested more in the conditions for a critical or negative philosophy than in developing a visionary or positive philosophy. This impression is confirmed by his stated goal of rehabilitating the concept of nihilism in a Nietzschean context, which is to say, as an affirmation of the insight that there can be no reality unaffected by our interpretations. However, it would be a mistake to reduce Vattimo's hermeneutic philosophy to a purely critical enterprise. On the contrary, in a lecture given later in spring 1994, Vattimo made clear that his 'nihilistic hermeneutics' was essentially a constructive and ethical project (a riposte to the stock complaint that philosophical nihilism tended to lead to a cynical resignation to the prospect of a war of all against all): 'There is no strict relation between nihilism and violence. In fact, even if one cannot attribute this to Nietzsche, one of the effects of nihilism may well be to undermine the reasons by which violence is justified and nourished.'[64] In other words, it is not the insight that all claims to reality are ultimately interpretations that leads to violence; rather, it is precisely those viewpoints that do *not* admit to being interpretations that tend to give rise to violent conflicts. Therein also lies the ethical value of nihilism: to the extent that each party concedes that its own perspective is ultimately an interpretation, it reduces its incentive for making coercive claims at the same time as it creates an opportunity to listen to other perspectives and viewpoints.

That said, another critical objection presents itself. If Vattimo's philosophy contains a visionary impulse in the form of a conviction that history has a redemptory quality, is there not a danger that this impulse, in its turn, takes the form of a new coercive claim? In other words, is the stubborn defence of weak thought not just a subtle way of launching a new strong claim – that there are no facts, only interpretations? This touches upon a problematic that the Romantics had already struggled with: the question of whether it is possible to articulate a visionary philosophy that does not express itself in utopian or totalitarian forms. In a way, this question had already been lurking in the wings of the debate over first principles, but it was actualized above all in the idea of a new, higher religion. As shown earlier, the Romantics' strategy for steering between Scylla and Charybdis – between absence of vision and utopian arrogance – was to focus their attention upon the temporal constitution of consciousness. In its inability to identify a moment outside of time, human thought quite simply could not claim to be able to capture the ideal more than fleetingly, as fragments in the eternal flow of time. However, the impossibility of grasping the ideal by means of philosophical thought did not mean that it was not detectable via other media such as art, poetry and myth. But it was only ever as fragments, and never unscathed by the ravages of time.

Now, Vattimo is not unaware of the objection that 'weak thought' runs the risk of becoming a strong or coercive claim. On the contrary, he makes the objection into one of his own by calling attention to the problem that hermeneutics – the insight that we unavoidably encounter the world in a mediated form – in the present day has been made into something of a common cultural property, the consequences of which has never been fully explored. People bandy about phrases like 'the death of metanarratives' or 'there is no uninterpreted reality' without ever noticing that, in time-honoured metaphysical fashion, they are thereby establishing a new, binding truth about the nature of reality. However, applying hermeneutics consistently means having to concede that even the insight as to the inescapability of interpretation is itself an interpretation – a historical truth rather than an objective structure of reality. Just like every other interpretation, this claim can only be defended by the force of sound argument: by asserting a narrative or account of specific historical events that appear to support the interpretation in question. In this sense, Vattimo argues, '[hermeneutics] also entails a philosophy of history (even if only the philosophy of the history of the end of the philosophy of history) that views hermeneutics as the result of a "nihilistic" process, in which metaphysical Being, meaning violence, consumes itself'.[65]

Not unlike the Romantic philosophers, then, Vattimo can be seen to turn his attention towards the temporal or historical character of consciousness in order to avoid the temptation of relapsing into 'strong' or metaphysical thinking. As historical beings, we always already find ourselves within a historical sequence, which implies that our critical understanding of history is itself historically conditioned. For example, to live in Europe during the latter part of the 1990s was to live with the experience of how particular kinds of coercive and authoritarian structures (colonialism, patriarchy, class society) were being steadily dismantled. When Vattimo claimed that the philosophical insight as to the unavoidability of interpretation was defensible only as a historical truth, his point was thus that these concrete historical developments formed the strongest argument in support of his position: it had *de facto* become increasingly unsustainable to preserve the illusion of an overarching and supposedly objective account of reality.[66]

It is here, too, that the anti-utopian elements in Vattimo's philosophy make their appearance. The claim that history contains a redemptory impulse can quite simply not be made from an external critical position, nor can it refer to some future state of fulfilment. On the contrary, it can only be made within the framework of a definite philosophical tradition, which, for Vattimo, is synonymous with the hermeneutic tradition that derives from the Christian theological tradition. Finally, in a seeming paradox, it is this manoeuvre that also prevents the claim about interpretative unavoidability from leading into a purely relativistic position:

> It is only in so far as it rediscovers its own provenance in the New Testament that this post-metaphysical thinking can take the form of a thinking of the event-like character of Being that is not simply reducible to a bare acceptance of the existent or to pure historical and cultural relativism. If you will: it is the fact of the Incarnation that confers on history the sense of a redemptive revelation, as opposed to a confused accumulation of happenings that unsettle the pure structured quality of true Being. That there is a redemptive (or in philosophical terms, emancipatory) sense to history, in spite, or precisely because, of its being a history of pronouncements and responses, of interpretations and not 'discoveries' or the ascendancy of 'true' presences, is only possible in the light of the doctrine of Incarnation.[67]

Vattimo's effort to cross-fertilize philosophy and a particular strain within religion represents an undeniably impressive attempt to navigate between objectivism and relativism, between absence of vision and utopian arrogance. At the same time, it is precisely here that perhaps the most serious objection to his philosophical argument makes itself felt, not least in light of the intellectual thread that this study has been following. Despite its universalistic impulse, Vattimo's emancipatory claim remains bound to a Christian theological framework. As a result, it runs up against the same problematic that accompanied the Romantics' dream of a new, higher religion, in which the universal ultimately remains synonymous with the Christian. In Vattimo's eyes the Christian tradition's universalizing impulse entails both a tolerance for the truth claims of other religions and a growing secularization and democratization of the Christian tradition itself. Yet the fact remains – as Vattimo repeatedly stresses – that this universalizing impulse can be articulated from within the Christian tradition alone.[68] The question that is left unanswered is thus: what happens to respecting the claims of other specific traditions to possess the truth?

The question is broached in an interesting fashion by Eugenio Trías's contribution to the Capri symposium. In light of contemporary geopolitical conflicts (the Balkan Wars, the First Gulf War, the escalating conflict in Rwanda), Trías's aim here is to formulate 'a wider *global* vision' that could unite an increasingly regionalized and divided world. Like Vattimo, he finds in religion a resource for this vision. However, the 'religion of the spirit' which Trías champions is in no way exclusively tied to Christianity. On the contrary, he presents it as a kind of 'eschatological horizon' uniting elements from all of the great religious and philosophical traditions.[69]

This notion of a metareligion can at first sight seem somewhat obsolete, not least given the debates among theologians of religion in recent years. A central feature of these debates has been the critique of the 'imperialist' aspect of the idea of a metareligion; another has been the questioning of the very possibility of formulating a truth claim that is not already embedded in particular (linguistic, mythological, cultural) forms of expression.[70] In order to do justice to Trías's concept of a religion of the spirit, it is therefore important to address his broader philosophical efforts around the time of the Capri symposium. In the same year as the symposium Trías published his comprehensive study *La edad del espíritu* ('The Age of the Spirit'), a journey through the history of ideas documenting the way in which human reason emerges from an array of different mythological traditions (Indian, Persian, Hebrew and Greek), which in various ways have shaped the concrete forms in which reason is expressed. The entire effort rested upon a fundamental idea that Trías had developed early on in his philosophical career, namely that reason is generated from prior revelation. It should be clarified immediately that the revelation Trías had in mind is not identical with any specific religion. This is, rather, a question of revelation in the deeper sense connoted by concepts such as 'mystery', 'the sacred' or 'the unspeakable'. Even so, this unspeakable could be discerned merely through the existing religious traditions. This leads to another of Trías's central concepts: the symbol. The religious symbol constitutes the locus in which the sacred manifests itself in the world, literally a 'throwing-together' (*sym-ballein*) of an unspeakable, noumenal aspect and its concrete manifestation. In turn, this '*symballic* event' assumes narrative form in the wealth of myths that has been preserved in the great religious and philosophical traditions.[71]

This leads back to reason. If the sacred reveals itself in symbols and is interpreted through myths, Trías imagines that down the years the different mythological traditions have generated a mode of rational self-reflection around such symbolic revelation. A key part of *La edad del espíritu* comprises the mapping and documenting of how the different traditions have given rise to different forms of self-reflection. In broad strokes Trías outlines a poetical-philosophical form that unites the Indian and Greek cultural spheres, while the Persian (Zoroastrian) and Hebrew (biblical) cultural spheres have developed a form of reflection that could more accurately be described as prophetical-sophiological. The two strands then merge in the Christian-Platonic tradition that forms the basis for Western civilization.[72]

This is not the place to offer a more detailed account of Trías's admittedly fascinating genealogy of the mythological roots of rational reflection. For now, I wish merely to highlight the fundamental conviction that Trías expresses in the course of his analysis of the history of ideas: reason, in its different historical forms of expression, has always emerged *a posteriori* from the symbolic revelation of the sacred. Indeed, this conviction forms the basis for the critical reading of Western modernity that Trías makes in the book's final section – which is of particular interest in order to properly understand his presentation at Capri. Trías here presents modernity as the great era of concealment, an epoch in which the sacred and its symbolic expressions were suppressed and obscured. While reason in all previous epochs had existed in a living relationship with the sacred, there appeared in modernity a reason which considered itself the ultimate revelation.

That the religious symbolizing of the sacred was suppressed during modernity did not, however, mean that the sacred as such was eliminated. It was merely displaced and manifested itself in other areas – in the *magia naturalis* of the Renaissance, in the allegorical form of the Baroque, and, later, in modern art and aesthetics. Nevertheless, philosophical reflection remained largely isolated from the symbolization of the sacred, leading to the slow impoverishment of reason and, eventually, the crisis that now affects Western rationality.[73]

The book concluded with a critique of civilization that Trías also took up in his presentation at Capri and that he further developed a couple of years later in his essay collection *Pensar la religión*. The path taken by modern reason is here presented as a Faustian adventure that is now coming to a tragic resolution. In its eagerness to wash its hands of any involvement with the sacred, reason (in its Western manifestation) has created a state of depthless surface, a disenchanted world in which nature has been emptied of value and humanity robbed of its dignity:

> Today, this reason is beginning to doubt itself. At the height of its hegemony and power, it reveals its macabre face, its terrifying and destructive design, its absolute, deadly force. This reason is beginning to lose certainty and legitimacy: in its domination, it shows its unstoppable, deadly character. Through a technoscience left to its own dynamics, it generates deadly arms capable of destroying every trace of life and humanity. Through the expansion of a capitalism radically mediated through its techno-scientific determination, it devastates the territorial and natural substratum that constitutes the sustaining provision for the world and for the inhabitants that give life and humanity to this world. It confronts the threshold of the final, definitive war, and the threshold of the unstoppable growth in its exploitation of the earth. It also defies the boundaries of its own technical expansion, in revealing the conditioning factor of solitude in its soundings of the cosmic world.[74]

How have we ended up in this soulless state? As already indicated, Trías identifies the root of the crisis of modern reason in the illusory notion of a self-constituted reason. Now, one does not need to use grand terms such as 'the sacred' or 'revelation' in order to highlight what is problematic about the positing of a self-defining reason. As a wide range of twentieth-century philosophers have argued, the very act of differentiating between things as being more or less reasonable in itself presupposes a narrative frame that supersedes individual reason. Although Trías concedes the force of this so-called linguistic turn, he nonetheless regards the postmodern philosophy which has come in its wake as profoundly unsatisfactory. In focusing exclusively on narrative and textuality, he argues, postmodernism has quite simply lost sight of the deeper cultural strata that determine such linguistic expressions in the first place.[75]

The way in which Trías distanced himself from postmodernism's preoccupation with language resembles in several respects Vattimo's scepticism towards a generalized hermeneutics. If Vattimo seeks to avoid the relativistic contradiction by attending to history as it *de facto* presents itself, Trías also aimed to 'capture the actual historical movements of the end of the century'.[76] Unsurprisingly, this effort to attend to the passage of actual historical events has led to similar outcomes for both philosophers. Like Vattimo, Trías identified the return of religion as the great *novum* of the present age, something that strengthened his conviction that there exists a deeper substratum which precedes the linguistic. In fact, he explains in 'Thinking Religion', religion *is* this substratum: 'It has been shown, above all in the bitter Yugoslavian conflict, that the real "point of difference" in a culture, that which can give rise to the Hegelian "struggle to the death", is not language at all ... but religion'.[77]

At the same time, these kinds of geopolitical conflicts attest to the acute situation in which the crisis of reason has left us. Contrary to the modern dream of a uniform social order governed by reason, the end of the Cold War has paved the way for a world fragmented into a riot of unstable and frequently conflict-beset centres. From this perspective, the return of religion is anything but a good omen; typically religion tends to intensify the world's conflicts. But for this very reason it is a matter of urgency that we begin to concern ourselves with religion; that we begin to 'think religion' before religion, in Trías's words, '"thinks us" in its specifically extreme form'.[78] Here, however, thinking religion does not mean, as it does for a certain strand of modern philosophy, reducing religion to superstition. It is, rather, a question of saving religion for what it is – 'the human's natural or connatural orientation towards the sacred'.[79] In other words, it is about saving religion simultaneously from a too-narrowly defined reason *and* from religion itself in its dogmatic and violent manifestations. All of which comes back to Trías's concept of a 'religion of the spirit', a critical horizon capable of taking us beyond the geopolitical conflicts of the present: 'It would, in fact, be a matter of combining the civilization of *reason* – which is general and uniform in its character – with the culture of *symbolic versatility* in all its various expressions and manifestations. Such is the *horizon* at this turn of the century, a horizon that may offer an alternative to the disquieting perspectives of widespread civil war, discriminate violence, or a growing inequality between different societies.'[80]

Is this not, once again, the Romantics' vision of a higher age in which freedom is united with order, and myth with reason? Like Vattimo, Trías makes no secret of his intellectual influences here and in the paragraph which follows indicates that it is perhaps a question of preparing for 'the emergence of a new religion: the true *religion of the spirit* already prophesied in the twelfth century by the Calabrian abbot Joachim of Fiore, and invoked afresh by Novalis and Schelling in the century of romanticism and idealism'.[81] Romantic influences are also present in *La edad del espíritu*, in which Trías portrays Romanticism as the great exception to the process of disenchantment that has been taking place during Western modernity. He sees Schelling in particular as the philosopher who, more clearly than any other, saw through the illusion of a self-grounding reason and thereby anticipated the synthesis between reason and its suppressed other that Trías predicts for the end of modernity. In the late

Schelling's philosophy of religion, he also finds an exact model for his own odyssey through the history of the emergence of reason from the great mythological traditions.[82]

Even so, Trías permitted himself a 'correction' of Schelling which, though slight, is not insignificant in this context. The correction relates to Schelling's view of the relation between myth and revelation, in which Schelling understood myth as a natural and unconscious revelation that only gained full and unifying expression with the Christian revelation.

> On the contrary, I believe that all mythology is already in itself revelation. A polycentric revelation that neither converges to nor diverges from any particular 'positive' religion.... As a matter of fact, revelation is already taking place in all the great religions and in their corresponding mythological cycles. In this sense, every religion constitutes a fragment, always necessary, of the religious event; a fragmentary piece of the great revelation that has its premise in the distinct messages revealed by each of these fractional samples that constitute the various positive religions.[83]

What Trías unambiguously states here is a refusal to privilege the Christian tradition over the other religious traditions. In contrast to Vattimo, he is careful to avoid making any kind of exclusive connection between the origins of his emancipatory vision and any one particular historical tradition; instead, each individual religion is presented as a fragment of 'the great textual web that constitutes the religious event in its entirety'.[84] It should also be noted that Trías avoids claiming to have narrowed down a universal philosophical core that would unite the different religious traditions. In a manner reminiscent of Schleiermacher's critique of the Enlightenment's abstract deism, Trías argues that religion has always only ever existed in and through its particular forms of expression. As was well known, this scepticism did not prevent Schleiermacher (any more than Novalis or Schelling) from ultimately choosing Christianity as the highest expression of religion. When Trías took up the Romantics' concept of a religion of the spirit, he wanted to go one stage further in this regard by mapping out a truly universal religion that would cut its privileged ties to the Christian West. The only question is whether the concept of 'religion' will allow itself to be disconnected quite so easily from the West in which it has originated.

Messianicity without Messianism

When Vattimo and Trías connected the notion of a redemptive series of historical events with the concept of the spirit, they inscribed themselves within a long tradition. Its embryo, as described in earlier chapters of this volume, already existed in the prophetic literature of antiquity, perhaps most clearly in Joel's prophesy of a time when the Lord would pour out his spirit over 'all flesh' (Joel 2:28–31). While the context makes clear that 'all flesh' in fact refers to the members of his own people, not humanity as such, the prophesy marks an important extension of the spirit's redemptive power: God's spiritual power would no longer be shared among only kings, warriors and wise men but would include young and old, men and women, enslaved and free. This generalization of redemption would assume central importance for how the early Christian movement understood itself, finding paradigmatic expression in the account of the pouring out of the spirit at the first Pentecost (Acts 2:1–13).

At the same time, a paradox hangs over this idea of redemption as having a continually widening scope, particularly when it is inserted into a temporal schema. It is as if the same spirit that explodes the boundaries of the existing community has to create new demarcations in order to raise itself up to new heights. The pattern is recognizable from the *adversus Iudaeos* tradition, in which the Christian church's claim to hold the keys to God's universal plan of salvation presupposed that the Jewish people were at the same time written out of the history of salvation. A thousand years later, Joachim of Fiore made a daring attempt to break down the church's restriction of the salvatory grace: not merely *populus gentilis* but also *populus iudaicus* would be included in the new outpouring of the spirit that would take place in the age of the spirit. Yet the dialectical pattern persisted even in Joachim's writings: ultimately, Jews would be welcomed into God's grace only after they had come to realize the truth of the Christian revelation. A few centuries later the pattern could be again discerned in Hegel's portrait of the journey of the spirit towards higher self-consciousness, which among many other things was a narrative of how the Jewish religion, trammelled by legalism and exclusivity, would have to be abandoned so that a truly free and civic religion – Prussian Protestantism – could be attained.

What happens to the Jew when Christianity is said to coincide with absolute truth? Derrida poses the question in 1974 in *Glas*, a deeply complex work containing, among other things, a comprehensive close reading of Hegel's early writings on the philosophy of religion. In a subtle fashion, Derrida outlines the way in which Hegel's ideas about family, love and ethical life are interwoven with the Christian religion, something that ultimately reveals itself as being the very matrix for the spirit's movements through history. Derrida affixes particular significance to the double function played by the family in Hegel's philosophy: on the one hand, as a specific element within the history of spirit; on the other, as a metaphorical model for the movement of history as such. The first function, Derrida explains, is expressed *inter alia* in Hegel's *Philosophy of Right* from the 1820s, which presents the loving Christian family as the seedbed from which 'ethical life' (*Sittlichkeit*) – the embodied ethics that Hegel contrasts with Kant's abstract 'morality' (*Moralität*) – springs. At the same time, this is merely a first stage. For ethical life to reach fulfilment, it is necessary that the father provides for his son's upbringing, education and, finally, departure from the family. Ethical life is in this way disseminated throughout civil society, whose principles are enshrined in turn in the state constitution.[85]

Hegel's philosophy of right is thus built upon an extended concept of the family – the private family is split up and attains perfection in the higher family comprised by civil society. It is precisely here that Derrida sees the second function of the family in Hegel's philosophy. The family is not merely part of the dialectic but also reveals in an emblematic fashion the pattern within the dialectical progression: the spirit reaches a higher degree of self-consciousness through the process in which the paterfamilias loses himself in his own offspring (the son) and becomes aware of himself as a citizen. The pattern is the same as that which Hegel identified in the Christian Trinity in his early philosophy of religion: God reveals himself first as a transcendent Father before emptying himself into the Son and finally being consummated in the Holy Spirit. The only difference is that the argument here is operating on an ontological – or, rather, ontotheological – level. In other words, the Christian Trinity in Hegel's philosophy is not merely an example of the dialectical progression of the spirit. Rather, Christianity has in a unique way shown itself to be the truth of existence: 'Just as German, the naturally speculative tongue, in certain of its truths relieves itself by itself in order to become the universal tongue, so a historically determinate religion becomes absolute religion'.[86]

Although *Glas* is a book about the family – 'Hegel's family', 'the concept of family according to Hegel' – it is equally a book about 'the bastard' (*le bâtard*), the figure who belongs to the family yet is rejected by it. 'Is there a place for the bastard in ontotheology or in the Hegelian family?'[87] Derrida invokes this rhetorical question as a way to direct attention towards the shadow narrative upon which Hegel's family philosophy is founded: when Hegel describes Christianity as the religion of the family, love and ethical life, he also devalues Judaism as the religion of law, fear and subordination. Like bastards, Judaism and Jews become the necessary antithesis which provides the basis for the Christian religion (and family). This is nowhere more evident, Derrida argues, than in Hegel's spiteful caricature of the patriarch Abraham in *The Spirit of Christianity and its Fate*. In Abraham, Hegel saw an archetype of the Jews' inability to be a part of moral, civic life. Abraham broke away from his forefathers by dreaming of complete freedom, only to instead end up in a relationship of utter dependency upon a violent and vengeful God. Abraham had created a family, admittedly, but it was a family which reflected the same relationship of fear and subordination as that between Israel and its God. Abraham was unable even to love his son, something that Hegel regarded as given paradigmatic figuration in both his circumcision and his near-complete sacrifice of Isaac: 'Both signify the curtailing, the cut, the transcendence, the absence or the subordination of love'.[88]

Just as a family sometimes needs illegitimacy in order to strengthen its sense of inner community, Hegel's speculative interpretation of Christianity needs this scurrilous portrait in order to achieve its full force. The loving God of Christianity is counterposed to the vengeful God of Judaism, the spirit of reconciliation to the dead letter of the law, and the inclusive community of the moral family to estrangement and fear. As John Caputo has observed, the problem with this gesture is not that it holds up Christianity as a religion of love and reconciliation – Christian theology is rich in resources to support such an interpretation. The problem is, rather, that this gesture results in a zero-sum game in which Judaism is permanently condemned to be the loser: 'God overcomes his alienated condition (= Judaism) in order to pitch his tent right here in Christian Prussia, or Christian Europe, or, let us say, more generally and more generously, the Christian West'.[89] Ultimately, the emancipatory movement of the spirit is only expressible within the metaphorical framework of Christianity.

Having sketched this background, let me now return to Vattimo's and Trías's contributions to the discussions at Capri. Derrida's critique of Hegel puts into particular perspective Vattimo's conflation of history's progressive developments and the *Wirkungsgeschichte* of Christian theology. Symptomatically, Vattimo also increases his emphasis upon the Christian Gospel's uniqueness by contrasting it with the image of God that he sees as characterizing the Old Testament and that he hears echoed in contemporary Jewish philosophers such as Levinas – and Derrida:

> In a certain sense, the God who at the end of the secularization process is recovered as wholly other is the God of the Old Testament (let me say this without any anti-Semitic implication), and not the God incarnate in Jesus Christ, of the New Testament revelation, and even less the God understood as spirit in the third age prophesied by Joachim of Fiore. The reference to Joachim clearly shows the radical difference between the position I am illustrating here and the one more common in contemporary culture, which understands the recovery of religion only as openness to the wholly other. I am thinking of the widespread influence of Emmanuel Levinas and of Derrida's deconstruction. In Joachim's terms, these positions go back to a theology of the first age, ignoring incarnation and consequently conceiving secularization as the fall in which God's transcendence as the wholly other can be revealed through a dialectical reversal. God's divinity would then consist in his radical alterity.[90]

It is not insignificant that Vattimo feels compelled in this context to disavow any kind of anti-Jewish intention. Understandably, the self-scrutinizing debates of the postwar years have made him acutely conscious of the dark side of Christianity's historico-theological tradition. It is presumably also in this light that Vattimo intends his listeners to understand the words that immediately follow the passage just quoted, in which he clarifies that the Christian tradition which he is so ardently defending in fact also *encompasses* the Jewish tradition: 'It is only in the hardening of dogmatic systems and church disciplines that the two souls of our tradition – Judaism and Christianity – are separated from and juxtaposed to each other'.[91]

Ironically, what Vattimo reveals here – through his declared sympathy for the Jewish tradition – is precisely the Achilles heel of the tradition that extends all the way from Joachim to idealism via Romanticism: an inability to acknowledge the value of Judaism in its own right. From the Old Testament to Derrida, the Jewish tradition remains a first stage in the journey of the spirit through history, a stage associated with transcendence, abstraction and alienation. Admittedly, in its more sympathetic manifestations – as in the work of Joachim, Schelling or Vattimo himself – Jews and the Jewish tradition are also included among the higher stages. Ultimately, however, it is always on the Christian tradition's terms, with the inevitable result that Christianity is presented as the quintessential framework of a genuinely inclusive, general or universal philosophy.

Trías's effort to separate 'the religion of spirit' from the primacy which Schelling ultimately accorded to Christianity represents an attempt to break free of this paradigm. But could this be done quite so easily? Is it not the case that merely by saying the word *religion* we are already speaking Latin? Derrida poses this very question in his own contribution to the Capri symposium, thereby subtly suggesting that the very idea of a truly universal religion, in both its origin and its purpose, is and will remain Christian in the broader sense of the word.[92] The question seems warranted when Trías's ambitious genealogy of the mythological roots of reason is considered. Even if Trías strives to present the different mythological traditions on similar terms, the very goal of approaching these different traditions in terms of religion already gives the game away – at least, if it turns out that the concept of 'religion' is not the empty and formal category that a certain established discourse has claimed, but is in fact impregnated with a series of characteristics revealing its affiliation with one particular tradition. If so, there might be included among these characteristics a certain idea about the origin and goal of religion, a fondness for triadic patterns and, last but not least, a conception of religion's progressive movement towards increasingly refined forms.[93]

To be fair, it must be pointed out that Trías explicitly rejects the term 'progression' in his survey of the great religious and philosophical traditions.[94] Nevertheless, he presents the history of religion as a gigantic teleological process whose later phases are deemed richer than the earlier ones. This pattern is reflected not only in the overarching division of epochs in *La edad del espíritu* – in which, to simplify greatly, religion goes from being 'wild' and 'unbridled' to 'cosmic' and 'ordered' before finally moving towards a harmonious synthesis of both aspects – but also at the level of his specific claims, as when he argues, in a commentary on the Christian notion of God's incarnation, that 'the atoning character of the messianic figure in Deutero-Isaiah is [here] radicalized'.[95] Not unlike Vattimo, Trías here seems to presuppose that the Jewish revelation is a less-developed original of the Christian, and both philosophers show very little interest in the continuing Jewish tradition. Both philosophers also share a seemingly unshakeable belief that history is gradually moving towards a fulfilment of the redemptive potential inherent in religion, notwithstanding the fact that Trías does not explicitly connect this potential to Christianity. Nor does either Vattimo or Trías seek to gloss over the sinister aspects of this process; both philosophers, as has been described above, offer a substantial critique of civilization. Nonetheless, these aspects ultimately tend to be represented as unavoidable stages on the way to a brighter future associated with the age of the spirit.

In his contribution to the conversation at Capri, Derrida strikes a quite different tone. Perhaps this is most easily explained by the fact that Derrida's entire life project, as Fredric Jameson once observed, can be seen as an attempt to demystify the strain of idealism that largely continues to define European philosophy.[96] *Glas* is illuminating in this respect, of course, but it should also be noted that Derrida was generally hesitant about the entire conceptual apparatus upon which idealism rests. This is especially true of the concept of the spirit. Interestingly, the book in which Derrida grapples with this concept at greatest length – *Of Spirit*, published in 1987 – is an attack on Heidegger, the philosopher who, more than any other, shaped his own critique of idealism. In order to demonstrate the concept's seductive power, it is nonetheless worth tracing its progress though Heidegger's writings. Derrida accordingly notes how the terms *Geist* and *geistig* were practically excluded from Heidegger's early philosophical works, but – significantly – began proliferating wildly in his political writings of the 1930s (above all in his notorious Rector's Speech of 1933) before receding again in his mature poetico-philosophical writings.[97]

Although the spirit concept signifies development, presence or, as in Heidegger's darker moments, the 'unyielding spiritual mission that forces the fate of the German people to bear the stamp of its history',[98] it is perhaps not so strange that Derrida, in his later writings, choses the philosopheme *ghost* instead of *spirit*.[99] In stark contrast to the spirit's steady if eventful development through history, Derrida's ghosts indicate that the time is out of joint and that presence is never as self-evident as it claims to be. This hesitancy about the spirit concept may also explain why Derrida articulates his vision of a new religion in terms of the messianic, rather than in the form of a 'religion of the spirit'. However, in order to grasp the subtle differences in how the messianic and the pneumatic motifs take concrete form in the Capri conversations, it is important to note that Derrida, despite his critical reservations, also shares the conviction that we can no more avoid the concept of religion than we can avoid the Western tradition which created it. In fact, Derrida aligns himself with perhaps the most famous of all Western attempts to get to grips with religion – Kant's ambition to think religion 'within the limits of reason alone'.[100]

Yet it is this very 'Kantian gesture' which allows Derrida to make critically visible a pattern that has seemingly escaped Vattimo and Trías – how the universal tends to merge with the Christian. When Kant critically ranked the different religions with regard to their moral-philosophical value, he naturally concluded that Christianity was the only true moral religion. Like no other religion, Christianity demonstrated the most important insight of practical philosophy, that the one unconditionally good thing is a 'good will'. At the same time, this very insight tended to make Christianity redundant as a *religion*. For Kant, Christian theology did not stand or fall with any specific historical revelation, which was why the element of Christianity that warranted preservation could ultimately be summarized by the postulates of practical reason. Like Hegel, Kant sublated religion into his own philosophy, which was another way of saying that true philosophy represented a higher form of Christianity. In his contribution at Capri Derrida coins the term 'globalatinization' (*mondialatinisation*) as a way of referring to this generalized form of Christianity, and he argues – in an allusion to Max Weber's famous thesis – that it is this 'alliance of Christianity, as the experience of the death of God, and tele-technoscientific capitalism' that subtly underpins the global dominance of the Christian West.[101]

Although the target of his critique is unmistakeable, Derrida aims, as always, at more than merely dismissing the line of argument that he is problematizing. There is thus both a seriousness and an honesty in his opening admission of affinity with the Enlightenment tradition and Kant's critical philosophy. It is in this light, too, that his attempt to repeat the Kantian gesture of thinking religion within the limits of reason alone should be understood. Like the other participants in the symposium, Derrida is concerned at the return of religion in the form of violence and extremism, and he professes

> an unreserved taste, if not an unconditional preference, for what, in politics, is called republican democracy as a universalizable model, binding philosophy to the public 'cause', to the *res publica*, to 'public-ness', once again to the light of day, once again to the 'lights' of the Enlightenment [*aux Lumières*], once again to the enlightened virtue of public space, emancipating it from all external power (non-lay, non-secular), for example from religious dogmatism, orthodoxy or authority (that is, from a certain rule of the *doxa* or of belief, which, however, does not mean from all faith).[102]

How, then, might it be possible to repeat this Kantian gesture without repeating its exclusionary aspect? How might it be possible to defend Kant's attempt to formulate a truly universal religion without immediately falling back on the Christian paradigm? To some extent the answer had already been given in *Specters of Marx*: by saving a particular spirit of religion – the prophetic tradition to which Marx arguably also belonged – which could then be directed critically against both religion in its dogmatic manifestations and a certain no less dogmatic Enlightenment tradition (whence Derrida's not insignificant remark in the quotation given above, that emancipation from *doxa* is not synonymous with the expulsion of all faith). In other words, it is by virtue of this more abstract spirit that it might be possible to rise above the exclusionary aspects of those concrete traditions and formulate a 'universalizable culture of singularities'.[103]

This touches upon a theme that recurred in a variety of forms in Derrida's philosophy in the years around the Capri seminar. In *Force of Law*, originally a series of lectures given in 1989–1990, he articulates this theme in terms of a productive tension between a deconstructible law (*droit*) and an undeconstructible justice (*justice*), by means of which he argues that our existing legal principles should be continually tested against a notion of justice that never allows itself to be reduced to any given system of justice.[104] In *The Gift of Death*, which appeared in 1999, a similar tension can be discerned when Derrida crosses swords with the Czech phenomenologist Jan Patočka. More precisely, Derrida shows how Patočka's genealogy of the notion of the human as a responsible subject has emerged from the Platonic-Christian tradition, commenting that on the face of it Patočka seems to be improperly propagandizing for a Christian view of humanity in phenomenological guise. Such is not the case, however. Although Patočka's concept of the responsible subject has been generated by a Christian theology of revelation, his deduction is none the less valid despite this particular revelation. Patočka thus illustrates a key phenomenon, namely that it is possible to repeat and refine certain structural elements of religious revelation (its idea of the responsible subject, its messianic hope, its faith in imminent justice, etc.) without thereby having to profess one's adherence to any particular dogma relating to the revelation in question. Derrida describes this phenomenon (which he also regards as characteristic of other thinkers in the phenomenological tradition, from Levinas to Paul Ricœur and Jean-Luc Marion) as a 'nondogmatic doublet of dogma', a mode of thinking which '"repeats" the possibility of religion without religion'.[105]

In corresponding fashion, Derrida coins the phrase 'messianicity without messianism' (*messianicité sans messianisme*) in his Capri presentation. 'Messianism' here is a metaphor for definite historical revelations, while 'messianicity' or 'the messianic' refers to a kind of formal structure that supersedes any particular religious revelation. Using rhetoric reminiscent of *Specters of Marx*, Derrida describes the messianic in terms of an 'opening to the future', an 'experience of faith' or 'an invincible desire for justice'. Yet these words should not be understood in a substantial or fixed sense. Derrida is not presenting a vision that relates to content, nor is this a matter of regulative ideals in line with Kant's ideas. As in *Force of Law*, the justice referred to here should be 'distinguished from right'; similarly, the striving for imminent justice is described as 'without horizon of expectation and without prophetic prefiguration'.[106] To further underscore the abstract, barren nature of what he means by the messianic, Derrida at this point choses to invoke *chora*, a concept taken from Plato's *Timaeus* that played a central role in his thinking around the time of the symposium.[107] *Chora*, like the messianic, lies outside any particular tradition, place or historical revelation; it would 'never permit itself to be sacralized, sanctified, humanized, theologized, cultivated, historicized' but denotes, rather, 'the very place of an infinite resistance'.[108]

Clearly, then, Derrida's attempt to repeat Kant's gesture does not lead to some well-defined, universal religion of reason. Rather, he takes the critical dissection of religion by reason to an extreme, to the point where only a series of critical neighbouring concepts (justice, messianicity, *chora*) remain. Only this 'desertification' of religion is capable of freeing a 'universal rationality' that makes it possible to rise above the violent potential of any particular religion. But are we not thereby lapsing back into the Enlightenment's totalizing universalism, one that excludes all faith even as it turns a blind eye to its own roots in a very specific theological tradition? Is Derrida not in fact repeating Marx's mistake of chasing away far too many ghosts, far too quickly? Derrida sees the temptation, a temptation to which not only Marx but also Kant, Hegel, and Heidegger succumbed. Each treated the historical religions as contingent expressions of a more general ontological structure which they claimed in their various ways to have captured in their philosophies. But is it really possible to capture this ontological structure, unaffected by religion's particular manifestations? It is here that Derrida's (self-)doubt sets in, a doubt that is evident in his Capri presentation and that he would formulate more extensively at a seminar at Villanova University in Pennsylvania later that year:

> The problem remains – and this is really a problem for me, an enigma – whether the religions, say, for instance, the religions of the Book, are but specific examples of this general structure, of messianicity. There is the general structure of messianicity, as the structure of experience, and on this groundless ground there have been religions, a history which one calls Judaism or Christianity and so on. That is a possibility, and then you would have a Heideggerian gesture, in style. You would have to go back from these religions to the fundamental ontological conditions of possibilities of religions, to describe the structure of messianicity on the groundless ground on which religions have been made possible. That is one hypothesis. The other hypothesis – and I confess that I hesitate between these two possibilities – is that the events of revelation, the biblical traditions, the Jewish, Christian, and Islamic traditions, have been absolute events, irreducible events which have unveiled this messianicity. We would not know what messianicity is without messianism, without these events which were Abraham, Moses, and Jesus Christ, and so on. In that case singular events would have unveiled or revealed these universal possibilities, and it is only on that condition that we can describe messianicity.[109]

Derrida returns on several occasions to this 'aporia',[110] yet never succumbs to the temptation to give one hypothesis priority over the other. On the contrary – and this is also the conclusion reached in his Capri presentation – he suggests that it is 'the respect for this singular indecision' which ultimately represents 'the chance of every responsible decision and of another "reflecting faith", of a new "tolerance"'.[111]

It is thus with important reservations that Derrida repeats Kant's gesture of thinking religion within the limits of reason alone. This is not because he ever wishes to declare reason finished; we have merely to remind ourselves that reason is never pure: that it is, for better or for worse, bound up with a faith that cannot be entirely separated from the religion for which reason seeks to establish limits. Put differently, it is a question of preserving the universal impulse of the Enlightenment tradition, without losing one's critical focus upon the particular tradition from which the universal is ultimately articulated.

By way of conclusion, let me return to the various ghosts and spirits which haunted the discussions at Capri. If Derrida was evasive about talk of a religion of the spirit, it was in all likelihood because he was sceptical about the kind of philosophy of history with which such talk is bound up. From Joachim of Fiore to German Romanticism, such talk has been underpinned by a theology (and thus an implicit teleology) which presents history as a steady if conflict-riven development towards gradual redemption. It was precisely this notion that Derrida challenged in *Specters of Marx* and, indeed, his entire philosophy. To quote Fredric Jameson yet again: 'Derrida's ghosts are these moments in which the present – and above all our current present, the wealthy, sunny, gleaming world of the postmodern and the end of history, of the new world system of late capitalism – unexpectedly betrays us'.[112] If Derrida preferred ghosts to spirits, it was thus because he feared that justice, our acute responsibility to the present, would be the ultimate victim as the spirit unfolded in the world as 'history'.

This is also the context in which Derrida's preference for the messianic over the pneumatic should be understood. With his strong conviction that justice demands that the time be out of joint, continually troubled by those who are not there, Derrida not only recalled Walter Benjamin's famous description of the messianic chips lying embedded in every instant of time's seemingly homogenous passage;[113] he also inscribed himself, albeit indirectly and perhaps unconsciously, in an older messianism that can be traced back to parts of rabbinic Judaism. This refers to that strand of anti-apocalypticism which sees in incomplete redemption a strength rather than a weakness: with the Messiah's continually deferred arrival, humanity's focus is instead directed towards its vocation of carrying out the work of justice in the world at all times.

Returning to the distinction between pneumatic and messianic motifs, it may be noted that a philosophy of history based on the idea of the presence of the spirit need not necessarily lead to apocalyptic and utopian visions. Quite the contrary. As illustrated in Chapter Two, there are obvious parallels between major strands within rabbinic messianism and the efforts of early Christian theology to legitimize Jesus's delayed return by means of reference to the spirit. The spirit here appears as a divine principle helping Christians to answer God's summons in the world – not as a call to leave the world behind. Joachim, too, can be seen in this light. Despite the demonstrably apocalyptical elements in his rhetoric, what he describes is by and large an anti-utopian vision; the *status* of the spirit signals, in other words, not the final goal of history in the form of a heavenly kingdom on earth, but a spiritual deepening of the present time.

This brief retrospective has enabled the identification of both an important similarity and an important difference between Vattimo and Trías on the one hand, and Derrida on the other. All three philosophers can be described as anti-utopian in an important sense. Just as Derrida rejects the notion that messianic justice might ever be attained, so, too, do Vattimo and Trías exclude the possibility that the age of the spirit ever be wholly realized. This conviction is ably expressed in the concluding pages of *La edad del espíritu* when Trías uses the image of a horizon that recedes even as we try to approach it.[114] And yet this very image encapsulates the crucial difference between these thinkers. Admittedly, Vattimo and Trías describe a horizon that recedes, but their image nonetheless suggests that we are moving, slowly but surely, towards a brighter future. Derrida is dubious about this image, partly because it tends to obscure the fact that as we approach one horizon, another is often darkening, but also because the messianic event demands 'a certain absence of horizon'. Justice, in other words, can never be calculated from a fixed horizon, but involves circumstances that are not foreseeable, among them the risk that, despite our best intentions, we might ultimately betray justice.[115]

Notes

1. H.-G. Gadamer. 1998. 'Dialogues in Capri', trans. J. Gaiger, in J. Derrida and G. Vattimo (eds), *Religion*, Cambridge: Polity Press, 208.
2. Ibid., 207.
3. Ibid.
4. I. Berlin. 1999. *The Roots of Romanticism: The A. W. Mellon Lectures in the Fine Arts, 1965*, ed. H. Hardy, London: Chatto and Windus, 34–40.
5. A. Olsson. 2000. *Läsningar av INTET*, Stockholm: Albert Bonniers Förlag, 17 (Eng. trans. by S. Donovan).
6. Hegel/Hölderlin/Schelling, 'Oldest Programme', 185.
7. Safranski, *Romanticism*, 115–116.
8. Berlin, *Roots of Romanticism*, 119.
9. Ibid., 145.
10. Ibid., 118, 127.
11. Ibid., 34–39.
12. G. Lukács. 1980. *The Destruction of Reason*, trans. P. Palmer, London: The Merlin Press, 11.
13. E. Voegelin. 2006. *Hitler and the Germans*, ed. and trans. D. Clemens and B. Purcell, Columbia and London: University of Missouri Press, 88. See also Novalis, *Schriften*, vol. 2, 554.
14. Voegelin, *Hitler*, 87–88.
15. Voegelin, *The New Science of Politics*, 107–132.
16. Ibid., 117–121.
17. Ibid., 112–113.
18. Ibid., 113.
19. Cf. e.g. Bloch, *Heritage*, 122–128; Taubes, *Occidental Eschatology*, 85–122; Lasky, *Utopia and Revolution*, 18–22; and N. Cohn. 1993. *The Pursuit of the Millennium: Revolutionary Millenarians and Mystical Anarchists of the Middle Ages*, London: Pimlico, 108–110. Of these authors only Bloch seems to have had any direct contact with Joachim's works, something which can partly be explained by the inaccessibility of the works (even today).

20. The latter question is not explicitly articulated in *Meaning in History*, but in several articles, e.g. K. Löwith. 1995. 'The Occasional Decisionism of Carl Schmitt', trans. G. Steiner, in R. Wolin (ed.), *Martin Heidegger and European Nihilism*, New York: Columbia University Press, 271–285.

21. K. Löwith. 1949. *Meaning in History*, Chicago and London: University of Chicago Press, 4.

22. Ibid., 60–114.

23. Ibid., 159.

24. See further H. Blumenberg. 1983. *The Legitimacy of the Modern Age*, trans. R.M. Wallace. Cambridge: The MIT Press. The so-called Löwith–Blumenberg debate is discussed further in J. Svenungsson. 2014. 'A Secular Utopia: Remarks on the Löwith–Blumenberg Debate', in E. Namli, J. Svenungsson and A. Vincent (eds), *Jewish Thought, Utopia and Revolution*, Amsterdam and New York: Rodopi, 69–84.

25. See e.g. R. Aron. 1955. *L'opium des intellectuels*, Paris: Calmann-Lévy; J.N. Shklar. 1957. *After Utopia: The Decline of Political Faith*, Princeton: Princeton University Press; D. Bell. 1960. *The End of Ideology: On the Exhaustion of Political Ideas in the Fifties*, New York: Free Press.

26. Safranski, *Romanticism*, 258–260.

27. See F.S. Saunders. 2000. *Who Paid the Piper? The CIA and the Cultural Cold War*, 2nd edn, London: Granta.

28. See e.g. Lasky, *Utopia and Revolution* (published in 1976).

29. Novalis, *Writings*, 148.

30. J. Derrida. 1994. *Specters of Marx: The State of the Debt, the Work of Mourning, and the New International*, trans. P. Kamuf, New York and London: Routledge, xviii.

31. Ibid., 39.

32. Ibid., 51–52.

33. Ibid., 80.

34. Ibid., 81–84.

35. Ibid., 45–47.

36. Ibid., 103–105, 159–164.

37. M. Sprinker. 1999. 'Introduction', in idem (ed.), *Ghostly Demarcations: A Symposium on Jacques Derrida's Specters of Marx*, London and New York: Verso, 2.

38. Derrida, *Specters of Marx*, 166–167.

39. Löwith, *Meaning in History*, 33–51.

40. Derrida, *Specters of Marx*, 89.

41. Ibid., 174.

42. See further G. Vattimo. 1998. 'Circumstances', trans. D. Webb, in Derrida and Vattimo (eds), *Religion*, vii–viii.

43. E. Trías, 1998. 'Thinking Religion: The Symbol and the Sacred', trans. D. Webb, in Derrida and Vattimo (eds), *Religion*, 99–100.

44. Novalis, *Writings*, 150.

45. See J. Derrida, 1998. 'Faith and Knowledge: The Two Sources of "Religion" at the Limits of Reason Alone', trans. S. Weber, in Derrida and Vattimo (eds), *Religion*, 8.

46. Gadamer, 'Dialogues', 207.

47. See M. Heidegger. 2002. *Off the Beaten Track*, ed. and trans. J. Young and K. Haynes, New York and Cambridge: Cambridge University Press, 157–199.

48. I am here primarily referring to Heidegger's late essay 'The Onto-theo-logical Constitution of Metaphysics', in M. Heidegger. 1969. *Identity and Difference*, trans. J. Stambaugh. Chicago: University of Chicago Press, 42–74.

49. G. Vattimo. 1998. 'The Trace of the Trace', trans. D. Webb, in Derrida and Vattimo (eds), *Religion*, 84.

50. Ibid., 82.

51. See G. Vattimo. 2012. 'Dialectics, Difference, Weak Thought', in P.A. Rovatti and G. Vattimo (eds), *Weak Thought*, trans. P. Carravetta, Albany: State University of New York Press, 39–52.
52. Vattimo, 'The Trace', 88.
53. Ibid., 92–93.
54. G. Vattimo. 1997. *Beyond Interpretation*, trans. D. Webb, Cambridge: Polity Press, 50.
55. See G. Vattimo (with P. Paterlini). 2009. *Not Being God: A Collaborative Autobiography*, trans. W. McCuaig, New York: Columbia University Press, 149–152.
56. G. Vattimo. 1999. *Belief*, trans. L. D'Isanto and D. Webb, Stanford: Stanford University Press, 28–38 (the Italian original appeared in 1996).
57. Vattimo, *Beyond Interpretation*, 48–49. Cf. also idem. 2002. *After Christianity*, trans. L. D'Isanto, New York: Columbia University Press, 25–39, and idem, *Not Being God*, 145–146.
58. See further Vattimo, *After Christianity*, 25–39; 57–68.
59. See Vattimo, *Beyond Interpretation*, 49; idem, *After Christianity*, 9, 32–36, 69–82.
60. See Vattimo, 'The Trace', 92. When Vattimo published the autobiography *Not Being God*, in 2006, he appears to have been less optimistic about the future.
61. Vattimo, *After Christianity*, 26–27.
62. Ibid., 98–102.
63. Vattimo, *Belief*, 47.
64. Vattimo, *Beyond Interpretation*, 29.
65. G. Vattimo. 2003 *Nihilism and Emancipation: Ethics, Politics, and Law*, trans. W. McCuaig, New York: Columbia University Press, 94.
66. Vattimo, *Beyond Interpretation*, 1–14.
67. Vattimo, 'The Trace', 92.
68. See e.g. ibid., 92–93; Vattimo, *Beyond Interpretation*, 47–48; Vattimo, *After Christianity*, 80–82, 90–91.
69. Trías, 'Thinking Religion', 99–102.
70. For an overview of these debates, see e.g. G. D'Costa. 2005. 'Theology of Religion', in D.F. Ford (ed.), *The Modern Theologians: An Introduction to Christian Theology since 1918*, 3rd edn, Oxford: Blackwell Publishing, 626–644.
71. E. Trías. 2006. *La edad del espíritu*, 2nd edn, Barcelona: Debolsillo, 33–57. Cf. also Trías, 'Thinking Religion', 102–106.
72. Trías, *La edad del espíritu*, 139–188.
73. Ibid., 411–450.
74. E. Trías. 1997. *Pensar la religión*, Barcelona: Destino, 55–56 (Eng. trans. by the author).
75. Ibid., 35–36.
76. Ibid., 36 (Eng. trans. by the author).
77. Trías, 'Thinking Religion', 100.
78. Trías, *Pensar la religión*, 37 (Eng. trans. by the author).
79. Ibid., 37–38 (Eng. trans. by the author).
80. Ibid., 67–68 (Eng. trans. by the author).
81. Ibid., 68 (Eng. trans. by the author). See also Trías, 'Thinking Religion', 99.
82. Trías, *La edad del espíritu*, 223; 495–514.
83. Trías, *Pensar la religión* , 22–23 (Eng. trans. by the author).
84. Ibid., 23 (Eng. trans. by the author).
85. J. Derrida. 1986. *Glas*, trans. J.P. Leavey and R. Rand, Lincoln and London: University of Nebraska Press, 4–18.
86. Ibid., 32.
87. Ibid., 6.
88. Ibid., 42.
89. J.D. Caputo. 2007. 'Spectral Hermeneutics: On the Weakness of God and the Theology of the Event', in J.W. Robbins (ed.), *After the Death of God*, New York: Columbia University Press, 69.

90. Vattimo, *After Christianity*, 37. Cf. idem, 'The Trace', 92–93.
91. Vattimo, *After Christianity*, 38.
92. Derrida, 'Faith and Knowledge', 14, 26–29.
93. See also T. Masuzawa. 2005. *The Invention of World Religions: Or, How European Universalism Was Preserved in the Language of Pluralism*, Chicago and London: University of Chicago Press.
94. See Trías, *La edad del espíritu*, 541.
95. Trías, *Pensar la religión*, 25 (Eng. trans. by the author).
96. F. Jameson. 1999. 'Marx's Purloined Letter', in M. Sprinker (ed.), *Ghostly Demarcations: A Symposium on Jacques Derrida's Specters of Marx*, London and New York: Verso, 50.
97. See J. Derrida. 1989. *Of Spirit: Heidegger and the Question*, trans. G. Bennington and R. Bowlby, Chicago: University of Chicago Press.
98. M. Heidegger. 1985. 'The Self-Assertion of the German University', trans. K. Harries, *Review of Metaphysics* 38:3, 470.
99. See Jameson, 'Marx's Purloined Letter', 36.
100. Derrida, 'Faith and Knowledge', 8.
101. Ibid., 13.
102. Ibid., 8.
103. Ibid., 18.
104. See further J. Derrida. 2002. 'Force of Law: The "Mystical Foundation of Authority"', trans. M. Quaintance, in E. Anidjar (ed.), *Acts of Religion*, London and New York: Routledge, 230–298.
105. J. Derrida. 1995. *The Gift of Death*, trans. D. Wills, Chicago and London: University of Chicago Press, 49.
106. Derrida, 'Faith and Knowledge', 17–18.
107. See J. Derrida. 1995. 'Khôra', trans. I. McLeod, in T. Dutoit (ed.), *On the Name*, Stanford: Stanford University Press, 89–130.
108. Derrida, 'Faith and Knowledge', 21.
109. J. Derrida. 1997. 'The Villanova Roundtable: A Conversation with Jacques Derrida', in J.D. Caputo (ed.), *Deconstruction in a Nutshell: A Conversation with Jacques Derrida*, New York: Fordham University Press, 23–24.
110. See J. Derrida. 1993. *Aporias: Dying – Awaiting (One Another at) the 'Limits of Truth'*, trans. T. Dutoit, Stanford: Stanford University Press.
111. Derrida, 'Faith and Knowledge', 21.
112. Jameson, 'Marx's Purloined Letter', 39.
113. W. Benjamin. 1999. *Illuminations*, trans. H. Zorn. London: Pimlico, 255.
114. Trías, *La edad del espíritu*, 541–542.
115. Derrida, 'Faith and Knowledge', 7.

CHAPTER 5

The Politics of History

In the early 1990s, the British theologian John Milbank made a name for himself with a controversial book entitled *Theology and Social Theory: Beyond Secular Reason*. In strident tones Milbank declared that the social theories which had propped up Western modernity were in fact 'theologies or antitheologies in disguise'.[1] Today, twenty-five years later, few will be provoked by such rhetoric. If anything, it is quite the reverse. In a *New Yorker* article published in 2009, James Wood called for a 'theologically engaged atheism', a phrase cited approvingly by Simon Critchley in a work published in 2012 under a hardly less controversial title, *The Faith of the Faithless: Experiments in Political Theology*.[2]

Between Milbank's and Critchley's books, a series of geopolitical upheavals, if not seismic shifts, had intervened. These epochal events included, of course, the attacks on the World Trade Center in New York on 11 September 2001, Islamist acts of terror that were quickly followed by a vicious circle of escalating political violence fuelled by religious rhetoric, in which 'the war on terror' continually revealed itself as based upon premises that differed only slightly from those of the religious terror it was intended to combat.[3] All this was compounded by a politically aware and increasingly influential strand of religious fundamentalism in Israel and by a newfound fascination in the trappings and symbols of Christianity among far-Right parties in Europe.

The picture that emerges here points to something important: like it or not, it has become increasingly difficult to analyse our current political reality without a knowledge of religion. Indeed, the only question is whether it has ever been possible to analyse political reality without a critical awareness of its covert theological premises. This was precisely the question that John Milbank tried to examine in his four-hundred-page study. And it is perhaps

---

Notes for this section begin on page 198.

here that the real seismic shift in the history of ideas of the last few decades has occurred. While the modern self-image of the West has largely assumed that politics is an autonomous sphere, separate from religion, leading political philosophers have recently posed the critical question of whether politics – consciously or unconsciously – is, in fact, always reliant upon norms and values that are not based upon politics itself.

This shift sheds light on contemporary philosophy's ever-growing interest in theological tropes. It is no exaggeration to say that the conversations that took place at Capri twenty years ago were merely the beginning of a debate that is still ongoing and that has been enhanced by the addition of a range of new voices. An interesting incident in this regard was the joint statement issued by Derrida and Jürgen Habermas in the years following the attacks on the Twin Towers. Those familiar with the 1980s debates over postmodernism will know that, at the time, Derrida and Habermas represented two diametrically opposed positions. Given this particular circumstance, it was widely regarded as a powerful gesture when both philosophers, in response to the invasion of Iraq in 2003, issued a joint appeal for European advocacy of 'a cosmopolitan order on the basis of international law' in order to counter the 'hegemonic unilateralism of the United States'. Their appeal brought together the arguments which the two philosophers had made in interviews given jointly in New York in the days immediately following the 11 September attacks, in which they had urged the necessity of a critical appraisal of Europe's unique political tradition.[4]

As the first decade of the new millennium wore on, Habermas, in whose thinking religion had hitherto not played a noticeable part, emerged as an influential voice in the debate over what he himself had termed 'a post-secular society'. Without downplaying his own conviction as to the necessity of a secular state, he repeatedly called for a renewed discussion of the 'pre-political' values which ultimately sustained democratic liberal states. In a number of settings – including his famous public dialogue with Joseph Ratzinger in autumn 2004 – he has also emphasized that the great religious traditions represent an inexhaustible source of such pre-political values.[5]

While Derrida and Habermas were united in their fundamentally Left-liberal stance – what Derrida in his Capri presentation called 'an unreserved taste ... for what, in politics, is called republican democracy as a universalizable model'[6] – their positions have in recent years been challenged by an explicitly anti-liberal Left whose leading lights are, among others, Giorgio Agamben, Alain Badiou and Slavoj Žižek. Drawing inspiration from such ostensibly disparate figures as Rousseau and Carl Schmitt, these philosophers have directed a series of powerful polemics against the liberal capitalist world order. It should be noted, of course, that both Habermas and the philosophers who participated in the Capri symposium were also strongly critical of the capitalist world order. Nevertheless, there is a watershed between the former and the latter groupings, as regards both the basis for their critiques and the proposed way forward. This watershed is perhaps best articulated by Žižek's provocative formulation, 'democracy is not to come, but to go' – pointedly directed at Derrida's indefatigable talk of 'a democracy to come'.[7]

This distinction will be discussed further below. For now, I wish merely to clarify this watershed somewhat. While Derrida, to the very end, was careful to defend liberal democracy as the least bad among existing forms of government, Žižek and the other philosophers mentioned above have expressed a growing dissatisfaction with parliamentary democracy as such. In light of how 'democracy as a universalizable model' has been *de facto* compromised during the 2000s – with the invasion of Iraq, Guantánamo Bay, Abu Ghraib – they have called for a more far-reaching critical discussion of the very premises of political debate. This also explains the attraction which a figure such as Carl Schmitt holds for several of these philosophers. Despite his notorious involvement with Nazism, Schmitt has turned out to offer considerable resources for a radicalized critique of parliamentary liberalism. Like few others, Schmitt captured the inherent failings of a system in which every political decision must ultimately be justified by the constitution itself. Schmitt's critique, whose immediate target was the weak governments of the Weimar Republic, speaks directly to our own postpolitical situation. Then as now, liberal democracies have tended to become snarled up in the political merry-go-round, incapable of acting in a world in which fundamental human values are continually disregarded.

In a series of widely discussed works, these contemporary philosophers have sought to break this deadlock by focusing attention upon theology as a potential resource for political thought. Interestingly, each of the historico-theological motifs examined in the present study has featured in this renewed politico-theological debate. The aim of this concluding chapter is to offer a deeper critical discussion of these three motifs by putting their current figurations into a dialogue with the historical background outlined in the preceding chapters. Once again, the selection of writers will be restricted, namely to Badiou, Agamben and Žižek. Each of these three philosophers has played a prominent part in an extended philosophical debate over the apostle Paul and his works that has been taking place over last decade. In this critical reading of these debates, I will clarify my own position and return to my starting question about the politico-philosophical value of the biblical tradition. The messianic, pneumatic and prophetic motifs will be considered in turn, in order to steadily narrow down what may be regarded as the enduring value of these far from unproblematic philosophical tropes in the Western historico-philosophical tradition.

Towards a Materialist Messianism

In recent decades European societies have rapidly become more multicultural on the ground while becoming less multicultural in attitude. This candid verdict was delivered some years ago by the American historian of ideas Mark Lilla. In light of the rapid accession of anti-immigrant parties to practically every parliament in Europe, the claim is hard to deny. Yet Lilla's comment was not primarily directed towards the newfound vigour of xenophobia in Europe. Instead, his polemic was targeted at European philosophy's rejection of the twentieth century's emphasis upon difference, pluralism and particularity, in favour of new politico-philosophical movements with universalistic qualities.[8]

Lilla's polemic could be countered by the claim that there were good grounds for renewed talk of universal political values. When one considers the actual developments of European societies in the last few decades, it is clear that identity politics and the promotion of particular rights have often been anything but the best means of furthering integration. The best of intentions have sometimes resulted in increased segregation, further eroding vital societal conversation about overarching values.

The philosopher who has perhaps most forcefully criticized liberal society's failure to unite people beyond particular identities is Alain Badiou. In one of the most obstinate recent analyses of contemporary culture, Badiou has acutely captured the cynical interaction between a wide range of identity politics and a market that systematically profits from our relentless pursuit of our own special interests. Cultural relativism has shown itself to fit hand in glove with capitalist market logic. While the latter needs to simulate diversity in order to conceal an underlying homogenization, the former gratefully welcomes all financial support for the promotion of local identities. In the process a boundless market for economic exploitation has come into existence. For every new identity there is a special magazine, for every new oppressed group a new 'free' radio station – in short, for every new subculture a new body of consumers. The devastating result is an ongoing collapse of public space in which no-one any longer considers anything really true. All that counts is that things sell, or that one's own identity is preserved.[9]

It is in the context of this politico-economic development that Badiou and an array of other philosophers have raised the question of a new universalism, a renewed public conversation about what unites people rather than what divides them. What is relevant for the present study is the extent to which this renewed conversation about the universal involves a *messianic* thematics, something that also accounts for the attraction which religion in general and Christianity in particular hold for these philosophers. In an era permeated by philosophical pessimism about the possibility of radical political change, the messianic element of religion presents unimagined possibilities.

While liberalism lulls people into pleasurable indifference towards the intrinsic injustice of capitalist society, the messianic hope has in all ages given people the courage to challenge the prevailing order. Of course, it should be noted that philosophers such as Badiou, Žižek and Agamben – all self-confessed atheists – are not in the least interested in religion in its concrete manifestations. Rather, their interest relates to the resources which religion commands on a structural level. In other words, religion has something to teach contemporary political philosophy by virtue of its form – its unique ability to create engaged subjects, people willing to live and die for their ideals – rather than its content.

This interest in the radical potential of religion has been nowhere more strikingly expressed than in the steadily growing philosophical literature on the apostle Paul. As if in illustration of this politico-theological trend, Mark Lilla's polemical commentary on the resurgence of European left-wing radicalism appeared within a longer article – in *The New York Review of Books* – reviewing several key works on the subject. Following this newfound interest in Paul back to its origins leads *inter alia* to Jacob Taubes's posthumously published study *The Political Theology of Paul* (the German original appeared in 1993), a radical political reading that was a particular inspiration for Agamben's celebrated commentary on Paul's Epistle to the Romans, *The Time that Remains*.[10] Another important impetus was given by Heidegger's phenomenological readings of Paul in the early 1920s, material that only became generally available in 1995 when it was published as the sixtieth volume of his collected works.[11]

At the same time, it should be noted that the real starting whistle for the debate over Paul came with Badiou's *Saint Paul: The Foundation of Universalism*, a short volume originally published in French in 1997. For his part, Badiou made no reference to Taubes or Heidegger; indeed, he showed no interest whatsoever in inscribing his reading of Paul within any specific theological or philosophical tradition. It is tempting to add that this is symptomatic of Badiou's entire philosophical career, which might be summarized as a passionate defence of the possibility of radical reorganization whatever the situation. This also sheds light on his fascination with Paul. For Badiou, the Christian church's leading apostle has no religious value whatsoever. What makes Paul of interest is his status as a revolutionary prototype, as the harbinger of a completely new kind of political subject.[12]

As Badiou sees it, Paul's 'unprecedented gesture' was to separate 'the truth' from any collective attempt to possess it. Instead, Paul proclaimed a truth that directed itself to every individual subject: 'There is no longer Jew or Greek, there is no longer slave or free, there is no longer male and female; for all of you are one in Christ Jesus' (Gal. 3:28). In so doing, he formulated the pattern of what Badiou terms a 'universal singularity', a bond between the subject and the proclaimed truth that does not derive from an ethnic origin, social class or gender identity. What gives the subject this true identity is, instead, a fidelity towards the revolutionary event – in Paul's case, the salvatory message of the risen Christ.[13]

In a timeless fashion, Paul showed the very possibility of a radical transformation of existing social and cultural orders: 'Ultimately it is a case of mobilizing a universal singularity both against the prevailing abstractions (legal then, economic now), and against communitarian or particularist protest'.[14] Behind these words can be discerned Badiou's critique of the unholy alliance between market liberalism and cultural relativism. Its corollary in the classical world was the alliance between the abstract universalism of the Roman Empire and the Jewish people's claim to have an exclusive covenant with God, manifested in their adherence to revealed law. Paul's announcement of the risen Christ involved a radical break with both. Against the abstract universalism of the Empire, he counterposed a truth that spoke to and engaged every individual subject: 'all of you are one in Christ Jesus'. Yet this did not mean that he sought a new, restricted community which would be united under the predicate 'Christian'. Paul's greatness lay precisely in how he undermined any claim to possess the truth on the basis of a particular identity or tradition.

It is also from this radical perspective that Badiou interprets Paul's talk of law and grace. For Badiou, grace denotes that which occurs 'without predicate' – the miracle of new life, the unforeseeable advent of an order other than the present one. Law is the opposite of grace. If grace is 'the maxim of universality', law is that which forces us to stand at our post: 'The law is always predicative, particular, and partial'.[15] Hence Paul's ambition to suspend the law. Paul saved the salvation message from remaining an internal Jewish concern by literally declaring the law invalid for non-Jews. The messianic event, the redemption, constitutes a break with the law, a 'pure excess over every prescription'.[16]

Let me pause here briefly and return to the historical manifestations of the messianic idea. Badiou presents the law as metonymous of the particular conditions that constrain or even prevent the messianic liberation (the event of grace). This runs directly contrary to how the law is routinely understood within both Jewish and Christian messianism. Early on within rabbinic Judaism there emerged a view of the law as a path by which humanity would steadily realize the messianic promise. God's grace was quite simply revealed in the gift of the law, thereby endowing humanity with a tool by which it might itself change the world to a better place by living a moral life. A similar thought is to be found within Christianity, inspired by the words of the Sermon on the Mount about how Jesus came not to abolish but to fulfil the law (Matt. 5:17). Not so much a break with particularity, Christian messianism was about preparing the world for the final redemption – the return of the Son of Man – by living in accordance with the specific message proclaimed by Jesus.

This discrepancy between Badiou's account of Paul and the historical manifestations of the messianic idea illuminates the relatively cool reception given to his writings among historians of religion. To be sure, Badiou makes clear that his interest in Paul is not historical in nature; what is of philosophical value is rather Paul's argument from principle. The only question is whether the principled argument which Badiou ascribes to Paul does not itself already presuppose a specific historical understanding of the texts. As several critics have noted, Badiou's lack of interest in the historical research on Paul means that he tends to inscribe himself within a very precise historical-hermeneutic paradigm from which most postwar historians have emphatically distanced themselves. A feature of this paradigm, which was a cornerstone of older Protestant biblical studies, is that it consistently contrasts Paul with his own Jewish faith and practices. Paul's radicalism, according to this view, lay in his readiness to take leave of the Jewish community and its claims to exclusivity.[17]

Modern scholarship on Paul has distanced itself from this paradigm not only because it rests upon an implicitly anti-Jewish dialectic that counterposes law to grace and identifies Christianity with the latter. Above all, it has done so because the paradigm runs directly contrary to what historians today know about Paul and Hellenic Judaism. Admittedly, few scholars would contest the claim that Paul's theology had clearly universalist features. Together with a growing number of Jews, Paul was convinced that Jesus of Nazareth was the messianic redeemer who had been promised to the Jewish people, and he was similarly convinced that the righteousness and grace of the God of Israel were so great that even non-Jews who had come to believe in Christ would share in the redemption. To give life to his conviction, Paul used the image of an olive tree: the Jewish covenant was like an olive trunk with deep roots, and onto this noble trunk God in his greatness had now permitted other boughs from wild olive trees to be grafted (Rom. 10:17–24). However, the universalism which appears here has little to do with what Badiou terms a singularly rooted universalism, opposed to any particular affiliation. Paul's aim was not to suspend the Jewish covenant but to broaden it to include non-Jews. Hence his involvement in the question of the law, which, for him, was primarily about a desire to settle the conditions for non-Jews' partaking in the covenant of God.

At the same time, it may be asked how significant these historical-critical objections to Badiou really are. If Badiou finds a radical universalism in Paul, does it matter that Paul's actual intention was to graft non-Jews onto his own, highly particular ethnic tree? Does not the greatness of these classic texts lie precisely in their capacity to generate meanings that reach beyond their author's intention? I believe it does; historical scholarship should not hobble the imaginative power of philosophy.[18] As regards Badiou's writings, it may also be added that bold new perspectives are hardly damaging to existing Pauline scholarship. Invoking the self-critical observation of a contemporary

New Testament scholar, one might say that Badiou has highlighted a radicalism in the biblical tradition that in both the Western church and the academic discipline of biblical studies has long lain dormant.[19] Even so, it can be asked whether the problematic which several historians have identified in Badiou's writings on Paul is not symptomatic of a broader pattern in Badiou's philosophy.

In what follows I will pursue this question by deepening my analysis of the messianic strain in Badiou's philosophy. Let me start by recalling the distinction between restorative and apocalyptic strands that Gershom Scholem and others have identified in the history of Jewish messianism. While the restorative strand emphasizes the importance of continuity, connecting messianic redemption to humanity's ongoing transformation of creation through the practice of justice, the apocalyptic strand conceives of redemption as an external, divine intervention that also involves a radical break with all previous history. With its emphasis upon disruption and reorganization, Badiou's political messianism is more easily connected to the apocalyptic than the restorative strand, albeit with the crucial difference, of course, that Badiou represents a wholly secular philosophical discourse. Given that he uses Paul as the starting point for his reflections on messianism, this should perhaps not come as a surprise. From the point of view of Scholem's distinction, even Paul can be seen as a highly apocalyptic thinker, shaped by his deep conviction as to the imminence of the final redemption.

For Badiou, however, this interpretation of Paul is really no more than a way to channel lines of thought which have long been a feature of his philosophy. Of particular significance in this regard is the study usually considered Badiou's magnum opus, *Being and Event*, published in French in 1988. In it, as his title indicates, Badiou introduces a distinction between 'being' and 'event'. Although ontology, the study of being, is conventionally held to belong to the domain of philosophy, Badiou argues that such need not be the case, and declares that only mathematics is qualified to deal with questions of being. This somewhat controversial claim allows Badiou, a philosopher schooled in mathematics, to invoke set theory in order to define being as pure multiplicity, prior to any unification into a higher principle or substance (God, the One). All that exist are singularities. Despite this, efforts are continually being made to structure and define these singularities, for example by ascribing to them identitarian predicates. Badiou coins the phrase état de la situation ('state of the situation') – in which état, significantly, connotes 'state' in both its general and political senses – to describe this inclusion of a number of singularities within an overarching whole.[20]

This is where the event comes into the picture. The event marks a break with the structuring entirety and a distancing from the long arm of ontology. The Event *is* not; it *happens*. For this reason, the event also cannot be explained or predicted from the order of being; seen from the 'state of the situation', it rather appears as a deviation: 'If there exists an event, *its belonging to the situation of its site is undecidable from the standpoint of the situation itself*'.[21] For Badiou, the event is also closely linked to the concept of truth. The event can be defined, quite simply, as 'the truth of the situation': that which reveals and makes visible whatever the official situation is concealing. However, for the truth-event not to be overlooked, for the event to be realized at all *as* truth, what is needed is the active intervention of a subject who acknowledges the event as truth (for instance, in Paul's announcement of the risen Christ). At the same time, Badiou notes that it is the event which primarily creates the subject; strictly speaking, the active subject comes into existence in the instant when it becomes able to distinguish the truth of the situation and to give it a name. In this way a mutual relationship emerges between the event that requires the subject's recognition and the subject that will be constituted by its 'fidelity' to the event.[22]

What, then, is an event in more concrete terms? Badiou gives a series of examples in addition to that already mentioned (the messianic event in its Pauline form). In the area of science, the breakthrough of modern physics is one example, as is Georg Cantor's set theory, which, as already noted, plays a central part in Badiou's own thinking. In the realm of art, it denotes innovations that do away with existing boundaries of aesthetic norms, such as Arnold Schoenberg's twelve-tone technique. In the realm of love, an event might also be something as obvious and yet extraordinary as a meeting between two people who fall in love. Yet the examples that occupy a central place in Badiou's philosophy are taken from politics: the French Revolution, the October Revolution in Russia, and May 1968. Even in a fairly abstract and theoretical work such as *Being and Event*, a clear political undertone can be detected. Behind Badiou's interest in sets and singularities lies a radical engagement with a concrete political reality based upon structural injustices. The ambiguity of the term état de la situation presents an illustrative example. In turning his attention to that which forms part of, yet is not acknowledged by, *l'état de la situation*, Badiou also delivers a scathing critique of the state apparatus in its current form, in which greater numbers of individuals now live within a particular state but without being counted as part of that state (those without papers or 'illegal' refugees).[23]

To understand Badiou's interest in disruption, events and reorganization, it is necessary to examine the political driving force behind his writing, which might be characterized as a desire to imagine politics beyond the state. For Badiou, true politics is allied with truth-events and revolutionary praxis. Only then is it possible to find a way beyond the capitalist form of organization and its devastating effects upon collective existence: 'Positively, it means that politics, in the sense of subjective mastery (the mastery of thought and praxis) over the future of humanity will have independent value, obeying its own atemporal norms like science and art. Politics will not be subordinated to power, to the State. It is, it will be, the force in the breast of the assembled and active people driving the State and its laws to extinction.'[24]

Badiou's work is often hailed as one of the more striking examples of the return of Marxism in contemporary philosophy. This truism needs modification, however, not least because he himself has repeatedly rejected the dialectical element of Marx's historical materialism in particular. His is similarly opposed to any notion that political action might find support or guidance in socio-economic patterns further back in history, and, equally, the idea that politics might be justified on rational or philosophical grounds. For Badiou, politics is about events that take place without originating in existing structures; it therefore requires *subjective* justification. 'Subjective' should not be confused here with 'individual'. Rather, it indicates that true politics always requires a subject, which, according to Badiou, can only be 'the people'. A political truth-event is thus an act by which a people declares itself a political subject and remains faithful to that declaration.[25]

Given this background, those who wish to find a historical model for Badiou's communism must, as Simon Critchley has argued, look to Rousseau rather than Marx.[26] In his study *The Faith of the Faithless*, which was alluded to at the start of this chapter, Critchley engages in a partly polemical argument with Badiou, in which he illuminates the latter's close relationship to Rousseau. In addition to the central role played by the people in Badiou's philosophy, their political philosophies are united by a series of thematic and structural qualities. Not the least of these are the voluntarist and decisionist elements; the political event is concentrated into an act of collective will through which the people constitutes itself. Both historical circumstances and concrete material relations are thereby accorded a secondary role (Badiou's textbook example is the Paris Commune of 1871, specifically 18 March, when the revolutionary workers of Paris seized power and took over the running of the city).[27] Another striking similarity is their anti-parliamentary quality. For both Rousseau and Badiou, the popular will can not be represented but only presented, an argument which Badiou made, among other occasions, in a widely discussed critique of France's presidential election in 2007.[28] Political struggle thus becomes a question of organizing the popular will – something that requires 'discipline', or, more precisely, political interventions without basis in party or state.[29]

Let me return at this point to the issue of whether the problematic aspects of Badiou's reading of Paul are indeed symptomatic of a larger pattern in his philosophy. A more pointed way of formulating the matter would be to say that the decisionist aspect of Badiou's philosophy makes it difficult for him to reconcile the apocalyptic messianism that he celebrates in Paul with the radical materialism that he has defended since his earliest writings. His interest in material conditions and circumstances is quite simply overshadowed by his fascination with the instant, the break and the new. In a seeming paradox, this means that he ultimately finds it difficult to do justice to Paul's messianism. The latter is apocalyptic in character, to be sure, but this does not mean that it is estranged from the particular material circumstances in which it was announced. On the contrary, Paul's interpretation of the Christ event is deeply rooted in the stories, traditions and divine promises which characterized Hellenistic Judaism.

These aspects have left little trace upon Badiou's reading of Paul. To quote the Jewish historian Daniel Boyarin, Badiou's account of Paul is permeated by a kind of 'Christian-Platonic spiritualization' that, when all is said and done, shows negligible interest in the concrete material circumstances that ultimately made Paul a 'singular' subject. What interests Badiou is the revolutionary structure of the event announced by Paul, not the unique mixture of memories, convictions and expectations that allowed the announced event – Christ's resurrection – to have any meaning for Paul and his listeners. Boyarin's concern, which relates not only to which liberties we can take with historical texts, is that this philosophical lack of interest in particular conditions and concrete identities easily blurs into a contempt for, or, at worst, denial of, particular identities.[30]

To judge from the debate that has arisen around Badiou's writings in recent years, such concerns are warranted. Of particular relevance in this context is the controversial essay collection which Badiou published in 2005 under the title *Uses of the Word 'Jew'*. In addition to an extract from Badiou's book on Paul and a contribution from his colleague Cécile Winter, the collection includes a series of essays on Israel, the Holocaust and 'the word "Jew"'.[31] Its overarching aim is to highlight how accusations of anti-Semitism are today used as a strategic ploy in order to silence criticism of Israel and its policies. Badiou's claim is certainly not without merit and most of those who have distanced themselves from the book have been careful to make clear that the issue for them is not that Israel's policies cannot or should not be criticized. The only question is at what price and at whose expense? Badiou's essays ultimately have very little to do with Israel and much more to do with Jews who today 'demand exceptional status' by virtue of having been the victims of Nazism. Briefly, Badiou's argument is based on the fact that the Nazis appropriated the Jews' 'religious fable' about being a chosen people and turned it against them. To claim that there is something unique about the Jewish experience is thus to continue to reaffirm the Nazis' perverted worldview.[32]

In his manifesto-like foreword, Badiou stresses that he has little time for this kind of 'sacralization' of 'the name "Jew"', by which 'the grace [sic] of having been an incomparable victim can be passed down not only to descendants and to the descendants of descendants but to all who come under the predicate in question'.[33] Instead, he wishes to advocate a position that is 'utterly irreconcilable' with such tendencies: 'Obviously, the key point is that I cannot accept in any way the victim ideology. ... That the Nazis and their accomplices exterminated millions of people they called "Jews" does not to my mind lend any new legitimacy to the identity predicate in question.'[34]

Beneath this line of argument can be discerned Badiou's larger challenge to identity politics and its tendency of undermining any radical vision of equality by means of irreconcilable, particular demands and privileges. Thus he forcefully rebuts any notion that his critique against 'the predicate "Jew"' involved any ill will towards Jews *per se*, underscoring his admiration for the numerous great philosophers, scientists, artists and revolutionaries of Jewish descent. And yet the question remains whether this supposedly disarming gesture in fact hides a deeper problematic in his reasoning. For when Badiou comes to point out Jews as the objects of his admiration, his canon revealingly comprises only figures who in one way or another have broken with Jewishness (even if, as has been noted, this can be questioned in the case of Paul): 'from the apostle Paul to Trotsky, including Spinoza, Marx and Freud, Jewish communitarianism has only underpinned creative universalism in so far as there have been new points of rupture with it'.[35]

Badiou should of course be taken at his word when he explicitly disavows any kind of anti-Jewish intentions. It is not here that the problem lies. Rather, it concerns an underlying inability to position himself in relation to differences and identities in a nuanced and reflective manner. Let me here briefly return to Badiou's critique of the interplay between identity politics and market liberalism. This critique is formulated in, among other places, the opening pages of *Saint Paul*, where Badiou rails against the unprecedented production of new identities in the current era: 'What inexhaustible potential for mercantile investments in this upsurge – taking the form of communities demanding recognition and so-called cultural singularities – of women, homosexuals, the disabled, Arabs! And these infinite combinations of predicative traits, what a godsend! Black homosexuals, disabled Serbs, Catholic pedophiles, moderate Muslims, married priests, ecologist yuppies, the submissive unemployed, prematurely aged youth!'[36]

What is particularly grating about Badiou's contemptuous inventory of 'communities demanding recognition' is how it lumps together every kind of difference. The demands for rights by black homosexuals and disabled Serbs seem to be neither more nor less legitimate than those of Catholic paedophiles. How is so nonchalant an attitude towards concrete social differences to be understood? As Eric Marty has argued, one possible answer lies in Badiou's stated aversion to the philosophy of difference that has been promoted by his peers ever since the 1960s. To be sure, everyone is entitled to their own view of the ostensibly ivory-towered fixation with linguistic structures that is associated with the names of Derrida, Lyotard or Kristeva, but the fact is that these linguistic interests were always inseparably bound up with a deep engagement with real social structures. It would be misdirected to insinuate that Badiou is lacking in social empathy. Nevertheless, I think Marty hits the mark when he connects Badiou's lack of interest in linguistic differences with his insensitivity to real social differences:

> What Badiou lacks is a proper understanding of the notion of difference, and that of course goes hand in hand with his failure to understand the signifier [*le signifiant*]. Badiou conceives of difference in substantialist terms, and thereby confuses difference with particularism, difference with hierarchy – and as a consequence he expresses a violent phobia of the very idea of difference. Hence, according to him, each and every difference must be rejected ('laid down', to use his own term) by reason of the content (particularity) it is based on or is the basis for. He is not able to envision a difference that unfolds through a system of relations established through this very difference. Neither is he able to understand the extent to which difference is one of the necessary conditions for authentic equality, for there is no equality without relational structures and there are no relational structures without difference.[37]

In this context, Badiou's almost mechanical way of talking about 'the predicate "Jew"' is illuminating. Indifference to the complexity that defines all historical concepts leads him to treat 'the predicate "Jew"' as a predicate that can be substituted interchangeably with any other; a predicate that is neither affected nor influenced by the fact of its having been for millennia a canvas for the projection of vitriolic representations, with violent consequences for the bearers of that predicate. Badiou's lack of interest in how meaning is generated from relational structures also blinds him to how he inscribes himself within a stereotyped pattern that throughout history has associated Christianity with openness and liberation while presenting Judaism in terms of closedness and exclusivity.

It would be a simplification, however, to relate Badiou's inability to deal with differences merely to his dissociation from poststructuralism. As already argued, it is, rather, about a deeper lack of interest in embodiment, empiricism and history – in short, in materiality. At this point it could be objected that Badiou's writings are brimming with historical examples that illustrate the material struggle for an emancipatory politics. On closer inspection, however, it is striking how often the bodies disappear and historical facts are twisted in order to fit into what ultimately comes to resemble an extremely idealistic historiography. Badiou's flattering presentation of Mao's Cultural Revolution in several of his later works is perhaps the most egregious example. Like Paul, Mao becomes in Badiou's account the emblem of a timeless political truth, and Badiou's lack of interest in the material circumstances that shaped Paul's life and works is reflected in a similar lack of interest in the material circumstances of Mao's rise: the terror, the purges, the systematic executions, the masses starved to death. Admittedly, after a protracted celebration of the Cultural Revolution in *The Century*, Badiou poses the question: 'What about the violence, often so extreme? The hundreds of thousands of dead? The persecutions, especially against intellectuals?' – only to adopt at once the idealist's stance of superior indifference to the reality of violence:

> One will say the same thing about them as about all those acts of violence that, to this very day, have marked the History of every somewhat expansive attempt to practice a free politics, to radically subvert the eternal order that subjects society to wealth and the wealthy, to power and the powerful, to science and scientists, to capital and its servants, and considers worthless what people think, worthless, the collective intelligence of workers, worthless, to tell the truth, any thought that is not homogenous to the order in which the ignoble rule of profit is perpetuated.[38]

Unsurprisingly, Badiou has attracted fierce criticism over the years for his unyielding defence of communism and for his unshakeable denunciation of capitalism.[39] However, I wish to stress that my own reservations relate not to Badiou's radical critique of the current world order but to his formulation of that critique. In other words, the problem is not that Badiou has inscribed himself within a Marxist tradition but that he has departed from it in the most fundamental respect: where Marx united the dream of messianic justice with a deep respect for the complexity of material reality, Badiou has nowhere succeeded in connecting messianism and materialism; event and history; the moment of revolt and the practice that ensures the permanence of justice.

Significantly, the most incisive criticism of Badiou, to my mind, has come from Marxist quarters, more precisely from the Trotskyist philosopher Daniel Bensaïd. In a series of articles, Bensaïd has pointed out the evasion of historical reality in Badiou's writings, an evasion that goes hand in hand with an unwillingness to involve oneself with the concrete conditions of political reality: 'this divorce between event and history (between the event and its historically determined conditions) tends to render politics if not unthinkable then at least impracticable'.[40] Politics is reduced to spectacular moments of will and decisiveness, in which the truth is determined by those who declare it. Once again the decisionist element in Badiou's philosophy appears, something that also aligns his philosophy with a certain type of theology: 'Detached from its historical conditions, pure diamond of truth, the event … is akin to a miracle. By the same token, a politics without politics is akin to a negative theology.'[41] Bensaïd's strongest objection to Badiou relates precisely to this quasi-theological quality, a quality that in modern French philosophy can be traced back to Simone Weil's political reflections. Like Badiou, Weil denounced faith in political parties in favour of an 'unconditional desire for truth'. Yet the question remains as to how political truth is to be attained when the mediating instance of party politics has been rejected. It is at this point, Bensaïd argues, that theology makes its entrance: 'The refusal of profane politics, with its impurities, uncertainties, and wobbly conventions, leads ineluctably back to theology and its jumble of graces, miracles, revelations, repentances, and pardons'.[42]

Bensaïd leaves no doubt that politics is better off without such theological muddle. Given Badiou's continual flirtation with terms such as 'terror', 'grace', 'discipline' and 'fidelity', one may be inclined to agree: the apocalyptic undertone to his social critique leaves little space for political virtues such as considerateness, self-criticism and the capacity to address ambiguities and tensions. At the same time, it may be asked whether politics has ever been able to dissociate itself entirely from theological presuppositions in the wider sense of the term. Is it not the case that all political reflection in some measure relies upon pre-political structures of thought, and that – to recall John Milbank's words, cited in the introduction to this chapter – we are always ultimately dealing with 'theologies or anti-theologies in disguise'? If such is the case, then it becomes a crucial task for political philosophy to distinguish critically between different forms of the theological motifs underpinning all conversation about the political. In light of this critical discussion of Badiou, I want to argue here that the apocalyptic and occasionally anti-historical messianism which finds expression in his writings constitutes a poor foundation upon which to construct a political philosophy. Yet this is not to say that the messianic motif no longer has a role to play as a politico-philosophical resource. In the next section, I will extend my consideration of the messianic by specifying what I myself regard as a more constructive formulation of the motif.

Law as Grace

In many respects Badiou's political messianism represents a legitimate reaction to social and economic developments in the twenty-first century. The problem lies in how this messianism is so focused upon the socially revolutionary event that it tends to obscure ideas about actual political projects or problems. However, the messianic motif need not lead to a political philosophy that distances itself from the concretely historical world. As discussed in earlier chapters, a tension between apocalyptic and restorative movements – to use Scholem's terminology – can be traced back as far as classical antiquity. Particularly during periods of oppression, persecution and suffering, the apocalyptic message of a radical break with history has provided people with hope and courage. For this reason, Scholem contends, we must never underestimate the political and social value of apocalypticism.[43] Nevertheless, it is unmistakeably the case that apocalyptic movements throughout history have often left behind them chaos and sometimes more acute suffering. The history of messianism includes a considerable number of messianic harbingers whose promises were never fulfilled – from Bar Kokhba in the second century AD to Sabbatai Zvi in the seventeenth century and the Hasidic Brooklyn rabbi Menachem Mendel Schneerson in the 1990s.

It is against this background that restorative messianism in both its Jewish and Christian manifestations should be understood. The theological reorganizations that took place within both traditions in late antiquity can be recalled here. In each case, it was a question of developing a theology of history which could make sense of the Messiah's postponed arrival (Judaism) or return (Christianity). In both cases, the apocalyptic elements were toned down in favour of a pragmatic stance which saw opportunity rather than failure in the passing of time. In the process, their view of messianic redemption was changed. Although both traditions remained faithful to the idea of an ultimate eschatological redemption, incomplete redemption in the present was to acquire a value in its own right. This process was reflected in aspects of rabbinic Judaism, by which *halakha*, cultivation of the law, became a way to gradually prepare the way for redemption. This was paralleled in the emergent Christian tradition by the idea that the kingdom of heaven had partially been inaugurated by Jesus's resurrection, which meant that Christians had a duty to live right here and now in a way that looked ahead to their final redemption.

Transferred to the level of principle, the dilemma of messianism is about whether it is possible to combine change and order; whether it is possible to articulate the dream of a more equitable world without such dreams changing into their opposite. In this sense the tension between restorative and apocalyptic tendencies within messianism lived on even after the secularization of the Jewish and Christian traditions. At this point, the anti-utopian messianism that emerged during Romanticism may be recalled. When Novalis in his lecture on Europe condemned the 'foolish striving to mould history and humanity and give them your own direction', he directed his critical reproof at the utopian arrogance of the French Revolution. In a way that captured the restorative quality of the older messianism, he developed a mode of visionary thought that also distanced itself from the apocalyptic fascination with disruption and the moment. It will be recalled that Novalis held a deep conviction that it was only by means of a laborious engagement with history that we might attain a deepened understanding of both the present and the future. But Romanticism's suspicion towards disruption and the moment was also rooted in a broader consideration of time's constitutive role in consciousness. There was, quite simply, something presumptuous about claiming that the ideal moment could ever be apprehended. By contrast, Romantic messianism was characterized by a kind of temporal transcendence, a critical awareness of the productive deferral of the ideal state. The messianic promise thereby became an ideal with whose continual realization humanity had been charged.

The discussions at Capri in 1994 represent a more recent example of this attempt to strike a balance between utopian arrogance and resigned loss of vision. Here too, I think, can be seen the crystallization of a mode of visionary thought that recycles key elements of restorative messianism. This is most clearly articulated in Derrida's concept of a 'messianicity without messianism', a generalized messianic structure that breaks away from and destabilizes the specific historical manifestations of the messianic. This 'desertification' of the messianic can be seen as an attempt to defend oneself against the potentially violent aspects of the apocalyptic cult of the immediate present. Linking the messianic event to specific historical episodes – as, for example, in Badiou's case, the Paris Commune or the Cultural Revolution – effectively prevents a critical examination of these episodes in a wider historical perspective. The messianic is identified with a moment to which the dignity of truth is ascribed, regardless of what preceded or followed it. Yet this is also the moment at which justice is betrayed. For what justice actually requires is that 'the time is out of joint' – that any specific historical moment is intersected by our responsibility for the past and the future. Once again, a temporal transcendence may be discerned, an insight into the risks attendant upon the belief in imminent messianic redemption: 'If the Messiah is at the gates of Rome among the beggars and lepers, one might think that his incognito protects or prevents him from coming, but, precisely, he is recognized; someone, haunted with questioning and unable to leave off, asks him: "When will you come?" [*Quand viendras-tu?*]'.[44]

This rabbinic anecdote – related by Maurice Blanchot and quoted by Derrida – can be interpreted as implying that the Messiah, in the strict sense of the word, belongs to the future; that justice is in a state of permanent deferral and thus in principle impossible. As such, it overlaps with a common criticism of Derrida, who has long been reproached by both theologians and philosophers for advocating a nihilistic position in which every substantial (ethical or epistemological) proposition is deferred to a future always beyond reach.[45] In fact, this criticism rests upon a serious misreading of the messianic strand in his philosophy. When Derrida refers to a Messiah whose arrival always lies in the future, he is not claiming that such a Messiah is impossible or absent. It is, rather, a way for him to underscore the fact that we should never take the presence of justice for granted. Even if the Messiah should one day reveal himself, we must therefore continue to call to him.[46]

The messianic age should thus not be mistaken for some chronologically distant future; indeed, it has little to do with chronology at all. In another version of the anecdote mentioned above, the Messiah replies to the enquiry as to when he will arrive with: 'Today'. When Rabbi Joshua, who has posed the question, later consults with the Prophet Elijah for clarification, he receives the answer: 'Today, if you hear his voice'. The time of the Messiah is the relation of every moment to the fulfilment of time, a qualitatively different time that intervenes in the seemingly homogenous passage of time in order to confront humanity with the possibility of pursuing at every moment the cause of justice in the world. This is also the rabbinic tradition invoked by Walter Benjamin in the famous final fragment of his theses on history: 'We know that the Jews were prohibited from investigating the future. The Torah and the prayers instruct them in remembrance, however. This stripped the future of its magic, to which all those succumb who turn to the soothsayers for enlightenment. This does not imply, however, that for the Jews the future turned into homogenous, empty time. For every second of time was the strait gate through which the Messiah might enter.'[47]

Returning now to the question of the politico-philosophical value of these various theological tropes, I want to argue that, for various reasons, this restorative strand of messianism is preferable to the apocalyptic. Where its apocalyptic strand tends to betray the complexity of historical reality, messianism's restorative variant shows, by contrast, the possibility of combining radical visions with practices that preserve the durability of justice. By means of emphasis upon the dialectic between memory and hope, past and future, it also becomes possible to avoid a potential evasion of historical responsibility that is inherent in apocalypticism's focus upon disruption, event and novelty. Benjamin is instructive here. To be sure, his theses on history related to event, disruption and the moment, yet this should not be mistaken for an evasion of history. Nor was his intention with these theses, as has sometimes been claimed, to distance himself from historical materialism. On the contrary, Benjamin sought to save historical materialism from what he termed 'homogenous, empty time' by restoring its revolutionary impulse. But this did not mean that he took recourse in apocalypticism. Like the prophets of antiquity, but also like the philosophers of Romanticism, Benjamin was instead interested in the redemptive power of memory: to offer resistance by extracting particular moments from the apparently homogenous course of historical events and allowing them to irrupt into the present like messianic chips, charged with redemptive force.[48]

Given this background, it is worth looking more closely at the contemporary philosopher who has most explicitly taken charge of Benjamin's messianic legacy – Giorgio Agamben. With Badiou, Agamben has been one of the more prominent voices in the ongoing philosophical debate over Paul. Like Badiou, Agamben belongs to a radical philosophical Left that in the last decade or so has created a distinct profile for itself by engaging in battles with both the corruption of contemporary politics and the paralysis of the academic Left by what is sometimes referred to as 'postpolitics'. Their resemblance ends there, however. If Badiou can be reproached for having neglected empirical reality, few philosophers of recent years have devoted so much intellectual energy to bodies, matter and history as Agamben. This is reflected above all in the title of his most famous work, *Homo Sacer: Sovereign Power and Bare Life* (published in Italian in 1995), the first in a series of studies which, from different perspectives, have shone light upon the intricate relationships between power, rule, economics and human bodies in Western politico-philosophical history.[49]

Agamben's interest in the historical and the particular is reflected in a reading of Paul that he first presented in *The Time that Remains* (2000). In its opening pages Agamben clarifies that his intention is to restore Paul to his Jewish context and to re-establish his letters as 'the fundamental messianic text for the Western tradition'. For this reason, he firmly rejects Badiou's claim that Paul might have intended to found a new religion. There has been a tacit consensus between church and synagogue throughout history that such was indeed the case: for Christianity, in order to guard its status as an independent tradition; for Judaism, in order to dissociate itself from any claim that Jesus of Nazareth might have been the promised messianic figure. In both cases, however, the issue boils down to a desire to avoid having to confront the radical nature of the messianism proclaimed by Paul.[50]

What did this radicalism comprise? Agamben locates it in Paul's teachings on the Christian *calling*. Where the focal point of Badiou's analysis of Paul is Galatians 3:28 ('There is no longer Jew or Greek…'), Agamben chooses to read Paul through another celebrated passage that bears citing in full:

> However that may be, let each of you lead the life that the Lord has assigned, to which God called you. This is my rule in all the churches. Was anyone at the time of his call already circumcised? Let him not seek to remove the marks of circumcision. Was anyone at the time of his call uncircumcised? Let him not seek circumcision. Circumcision is nothing, and uncircumcision is nothing; but obeying the commandments of God is everything. Let each of you remain in the condition in which you were called. Were you a slave when called? Do not be concerned about it. Even if you can gain your freedom, make use of your present condition now more than ever. For whoever was called in the Lord as a slave is a freed person belonging to the Lord, just as whoever was free when called is a slave of Christ. You were bought with a price; do not become slaves of human masters. In whatever condition you were called, brothers and sisters, there remain with God. Now concerning virgins, I have no command of the Lord, but I give my opinion as one who by the Lord's mercy is trustworthy. I think that, in view of the impending crisis, it is well for you to remain as you are. Are you bound to a wife? Do not seek to be free. Are you free from a wife? Do not seek a wife. But if you marry, you do not sin, and if a virgin marries, she does not sin. Yet those who marry will experience distress in this life, and I would spare you that. I mean, brothers and sisters, the appointed time has grown short; from now on, let even those who have wives be as though they had none, and those who mourn as though they were not mourning, and those who rejoice as though they were not rejoicing, and those who buy as though they had no possessions, and those who deal with the world as though they had no dealings with it. For the present form of this world is passing away (1 Cor. 7:17–31).

This text can be seen as an elaboration of the meaning of the famous passage in Galatians, and it is significant that Agamben chooses the longer exposition of the two. For Agamben, Paul makes clear here that being 'a slave of Christ' supersedes all other callings. In other words, the messianic calling relativizes the meaning of being Jew or Greek; man or woman; enslaved or free. Christians are urged to live 'as though' the actual legal relationships that define their lives no longer have any significance. At the same time, Agamben is careful to stress that this does not mean that these existing identities have been suspended in the sense of ceasing to exist. What makes Paul's description of the Christ as 'a new creation' (2 Cor. 5:17) so radical is that the old identity remains and yet is transformed through the Christian calling.[51]

At this point the differences between Agamben's and Badiou's readings of Paul start to become clear. Agamben does agree with Badiou about Paul having been convinced that Christ had suspended the law and thereby torn down the wall separating Jews from non-Jews. But what does this really signify? Badiou's reply is that this conviction of Paul's has laid the foundations for the idea of the universal human. For Agamben, who enters into a direct polemic with Badiou on this question, such a claim represents a projection of modern dreams of equality, tolerance and respect onto a thinker from antiquity whose worldview could not have been more different:

> For Paul, it is not a matter of 'tolerating' or getting past differences in order to pinpoint sameness or a universal lurking beyond. The universal is not a transcendent principle through which differences may be perceived – such a perspective of transcendence is not available to Paul. Rather, this 'transcendental' involves an operation that divides the divisions of the law themselves and renders them inoperative, without ever reaching any final ground. No universal man, no Christian can be found in the depths of the Jew or the Greek, neither as a principle nor as an end; all that is left is a remnant and the impossibility of the Jew or the Greek to coincide with himself.[52]

Agamben is not objecting solely on historical grounds. At a more principled level he is fundamentally sceptical of the abstract universalism which Badiou discerns in Paul's epistles. However, the fact that Paul does not formulate the model for a (supposedly) universal human in no way weakens his radicalism. Quite the reverse. Paul instead challenges us to reflect in a new way upon the broader tension between particular and universal. A more careful reading of Paul reveals, above all, that the choice is not between self-inclusive particular identities on the one hand and, on the other, a neutral universalism that disavows the importance of such identities. Paul was considerably more sophisticated than that, as evidenced by his teaching on the issue of vocation. Being called to Christ means that the potentially oppressive differences (enslaved/free, Jewish/Greek, circumcised/uncircumcised etc.) by which the law separates people will be disrupted and changed in the name of another difference which has not been asserted in the name of the law: that between flesh and spirit (or 'breath', *soffio*, as Agamben chooses to translate *pneuma*). To live life in the spirit, which is the meaning of the messianic calling, is to take a path in life that cuts directly across all others. This is what Agamben has in mind when he writes that the universal, as Paul describes it, is a movement that 'divides the divisions of the law'. In other words, Paul undermines the very division to which the law gives rise, not in order to dissolve it into some neutral universalism, but in order to radicalize that division and thereby show that no identity is ever definitive.[53]

Although this line of reasoning might seem to rely upon hair-splitting distinctions, it in fact has important consequences for Agamben's politico-philosophical argument more broadly. In contrast to Badiou, Agamben identifies in Paul's epistles a radicalism that does not result in an indifference to the specific material circumstances which govern every concrete, material existence. This does not mean, however, that Agamben has any patience with the essentializing of particular identities that results from an excessive application of identity politics. Extending Paul's teachings on the Christian calling, Agamben instead reveals the complexity and porousness of all identities, something that opens up the possibility of maintaining a respect for differences without laying claim to exclusiveness. For a concrete example, Badiou's critique of the way that anti-Semitism has historically been differentiated from other forms of racial oppression might be recalled. While Badiou's solution is to abandon any claim to special treatment, that suggested by Agamben's line of argument would instead be to take every particular form of oppression even more seriously. To take Badiou's own example, then, the problem is not that people accord a special status to the Nazi genocide of the Jews by asserting the uniqueness of the relevant political and historical factors; rather, the problem lies in the fact that one does not accord a sufficiently special status to other genocides. In a nutshell, a good analysis of social and racial oppression needs *more* difference, not less.

The differing emphases so far highlighted in Badiou's and Agamben's respective readings of Paul can be traced back to a more fundamental difference relating to their understanding of messianic time. As his title, *The Time that Remains*, indicates, messianic time is the focus of Agamben's reading of Paul. Yet the time that he identifies is significantly different from Badiou's. Whereas Badiou is interested in the messianic event as a radical reorganization, an irruption that cannot be foreseen from the current order of being, Agamben has little sympathy for such apocalyptic readings. With an assurance that would disconcert most historically oriented Pauline scholars, Agamben instead insists that Paul should in no way be considered an apocalyptic thinker: whereas an apocalyptic mind contemplates the end of time and awaits the imminent advent of a new heaven and a new earth, Paul is preoccupied with the time that remains before the end of time. However, this remainder or 'remnant' should not be mistaken for chronological time. Rather, this is a matter of a parallel time, a qualitatively different time that interrupts chronological time and transforms it from within.[54]

Here Agamben puts his finger on what theologians call 'realized eschatology': the idea that the messianic redemption that follows upon Christ's resurrection has already partially begun. To live in expectation of parousia, Christ's return, is thus to live in the tension between 'already' and 'not yet'. This again touches upon the messianic calling, which is precisely about living in a penultimate time *as if* the end of days had already begun. This should not be confused with escapism, a longing for a world beyond the clouds, which takes the joy out of life here and now. On the contrary, this is about intensifying the present time, for which reason, Agamben stresses, Paul speaks about the messianic time as 'the time of the now' *ho nyn kairos* (cf. e.g. Rom. 11:5).[55] In other words, messianic redemption represents the possibility of at every moment bringing time to fulfilment. In a latter essay, Agamben even goes so far as to stress that '[c]ontrary to the contemporary eschatological interpretation, it should not be forgotten that the time of the messiah cannot be, for Paul, a future time'.[56]

Agamben is both right and wrong in making this claim. He is right in the sense that Paul was indeed interested in the 'time that remains'; his epistles are nothing less than a kind of handbook on how the early congregations should live in the remaining time before the Messiah's return. It is also true that Paul represents a realized eschatology, the theological idea that the kingdom of heaven has already begun and that 'the saints' have therefore been summoned to rise above their worldly existence in order to live a life in the spirit. Yet Agamben is mistaken in denying that Paul's worldview contains any apocalyptic elements and that Paul imagines the age of the Messiah as a time that actually lies in the future. When Paul writes that 'the appointed time has grown short' (1 Cor. 7:29) or that 'the day of the Lord will come like a thief in the night' (1 Thess. 5:2), he unequivocally means that the Messiah is just around the corner.[57]

When Agamben quotes these passages, he instead connects them to Benjamin's messianic chips, which irrupt into every moment, filling empty and homogenous time with revolutionary force. The only question is whether Agamben is not here guilty of the same anachronism of which he accuses Badiou (in which it is worth mentioning that Badiou is actually on the right track as regards the apocalyptic aspect of Paul). As noted earlier, Benjamin's messianism can be inscribed within the restorative strand that emerged early on within rabbinic Judaism and which to some extent reverberated in the efforts of the Christian tradition to come to terms with the delay of parousia. This restorative strand was not present from the start, however, but emerged only gradually as the rabbinic (and, in the Christian case, ecclesiastical) authorities sought to come to terms with a proliferation of popular apocalyptic movements. In other words, Agamben tends to ascribe to the Pauline texts a form of messianism which had not yet assumed a definite shape.

All that notwithstanding, I still wish to argue that the restorative messianism to which Agamben has given voice in contemporary political philosophy remains preferable to Badiou's intellectual romance with apocalyptic interruption (my objection, in other words, concerns not the Benjaminian messianism advocated by Agamben but, rather, the fact that Paul can scarcely be claimed to have been its harbinger). While Agamben avoids the temptation of playing memory off against hope, matter against spirit and the particular against the universal, there is nonetheless a point at which his reading of Paul tends to inscribe itself within that most hardy of stereotypes: the polarizing notion of law versus grace (or faith). Like Badiou, Agamben depicts the law as a metonym for subjugation, oppression and potential violence. The concept of law thereby fulfils a primarily negative function, not unlike that of the law in earlier periods within the *adversus Iudaeos* tradition, in which the 'legalistic' tradition of Judaism was counterposed to Christianity's status as the religion of love and mercy. It would, however, be somewhat far-fetched to trace the negative connotations of the concept of law in contemporary philosophy back to the anti-Jewish polemics of the medieval period. In fact, pejorative connotations of the law persisted in secularized form during modernity, leaving their mark on both Marxist and psychoanalytically oriented philosophers.

If nothing else, the fact that this antinomian element need not be interlaced with anti-Jewish polemic will be evident from even the most cursory examination of the two thinkers who, more than any others, have inspired Agamben's reading of Paul. One is the controversial rabbi and philosopher Jacob Taubes, whose *Political Theology of Paul*, mentioned earlier, portrays Paul as a political radical who spread the good news that Christ had redeemed humanity from Jewish as well as Roman law.[58] The other is Benjamin, who has exerted a major influence not only on Agamben's account of Paul more generally but on his account of Paul's concept of law in particular. More precisely, Agamben identifies in the writings of Paul a prototypical version of Benjamin's critical retort to Carl Schmitt's theory of the state of emergency, or, literally, 'state of exception' (*Ausnahmezustand*).

At this point, it is worth considering Schmitt's theory more closely. In a nutshell, Schmitt, as part of his critique of the liberal state, defines the sovereign as the one who has the power to inaugurate a state of exception. To avoid the feedback loop of the liberal state constitution, what is needed is a legally regulated possibility, under exceptional circumstances, to take the decision to pursue a course of action that exceeds the existing legal framework: '[the sovereign] decides whether there is an extreme emergency as well as what must be done to eliminate it. Although he stands outside the normally valid legal system, he nevertheless belongs to it, for it is he who must decide whether the constitution needs to be suspended in its entirety.'[59] The paradoxical situation which then arises is that suspension of the law is itself written into law; the sovereign decides on the state of exception and simultaneously guarantees its basis in the legal system.

Schmitt's notorious theory has become the focus of contemporary politico-philosophical debates as a direct result of the realpolitik developments at the turn of the century. In the wake of the terrorist attacks on New York and Washington DC, a number of exceptional measures have been taken in various parts of the world, with 'national security' or 'the War on Terror' being invoked to legitimize forms of coercion and violence that exceed existing principles of justice. It is also in this light that Agamben's interest in Schmitt in his study *State of Exception*, first published in Italian in 2005, a few years after his commentary on Paul's letters, must be understood. By constructing a legal form for something that cannot have legal form, Schmitt's right-wing revolutionary theory functions as a kind of distorting mirror to the subtle absolutism that is currently undermining Western democracies. The only difference is that Schmitt imagined the state of exception as precisely an *exception* whose purpose was to guarantee the normal state of affairs, while today's supposedly democratic governments tend to make mechanisms of the state of exception into a rule.

> Faced with the unstoppable progression of what has been called a 'global civil war', the state of exception tends increasingly to appear as the dominant paradigm of government in contemporary politics. This transformation of a provisional and exceptional measure into a technique of government threatens radically to alter – in fact, has already palpably altered – the structure and meaning of the traditional distinction between constitutional forms. Indeed, from this perspective, the state of exception appears as a threshold of indeterminacy between democracy and absolutism.[60]

Benjamin foresaw this tendency early on. In the eighth of his 'Theses on the Philosophy of History', written only a few months before his death in 1940, he states: 'The tradition of the oppressed teaches us that the "state of emergency" in which we live is not the exception but the rule'. Yet the fragment does not include any call to fight for the restoration of the rule of law. Instead, Benjamin declares that the task now in hand is to bring about a 'real state of emergency' in order to thereby strengthen the position of resistance in 'the struggle against Fascism'.[61] The fragment can be seen as a late echo of the famous essay which Benjamin had published back in 1921 under the title 'Critique of Violence' and which, according to Agamben, was the opening salvo in a critical exchange between Benjamin and Schmitt that continued for many years. Even at this early stage, Benjamin evoked a state in which militarism and police violence rendered the boundary between law and violence arbitrary. Against this lawless or 'mythical' violence, he offers at the end of his essay a 'divine', 'pure' or 'revolutionary' violence that neither establishes nor maintains justice, but rather aims to abolish it: 'But if the existence of violence outside the law, as pure immediate violence, is assured, this furnishes the proof that revolutionary violence, the highest manifestation of unalloyed violence by man, is possible, and by what means'.[62]

Whereas Schmitt's theory of a state of exception sought to bring violence back within a judicial context (precisely by enshrining the state of exception in law), Benjamin's idea was that a pure revolutionary violence would shatter the whole illusion that lawless violence can remain in a legitimate relationship with the legal order. It is this ambition of Benjamin's that Agamben seizes upon. Where Schmitt formulated the very logic behind the state of exception that is now attaining its 'its maximum worldwide deployment',[63] Benjamin showed a way to dismantle this logic by securing a locus of resistance outside the law. The only question is: What guarantees that this new locus does not in turn degenerate into a platform for arbitrary violence? Benjamin's answer was that once this happens we are no longer dealing with a pure or divine violence. Pure violence can never appear as a presiding or executive violence; only as a critical unmasking of the symbiosis between violence and justice. Here can be discerned the messianic strain in Benjamin's thought that emerged in full force in his theses of 1940, whose reference to a 'real state of emergency' should not be mistaken for an appeal to lawlessness for its own sake. Rather, as Agamben explains, it is a matter of not confusing existing judicial orders with justice as such: 'What opens a passage toward justice is not the erasure of law, but its deactivation and inactivity [*inoperosità*] – that is, another use of the law'.[64]

At this point Agamben's reading of Paul should be recalled. Benjamin challenged the law in the name of a higher justice, and Agamben finds prototypical formulation of this gesture in Paul. Just as Benjamin revealed how Schmitt's theory of the state of exception grinds to a halt when the state of exception becomes the rule, Paul showed how Jewish law, with its elaborate regulations, ultimately constrained the individual in such a fashion that the law ceased to have a normative function. Paul expressed this most pithily in his self-scrutinizing reflections on the law in the seventh chapter of his Letter to the Romans: 'What then should we say? That the law is sin? By no means! Yet, if it had not been for the law, I would not have known sin. I would not have known what it is to covet if the law had not said, "You shall not covet." But sin, seizing an opportunity in the commandment, produced in me all kinds of covetousness' (Rom. 7:7–8). Paul here gives a name to a situation in which it has become impossible to tell the difference between being within the law and being outside it; in which legal regulations snare humanity in unending self-reproach; and in which those who seek to follow the law in fact end up breaking it.[65]

Agamben emphasizes that, for Paul, the way out of this dead-end is through Christ, since Christ marks 'the end of the law' (Rom. 10:4). In accordance with his precept that the individual is summoned to be 'a slave of Christ', Paul dissolved the very distinction between those who were under the law and those who were without law (Jews and non-Jews) – not by extending the regulations of the law to include non-Jews but by showing that the law in its existing form had become ineffective. Yet Agamben underscores that, for Paul, dissolving the law was not merely an act of negation. In criticizing the law, what Paul had in mind were its normative regulations, not the very idea of living a moral life. Thus Paul could insist, as, for example, in Chapter Thirteen of his Letter to the Romans, that 'the one who loves another has fulfilled the law' and that love is 'the fulfilling of the law' (Rom. 13:8,10). In other words, Paul calls into question a particular use of the law in the name of another, higher use, for which reason he is able to make a rhetorical contrast between 'the law of works' and 'the law of faith' (Rom. 3:27). The messianic suspension of the law is thus revealed as being ultimately a struggle within the law itself; an attempt, in the name of the promise contained in the law, to suspend its specific regulations.[66]

Despite Agamben's sensitivity to the complexity of the law in Paul, his reading nonetheless results in a polarizing schema in which law – in the sense of regulations, decrees and acts – is counterposed to a general promise of justice that lies hidden within the law itself. Ultimately, the true purpose of the law seems to be to dissolve itself in its positive form. This is not the place in which to offer a more thoroughgoing discussion of the actual significance of the law in the Pauline texts. Nonetheless, I wish to raise a question about the fundamental significance of the antinomian qualities shared by Badiou's and Agamben's readings of Paul. Specifically, I contend that it is here that the gravest flaw in the messianic motif as it has reappeared in contemporary politico-philosophical debate is found. Setting up the law as the opposite of messianic liberation leaves little or no space for the law as something good *in itself*, which is what it has been for most of the history of the Jewish tradition and to some extent in Christian theology also.

Although the current debate over Paul is about the law as a theologeme and a philosopheme – that is to say, as metonymic of more profound theological and philosophical points of principle – the tendency to depict the law as an obstacle to emancipation, rather than its precondition, has important consequences at the concrete politico-philosophical level. When Agamben argues that we live in a state of exception that has today attained its 'maximum worldwide deployment', his illustrative examples range from the countless violations committed in the name of the 'War on Terror' to the subtle shift from legislative to executive power that has taken place in several Western democracies and that has in practice resulted in political laws becoming increasingly subordinate to those of the market.

It goes without question that these developments should be made visible and criticized. My objection concerns the way in which this critique is formulated and delivered. By drawing on terms such as 'violence' and 'state of exception' – rather than, for example, 'corruption' and 'democratic deficit' – to describe ongoing societal developments, one does not merely create a problematic kind of conceptual inflation; one also risks obscuring the progressive judicial developments that are *de facto* taking place in democratic societies. In *State of Exception*, Agamben portrays the current judicial-political system as a 'killing machine' which has 'continued to function almost without interruption from World War One, through fascism and National Socialism, and up to our own time'.[67] What this monolithic historical description entirely overlooks is that the period since 1918 (and since 1945 in particular) has also coincided with the emergence of supranational legal institutions and conventions intended to strengthen the international legal system and thereby create stronger protections *against* abuse and violence. Naturally, this development does not mean that Agamben's critique is without its merits – international law is a vast edifice whose actual authority remains weak. Yet it nonetheless serves to remind us that the law as it currently stands is not *synonymous* with violence, coercion or repression. Whatever the continual shortcomings of the law, efforts are being continually made, nationally and internationally, to develop and strengthen legal protections for groups and individuals who have previously been the target of oppression and discrimination.

It is significant that Agamben's critique entirely omits these progressive aspects of the current judicial-political order. Following Benjamin, he invariably insists upon 'the law' as an obstacle to emancipation, thereby revealing an inability to acknowledge that legal norms can also act as a radical force that shapes and challenges existing social norms in a progressive direction (environmental legislation and anti-discrimination laws are both illustrative examples). Indeed, Agamben's refusal to assign the law any kind of constructive role is symptomatic of a more fundamental problem in contemporary political messianism: an absence of plausible alternatives to the parliamentary democracy that is being rejected. Like Badiou, Agamben seeks to find a basis for political opposition to the current state and legal systems. The problem is that his critique does not go beyond mere opposition. For his part, Agamben ends up embracing Benjamin's idea of a permanent state of exception: 'From the real state of exception in which we live, it is not possible to return to the state of law [*stato di diritto*], for at issue now are the very concepts of "state" and "law"'.[68] The question that needs answering is: which institutions and practices should provide the basis for justice in a post-statist and post-judicial society? To use more theological terms, the permanent state of exception is distinctly reminiscent of the Garden of Eden.[69]

It might reasonably be objected here that I am disregarding the deeper implications of the *messianic* strand within contemporary radical political philosophies; after all, Badiou and Agamben have called not for lawlessness but for a questioning of the existing judicial system in the name of a more radical notion of justice. That their politico-philosophical efforts have not become stuck in a purely negative critique can also be seen from their respective readings of Paul, in which Badiou and Agamben, despite their substantial differences, both conclude by embracing a higher law – the law of 'faith' or 'spirit' – above and beyond that which binds humanity in political and moral unfreedom.

The question is simply whether this is not in fact the greatest problem of all. Even if the messianic strand does call for a constructive critique of existing judicial-political structures, the antinomian elements in Badiou's and Agamben's thought nonetheless lead to their celebrating purity of faith over the decrees of the law. Let me return for a moment to Benjamin's essay on violence in order to highlight the problem of this zeal for purity. To be sure, Benjamin insists that no-one can lay claim to represent 'pure' or 'divine' violence since this would never 'be recognizable as such with certainty'.[70] Nonetheless, he takes pains to distinguish 'divine' violence from 'mythical' violence, thereby revealing his own confidence in a pure violence that is not merely the means to an end. This faith is echoed by the concluding words of Agamben's *State of Exception*: 'We will then have before us a "pure" right, in the sense in which Benjamin speaks of a "pure" language and a "pure" violence. To a word that does not bind, that neither commands nor prohibits anything, but says only itself, would correspond an action as pure means, which shows only itself, without any relation to an end.'[71] Although the influence of Benjamin is less immediate in Badiou's writings, a similar faith can be descried in his conviction that the revolutionary political act can never find support in existing judicial-political structures, having its sole legitimate foundation in the engaged revolutionary subject.

It is precisely this faith in pure resistance, untainted justice and radical breaks that I wish to question. As Derrida has remarked in a famous commentary to the text, Benjamin's essay, despite its greatness, relies upon a deeply problematic notion that 'divine' violence could ever be distinguished from 'mythical' violence. There exists no pure violence beyond the violence implied in the foundation of law and the violence implied in the conservation of law, no more than there exists any pure position of resistance beyond the system against which that resistance is directed. On the contrary, the very quest for purity itself tends to give rise to a kind of violence that is anything but pure.[72]

The distinction between law in the sense of normative regulations and the notion of a 'higher' law of the spirit championed by both Agamben and Badiou may be considered from another angle. As Emmanuel Levinas has noted in one of his Talmudic readings, it has always been tempting to summarize the Bible's complex legal systems in a few 'spiritual' principles: 'Everyone is seduced by what might be called the angelic essence of the Torah, to which many verses and commandments can be reduced. This "internalization" of the Law enchants our liberal souls and we are inclined to reject anything which seems to resist the "rationality" or the "morality" of the Torah.'[73] The only question is: what is lost in this eagerness to abandon the concrete aspects of the law? Whereas the law, with its seemingly superfluous decrees and regulations, binds us to our finitude, history and physicality, the injunction to suspend the law seduces us with a fantasy of being able to rise above our material complexity and acquire an angelic view of the world. The problem with angels, to quote Levinas again, is simply that they are not human: 'as a purely spiritual being, … [the Angel] has no need to eat, or take, or give, or work, or even not to work on the Shabbat! He is a principle of generosity, but no more than a principle'.[74]

In contrast to those longstanding stereotypes that associate the law with coercion and prohibitions, the law here appears in all its *affirmative* force. Rather than restricting and denying humanity in its everyday temporal existence, the law in its Jewish setting represents more than anything a recognition of our concretely embodied life. Thus, for example, Yeshayahu Leibowitz, writing in a similar spirit to Levinas, has observed that '[t]he Judaism of the Halakhah despises rhetoric, avoids pathos, abjures the visionary.... It prevents flight from one's functions and tasks in this inferior world to an imaginary world in which is all good, beautiful, and sublime. Not by chance are so many of the Mitzvoth concerned with the body, procreation and birth, food and drink, sexual life, diseases, and the corpse'.[75]

If the law in this theological sense symbolizes all those tiny practices that tie us to the everyday, that enjoin us to remember and that safeguard our physical being, it is also here that its politico-philosophical value lies. The law becomes a metonym for the realpolitik demands of reality, protecting us from the illusory attempt to escape the contradictions, tensions and unstable conventions that define everyday politics. As has been illustrated above, it is precisely here that the weakness lies in a political messianism that plays off law against grace. The temptation to replace law with grace is inextricable from the temptation to evade the contradiction between conditional practices and unconditional principles. Yet political reality unfolds within precisely this field of tensions. To be sure, politics can require moments of will and determination, but it also relies to a great degree on compromise, mediation and the ability to relate to the unforeseeable. The theological figure for such a perspective is a messianism that sees the law not as an obstacle to redemption but rather as God's answer to humanity's longing for redemption. Law is not the opposite of grace but a tool given by God so that humanity itself can change its historical conditions for the better.

On Spirits and Ghosts

Badiou's and Agamben's polarizing of law and grace can be problematized from other vantage points than the politico-philosophical. A third prominent voice in the philosophical debate over Paul is Slavoj Žižek, whose psychoanalytically oriented critique can shed light on how the pneumatic motif is being foregrounded in the present moment. Although Žižek proceeds in large part from the reading of Paul established by Badiou in *Saint Paul* in 1997, their readings differ in one crucial respect, namely on the issue of law. Briefly, Žižek poses the question of whether Badiou, in his eagerness to suspend the law, in fact swathes himself in a higher, invisible, but no less oppressive law. Beneath this critique can be discerned Badiou's and Žižek's differing relationship to Jacques Lacan, an important influence on both philosophers.

For Badiou, psychoanalysis provides a crucial insight into the intricate bond between law and desire; that is, how the law – to invoke Paul once again – elicits the very desire to transgress it. Yet Lacan, who was himself fascinated by Paul's meditations on law and desire, never offered a way out of this morbid conflation of prohibition and transgression. On the contrary, argues Badiou, in psychoanalysis the subject remains bound to 'the order of being' and thus incapable of conceptualizing a space beyond the law. However, as described above, the belief that the subject can indeed rise above the oppressive structures of being forms the very backbone of Badiou's philosophy in general and his reading of Paul's texts in particular.[76]

Žižek engaged with Badiou's reading of Paul barely two years after the publication of *Saint Paul*. In *The Ticklish Subject* (1999), he reproached his colleague not only for having underestimated the complexity of the subject's economy of desire. In his strong faith in a radical break with the law, argued Žižek, Badiou had quite simply missed Lacan's point – that what is illusory is the very belief that we can shake off the law by simply suspending it.[77] That Badiou's reading of Paul tends to cloak itself in a more subtle reliance upon the law is, incidentally, confirmed by an interesting slip in his own argument. To the question of how the radical subject generated by the event might actually stand outside the law, Badiou replies in *Saint Paul* that the love or grace that replaces the law can equally well be formulated in terms of a 'law of the break with law'.[78]

What, then, is this subtle form of law that reveals itself beyond the suspension of the law in its manifest or positive form? Žižek elaborated his answer a few years later, by which time Agamben had also published his reading of Paul. In *The Puppet and the Dwarf* (2003), Žižek delivered a polemic against Agamben, whose reading of Paul, he claimed, even more clearly than Badiou's, ends up defending a higher law beyond 'the law of works'. The basis for Žižek's critique is Lacan's thesis that 'the big Other' (*le grand Autre*) – the guarantor of the symbolic order within which we are socialized – no longer exists. In the modern era, Žižek contends, traditional norms, regulations and decrees have been modified, with the result that the established connection between law and transgression has been dissolved; in other words, when a norm loses its power, so, too, does its transgression. This does not mean, however, that we have been liberated from the law. On the contrary, it is here that the truly intricate game of the law begins. Believing that we have liberated ourselves from the burdensome norms of tradition, we fail to notice that we have in fact internalized the big Other in the form of the obscene law of the superego. As an example, Žižek invokes the 'permissive', experiential culture of late capitalism, which urges us to enjoy sex without guilt. In the superego's coercive injunction to take pleasure, the 'underside' of traditional (prohibitive) law reveals itself. The result is that late-capitalist subjects find themselves in a state of continual angst and dissatisfaction because they are not enjoying themselves sufficiently, sufficiently well or in a sufficiently sophisticated manner.[79]

The dictum of modern atheism, 'if God is dead, everything is permitted', is therefore misleading. On the contrary, if God does not exist, then everything is forbidden, something Lacan also noted. It is this generalization and internationalization of the law that preoccupies Žižek in his critique of Badiou and Agamben. There is an interesting parallel here to Levinas's remarks on the treacherousness of trying to extract an 'angelic essence' from Jewish law. Nonetheless, they have quite different aims; not only because Žižek develops his argument from within a psychoanalytic discourse, but because they represent two essentially different relationships to the law. This much is evident from Žižek's broader critique of Agamben, which not only targets the latter's inability to supersede the law without cloaking himself in the 'hyperbolic' law of the superego. Žižek's real objection in fact concerns the way in which Agamben downplays the universal impulse of Paul's texts. On this issue, Žižek unequivocally follows Badiou, insisting that the only road to a radical universalism runs through the suspension of particular identities. Where Levinas's critique aims at reconciling the law with its concretion and materiality, Žižek quite simply aims to radicalize this break with the law; not merely with the prohibitive law but also with the obscene law of the superego (the compulsive transgression). Only by means of this double movement, he proposes, can a true universalism come into existence.[80]

By this point it should be clear that Žižek's concern is not limited to psychoanalysis. Every bit as much as Badiou and Agamben, he is interested in the politico-philosophical consequences of Paul's reflections on the law. In showing how the law generates transgression, Paul speaks directly to the present cultural situation, in which an eagerness to continually transgress and contest an order regarded as oppressive has made us blind to the inherent laws of transgression itself. Žižek offers as an example the utter conventionality with which contemporary art ceaselessly seeks to challenge received norms and taboos: 'is there anything more dull, opportunistic, and sterile than to succumb to the superego injunction of incessantly inventing new artistic transgressions and provocations?'[81] The pattern is also visible in the realm of religion – the 'free-thinking' neo-atheist whose struggle against superstition takes on all the characteristics of religious zealotry – or, come to that, some aspects of international politics, as when warring 'democratic' nations are willing to stoop to torture in order to fight 'anti-democratic' fundamentalism.[82]

Would it be possible to move beyond the law, not merely in its definite form, but also when it functions as a diffuse meta-law generating subtler but no less violent varieties of oppression? Žižek's reply is that such an avenue exists, and that its path runs through the 'perverse' or 'subversive' core of Christianity. In order to reach this core, however, it is necessary to grasp the dialectical element of Christian theology. In other words, it is not enough to announce, as Badiou does, an absolute break with law and grace; for true grace to be revealed, a double negation is required. This was precisely what occurred on the Cross. By extending Hegel's historico-philosophical account of Christian doctrine of God, Žižek portrays the Christian idea of the Cross as a decisive moment in the history of human thought. What was revealed on the Cross was *both* God's alienation from himself ('Father, why have you forsaken me?') *and* humanity's alienation from God (a powerless God is not a credible God). This double alienation is not the end of the road, however. Though God in his capacity as transcendent Father ('the Absolute In-Itself') has, as a first step, been sublated in the Son ('God-for-us'), the Son has been sublated in turn in the Holy Spirit.[83]

The question is whether this Hegelian trope does not in fact lead to an even stronger assertion of an absolute or divine substance – absolute Spirit – as the basis for all reality. Like many contemporary thinkers, Žižek defends himself against such a reading of Hegel: 'The point this reading misses is the ultimate lesson to be learned from the divine Incarnation: the finite existence of mortal humans is the only site of the Spirit, the site where the Spirit achieves its actuality'.[84] It is also at this point that Christianity's truly emancipatory potential reveals itself. By experiencing heaven as empty, seeing that there is no absolute being that guarantees the meaning of life, humans are at last freed to affirm themselves as finite beings, with the ability to change their own fate:

> 'Holy Spirit' designates a new collective held together not only by a Master-Signifier, but by fidelity to a Cause, by the effort to draw a new line of separation that runs 'beyond Good and Evil', that is to say, that runs across and suspends the distinctions of the existing social body. The key dimension of Paul's gesture is thus his break with any form of communitarianism: his universe is no longer that of the multitude of groups that want to 'find their voice', and assert their particular identity, their 'way of life', but that of a fighting collective grounded in the reference to an unconditional universalism.[85]

The quotation reveals Žižek's proximity to Badiou, even as his broader argument makes clear the difference between them: Badiou's stated anti-dialectical view of suspending the law versus Žižek's emphasis upon the necessity of the dialectic. The double negation revealed on the Cross, says Žižek, has served to abolish not only God as the big Other but also the big Other's supplement in the form of the obscene superego. Only by means of this dialectical movement is it possible to achieve a genuine suspension of the law, a suspension that will permit us to go beyond not only the explicit law with its decrees and regulations, but also the diffuse meta-law that constitutes its shadow.[86]

By constructing the relation between law and grace in dialectical terms, Žižek ends up, to my mind, with a considerably more dynamic and complex perspective than Badiou's. This means, at least for this stage of his argument, that he distances himself from the stereotyping formula that connects Judaism with reactionary particularism (the law) and Christianity with emancipatory universalism (grace). Instead, Žižek emphasizes that the two traditions are interwoven and that Hellenistic diaspora Judaism to a considerable degree anticipated Christianity's suspension of the law in the sense of a dominant social order. Where Roman law sought to regulate the lives of its citizens, the Jews' fidelity to a higher, divine justice constituted a challenge to the imperial order. It is precisely this cosmopolitan impulse in Judaism that is fulfilled in Christianity, one consequence of which is that a Christian theology that believes itself to be making a sharp break with Jewish law continually risks betraying this cosmopolitan quality by falling back upon a self-encompassing imperial violence.[87]

Even so, Žižek continues to regard Judaism as incapable of suspending the law in its 'hyperbolic' sense. He highlights the contrast between Job and Jesus as an illustrative example. Both cried out in despair to a heaven that, by remaining silent, dispelled the illusion of God the merciful Father. In both cases, their suffering was cruel, meaningless and unfathomable. The difference is that Job, the suffering human, remained trapped in an alienated relationship to a God who, in his unfathomableness, had turned his face away, while Christ, the son of God, transformed the gap between God and humanity into a gap within God himself. If the story of Job thereby seeks to conceal the powerlessness of the big Other, the story of Christ, by contrast, serves to expose God's impotence: 'Christianity is the religion of Revelation: everything is revealed in it, no obscene superego supplement accompanies its public message'.[88]

Judaism, as represented here by Job, was never capable of taking the decisive step, Žižek contends. Instead of bringing the truth of God's powerlessness into the light of day and allowing the ghost to be revealed, the suppressed insight of God's powerlessness remained the secret that held together the Jewish community throughout history (and that, according to Žižek, also preserved its vitality: 'they refused to give up their ghost, to cut off the link to their secret, disavowed tradition'[89]). As the Jews remained shackled to their ghost, their delimited community, it seemed only natural that the baton of history should have passed to Christianity. Paul's great achievement was to put this event into words:

> Saint Paul conceives of the Christian community as the new incarnation of the chosen people: it is Christians who are the true 'children of Abraham'. What was, in its first incarnation, a distinct ethnic group is now a community of free believers that suspends all ethnic divisions (or, rather, cuts a line of separation *within* each ethnic group) – the chosen people are those who have faith in Christ. Thus we have a kind of *'transubstantiation' of the chosen people*: God kept his promise of redemption to the Jewish people, but, in the process itself, he changed the identity of the chosen people.[90]

While Žižek initially seems to offer a more complex view of the relationship between law and grace, the Jewish and the Christian, his dialectical reading in fact ends in a reinforced polarity: 'It is *only* Christianity which properly completes the Law by, in effect, getting rid of the undead reminder – and, of course, this completion is the Law's self-sublation, its transmutation into Love'.[91] The dialectical movement also means that Žižek replaces Badiou's and Agamben's bipartite schema with a tripartite one, with the result that he focuses less on the messianic motif and more on the pneumatic: redemption is not fulfilled by the messianic event but by the Holy Spirit, the power that binds together and actuates the emancipatory political collective.[92]

Žižek's focus on the spirit as the third element of a redemptive dialectical movement foregrounds the line running from Joachim of Fiore, via Romanticism, to those late-twentieth-century philosophers who resurrected the spirit concept in order to formulate progressive political visions. It thereby also illustrates the problematic that accompanies this specific history of effects. As has been argued at several points in the present study, the idea of the development of the spirit contains a paradoxical tension between expansion and exclusion: the same spirit that widens the boundaries of the existing community tends to create new, exclusionary demarcations as it moves towards the higher stages of history. This pattern is perhaps most clearly articulated in Hegel's polarization of the spirit of Judaism and that of Christianity, with Judaism being presented as an ossified religion that has long ago played out its historical role.

As has already been indicated, Hegel is also the philosopher that Žižek draws on most explicitly in his analysis of Christian theology ('Hegel is *the* Christian philosopher'[93]), something that explains, while hardly excusing, the breathtaking stereotyping in which he indulges himself. While it can be said in Hegel's defence that the notion of Judaism as an undead reminder was, if not a commonplace, at least widespread among intellectuals at that time, the same can hardly be said of Žižek's present-day remarks on the subject:

> The problem of shofar – the voice of the dying father rendered in the Jewish ritual by the low, ominously reverberating sound of a horn – is that of the rise of the Law out of the Father's death: Lacan's point is that, in order for the Law to arise, the Father should not wholly die, a part of him should survive and sustain the Law. This is why shofar occurs in Judaism, the religion of the dead God – monotheism is as such the religion of a dead God. Shofar is not a pagan reminder, a sign of the death of the pagan God, but something generated by the monotheistic turn. The shift from Judaism to Christianity is discernable precisely in the shift from shofar – the cry of the dying God-*Father* – to 'Father, why have you forsaken me!', the cry of the dying *son* on the cross.[94]

Žižek's damning image of Judaism has been the focus of much debate over the years, and it is not my intention to prolong that debate here (in this context it should be clarified that the shofar, the horn used at specific moments in the Jewish liturgy, has few associations with the death or absence of God and, rather, alludes to repentance and reconciliation).[95] Rather, what interests me are the larger philosophical implications of his supersessionist line of argument. Just like Vattimo – and that whole line of thinkers extending back from Hegel to Joachim – Žižek advances the thesis that a genuinely emancipatory philosophy can only be formulated within the framework of the Christian legacy (hence the subtitle of one of his more talked-about works, *The Fragile Absolute – Or, Why Is the Christian Legacy Worth Fighting For?*, published in 2000). This categorical stance, which is hardly representative of the majority of contemporary Christian theologians, has brought Žižek allies from unexpected quarters. I wish to consider one of these alliances in order to pin down more clearly the problematic aspect of his position.

This chapter opened with reference to John Milbank's groundbreaking and hotly debated work, *Theology and Social Theory*, published in 1990. In retrospect, this book can be seen to have launched a new, politically radical but theologically conservative trend within contemporary academic theology. A decade later, Milbank emerged as the leading figure of 'radical orthodoxy', a loose grouping of British theologians whose goal – as stated in their collaborative work *Radical Orthodoxy* (1999) – was to recover the voice of theology in the secular public sphere (an ambition which Milbank had already declared in *Theology and Social Theory*). What unified these theologians was a strong emphasis not only on Christian practice (in both the liturgical and social sense), but also on the Christian community as a culture that stood in marked contrast to the dominant secular culture.[96]

These qualities ostensibly have little in common with the 'subversive core' that prompts Žižek to claim that the Christian legacy is worth fighting for. As a self-confessed atheist and materialist, he has little time for Christian practice in its traditional sense and argues that Christianity's real challenge today is to abandon its 'institutional organization' and 'specific religious experience' in order to unleash its radical political potential.[97] Nevertheless, in the past decade Žižek and Milbank have conducted a lively debate that has resulted in a series of joint publications.[98] The key to this unexpected intellectual agreement becomes clearer when one recalls Milbank's aim in *Theology and Social Theory* – to challenge the modern myth of a self-constituting secular politics. Milbank and Žižek are united not only in their critique of political liberalism but also in their opposition to the traditional academic Left's inability to confront the repressive structures of capitalist society. Their critical targets are deconstructionist philosophers as well as liberal theologians – all these (in Milbank's words) 'craven, weak, sentimental theologians, … who claim to believe in some sort of remote, abstract, transcendent deity and who yet compromise the universal claims of Christianity in favor of mystical relativism, glorification of hypostasized uncertainty, and practical indulgence in the malignly infinite air-shuttle of mindless "dialogue"'.[99]

Can any discipline thus offer resistance to the sinister logic of capitalist society? Žižek and Milbank pose this rhetorical question in the foreword to one of their joint publications and reply that such a discipline exists and its name is *theology*. Now, as noted previously, this is a question, not of theology in general, but of an 'uncompromising' Pauline theology with the ability to break free of the 'ironic, postmodern deadlock' and 'risk the Absolute in the face of the shifting sands of relativism'.[100] It should be clarified here that 'the Absolute' has a somewhat different connotation for each author; for Milbank, it is identical with God's transcendent reality as revealed in Christ, while Žižek, as has been shown here, entirely rejects the idea of both a transcendent Father and an immanent Son. For his part, Žižek situates the absolute in a dialectical movement that, thanks to humanity's emancipation from all sacral illusions, results in the emergence of a combative political collective.[101] Despite their fundamentally different worldviews – theological realism versus dialectical materialism – Žižek and Milbank nonetheless remain in touching agreement that the road to genuine emancipation lies through Christianity alone: '*only* Christianity ... allows differences to coexist peaceably, and so ... permits differences to flourish (and the neighbor to appear)'.[102]

The debate between Milbank and Žižek is illuminating on several counts, but perhaps most because it sheds light on the simultaneously abstract and arrogant universalism that they both champion in the name of Christian theology. In a declamatory fashion, they insist that the Christian Cross is a bulwark against 'the shifting sands of relativism'. What the substantive meaning of the Christian story of the Cross is – the revelation of a transcendent God or the revelation that there never was any God – reveals itself to be of secondary importance. The same holds true of the practical consequences of the story of the Cross – a liturgically conscious Christian community or the dissolution of the church as an institutional organization. In other words, Milbank and Žižek seem to be so eager to defend the exclusivity and superiority of Christian truth that they are prepared to disregard the fact that the truth which they are defending in fact has very different meanings depending on its concrete manifestation.

To be sure, Žižek would under no circumstances admit the charge of championing an abstract universalism, let alone an arrogant one. On the contrary, this is the very premise of his critique of existing universalist projects relating to human rights: in the name of a putatively universal perspective, we in fact privilege certain groups while excluding others. A radical political universalism must instead take as its starting point that which is excluded, 'the Remainder' that has already and in advance been deprived of its place within 'official' universality: 'it is those who are excluded, with no proper place within the global order, who directly embody true universality, who represent the Whole in contrast to all others who stand only for their particular interests'.[103] Behind these words can be discerned Badiou's concept of a 'universal singularity', an assertion of universality which presupposes the absolute equality of every subject and which thereby cuts directly across any claim to particularity.

Naturally, Žižek's reference to 'the Remainder' as the true bearer of the universal can be seen as a bulwark against the arrogant tendencies highlighted above. Any discussion of the universal that does not continually scrutinize itself for the exclusion of marginal voices runs the risk of ending up as a covert form of colonialism. Even so, I want to argue that Žižek undermines the potential of his own argument by categorically rejecting the particular. Just as his debate with Milbank reveals that Žižek, in his desire to reach formal agreement upon the superiority of Christianity, is prepared to ignore the significance of the particular content of the Christian tradition, so, too, does his notion of the universal require him to disregard the particular attributes of those 'with no proper place within the global order'. Upon closer inspection, 'the Remainder' reveals itself to be an empty figure, a pure principle from which Žižek can make the argument that true emancipation derives from the margins. Had he instead taken an interest in the real subjects of 'the Remainder' – people of differing cultural backgrounds with potentially conflicting ideological, political and religious conceptions of freedom and justice – he would have been forced to concede the complexity and nuance that necessarily characterize any responsible discussion of universal human emancipation.[104]

It must be underscored here that my objection does not relate to the ambition of formulating universal emancipatory visions itself. On the contrary: this is certainly one of contemporary political philosophy's more pressing tasks. Nor does my objection relate to the fact that Žižek situates claims to universality within the framework of Christian theology. The problem is Žižek's categorical assertion that *only* the Christian tradition is capable of articulating truly emancipatory visions – an assertion that is both false and counter-productive. Ironically, he is at the same time strikingly uninterested in the specific content of the Christian tradition, with the result that he never undertakes the critical self-reflection that is a precondition for any claim to universality that does not assert itself at the expense of other traditions.

Žižek's unwillingness to engage with the particular parallels his (and Badiou's) lack of interest in the historical, the empirical and the material. They may be full of revolutionary pathos, but disappointment awaits any reader of Žižek's writings looking for substantial reflection upon the concrete conditions of possibility for the revolutionary project. Žižek would in all likelihood reply that such reflection is futile insofar as the authentically revolutionary event is characterized by the fact that it can never be announced or predicted from a position within the current order: 'there is no Event outside the engaged subjective decision which creates it – if we wait for the time to become ripe for the Event, the Event will never occur. ... Authentic revolution, in contrast, always occurs in an absolute Present'.[105] Here, too, Badiou's influence can be seen clearly, raising once again the question of how so decisionist a stance can escape the arbitrariness of violence.

While Žižek broadly mirrors Badiou in showing little or no interest in the concrete and institutional aspects of political reality, there is nonetheless an important difference between them as regards their respective understanding of the revolutionary project's future. This difference leads back to the different functions which the messianic and pneumatic motifs perform in their thinking. Earlier in this chapter, Badiou and Agamben were criticized for subscribing to a kind a political messianism that resulted in a vision of pure resistance beyond state, party and laws. For Žižek, this reactive stance is symptomatic of a mode of thought that is unable to carry out the double movement of the dialectic. In other words, it is not enough merely to separate politics from the state; a fully emancipatory movement requires a 'negation of the negation', which in practice means a revolutionary recapture of the state. Žižek has a specific name for this third movement in the dialectical movement: *the dictatorship of the proletariat*.[106]

Provocative formulations are part of Žižek's philosophical jargon, and what he means by 'the dictatorship of the proletariat' differs in part from what the concept has historically denoted. What Žižek is calling for is 'the tremulous moment when the complex web of representations is suspended due to the direct intrusion of universality into the political field'.[107] In other words, this is a question of the proletariat's instituting of a radically egalitarian order, something which accordingly requires more than a reactive distancing from that of the state. Behind this argument can be discerned the central idea in Žižek's reading of Paul: the emancipatory movement will not be realized through suspension of the exterior law (the death of the Father) but only by means of that double sublation by which Christ (the dead Son) is resurrected in the form of the animating spirit (the Holy Spirit) of the political avant-garde in struggle. It is thus this third, affirmative element that differentiates Žižek's pneumatic vision from Badiou's (and Agamben's) messianic negation of the state and the law.

The only question is what prevents Žižek's version of the dictatorship of the proletariat from developing into a dictatorship in its conventional sense – or what the dictatorship of the proletariat hitherto has developed into in its historical manifestations. Žižek's reply is that in his dictatorship the proletariat is constituted by 'the Remainder' or what, borrowing Jacques Rancière's formulation, he calls 'the part of no-part' (*la part des sans-part*): 'Insofar as the proletariat designates the "part of no-part" which stands for universality, the "dictatorship of the proletariat" is the power of universality where those who are the "part of no-part" set the tone. ... [A]s the part of no-part, they lack the particular features that would legitimate their place within the social body – they belong to the set of society without belonging to any of its subsets.'[108]

What prevents Žižek's emancipatory vision from degenerating into an oppressive dictatorship is thus that 'the new rulers' are directly and immediately related to 'the part of no-part'.[109] The only problem, as already argued above, is that this part, in Žižek's account, is devoid of any kind of particularity. This downplaying of the fact that even those officially denied an identity (sexual, cultural, religious or other) are concrete subjects, indivisible from their identities, is also a precondition of Žižek's assertion of 'the Remainder' as a guarantor of the universal. In other words, by neglecting the diversity of the substantial visions of justice and liberation represented by the subjects of 'the Remainder', Žižek is able to hold up 'the Remainder' as the bearer of a universal emancipatory potential.

Another question that is left hanging is who or what will speak for 'the Remainder' and thereby represent the universal. Taken together with the decisionist aspect of his ideas, Žižek's rhetoric, which is replete with terms such as 'terror', 'dictatorship' and 'violence', hardly inspires confidence. On the contrary, it reinforces the impression of an arrogant universalism that offers few critical obstacles to the elevation of its own concept of the revolutionary event to the status of an unimpeachable truth. When one adds to this picture Žižek's protracted flirtation with exclusivistic forms of Christian theology (Hegel, Chesterton, Milbank), his philosophical project ultimately comes to resemble an extreme position within the Joachite-Romantic tradition.

At this point the ambiguity that attaches to the spirit as a historico-philosophical motif is encountered once again. While references to the spirit have at all times inspired oppressed groups to call into question and break with repressive structures, this emancipatory impulse has also at times tended to bleed into its opposite – the flight from the body and towards a purely spiritual world; the dream of a radical departure at the expense of memory and history; the assertion of the universal by means of a denial or outright obliteration of the particular. Žižek's presentation of the universal is symptomatic in all these respects and reveals the precariousness of invoking the pneumatic motif as a critical resource in contemporary politico-philosophical debate.

Does this mean that the concept of spirit has played out its role? My own view is that such is not the case, even if this concept, like the messianic, needs to be criticized and modified. In this respect I align myself with a long line of theologians who in recent years have returned to the biblical concept of spirit in order to criticize its later evolution within the Western tradition. As argued in the first chapter of this book, both the Hebraic *ruach* and the Greek *pneuma* are characterized by a semantic complexity that is partly lost by translation into the considerably narrower Latin term *spiritus*. What differentiates the biblical concept of 'spirit' above all is that it is not involved in the dualism between spirit and matter that characterizes the concept's subsequent manifestations in Christian theology. The prophetic literature in particular contains numerous examples of how *ruach* in fact seems to be a kind of pathos that is closely bound up with humanity's physical existence. When theologians today recuperate the biblical concept of spirit, they therefore do so with the goal of settling accounts with a contempt for the bodily and material reality that has been an enduring feature of elements within the Christian tradition.[110]

Nonetheless, my own view is that it is not enough to hold up the biblical spirit concept as a critical contrast to the problematic aspects of the reception history that runs from Joachim, via Romanticism, to contemporary philosophers such as Vattimo and Žižek. It is also important to clarify that many of these more problematic aspects only arose when the concept was inserted into a temporal schema. As shown in Chapter Two, this took place early in the first millennium in tandem with the emergence of a theology of history in which the spirit, among other things, became a means of differentiating Christianity from Judaism. Within the emerging *adversus Iudaeos* genre, Christian faith was presented in terms of spiritual superiority, while the Jewish religion was described as hopelessly in thrall to the past, the material and the literal. And thus it was here that a basis was established for a dialectical theology of history, which was confirmed by Joachim and which then lived on in more or less secularized form in German Romanticism and idealism. The problem, as identified by Derrida in *Glas*, is that this kind of theology of history tends to result in a zero-sum game in which the 'earlier' stages must be abandoned in order for the spirit to be fully realized.

Might it be possible to find another concept of spirit, or rather another way of interpreting the complex motif that the spirit constitutes in the Western theological and philosophical tradition? Returning to the earlier discussion of spirits and ghosts in relation to Derrida's critique of idealism, if Žižek (inspired by Freud) ridicules the Jewish faith because it 'refuses to give up its ghost', perhaps it is in fact this ghost – a visitation by the events of the past – that protects us from a decisionist worship of Presence and the Now. Against spiritual fervour and overweening confidence in the present moment, what the absent presence of the ghost creates is self-doubt. Not least, the value of this kind of self-doubting stance lies in the fact that it helps us to see – *pace* Žižek and Badiou – that there is usually more than one truth in any given situation and that it can require time, knowledge and persistence in order to differentiate one truth from another (the complex geopolitical developments in the Arab world during the 2010s are a stark reminder of this).[111] What above all makes the ghost a fruitful trope is, however, that it disrupts the coercive temporal schema which pits new against old; impulse against memory; event against history. The ghost, the spectral remainder, teaches, if anything, that responsibility for the past is always implicated in 'Presence' and 'the Now', and therefore the subjects of history must never be abandoned for the sake of some transitorily acclaimed 'Event' or 'Truth'.

Must the ghost therefore be counterposed to the spirit? The answer, I think, is no. On the contrary, the whole point of the ghost as a philosopheme is precisely that it opposes such zero-sum games. Rather than abandoning the idea of the spirit, it is thus a question of rediscovering a more spectral, elusive and intangible concept of spirit. Even though Derrida himself never made this connection, some interesting points of convergence between the ghost and the biblical concept of spirit that contemporary theologians are trying to recover can be discerned here. *Ruach*, in the form which it takes in both the historical and prophetic books, is precisely characterized by the fact that it can never be grasped, controlled or manipulated by human beings. Humanity is endowed with God's spirit on God's terms, and just as unexpectedly as the spirit can descend upon the man or woman of God, so, too, can it abandon humanity. The symbolism is powerful if it is recalled that *ruach*, particularly in the prophetic literature, is intimately associated with justice and righteousness. Indeed, to return to Fredric Jameson's words, it may well be that *ruach*, like Derrida's ghosts, denotes 'these moments in which the present ... unexpectedly betrays us'.[112] If 'the present' here denotes the smug conviction that we are standing on the side of Truth and Justice, *ruach* reminds us of what is treacherous in this conviction: the moment when we think we hold justice in our hands is not infrequently the very moment that it slips between our fingers.

Prophetic Justice

This study had its point of departure in the classical books of prophesy. It was in this literature, authored more than two thousand years ago, that the idea of God as the God of all humanity was first formulated. Intimately connected to this idea is the notion of God as the Lord of history and thence the notion of history as divine. That history is divine does not mean that the prophets saw it as a divinely dictated scroll lying ready to be unrolled. It is, rather, a question of humanity's involvement in a drama in which we, as God's creations, have a vocation to realize the higher form of justice that is the ultimate meaning and purpose of history.

It is in this light that the emergence and solidification not only of the messianic motif but also of the pneumatic motif in the biblical tradition should be viewed. As this study has been intended to show, both these motifs have given rise to an ambivalent reception history in which dreams of future justice have repeatedly spilled over into utopian projects that have ultimately done violence to that justice. Nonetheless, I have chosen, albeit with certain critical reservations, to argue that the motifs have a lasting politico-philosophical value. But what about prophetism, that more overarching theme that involves the very idea that history contains a redemptive impulse and that this impulse is bound up with a higher, divine justice? Does this motif also have anything to contribute to contemporary politico-philosophical discussion?

Given the history of the twentieth century, there are good grounds for scepticism. Let me here return to the critical voices that in the mid-twentieth century sought to understand the links between the West's historico-theological tradition and the totalitarian movements of modernity. Although such critiques were often unnuanced, they were not without basis. The utopian elements of totalitarian ideologies can, via a complex reception history, be connected to aspects of Romanticism, which can in turn be traced back to parts of the Jewish and Christian historico-theological tradition. From a contemporary perspective, too, there are certain problems entailed by reinvoking the prophetic tradition as an inspiration for emancipatory visions. The politico-philosophical discussion that has been the focus of this final chapter highlights several of these problems, above all the way in which decisionist elements are being combined with more or less explicitly theological tropes.

In connection with these decisionist elements it is also highly telling that Carl Schmitt has emerged as a recurrent point of reference in these contemporary debates. To further narrow down the problematic in the politico-philosophical position represented by Agamben, Badiou and Žižek (despite their internal differences), it may be helpful to pause for a moment to consider an article which Karl Löwith published in 1935 under the title 'The Occasional Decisionism of Carl Schmitt'. At this point Löwith's *Meaning in History*, his great settling of accounts with the Western historico-theological tradition, lay more than a decade in the future. Nonetheless, several key aspects of his critique were already discernible, and it would seem that what clarified the pattern for him were Schmitt's actions and positions in the early 1930s. Löwith situated Schmitt within a generation of Germans who had grown up with and been shaped by the nineteenth-century historico-philosophical tradition. It was also in the nineteenth century that he found the roots of the decisionist elements in Schmitt's thinking. In a way that anticipated his thesis in *Meaning in History*, Löwith argued that transhistorical notions of truth and meaning at that time began to be projected upon the actual historical course of events, his example *par excellence* being Marxism.[113]

Although Marx and his followers still believed in history as a rational process containing both meaning and purpose, this changed during the following century. The First World War sounded the death knell for the nineteenth century's cultural optimism and, with them, any faith that history described a journey towards a brighter future. The recurrent crises of the Weimar Republic were regarded by many German intellectuals as an expression of the general decline of the West, and Schmitt was no exception. They were also fuel for Schmitt's emergent critique of parliamentary democracy. The weak governments and frequent new elections of this period revealed with admirable clarity liberalism's tendency to become mired in endless deliberations and chronic inability to act. Once this critique had been formulated, it was only a short step to the hard-bitten rhetoric that asserted the necessity of will and determination

(*Entschlossenheit*) in order to overcome Germany's palpable symptoms of exhaustion.

Determination about what? It was here that the shift away from the nineteenth-century philosophies revealed itself. When both classical theology of history and modern philosophies of history have been forfeited, there remain no criteria for truth or action beyond the 'actual' (*faktische*) historical situation. What would once have been determination to reach a higher (supra- or intra-historical) goal was now merely determination for determination's sake: 'What Schmitt defends is a politics of sovereign decision, but one in which content is merely a product of the accidental *occasio* of the political situation which happens to prevail at the moment'.[114] In other words, Schmitt's 'occasional decisionism' meant the abandonment of faith in political negotiations based on overarching moral principles in favour of resolute decisions based solely upon the actual situation. With this philosophical starting point, it is perhaps not entirely surprising that Schmitt in 1933 should have decided to lend his support to the cause of National Socialism.

To return to the contemporary politico-philosophical discussion: although Schmitt is a recurrent point of reference in this discussion, it is not wholly obvious that Löwith's critique of Schmitt the right-wing revolutionary should be connected to radical leftist theoreticians such as Agamben, Badiou and Žižek. When Schmitt is invoked – most explicitly by Agamben – it is, as I have shown, best understood as an attempt to hold up a distorting mirror to the abuse of power that is currently eroding the credibility of Western democracies. The image presented of Schmitt is thus highly polemical; one in which his anti-Semitism and advocacy of the Nazi cause is by no means toned down or glossed over.[115]

Nonetheless, Agamben, Badiou and Žižek are united with Schmitt in explicitly rejecting liberalism and parliamentary democracy. As argued earlier in the discussion of Agamben, this means among other things that they fail to attribute a progressive force to existing judicial and political structures. On the contrary, they portray 'the law' as metonymic of violence, coercion and repression. In the same way as Schmitt criticized contemporary champions of legal positivism for ending up in a stance of relativism, Agamben, Badiou and Žižek now reproach Left-liberal thinkers such as Derrida and Vattimo (though it should be mentioned in passing that Vattimo during the 2000s distanced himself from his former advocacy of social democracy[116]) for being locked into an anti-essentialist rhetoric that in practice merely supports the logic of capitalist society. With a view to breaking this 'ironic, postmodern deadlock', they invoke quasi-theological – and typically capitalized – entities such as 'Truth', 'the Event' or 'the Absolute'. Yet it is precisely here that Löwith's critique comes into play, since the effort to break with the phenomenologically and hermeneutically oriented philosophy that predominated in the late twentieth century should not be mistaken for a desire to reinstate older, metaphysical concepts of truth, subjectivity or the absolute. On the contrary, these concepts are accorded a radically contingent facticity by the revolutionary event:

> The undecidability of the Event thus means that an Event does not possess any ontological guarantee. It cannot be reduced to (or deduced, generated from) a (previous) situation; it emerges 'out of nothing' (the Nothing that was the ontological truth of this previous situation). Thus there is no neutral gaze of knowledge that can discern the Event in its effects: a decision is always already there – that is, one can discern the signs of an Event in the situation only from a previous decision for truth, just as in Jansenist theology, in which divine miracles are legible as such only to those who have already decided for faith.[117]

What Žižek – who here sets out Badiou's philosophy with approval – is saying in other words is that radical political action can never find support in exterior judicial-political procedures but rather rests entirely upon the decision and conviction of the engaged revolutionary subject. Just as with Schmitt, all criteria that go beyond the political situation at hand are eliminated, the engaged decision itself becoming the sole basis for truth. At this point, however, it is worth emphasizing once again the clearly opposing political ambitions and ideals which motivate both thinkers. For Schmitt, the actual political situation was equivalent to the present distinction between 'friend or foe', and the decision – which sought to preserve the prevailing order – belonged to the sovereign; for Žižek, the situation is equivalent to the revolutionary event, and the decision devolves upon the person who by definition has no power or status in the prevailing order.

Nonetheless, at a structural level the problematic remains the same: politics is placed above morals and the ultimate point of reference is a decision grounded upon a 'Nothing'. To be sure, putting engaged, subjective conviction above dialogue and negotiation can seem justified in a climate in which politics is increasingly carried out far above the head of the subject supposedly represented by the institutions of politics. And yet the price of decisionist rhetoric is the removal of all barriers to the enshrining of a perverted situation as a political truth. Žižek and Badiou reject the possibility that the 'truth' of an event – the French Revolution, the Paris Commune or the Cultural Revolution, just to take their own staple examples – might be the object of further historical or moral discussion. 'Truth' never belongs to spectators, only actors, 'those who have already decided for faith'. The only question is what happens to those within a particular episode who are not convinced of 'the truth of the Event' or, indeed, have a quite different notion of where truth inheres. An indirect but wholly adequate answer may be obtained from the 'typology' of different 'political subjects' that Badiou develops under the heading 'Formal Theory of the Subject' in *Logics of Worlds*. To 'the faithful subject' (*le sujet fidèle*), Badiou here counterposes 'the reactive subject' (*le sujet réactif*), who is characterized by its 'no to the event'. Examples of this 'reactive' spirit range from the leaders of the Thermidor coup (who put an end to the Jacobin Reign of Terror), via the revisionists in 1970s China (who undermined Maoism), to Badiou's own opponents in the present day.[118]

Like his conviction that equality demands 'discipline' (whence his admiration for the Jacobins), Badiou's 'typology of the subject' reveals the razor-thin dividing line between radical egalitarianism and anti-democratic elitism. His tendency towards antidemocratic elitism also reveals his proximity to Schmitt on precisely the aspect criticized by Löwith. Schmitt's secularization thesis (taken up in passing in Chapter Four), in a nutshell, stipulates that modern political concepts constitute secularized forms of older theological concepts. This general observation, as has been described, appealed also to Löwith. But unlike Löwith, who wished to break with the entire politico-theological tradition, Schmitt was interested in preserving an extra-political (or, more precisely, extra-parliamentary) authority that was theological as regards its structure, yet also dissociated from traditional theological metaphysics. Here is the normative aspect of Schmitt's political theology: in a crucial contrast to liberal constitutionalism, Schmitt restores the theological sovereign in a secular guise.[119] Interestingly, it is precisely this gesture that, formally speaking, is being repeated in contemporary politico-philosophical critiques of parliamentary liberalism – with the not inconsequential difference that the gesture itself is again being draped in explicitly theological language (albeit without its traditional content). In this combination of decisionism and a select number of theological concepts ('grace' rather than 'law', 'spirit' rather than 'letter', etc.), can also be found a renaissance of the potentially authoritarian qualities that Löwith identified as the tragic culmination of the Western politico-theological tradition: a quasi-theologically legitimated worship of the present and the moment, which in its most extreme forms regards the actual course of historical events as self-justifying.

As has been shown throughout this study, this view of history is fundamentally challenged by the prophetic tradition. In contrast to the inflated rhetoric that announces a revolutionary overthrow, prophetism is concerned with a more unobtrusive mode of thought, albeit one that is no less thoroughly radical. Such a philosophy rests upon the insight that real change takes time and requires continuity; the revolutionary transformation of views on gender during the last century, like the equally revolutionary transformation of views of sexual orientation during recent decades, offers an illustrative example. However, these examples are also illustrative in that they remind us that what we call justice is a never-completed task and that we can thus never be complacent about existing systems of justice.

The idea of a justice that supersedes existing judicial orders must be counted one of the most valuable elements of the prophetic tradition. Of the contemporary authors considered in this study, it is perhaps above all Jacques Derrida who has sought to pin down the relationship between the political and the values that supersede the political in terms of 'law' and 'justice'.

In *Force of Law* Derrida underscores that the law, in the sense of existing judicial-political structures, is always possible to deconstruct, while justice itself, 'if there is such as thing', is impossible to deconstruct. 'Justice' should not be mistaken here for a pre-formulated ideal or a regulative idea in Kant's sense. On the contrary, justice is associated with a radical indeterminacy or even impossibility. The thrust of this argument is that a political or judicial action, to remain just, can never blindly rely upon a fixed norm or rule. Justice always demands unique decisions in unique situations – decisions that always run the risk of being to justice's disadvantage. But for this very reason the critical conversation about justice must continue. What makes justice possible is thus the insight into its impossibility – into the impossibility of ever fully realizing it.[120]

On precisely this issue there is an interesting parallel between Derrida and Agamben that deserves to be highlighted in order to further narrow down the difference between the various positions which I have sought to clarify. As mentioned, both have published extensive readings of Benjamin's 1921 essay on violence. Agamben's reading concludes with a defence of Benjamin's efforts to unmask 'mythical violence' in the name of 'pure' or 'divine violence'. However, this critique of the existing justice system does not mean that the idea of justice as such should be abandoned. Agamben clarifies his position in a passage quoted earlier: 'The decisive point here is that the law ... is not justice, but only the gate that leads to it. What opens a passage toward justice is not the erasure of law, but its deactivation and inactivity [*inoperosità*] – that is, another use of the law.'[121] This suggestion of a justice beyond the law seems almost identical to Derrida's deconstructionist understanding of law and justice, which he formulates as follows: 'I want to insist at once to reserve the possibility of a justice, indeed of a law [*loi*] that not only exceeds or contradicts law [*droit*] but also, perhaps, has no relation to law, or maintains such a strange relation to it that it may just as well demand law as exclude it'.[122]

The difference between them first appears when Agamben, writing on the issue of the dissonance between law and justice, clarifies that '[o]bviously, it is not a question here of a transitional phase that never achieves its end, nor of a process of infinite deconstruction that, in maintaining the law in a spectral life, can no longer get to the bottom of it'.[123] What separates Agamben from Derrida is a conviction that there is no way back to the 'state' or 'rule of law' (*stato di diritto*) in its current form, which is why he is also reluctant to uphold the law in a 'spectral' guise. The alternative Agamben proposes is, rather, to assume a position of radical resistance of the kind evoked by Benjamin in his concept of a pure or divine violence. As discussed previously, Derrida is more appreciative of 'spectrality' and his concern is that precisely this claim to purity contains within it a violence that is neither pure nor divine. For this reason he also has little patience with a resistance that in advance positions itself beyond the rule of law:

This excess of justice over law and calculation, this overflowing of the unrepresentable over the determinable, cannot and should not [*ne peut pas et ne doit pas*] serve as an alibi for staying out of juridico-political battles, within an institution or a state, between institutions or states. Abandoned to itself, the incalculable and giving [*donatrice*] idea of justice is always very close to the bad, even to the worst for it can always be reappropriated by the most perverse calculation.[124]

It may nonetheless be asked whether Agamben does not have a point when he objects that Derrida's deconstructionist philosophy risks turning into an endless deferral, a 'spectral life' that never succeeds in reaching a conclusion. This objection has also been levelled by Badiou and Žižek, who accuse Derrida in similar terms for having become mired in permanent indecision, with the result that the revolutionary event is always postponed: 'The fundamental lesson of postmodernist politics is that *there is no Event*, that "nothing really happens", that the truth-Event is a passing, illusory short circuit, a false identification to be dispelled sooner or later by the reassertion of difference or, at best, the fleeting promise of the redemption to come, toward which we have to maintain a proper distance in order to avoid catastrophic "totalitarian" consequences'.[125]

In order to put this polemic in perspective, it is worth noting once again that the critique is an almost verbatim repetition of Schmitt's charges against parliamentary democracy ('endless discussion', 'indecision' etc.). It is thereby also possible to pin down what is ultimately at stake in this debate. While Derrida to the end defended liberal democracy as the least bad of existing forms of government, several leading contemporary political philosophers dismiss parliamentary democracy as such. The division is nicely summarized in Žižek's pointed slogan *democracy is not to come, but to go*, which makes a direct riposte to Derrida's idea of a 'democracy to come'. Now, it is not difficult to feel sympathy for the former perspective if, like Žižek, Agamben and Badiou, one foregrounds the rights violations currently taking place in the name of Western democracy, not to mention the at times startling democratic deficit within Western societies. But will this argument suffice in order to reject parliamentary democracy as such?

The question is warranted not only for the reason that Žižek, Agamben and Badiou offer little by way of alternative to the liberal democracy which they repudiate. It is also warranted because the image that emerges is one-sided. The democratic process is undeniably a narrative of continual defeats and failings – but it is also a narrative of enhanced protection for women, children and minorities; of enhanced environmental legislation and of improved conventions for minimizing armed conflict, torture and persecution. To reject liberal democracy as such merely by highlighting its deviations is quite simply to forget that it is only by virtue of the very idea of democracy that we are outraged by the crimes committed in its name. For this reason, Derrida's *democracy to come* – democracy as the name for a never-completed task – is always preferable to Žižek's *democracy to go*. If the vital critique of democracy is to have any higher purpose than societal overthrow for the sake of overthrow, it must quite simply have an idea, however open and provisional, of what it is seeking to achieve. The challenge of the prophetic tradition ultimately involves this unwavering defence of a justice to come: one that never allows itself to be restricted to existing systems of law but that also can never be articulated independently of those systems.

Notes

1. J. Milbank. 1990. *Theology and Social Theory: Beyond Secular Reason*, Oxford and Malden: Blackwell, 3.

2. S. Critchley. 2012. *The Faith of the Faithless: Experiments in Political Theology*, London and New York: Verso, 19.

3. See also V.J. Seidler. 2013. *Remembering 9/11: Terror, Trauma and Social Theory*, New York: Palgrave Macmillan.

4. J. Derrida and J. Habermas. 2003. 'February 15, or What Binds Europeans Together: A Plea for a Common Foreign Policy, Beginning in the Core of Europe'. Retrieved 24 July 2014 from http://platypus1917.org/wp-content/uploads/archive/rgroups/2006-chicago/habermas-derrida_europe.pdf. The interviews from September 2001 were later published in G. Borradori. 2003. *Philosophy in a Time of Terror: Dialogues with Jürgen Habermas and Jacques Derrida*, Chicago and London: University of Chicago Press.

5. See Benedictus XVI and J. Habermas. 2006. *Dialectics of Secularization: On Reason and Religion*, trans. B. McNeil, San Francisco: Ignatius Press.

6. Derrida, 'Faith and Knowledge', 8.

7. S. Žižek. 2009. 'Dialectical Clarity versus the Misty Conceit of Paradox', in C. Davis (ed.), *The Monstrosity of Christ: Paradox or Dialectic?* Cambridge and London: The MIT Press, 255.

8. See M. Lilla. 2008. 'A New, Political Saint Paul?', *The New York Review of Books* 55:16.

9. A. Badiou. 2003. *Saint Paul: The Foundation of Universalism*, trans. R. Brassier. Stanford: Stanford University Press, 4–30.

10. See J. Taubes. 2004. *The Political Theology of Paul*, trans. D. Hollander, Stanford: Stanford University Press; G. Agamben. 2005. *The Time that Remains: A Commentary on the Letter to the Romans*, trans. P. Daley, Stanford: Stanford University Press.

11. See M. Heidegger. 1995. *Gesamtausgabe*, vol. 60, *Phänomenologie des Religiösen Lebens*, Frankfurt am Main: Vittorio Klostermann.

12. Badiou, *Saint Paul*, 1–3.

13. Ibid., 4–15.

14. Ibid., 14.

15. Ibid., 76.

16. Ibid., 57.

17. See e.g. J.D. Caputo and L.M. Alcoff (eds). 2009. *St. Paul among the Philosophers*, Bloomington and Indianapolis: Indiana University Press.

18. See also H. Ruin. 2010. 'Faith, Grace, and the Destruction of Tradition: A Hermeneutic-Genealogical Reading of the Pauline Letters', *Journal for Cultural and Religious Theory* 2:1, 17.

19. W. Blanton. 2007. 'Disturbing Politics: Neo-Paulinism and the Scrambling of Religious and Secular Identities', *Dialog: A Journal of Theology* 46:1, 4–5.

20. A. Badiou. 2005. *Being and Event*, trans. O. Feltham, London and New York: Continuum, 93–103.

21. Ibid., 181.

22. Ibid., 201–211, 232–239.
23. See ibid., 104–111, 173–177.
24. A. Badiou. 2011. 'The Democratic Emblem', trans. W. McCuaig, in G. Agamben, A. Badiou, D. Bensaïd, W. Brown, J.-L. Nancy, J. Ranciere, K. Ross and S. Zizek, *Democracy in what State?* New York: Columbia University Press, 14.
25. See A. Badiou. 2010. 'The Idea of Communism', in C. Douzinas and S. Žižek (eds), *The Idea of Communism*, London and New York: Verso, 1–14.
26. Critchley, *Faith of the Faithless*, 26.
27. Cf. e.g. A. Badiou. 2009. *Logics of Worlds: Being and Event II*, trans. E. Toscano, London and New York: Continuum, 363–380.
28. A. Badiou. 2008. *The Meaning of Sarkozy*, trans. D. Fernbach, London and New York: Verso.
29. Critchley, *Faith of the Faithless*, 93–102.
30. D. Boyarin. 2009. 'Paul among the Antiphilosophers; or, Saul among the Sophists', in Caputo and Alcoff (eds), *St. Paul among the Philosophers*, 109–141.
31. In the English edition (2006), the essays are gathered in a larger collection of essays under the heading *Polemics* (trans. S. Corcoran, London and New York: Verso), 155–254.
32. Ibid., 159–171.
33. Ibid., 160.
34. Ibid., 161.
35. Ibid., 162–163.
36. Badiou, *Saint Paul*, 10.
37. É. Marty. 2007. *Une querelle avec Alain Badiou, philosophe*, Paris: Gallimard, 27–28 (Eng. trans. by the author).
38. A. Badiou. 2007. *The Century*, trans. A. Toscano, Cambridge and Malden: Polity Press, 62–63. See also idem, *Logics of Worlds*, 20–27.
39. See e.g. Marty, *Une querelle*, 17–23, and P. Raynaud. 2006. *L'extrême gauche plurielle*, Paris: Autrement, 149–170.
40. D. Bensaïd. 2001. 'Alain Badiou and the Miracle of the Event'. Retrieved 24 July 2014 from ftp://ftp2.marxau21.fr/marxau/reserve/BENSAID_Badiou_and_the_Miracle_of_Event.pdf.
41. Ibid.
42. D. Bensaïd. 2011. 'Permanent Scandal', trans. W. McCuaig, in Agamben et al., *Democracy in what State?*, 42.
43. See Scholem, 'Messianic Idea', 19.
44. M. Blanchot, quoted in J. Derrida. 2005. *The Politics of Friendship*, trans. G. Collins, London and New York: Verso, 46, n. 14.
45. See e.g. Milbank, *Theology and Social Theory*, 302–313; Vattimo, *After Christianity*, 37; M. Volf. 2011. *A Public Faith: How Followers of Christ Should Serve the Common Good*, Grand Rapids: Brazos Press, 46–48; S. Žižek. 2003. *The Puppet and the Dwarf: The Perverse Core of Christianity*, London and New York: Verso, 139–143.
46. Derrida, *Politics of Friendship*, 46, n. 14.
47. Benjamin, *Illuminations*, 255.
48. See ibid., 252–255. See also M. Löwy. 2005. *Fire Alarm: Reading Walter Benjamin's 'On the Concept of History'*, trans. C. Turner, London: Verso.
49. See further G. Agamben. 1998. *Homo Sacer: Sovereign Power and Bare Life*, trans. D. Heller-Roazen, Stanford: Stanford University Press.
50. Agamben, *The Time that Remains*, 1–3.
51. Ibid., 26–27.
52. Ibid., 52–53.
53. Ibid., 44–58.
54. Ibid., 62–65.
55. Ibid., 69–72.

56. G. Agamben. 2012. *The Church and the Kingdom*, trans. L. de la Durantaye, London and New York: Seagull Books, 26.

57. See e.g. M.C. de Boer. 2003. 'Paul and Apocalyptic Eschatology', in Collins et al. (eds), *The Continuum History of Apocalypticism*, 166–194; D.B. Martin. 2009. 'The Promise of Teleology, the Constraints of Epistemology, and the Universal Vision in Paul', in Caputo and Alcoff (eds), *St. Paul among the Philosophers*, 109–141.

58. See also Taubes, *Political Theology*.

59. C. Schmitt. 2005. *Political Theology: Four Chapters on the Concept of Sovereignty*, trans. G. Schwab, Chicago: University of Chicago Press, 7.

60. G. Agamben. 2005. *State of Exception*, trans. K. Attell, Chicago: University of Chicago Press, 2–3.

61. Benjamin, *Illuminations*, 248–249.

62. W. Benjamin. 1986. *Reflections: Essays, Aphorisms, Autobiographical Writings*, trans. E. Jephcott, New York: Schocken Books, 300.

63. Agamben, *State of Exception*, 87.

64. Ibid., 64.

65. Agamben, *The Time that Remains*, 104–108.

66. Ibid., 93–99, 104–108, 115–121.

67. Agamben, *State of Exception*, 86–87.

68. Ibid., 87.

69. On these critical points, see also V. Liska. 2008. *Giorgio Agambens leerer Messianismus*, Vienna: Schleebrügge Editor, and A. Bielik-Robson. 2010. 'A Broken Constellation: Agamben's Theology between Tragedy and Messianism', *Telos* 152, 103–126.

70. Benjamin, *Reflections*, 300.

71. Agamben, *State of Exception*, 88.

72. Derrida, 'Force of Law', 258–298.

73. E. Levinas. 1990. *The Levinas Reader*, trans. S. Hand, Oxford and Cambridge: Basil Blackwell, 219.

74. Ibid.

75. Y. Leibowitz. 1992. *Judaism, Human Values, and the Jewish State*, Cambridge and London: Harvard University Press, 13.

76. See Badiou, *Saint Paul*, 75–85.

77. See further S. Žižek. 1999. *The Ticklish Subject: The Absent Center of Political Ontology*, London and New York: Verso, 162–167.

78. Badiou, *Saint Paul*, 89.

79. Žižek, *The Puppet*, 53–57.

80. Ibid., 93–121. I develop my critical reading of Levinas' and Žižek's different understandings of the law in J. Svenungsson. 2010. 'Wrestling with Angels: Or, How to Avoid Decisionist Messianic Romances', *International Journal of Zizek Studies* 4:4 (online).

81. Žižek, *The Puppet*, 35.

82. Ibid., 35–37.

83. Ibid., 123–130 and S. Žižek. 2009. 'The Fear of Four Words: A Modest Plea for the Hegelian Reading of Christianity', in C. Davis (ed.), *The Monstrosity of Christ: Paradox or Dialectic?* Cambridge and London: The MIT Press, 50–61.

84. Žižek, 'The Fear', 60.

85. Žižek, *The Puppet*, 130.

86. Ibid., 127; see also S. Žižek. 2000. *The Fragile Absolute – Or, Why is the Christian Legacy Worth Fighting For?* London and New York: Verso, 143–160.

87. Žižek, *The Puppet*, 188–120. See also S. Žižek. 2001. *On Belief*, London and New York: Routledge, 127–137.

88. Žižek, *The Puppet*, 127.

89. Ibid., 128.

90. Ibid., 130.

91. Žižek, 'Dialectical Clarity', 296 (my emphasis).
92. Ibid., 295–296.
93. Ibid., 291 (this could be compared to the central role that Schelling plays in Žižek's earlier works).
94. Ibid., 296.
95. See e.g. the animated debate that took place between Žižek and Adam Kirsch in *The New Republic* in 2008/2009: A. Kirsch. 2008. 'The Deadly Jester', *The New Republic*, 3 Dec.; S. Žižek. 2009. 'Who Are You Calling Anti-Semitic?', 7 Jan.; and A. Kirsch. 2009. 'Still the Most Dangerous Philosopher in the West', 7 Jan. See also John Gray's critical review, 'The Violent Visions of Slavoj Žižek', *New York Review of Books* 59:12, and Žižek's reply 'Not Less Than Nothing, But Simply Nothing' (2012). Retrieved 24 July 2014 from http://www.versobooks.com/blogs/1046-not-less-than-nothing-but-simply-nothing. For a theological critique of the supersessionist tendency in Žižek, see O. Sigurdson. 2012. *Theology and Marxism in Eagleton and Žižek: A Conspiracy of Hope*, New York: Palgrave Macmillan, 104–107.
96. See further J. Milbank, C. Pickstock and G. Ward. 1999. 'Introduction: Suspending the Material: The Turn of Radical Orthodoxy', in eidem (eds), *Radical Orthodoxy: A New Theology*, London: Routledge, 1–20; J. Milbank, *Theology and Social Theory*, 1–6.
97. Žižek, *The Puppet*, 171.
98. See e.g. C. Davis, J. Milbank and S. Žižek (eds). 2005. *Theology and the Political: The New Debate*, Durham and London: Duke University Press; C. Davis (ed.). 2009. *The Monstrosity of Christ: Paradox or Dialectic?* Cambridge and London: The MIT Press; C. Davis, J. Milbank and S. Žižek (eds). 2010. *Paul's New Movement: Continental Philosophy and the Future of Christian Theology*, Grand Rapids: Brazos Press.
99. J. Milbank. 2009. 'The Double Glory, or Paradox versus Dialectics: On Not Quite Agreeing with Slavoj Žižek', in Davis (ed.), *The Monstrosity of Christ*, 111.
100. C. Davis, J. Milbank and S. Žižek, 'Introduction', in eidem (eds), *Paul's New Movement*, 6.
101. Cf. S. Žižek. 2012. 'Christianity against the Sacred', in idem and B. Gunjević (eds), *God in Pain: Inversions of Apocalypse*, New York: Seven Stories Press, 43–72.
102. Davis et al., 'Introduction', 12 (my emphasis).
103. Žižek, *The Puppet*, 109.
104. For a thought-provoking discussion of this complexity, see E. Namli. 2013. 'Universal Rights versus Sharia? Reflections on the Moral and Legal Dimensions of Human Rights Law and Sharia', *Religion and Human Rights* 8, 139–161.
105. Žižek, *The Puppet*, 135.
106. S. Žižek. 2008. *In Defense of Lost Causes*, London and New York: Verso, 406–412; cf. also idem, 'Dialectical Clarity', 291–292.
107. Žižek, *In Defense of Lost Causes*, 415.
108. Ibid., 413.
109. Ibid., 419.
110. See e.g. J. Comblin. 2004. *The Holy Spirit and Liberation*, Eugene: Wipf and Stock; S. Bergmann. 2005. *Creation Set Free: The Spirit as Liberator of Nature*, Grand Rapids: Eerdmans; D. Edwards. 2004. *Breath of Life: A Theology of the Creator Spirit*, Maryknoll: Orbis; E. Rogers. 2005. *After the Spirit: A Constructive Pneumatology from Resources outside the Modern West*, Grand Rapids: Eerdmans; M.I. Wallace. 1996. *Fragments of the Spirit: Nature, Violence and the Renewal of Creation*, New York: Continuum.
111. Cf. S. Žižek. 2010. 'Paul and the Truth Event', in Davis et al. (eds), *Paul's New Movement*, 77.
112. Jameson, 'Marx's Purloined Letter', 39.
113. Löwith, 'Occasional Decisionism'.
114. Ibid., 144.
115. In addition to the earlier discussion of Agamben's reception of Schmitt in the present volume, see S. Žižek. 1999. 'Carl Schmitt in the Age of Post-Politics', in C. Mouffe (ed.), *The Challenge of Carl Schmitt*, London and New York: Verso, 18–37. For a discussion of the relation

between Badiou and Schmitt, see C. Wright. 2008. 'Event or Exception? Disentangling Badiou from Schmitt, or, Towards a Politics of the Void', *Theory & Event* 11 (online). As the title indicates, Wright's endeavour is to disentangle Badiou's theory of the event from Schmitt's authoritarian philosophy. Although I concur with the general argument, it is nevertheless my contention that Wright evades, as I see it, the most problematic feature that unites their theories, namely their decisionist stance.

116. See further G. Vattimo. 2007. *Ecce comu: Come si ri-diventata ciò che si era*, Rome: Fazi Editore; see also F. Depoortere. 2010. 'Christianity and Politics: A Biographical-Theoretical Reading of Gianni Vattimo and Alain Badiou', in L. Boeve and C. Brabant (eds), *Between Philosophy and Theology: Contemporary Interpretations of Christianity*, Burlington: Ashgate, 193–212.

117. Žižek, 'Paul and the Truth Event', 83.

118. Badiou, *Logics of Worlds*, 43–78.

119. See further Schmitt, *Political Theology*, 36–66.

120. Derrida, 'Force of Law', 242–258.

121. Agamben, *State of Exception*, 64.

122. Derrida, 'Force of Law', 233.

123. Agamben, *State of Exception*, 64. Cf. also idem, *The Time that Remains*, 101–104.

124. Derrida, 'Force of Law', 257.

125. Žižek, 'Paul and the Truth Event', 81.

POSTSCRIPT

A Theopolitical Vision

Is religion only ever a burden upon modern political thought and action? Looking at the world in its present state, it is admittedly tempting to answer the question in the affirmative. What was seen twenty-five years ago as anomalous backlashes to a steadily secularized political reality – the Rushdie Affair or the resurgence of religion as a culturally formative power in the Balkan Wars – has become commonplace in today's world. Be it in the form of national separatism or of grandiose universalist ambitions, religious extremism increasingly tends to undermine healthy political processes.

But do these ominous developments mean that all that can be said about religion and politics has been said and that we should once and for all throw the theological baggage of our past overboard? I am not persuaded that matters are quite so black and white. As I have shown in this study, the focus of which has been the Western religious legacy, religious traditions are dynamic entities, ongoing negotiations between different interpretations. It should therefore not be surprising that Western theology of history has given rise to a complex and ambiguous reception history. There is a dark side that encompasses contempt for history, supersessionism, political utopianism and arrogant universalism. But parallel with these qualities there runs a vein that is critical of utopia; one that contains insights into humanity's finite nature and thus its inability to possess the ideal or the absolute.

This ambivalence not infrequently cuts across one and the same author. The writings of Joachim of Fiore reveal a patient exploration of how history's various epochs are organically interwoven with each other – which did not prevent him from also being an apocalyptically-inclined thinker who believed himself capable of identifying the exact year in which 'the Age of the Spirit' would begin. Like other Romantics, Friedrich Schleiermacher harboured deep feelings for the uniqueness of humanity's historical existence and emphasized

---

Notes for this section begin on page 206.

the importance of the unique forms taken by religious traditions – but was nonetheless willing to enjoin spiritually mature individuals to reject their own particular tradition in favour of a 'religion of the spirit'. Gianni Vattimo's entire life's work is an attempt to defend the hermeneutic insight that humanity is an interpreting creature – at the same time as he forcefully asserts, in the name of such 'weak thought', that the Christian tradition contains the very matrix of any genuinely universal and emancipatory philosophy.

In light of this ambivalence, I should like to recall once again John Milbank's statement that supposedly secular political thought in some measure always rests upon 'theologies or anti-theologies in disguise'. If these words contain anything of importance, it is essential to conduct a critical discussion of better and worse 'theologies' in the sense of pre-political values and concepts (for the reasons given in Chapter Five, my own view is that Milbank's own theological position belongs among the worse). In other words, if the Western historico-theological tradition – which includes a wealth of such values and concepts – has an ambivalent potential, then the examination of this tradition should be an urgent task for political philosophy.

This is also where I think the categorical rejection of the political value of biblical tradition by anti-utopian thinkers from Karl Löwith to John Gray falls short. If these thinkers are convinced that modern politics is better off without its theological past, one is bound to ask whether they have not abandoned the tradition too soon. Whether we want it or not, the biblical legacy, in all its varieties, remains the crucible in which the political and intellectual cultures of the West have been moulded. To distance oneself from this legacy instead of making claims on it as a common cultural concern is, arguably, to hand it over to the groupings within both Judaism and Christianity who define their respective traditions in a manner that fairly well corresponds to the excesses that the anti-utopian critics see as representative of biblical religion (dangerous utopianism, theocratic fantasies, forsaking of the present in the name of a future goal). Most importantly, however, to do away with the biblical legacy for politico-philosophical reasons is also to fail to acknowledge that religion may in fact offer important resources for constructive political engagement. One of the aims of this study has therefore been to identify lines of thought in both Jewish and Christian theology of history that I believe can serve as critical tools in the ongoing debates on issues such as universal rights, plurality, identity, justice and democracy.

Yet the politico-philosophical challenge is not only to conduct a critical discussion of different pre-political 'theologies'. An equally important question relates to the very relationship between the political and those values that precede or, rather, supersede the political. This question goes to the very heart of the prophetic tradition and foregrounds once again the distinction between 'political theology' and 'theopolitics'. If the former concept denotes a tendency to undergird politics with theological claims, the latter denotes, rather, an understanding of a prophet-inspired idea of justice that always supersedes existing judicial-political systems. On the level of principle, only 'theopolitics' is capable of sustaining the distinction between the political and an authority that remains transcendent to the political, whereas 'political theology' entails that politics and theology dissolve into each other. At a practical level, however, the boundary between the two concepts is razor-thin, and, as described in Chapter One, an awareness that such is the case can be traced back as far as the biblical literature.

This is reflected, not least, in the Deuteronomistic History, in which an image of the prophet inspired by Moses is critically counterposed to the kings who continually tend to confuse their own power with that of God. Against these worldly potentates' tendency to seek theological sanction for their own exercise of power, the prophets invoke a God whose power and justice supersede any human order. During the Middle Ages, this politico-theological ambition received inspiration from Eusebius's theology, while Joachim's idea of an *Ecclesia spiritualis* in the Age of the Spirit constituted a kind of theopolitical vision that contrasted with the worldly orders of political power. In the modern era, Hegel's Christian philosophy of the state can be contrasted with Schelling's notion of a 'truly universal church' that can be built 'only in the spirit' and thus can never permit itself to be trammelled within existing political structures. Moving finally into the twentieth century, our path leads naturally to Carl Schmitt's quasi-theologically motivated sovereign, at the same time as we find countless attempts to defend against the potentially totalitarian qualities of new, secular political theologies. Among these attempts is, not least, Martin Buber's reading of the prophetic literature, whence his own thinking derives and whence he coins the term 'theopolitics'.

If there is an unstated addressee of Buber's critique, it is undoubtedly the messianic claims of political Zionism rather than Schmitt's theory of the sovereign. For Buber, Judaism is the bearer of a universalistic tradition that runs contrary to all forms of theologically motivated political power.[1] What Buber understands by theopolitics is the notion of a prophet-inspired resistance to worldly autocracy, based upon God's demands for truth and justice. This notion also includes the vocation to enact, in an exemplary way, a higher justice among the nations (which is also the foundation for Buber's 'spiritual Zionism'). However, once again there is a thin line between theopolitics and political theology, for how is it possible to guarantee that the vocation to provide an exemplary image of divine justice does not degenerate into ambitions for political power in God's name? For Buber, no such guarantees exist, for which reason the prophetic vocation is without end. 'Prophetic theopolitics' here becomes instead a name for the unattainability of the ideal: it is because God's justice eternally supersedes humanity's ordering of the world that it remains an eternally unrealized task.[2]

It should be remembered at this point that the prophets never imagined everything that took place on earth to be a reflection of God's will. History was, rather, a space where God put humanity's will to the test, challenging it to overthrow systems of worldly injustice in the name of a higher justice. To speak of history as divine was, in this light, to acknowledge humanity's radical historicity without excluding the need for a struggle for something higher in whose name the freedom of humanity could be asserted against those who might try to curtail or reify it. Here is perhaps the single most important insight granted by the prophetic tradition – that what Buber calls 'the theopolitical hour' has always already chimed, that the moment for justice is now, and that at every moment history stands ready to be put on trial by an authority that is not reducible to history itself.

Notes

1. See M. Buber. 1967. 'The Silent Question', in N.N. Glatzer (ed.), *Martin Buber: On Judaism*, New York: Schocken Books, 207.

2. See Buber, *Prophetic Faith*, 126–154.

Bibliography

Agamben, G. 1998. *Homo Sacer: Sovereign Power and Bare Life*, trans. D. Heller-Roazen, Stanford: Stanford University Press.
——. 2005. *State of Exception*, trans. K. Attell, Chicago: University of Chicago Press.
——. 2005. *The Time that Remains: A Commentary on the Letter to the Romans*, trans. P. Daley, Stanford: Stanford University Press.
——. 2012. *The Church and the Kingdom*, trans. L. de la Durantaye, London and New York: Seagull Books.
Allison, D.C. 2003. 'The Eschatology of Jesus', in J.J. Collins, B. McGinn and S.J. Stein (eds), *The Continuum History of Apocalypticism*, New York and London: Continuum, 139–165.
Aron, R. 1955. *L'opium des intellectuels*, Paris: Calmann-Lévy.
Asurmendi, J. 1985. *Le prophétisme. Des origines à l'époque moderne*, Paris: Nouvelle cité.
Augustine. 2013. *The Works of Saint Augustine: A Translation for the 21st Century*, vol. 7, *The City of God (Books XI–XXII)*, trans. W. Babcock, New York: New City Press.
Badiou, A. 2003. *Saint Paul: The Foundation of Universalism*, trans. R. Brassier, Stanford: Stanford University Press.
——. 2005. *Being and Event*, trans. O. Feltham, London and New York: Continuum.
——. 2006. *Polemics*, trans. S. Corcoran, London and New York: Verso.
——. 2007. *The Century*, trans. A. Toscano, Cambridge and Malden: Polity Press.
——. 2008. *The Meaning of Sarkozy*, trans. D. Fernbach, London and New York: Verso.
——. 2009. *Logics of Worlds: Being and Event II*, trans. E. Toscano, London and New York: Continuum.
——. 2010. 'The Idea of Communism', in C. Douzinas and S. Žižek (eds), *The Idea of Communism*, London and New York: Verso, 1–14.
——. 2011. 'The Democratic Emblem', trans. W. McCuaig, in G. Agamben, A. Badiou, D. Bensaïd, W. Brown, J.-L. Nancy, J. Ranciere, K. Ross and S. Zizek, *Democracy in what State?* New York: Columbia University Press, 6–15.
Banon, D. 1998. *Le messianisme*, Paris: PUF.
Bell, D. 1960. *The End of Ideology: On the Exhaustion of Political Ideas in the Fifties*, New York: Free Press.
Benedictus XVI and J. Habermas. 2006. *Dialectics of Secularization: On Reason and Religion*, trans. B. McNeil, San Francisco: Ignatius Press.
Benjamin, W. 1986. *Reflections: Essays, Aphorisms, Autobiographical Writings*, trans. E. Jephcott, New York: Schocken Books.
——. 1999. *Illuminations*, trans. H. Zorn, London: Pimlico.

Bensaïd, D. 2001. 'Alain Badiou and the Miracle of the Event'. Retrieved 24 July 2014 from ftp://ftp2.marxau21.fr/marxau/reserve/BENSAID_Badiou_and_the_Miracle_of_Event.pdf.
———. 2011. 'Permanent Scandal', trans. W. McCuaig, in G. Agamben et al., *Democracy in what State?* New York: Columbia University Press, 16–43.
Bergmann, S. 2005. *Creation Set Free: The Spirit as Liberator of Nature*, Grand Rapids: Eerdmans.
Berlin, I. 1999. *The Roots of Romanticism: The A.W. Mellon Lectures in the Fine Arts, 1965*, ed. H. Hardy, London: Chatto and Windus.
Bielik-Robson, A. 2010. 'A Broken Constellation: Agamben's Theology between Tragedy and Messianism', *Telos* 152, 103–126.
Birnbaum, D. 1990. 'Det romantiska fragmentet', in Novalis, *Fragment*, Lund: Propexus, 143–182.
Blanton, W. 2007. 'Disturbing Politics: Neo-Paulinism and the Scrambling of Religious and Secular Identities', *Dialog: A Journal of Theology* 46:1, 3–13.
Blenkinsopp, J. 1983. *A History of Prophecy in Israel*, 2nd edn, Louisville and London: Westminster John Knox Press.
Bloch, E. 1991. *Heritage of our Times*, trans. N. and S. Plaice, Oxford: Polity Press.
Blum, M. 2010. *"Ich wäre ein Judenfeind?": Zum Antijudaismus in Friedrich Schleiermachers Theologie und Pädagogik*, Cologne: Böhlau Verlag.
Blumenberg, H. 1983. *The Legitimacy of the Modern Age*, trans. R.M. Wallace, Cambridge: The MIT Press.
Borradori, G. 2003. *Philosophy in a Time of Terror: Dialogues with Jürgen Habermas and Jacques Derrida*, Chicago and London: University of Chicago Press.
Bowie, A. 1993. *Schelling and Modern European Philosophy: An Introduction*, London and New York: Routledge.
———. 1997. *From Romanticism to Critical Theory: The Philosophy of German Literary Theory*, London and New York: Routledge.
———. 2009. 'Romantic Philosophy and Religion', in N. Saul (ed.), *The Cambridge Companion to German Romanticism*, Cambridge and New York: Cambridge University Press, 175–190.
Boyarin, D. 2009. 'Paul among the Antiphilosophers; or, Saul among the Sophists', in J.D. Caputo and L.M. Alcoff (eds), *St. Paul among the Philosophers*, Bloomington and Indianapolis: Indiana University Press, 109–141.
Brueggemann, W. 1986. *Hopeful Imagination: Prophetic Voices in Exile*, Minneapolis: Augsburg Fortress Publishers.
———. 2000. *Texts that Linger, Words that Explode: Listening to Prophetic Voices*, Minneapolis: Augsburg Fortress Publishers.
———. 2001. *The Prophetic Imagination*, 2nd edn, Minneapolis: Fortress Press.
Brumlik, M. 2000. *Deutscher Geist und Judenhass: Das Verhältnis des philosophischen Idealismus zum Judentum*, Munich: Luchterhand.
Buber, M. 1949. *The Prophetic Faith*, trans. C. Witton-Davies, New York: Collier Books.
———. 1967. 'The Silent Question', in N.N. Glatzer (ed.), *Martin Buber: On Judaism*, New York: Schocken Books, 202–213.
Caputo, J.D. 2007. 'Spectral Hermeneutics: On the Weakness of God and the Theology of the Event', in J.W. Robbins (ed.), *After the Death of God*, New York: Columbia University Press, 47–88.
Caputo, J.D. and L.M. Alcoff (eds). 2009. *St. Paul among the Philosophers*, Bloomington and Indianapolis: Indiana University Press.
Carroll, J. 2001. *Constantine's Sword: The Church and the Jews*, Boston and New York: Houghton Mifflin Company.
Cohn, N. 1993. *Cosmos, Chaos and the World to Come: The Ancient Roots of Apocalyptic Faith*, New Haven and London: Yale University Press.
———. 1993. *The Pursuit of the Millennium: Revolutionary Millenarians and Mystical Anarchists of the Middle Ages*, London: Pimlico.

Collins, J.J. 1989. *The Apocalyptic Imagination: An Introduction to the Jewish Matrix of Christianity*, New York: Crossroad.
——. 2003. 'From Prophecy to Apocalypticism: The Expectation of the End', in J.J. Collins, B. McGinn and S.J. Stein (eds), *The Continuum History of Apocalypticism*, New York and London: Continuum, 64–88.
Comblin, J. 2004. *The Holy Spirit and Liberation*, Eugene: Wipf and Stock.
Congar, Y. 1997. *I Believe in the Holy Spirit*, trans. D. Smith, New York: Crossroad.
Critchley, S. 2012. *The Faith of the Faithless: Experiments in Political Theology*, London and New York: Verso.
Davis, C. (ed.). 2009. *The Monstrosity of Christ: Paradox or Dialectic?* Cambridge and London: The MIT Press.
Davis, C., J. Milbank and S. Žižek (eds). 2005. *Theology and the Political: The New Debate*, Durham and London: Duke University Press.
—— (eds). 2010. *Paul's New Movement: Continental Philosophy and the Future of Christian Theology*, Grand Rapids: Brazos Press.
——. 2010. 'Introduction', in C. Davis, J. Milbank and S. Žižek (eds), *Paul's New Movement: Continental Philosophy and the Future of Christian Theology*, Grand Rapids: Brazos Press, 1–17.
D'Costa, G. 2005. 'Theology of Religion', in D.F. Ford (ed.), *The Modern Theologians: An Introduction to Christian Theology since 1918*, 3rd edn, Oxford: Blackwell Publishing, 626–644.
De Boer, M.C. 2003. 'Paul and Apocalyptic Eschatology', in J.J. Collins, B. McGinn and S.J. Stein (eds), *The Continuum History of Apocalypticism*, New York: Continuum, 166–194.
De Lubac, H. 1978. *Paradoxes of Faith*, trans. P. Simon and S. Kreilkamp, San Francisco: Ignatus Press.
——. 1979/1980. *La postérité de Joachim de Flore*, vols 1–2, Paris: Lethielleux.
De Man, P. 1983. *Blindness and Insight*, London: Methuen & Co.
Depoortere, F. 2010. 'Christianity and Politics: A Biographical-Theoretical Reading of Gianni Vattimo and Alain Badiou', in L. Boeve and C. Brabant (eds), *Between Philosophy and Theology: Contemporary Interpretations of Christianity*, Burlington: Ashgate, 193–212.
Derrida, J. 1986. *Glas*, trans. J.P. Leavey and R. Rand, Lincoln and London: University of Nebraska Press.
——. 1989. *Of Spirit: Heidegger and the Question*, trans. G. Bennington and R. Bowlby, Chicago: University of Chicago Press.
——. 1993. *Aporias: Dying – Awaiting (One Another at) the 'Limits of Truth'*, trans. T. Dutoit, Stanford: Stanford University Press.
——. 1994. *Specters of Marx: The State of the Debt, the Work of Mourning, and the New International*, trans. P. Kamuf, New York and London: Routledge.
——. 1995. *The Gift of Death*, trans. D. Wills, Chicago and London: University of Chicago Press.
——. 1995. 'Khôra', trans. I. McLeod, in T. Dutoit (ed.), *On the Name*, Stanford: Stanford University Press, 89–130.
——. 1997. 'The Villanova Roundtable: A Conversation with Jacques Derrida', in J.D. Caputo (ed.), *Deconstruction in a Nutshell: A Conversation with Jacques Derrida*, New York: Fordham University Press, 3–28.
——. 1998. 'Faith and Knowledge: The Two Sources of "Religion" at the Limits of Reason Alone', trans. S. Weber, in J. Derrida and G. Vattimo (eds), *Religion*, Cambridge: Polity Press, 1–78.
——. 2002. 'Force of Law: The "Mystical Foundation of Authority"', trans. M. Quaintance, in E. Anidjar (ed.), *Acts of Religion*, London and New York: Routledge, 230–298.
——. 2005. *The Politics of Friendship*, trans. G. Collins, London and New York: Verso.
Derrida, J. and J. Habermas. 2003. 'February 15, or What Binds Europeans Together: A Plea for a Common Foreign Policy, Beginning in the Core of Europe'. Retrieved 24 July 2014 from http://platypus1917.org/wp-content/uploads/archive/rgroups/2006-chicago/habermas-derrida_europe.pdf.

Dibelius, M. 1968. *Aufsätze zur Apostelgeschichte*, 5th edn, Göttingen: Vandenhoeck and Ruprecht.
Dietrich, W. 2002. *"Theopolitik": Studien zur Theologie und Ethik des Alten Testaments*, Neukirchen-Vluyn: Neukirchener Verlag.
Dunn, J.D.G. (ed.). 1999. *Jews and Christians: The Parting of the Ways AD 70 to 135*, Grand Rapids: Eerdmans.
Edwards, D. 2004. *Breath of Life: A Theology of the Creator Spirit*, Maryknoll: Orbis.
Eusebius. 1953. *Ecclesiastical History (Books I–V)*, trans. R.J. Deferrari, Washington: Catholic University of America Press.
———. 1955. *Ecclesiastical History (Books VI–X)*, trans. R.J. Deferrari, Washington: Catholic University of America Press.
Frank, M. 1972. *Das Problem der "Zeit" in der deutschen Romantik: Zeitbewußtsein und Bewußtsein von Zeitlichkeit in der frühromantischen Philosophie und in Tiecks Dichtung*, Munich: Winkler Verlag.
———. 1982. *Der kommende Gott. Vorlesungen über die Neue Mythologie*, vol. 1, Frankfurt am Main: Suhrkamp.
———. 1985. *Eine Einführung in Schellings Philosophie*, Frankfurt am Main: Suhrkamp.
———. 1997. *"Unendliche Annäherung": Die Anfänge der philosophischen Frühromantik*, Frankfurt am Main: Suhrkamp.
Fredriksen, P. 2002. 'The Birth of Christianity and the Origins of Christian Anti-Judaism', in P. Fredriksen and A. Reinhartz (eds), *Jesus, Judaism and Christian Anti-Judaism: Reading the New Testament after the Holocaust*, Louisville: Westminster John Knox Press, 8–30.
Gadamer, H.-G. 1998. 'Dialogues in Capri', trans. J. Gaiger, in J. Derrida and G. Vattimo (eds), *Religion*, Cambridge: Polity Press, 200–211.
Girard, R. 2001. *I See Satan Fall Like Lightning*, trans. J.G. Williams, Maryknoll: Orbis Books.
Gould, W. and M. Reeves. 2001. *Joachim of Fiore and the Myth of the Eternal Evangel in the Nineteenth and Twentieth Centuries*, 2nd edn, Oxford: Clarendon Press.
Gray, J. 2008. *Black Mass: Apocalyptic Religion and the Death of Utopia*, London: Penguin Books.
———. 2012. 'The Violent Visions of Slavoj Žižek', *New York Review of Books* 59:12.
Gross, B. 1994. *Messianisme et histoire juive*, Paris: Berg International Éditeurs.
Hegel, G.F.W. 1971. *Early Theological Writings*, trans. T.M. Knox, Philadelphia: University of Pennsylvania Press.
Heidegger, M. 1969. *Identity and Difference*, trans. J. Stambaugh, Chicago: University of Chicago Press.
———. 1985. 'The Self-Assertion of the German University', trans. K. Harries, *Review of Metaphysics* 38:3, 470–480.
———. 1995. *Gesamtausgabe*, vol. 60, *Phänomenologie des Religiösen Lebens*, Frankfurt am Main: Vittorio Klostermann.
———. 2002. *Off the Beaten Track*, ed. and trans. J. Young and K. Haynes, New York and Cambridge: Cambridge University Press.
Henrich, D. 1965/1966. 'Hölderlin über Urteil und Sein. Eine Studie zur Entstehungsgeschichte des Idealismus', *Hölderlin-Jahrbuch* 14, 73–96.
———. 1991. *Konstellationen: Probleme und Debatten am Ursprung der idealistischen Philosophie (1789–1795)*, Stuttgart: Klett-Cotta.
———. 2004. *Grundlegung aus dem Ich: Untersuchungen zur Vorgeschichte des Idealismus: Tübingen – Jena (1790–1794)*, Frankfurt am Main: Suhrkamp.
Heschel, A.J. 1982. *Maimonides: A Biography*, New York: Farrar, Strauss, Giroux.
———. 2001. *The Prophets*, vols 1–2, New York: Harper Perennial Classics.
Hirsch-Reich, B. 1966. 'Joachim von Fiore und das Judentum', in P. Wilpert (ed.), *Judentum im Mittelalter: Beiträge zum christlich-jüdischen Gespräch*, Berlin: Walter de Gruyter & Co, 228–263.
Hölderlin, F. 1961. *Sämtliche Werke: Große Stuttgarter Ausgabe*, vol. 4, ed. F. Beißner, Stuttgart: Kohlhammer.

—— [and/or G.W.F. Hegel and/or F.W.J. Schelling]. 2003. 'Oldest Programme for a System of German Idealism', in J.M. Bernstein (ed.), *Classic and Romantic German Aesthetics*, Cambridge: Cambridge University Press, 185–187.

——. 2008. *Hyperion, or, The Hermit in Greece*, trans. R. Benjamin, Brooklyn: Archipelago Books.

Horbury, W. 2003. *Messianism among Jews and Christians: Biblical and Historical Studies*, London and New York: T&T Clark.

Jameson, F. 1999. 'Marx's Purloined Letter', in M. Sprinker (ed.), *Ghostly Demarcations: A Symposium on Jacques Derrida's Specters of Marx*, London and New York: Verso, 26–67.

Joachim of Fiore. 1957. *Adversus Iudeos*, The Latin Library. Source of the database: Arseneo Frugoni (ed.), *Fonti per la storia d'Italia* 95, Rome: Istituto Storico Italiano per il Medio Evo.

——. 1964. *Expositio in Apocalypsim*, unaltered reproduction from 1527, Frankfurt am Main: Minerva.

——. 1983. *Liber de Concordia Novi ac Veteris Testamenti*, in E.R. Daniel (ed.), *Transactions of the American Philosophical Society* 73:8, Philadelphia.

——. 1999. *Expositio de Prophetia Ignota*, in M. Kaup (ed.), *Gioacchino da Fiore: Commento a una profezia ignota*, Rome: Viella, 147–181.

——. 2009. *Psalterium Decem Chordarum*, Monumenta Germaniae Historica, vol. 20, ed. K.V. Selge, Hannover: Hahnsche Buchhandlung.

Johnson, A.P. 2014. *Eusebius*, London and New York: I.B. Tauris.

Kant, I. 1992. *The Conflict of the Faculties*, trans. M.J. Gregor, Lincoln and London: University of Nebraska Press.

Kaufmann, Y. 1960. *The Religion of Israel: From Its Beginnings to the Babylonian Exile*, trans. M. Greenberg, Chicago: University of Chicago Press.

Kirsch, A. 2008. 'The Deadly Jester', *The New Republic*, 3 Dec.

——. 2009. 'Still the Most Dangerous Philosopher in the West', *The New Republic*, 7 Jan.

Kraus, H.J. 1982. *Geschichte der historisch-kritischen Erforschung des Alten Testaments*, 3rd edn, Neukirchen-Vluyn: Neukirchener Verlag.

Kubik, A. 2011. 'Restauration oder Liberalisierung? Christentumsteoretische Aspekte in Novalis' "Die Christenheit oder Europa"', in M. Pirholt (ed.), *Constructions of German Romanticism: Six Studies*, Uppsala: Historia litterarum, 45–77.

Lasker, D.J. 2007. *Jewish Philosophical Polemics against Christianity in the Middle Ages*, 2nd edn, Oxford and Portland: The Littman Library of Jewish Civilization.

Lasky, M.J. 1976. *Utopia and Revolution: On the Origins of a Metaphor*, Chicago: University of Chicago Press.

Leibowitz, Y. 1992. *Judaism, Human Values, and the Jewish State*, Cambridge and London: Harvard University Press.

Lerner, R. 2001. *The Feast of Saint Abraham: Medieval Millenarians and the Jews*, Philadelphia: University of Pennsylvania Press.

Levinas, E. 1990. *The Levinas Reader*, trans. S. Hand, Oxford and Cambridge: Basil Blackwell.

Lévy, R. 2005. 'Le messianisme de Maïmonide', *Cahiers d'études Lévinassiennes: Messianisme* 4, 151–176.

Lilla, M. 2007. *The Stillborn God: Religion, Politics, and the Modern West*, New York: Alfred A. Knopf.

——. 2008. 'A New, Political Saint Paul?', *The New York Review of Books* 55:16.

Liska, V. 2008. *Giorgio Agambens leerer Messianismus*, Vienna: Schleebrügge Editor.

Löwith, K. 1949. *Meaning in History*, Chicago and London: University of Chicago Press.

——. 1995. 'The Occasional Decisionism of Carl Schmitt', trans. G. Steiner, in R. Wolin (ed.), *Martin Heidegger and European Nihilism*, New York: Columbia University Press, 271–285.

Löwy, M. 2005. *Fire Alarm: Reading Walter Benjamin's 'On the Concept of History'*, trans. C. Turner, London: Verso.

Lukács, G. 1955. *Die Zerstörung der Vernunft: Der Weg des Irrationalismus von Schelling zu Hitler*, Berlin: Aufbau Verlag.

———. 1980. *The Destruction of Reason*, trans. P. Palmer, London: The Merlin Press.
Mack, M. 2003. *German Idealism and the Jew: The Inner Anti-Semitism of Philosophy and German Jewish Responses*, Chicago and London: University of Chicago Press.
Mähl, H.-J. 1965. *Die Idee des goldenen Zeitalters im Werk des Novalis: Studien zur Wesensbestimmung der Frühromantischen Utopie und zu ihren ideengeschichtlichen Voraussetzungen*, Heidelberg: Carl Winter Universitätsverlag.
Maimonides, 1949. *The Code of Maimonides. Book Fourteen: The Book of Judges*, trans. A.M. Hershman, New Haven: Yale University Press.
Marguerat, D. 1999. *La première histoire du Christianisme: Les Actes des apôtres*, Paris and Geneva: Cerf/Labor et Fides.
Martin, D.B. 2009. 'The Promise of Teleology, the Constraints of Epistemology, and the Universal Vision in Paul', in J.D. Caputo and L.M. Alcoff (eds), *St. Paul among the Philosophers*, Bloomington and Indianapolis: Indiana University Press, 109–141.
Marty, É. 2007. *Une querelle avec Alain Badiou, philosophe*, Paris: Gallimard.
Masuzawa, T. 2005. *The Invention of World Religions: Or, How European Universalism Was Preserved in the Language of Pluralism*, Chicago and London: University of Chicago Press.
McGinn, B. (ed.). 1979. *Apocalyptic Spirituality: Treatises and Letters of Lactantius, Adso of Montier-en-Der, Joachim of Fiore, the Franciscan Spirituals, Savonarola*, New York: Paulist Press.
———. 1979. *Visions of the End: Apocalyptic Traditions in the Middle Ages*, New York: Columbia University Press.
———. 1985. *The Calabrian Abbot: Joachim of Fiore in the History of Western Thought*, New York: Macmillan.
McIntyre, J. 1979. *The Shape of Pneumatology: Studies in the Doctrine of the Holy Spirit*, Edinburgh: T&T Clark.
Milbank, J. 1990. *Theology and Social Theory: Beyond Secular Reason*, Oxford and Malden: Blackwell.
———. 2009. 'The Double Glory, or Paradox versus Dialectics: On Not Quite Agreeing with Slavoj Žižek', in C. Davis (ed.), *The Monstrosity of Christ: Paradox or Dialectic?*, Cambridge and London: The MIT Press, 110–233.
Milbank, J., C. Pickstock and G. Ward. 1999. 'Introduction: Suspending the Material: The Turn of Radical Orthodoxy', in eidem (eds), *Radical Orthodoxy: A New Theology*, London: Routledge, 1–20.
Montague, G.T. 2006. *The Holy Spirit: The Growth of a Biblical Tradition*, Eugene: Wipf and Stock.
Müller, G., K. Ries and P. Ziche (eds). 2001. *Die Universität Jena: Tradition und Innovation um 1800*, Stuttgart: Franz Steiner Verlag.
Namli, E. 2013. 'Universal Rights versus Sharia? Reflections on the Moral and Legal Dimensions of Human Rights Law and Sharia', *Religion and Human Rights* 8, 139–161.
Nietzsche, F. 1989. *On the Genealogy of Morals; Ecce Homo*, trans. W. Kaufmann and R.J. Hollingdale, New York: Vintage.
Novalis. 1975. *Schriften*, vol. 4, *Tagebücher, Briefwechsel, Zeitgenössische Zeugnisse*, ed. R. Samuel, H.-J. Mähl and G. Schulz, Stuttgart: Kohlhammer.
———. 1981. *Schriften*, vol. 2, *Das philosophische Werk I*, ed. R. Samuel, H.-J. Mähl and G. Schulz, Stuttgart: Kohlhammer.
———. 1983. *Schriften*, vol. 3, *Das philosophische Werk II*, ed. R. Samuel, H.-J. Mähl and G. Schulz, Stuttgart: Kohlhammer.
———. 1997. *Philosophical Writings*, ed. and trans. M.M. Stoljar, Albany: State University of New York Press.
O'Brien, W.A. 1995. *Novalis: Signs of Revolution*, Durham and London: Duke University Press.
Olsson, A. 2000. *Läsningar av INTET*, Stockholm: Albert Bonniers Förlag.
Pelikan, J. 1966. *The Finality of Jesus Christ in an Age of Universal History: A Dilemma of the Third Century*, Richmond: John Knox Press.
Raynaud, P. 2006. *L'extrême gauche plurielle*, Paris: Autrement.

Redin, J. 2003. *Ars inventrix: En studie av Friedrich von Hardenbergs (Novalis) paraestetiska projekt*, Uppsala: Uppsala universitet.
Reeves, M. 1999. *Joachim of Fiore and the Prophetic Future: A Medieval Study in Historical Thinking*, 2nd edn, Stroud: Sutton Publishing.
Riedl, M. 2004. *Joachim von Fiore: Denker der vollendeten Menschheit*, Würzburg: Königshausen and Neumann.
Rogers, E. 2005. *After the Spirit: A Constructive Pneumatology from Resources outside the Modern West*, Grand Rapids: Eerdmans.
Rosenberg, A. 1977. *Joachim von Fiore: Das Reich des Heiligen Geistes*, Bietigheim: Turm Verlag.
Rowland, C. 2002. *Christian Origins: The Setting and Character of the Most Important Messianic Sect of Judaism*, 2nd edn, London: SPCK.
Ruin, H. 2010. 'Faith, Grace, and the Destruction of Tradition: A Hermeneutic-Genealogical Reading of the Pauline Letters', *Journal for Cultural and Religious Theory* 2:1, 16–34.
Sá Cavalcante Schuback, M. 2005. 'The Work of Experience: Schelling on Thinking beyond Image and Concept', in J.M. Wirth (ed.), *Schelling Now: Contemporary Readings*, Bloomington and Indianapolis: Indiana University Press, 66–83.
Safranski, R. 2014. *Romanticism: A German Affair*, trans. R.E. Goodwin, Evanston: Northwestern University Press.
Saunders, F.S. 2000. *Who Paid the Piper? The CIA and the Cultural Cold War*, 2nd edn, London: Granta.
Schelling, F.W.J. 1977. *Philosophie der Offenbarung 1841/42*, ed. M. Frank, Frankfurt am Main: Suhrkamp.
——. 2008. *Vorlesungen über die Methode des akademischen Studiums*, Norderstedt: Books on Demand.
Scheuer, B. 2008. *The Return of YHWH: The Tension between Deliverance and Repentance in Isaiah 40–55*, Berlin: Walter de Gruyter.
Schlegel, F. 1967. *Kritische Ausgabe*, vol. 2: *Charakteristiken und Kritiken I (1796–1801)*, ed. H. Eichner, Paderborn: Verlag Ferdinand Schöningh.
Schleiermacher, F. 1984. *Briefe bei Gelegenheit der politisch theologischen Aufgabe und des Sendschreibens jüdischer Hausväter*, KGA, vol. 1.2, *Schriften aus der Berliner Zeit 1796–1799*, ed. G. Meckenstock, Berlin and New York: Walter de Gruyter, 327–361.
——. 1996. *On Religion: Speeches to its Cultured Despisers*, 2nd edn, ed. and trans. R. Crouter, Cambridge: Cambridge University Press.
——. 2001. *Dialektik*, ed. M. Frank, Frankfurt am Main: Suhrkamp.
Schmidt, W.H. 1984. 'Geist/Heiliger Geist/Geistesgaben: I. Altes Testament', in *Theologische Realenzyklopädie*, vol. 12. Berlin and New York: Walter de Gruyter, 170–173.
Schmidt-Biggemann, W. 1998. *Philosophia perennis: Historische Umrisse abendländischer Spiritualität in Antike, Mittelalter und Früher Neuzeit*, Frankfurt am Main: Suhrkamp.
Schmitt, C. 2005. *Political Theology: Four Chapters on the Concept of Sovereignty*, trans. G. Schwab, Chicago: University of Chicago Press.
Scholem, G. 1971. 'Toward an Understanding of the Messianic Idea in Judaism', trans. M.A. Meyer, in G. Scholem, *The Messianic Idea in Judaism and Other Essays on Jewish Spirituality*, New York: Schocken Books, 1–36.
Seidler, V.J. 2013. *Remembering 9/11: Terror, Trauma and Social Theory*, New York: Palgrave Macmillan.
Shklar, J.N. 1957. *After Utopia: The Decline of Political Faith*, Princeton: Princeton University Press.
Sigurdson, O. 2012. *Theology and Marxism in Eagleton and Žižek: A Conspiracy of Hope*, New York: Palgrave Macmillan.
Sprinker, M. 1999. 'Introduction', in M. Sprinker (ed.), *Ghostly Demarcations: A Symposium on Jacques Derrida's Specters of Marx*, London and New York: Verso, 1–4.
Strauß, H. 'Messias/Messianische Bewegungen: I. Altes Testament', in *Theologische Realenzyklopädie*, vol. 22, Berlin and New York: Walter de Gruyter, 617–621.

Svenungsson, J. 2010. 'Wrestling with Angels: Or, How to Avoid Decisionist Messianic Romances', *International Journal of Zizek Studies* 4:4 (online).

——. 2014. 'A Secular Utopia: Remarks on the Löwith–Blumenberg Debate', in E. Namli, J. Svenungsson and A. Vincent (eds), *Jewish Thought, Utopia and Revolution*, Amsterdam and New York: Rodopi, 69–84.

Szondi, P. 1976. *Satz und Gegensatz*, Frankfurt am Main: Suhrkamp.

Taubes, J. 2004. *The Political Theology of Paul*, trans. D. Hollander, Stanford: Stanford University Press.

——. 2009. *Occidental Eschatology*, trans. D. Ratmoko, Stanford: Stanford University Press.

Tertullian. 1950. 'Apology', in *Apologetical Works and Minucius Felix Octavius*, trans. R. Arbersmann, E.J. Daly and E.A. Quain, Washington: Catholic University of America Press, 1–126.

Trías, E. 1997. *Pensar la religión*, Barcelona: Destino.

——. 1998. 'Thinking Religion: The Symbol and the Sacred', trans. D. Webb, in J. Derrida and G. Vattimo (eds), *Religion*, Cambridge: Polity Press, 95–110.

——. 2006. *La edad del espíritu*, 2nd edn, Barcelona: Debolsillo.

VanderKam, J.C. 2003. 'Messianism and Apocalypticism', in J.J. Collins, B. McGinn and S.J. Stein (eds), *The Continuum History of Apocalypticism*, New York and London: Continuum, 112–138.

Vattimo, G. 1997. *Beyond Interpretation*, trans. D. Webb, Cambridge: Polity Press.

——. 1998. 'Circumstances', trans. D. Webb, in J. Derrida and G. Vattimo (eds), *Religion*, Cambridge: Polity Press, vii–viii.

——. 1998. 'The Trace of the Trace', trans. D. Webb, in J. Derrida and G. Vattimo (eds), *Religion*, Cambridge: Polity Press, 79–94.

——. 1999. *Belief*, trans. L. D'Isanto and D. Webb, Stanford: Stanford University Press.

——. 2002. *After Christianity*, trans. L. D'Isanto, New York: Columbia University Press.

——. 2003. *Nihilism and Emancipation: Ethics, Politics, and Law*, trans. W. McCuaig, New York: Columbia University Press.

——. 2007. *Ecce comu: Come si ri-diventata ciò che si era*, Rome: Fazi Editore.

——. 2012. 'Dialectics, Difference, Weak Thought', in P.A. Rovatti and G. Vattimo (eds), *Weak Thought*, trans. P. Carravetta, Albany: State University of New York Press, 39–52.

Vattimo, G. (with P. Paterlini). 2009. *Not Being God: A Collaborative Autobiography*, trans. W. McCuaig, New York: Columbia University Press.

Voegelin, E. 1952. *The New Science of Politics*, Chicago: University of Chicago Press.

——. 2006. *Hitler and the Germans*, ed. and trans. D. Clemens and B. Purcell, Columbia and London: University of Missouri Press.

Volf, M. 2011. *A Public Faith: How Followers of Christ Should Serve the Common Good*, Grand Rapids: Brazos Press.

Voltaire. 2010. *La philosophie de l'histoire*, Paris: Nabu Press.

Wagner, T. 2006. *Gottes Herrschaft: Eine Analyse der Denkschrift (Jes 6,1–9,6)*, Leiden and Boston: Brill.

Wallace, M.I. 1996. *Fragments of the Spirit: Nature, Violence and the Renewal of Creation*, New York: Continuum.

Williams, R. 2005. *Why Study the Past: The Quest for the Historical Church*, London: Darton, Longman and Todd Ltd.

Wright, C. 2008. 'Event or Exception? Disentangling Badiou from Schmitt, or, Towards a Politics of the Void', *Theory & Event* 11 (online).

Yovel, Y. 1998. *Dark Riddle: Hegel, Nietzsche and the Jews*, Cambridge: Polity Press.

Zetterholm, K. 2007. 'Elijah and the Messiah as Spokesmen of Rabbinic Ideology', in M. Zetterholm (ed.), *The Messiah in Early Judaism and Christianity*, Minneapolis: Fortress Press, 57–78.

Žižek, S. 1999. 'Carl Schmitt in the Age of Post-Politics', in C. Mouffe (ed.), *The Challenge of Carl Schmitt*, London and New York: Verso, 18–37.

——. 1999. *The Ticklish Subject: The Absent Center of Political Ontology*, London and New York: Verso.
——. 2000. *The Fragile Absolute – Or, Why is the Christian Legacy Worth Fighting For?* London and New York: Verso.
——. 2001. *On Belief*, London and New York: Routledge.
——. 2003. *The Puppet and the Dwarf: The Perverse Core of Christianity*, London and New York: Verso.
——. 2008. *In Defense of Lost Causes*, London and New York: Verso.
——. 2009. 'Dialectical Clarity versus the Misty Conceit of Paradox', in C. Davis (ed.), *The Monstrosity of Christ: Paradox or Dialectic?* Cambridge and London: The MIT Press, 234–305.
——. 2009. 'The Fear of Four Words: A Modest Plea for the Hegelian Reading of Christianity', in C. Davis (ed.), *The Monstrosity of Christ: Paradox or Dialectic?* Cambridge and London: The MIT Press, 24–109.
——. 2009. 'Who Are You Calling Anti-Semitic?', *The New Republic*, 7 Jan.
——. 2010. 'Paul and the Truth Event', in C. Davis, J. Milbank and S. Žižek (eds), *Paul's New Movement: Continental Philosophy and the Future of Christian Theology*, Grand Rapids: Brazos Press, 74–99.
——. 2012. 'Christianity against the Sacred', in S. Žižek and B. Gunjević (eds), *God in Pain: Inversions of Apocalypse*, New York: Seven Stories Press, 43–72.
——. 2012. 'Not Less than Nothing, but Simply Nothing'. Retrieved 24 July 2014 from http://www.versobooks.com/blogs/1046-not-less-than-nothing-but-simply-nothing.

Index

Abu Ghraib prison, 153
Adam of Perseigne, 45, 47
Adorno, Theodor W., vii
Agamben, Giorgio, xii–xiii, 152–153, 155,
 168–181, 184, 188, 192–193, 196–197
alienation, 98, 141, 182–183. *See also*
 materialism.
Amos, 4, 7, 11, 26, 122
Anti-Christ, 45
anti-Jewish stereotypes (tropes), ix, 4, 96–99,
 140, 157, 173, 184.
 adversus (contra) Iudaeos, 41, 56, 60, 96–97,
 99, 138, 173, 190
 See also anti-Semitism and
 supersessionism.
antinomianism, xiii, 173, 176–177. *See also* law.
anti-Semitism, 121, 161, 171, 193. *See also*
 anti-Jewish stereotypes.
anti-utopianism, viii–ix, xi, 15, 109, 114, 132,
 146–147, 166, 204. *See also* critique of
 ideology.
apocalypticism, xiii, 14, 16, 22–24, 31, 36–40,
 43–45, 51, 54–55, 58–59, 88–89, 146,
 158, 161, 165–168, 171–172, 203.
 Book of Daniel, 14
 Book of Joel, 31
 Joachim of Fiore, 37, 44–45, 51, 58–59
 See also apocalyptic messianism.
Arab world, 190
Aron, Raymond, 116
Assyrian Empire, 5, 8, 18
atheism, 106, 151, 155, 181, 185
Augustine, viii, 37–38, 42–43, 51–52, 59, 113,
 127

Babylonian exile, 4, 7, 14, 17–20, 30

Badiou, Alain, xii–xiii, 152–165, 167–173,
 176–184, 186–188, 190, 192–195, 197
Bakunin, Mikhail, 81
Balkan Wars, 122–123, 133, 136, 203
Bar Kokhba revolt, 38, 49, 55, 165
Bell, Daniel, 116
Benedict of Nursia, 50–51, 53
Benjamin, Walter, 146, 167–168, 172–175,
 177–178, 196
 on 'divine' ('pure', 'revolutionary') violence,
 174–175, 178, 196
 on 'mythical' violence, 174, 178, 196.
Bensaïd, Daniel, 164–165
Berlin, Isaiah, vii, 108, 110–112
Bernard McGinn, 41
Bible (Scriptures), viii, x, 10, 40, 43, 45–46, 48,
 51–53, 57, 60, 69, 75, 93, 97, 118, 124,
 129–130, 178, 205
 Hebrew Bible, x, 3, 12, 14, 24–25
 New Testament, 2, 24, 37–39, 46, 57–58, 60,
 133, 140, 158
 Old Testament, x, 17, 33n4, 46, 60, 121, 129,
 140–141
 Septuagint, 25
 Torah, 38, 54–55, 57–58, 168, 178
Blanchot, Maurice, 167
Bloch, Ernst, viii, 147n19
Blumenberg, Hans, 115–116, 148n24
Böhme, Jacob, 80
Bousset, Jacques-Bénigne, viii
Boyarin, Daniel, 161
Brentano, Clemens, 110
Brentano, Franz, 71
Brueggemann, Walter, 15–16
Buber, Martin, viii, xi, 3, 13, 53, 205–206
Buffon, Georges-Louis Leclerc, 111

Burckhardt, Jacob, viii

Calabria, 44, 56–57
capitalism, 120, 135, 143, 164, 180,
   capitalist democracy, 106
   capitalist market logic, 154
   capitalist society, 155, 185–185, 193
   capitalist world (order), 119, 152–153, 159
   late capitalism, 146, 180
   neo-capitalism, 121
Capri symposium, xii, 105–108, 117–118, 122–127, 130, 133–135, 140–146, 152, 166
Cantor, Georg, 159
Catholicism, 69, 81–82, 93, 109, 128, 130
Cistercian Order, 44
Chesterton, G.K., 189
China, 195
Christ, 3, 35–36, 39–40, 43, 48–51, 55, 75, 77, 82–83, 91, 94–95, 128–129, 140, 145, 155–156, 159, 161, 169–171, 173, 175, 183, 186, 188. *See also* Jesus of Nazareth.
Christianity, ix–xi, 1–4, 12, 17–18, 22–24, 29, 32, 36, 38–41, 43, 49, 54–56, 61, 67–68, 70–71, 89–91, 94–95, 97–100, 105, 112, 125, 127–131, 133, 137–143, 145, 151, 154, 156–157, 163, 166, 169, 173, 182–187, 190, 204
   Christian church, 2, 23, 40–43, 45, 48–51–54, 78, 80–82, 92–95, 99, 114, 116, 129, 130, 138, 155, 158, 169, 181, 186
   Christian creed, 24
   Christian tradition (legacy), xii, 1, 3, 24, 35–36, 38, 42–43, 48–49, 51, 55, 59, 68, 93–94, 98, 128–130, 133, 137, 140–141, 144, 166, 172, 185, 187, 190, 204
classless society. *See* communism.
Cohn, Norman, viii
Cold War, 105, 117–118, 123, 136
colonialism, 130, 132, 187
communism, 106, 113–114, 119–120; 160, 164
   Communist Manifesto, 119, 121
   Communist Party, 121
   classless society, 113–114
   dictatorship of the proletariat, 188
communitarianism, 156, 162, 182
Comte, Auguste, viii, 113, 115
Condorcet, Nicolas, viii, 111, 113
Congress for Cultural Freedom, 116
Constantine the Great, 40–42
constitutionalism, 195
cosmopolitism, 32, 68–69, 94, 109, 152, 183
Covenant (Jewish), 6, 23, 35, 156–157
'Old Covenant', 41
'New Covenant', 41
Critchley, Simon, 151, 160
cultural relativism. *See* relativism
Cultural Revolution. *See* revolution.

de Lubac, Henri, 1–2, 32, 80
de Man, Paul, 89
death of God, 93, 105, 124–125, 143, 181
   Holocaust, 161
decisionism, xiii, 160, 164, 188–190, 192–195
decolonization, 127
deconstruction, xii, 144, 196
   deconstructionist philosophy, 185, 197
deism, 137
democracy, 106, 113, 130, 143, 152–153, 174, 177, 181, 192–193, 197–198, 204
   democratic society (state), 116–117, 152, 174, 176
   democratization, 133
Derrida, Jacques, ix, xii–xiii, 105, 107–108, 118–123, 138–147, 152–153m 162, 167, 178, 190–191, 193, 195–197
Descartes, René, 108
Deuteronomistic History, 13, 25, 205
dictatorship of the proletariat. *See* communism.

Eastern bloc, 106, 116–117, 123
embodiment, 76, 163, 179. *See also* materiality.
Egypt, 4–5, 8, 16, 19
End of Days, 39, 43, 50, 54, 57, 97, 171. *See also* Last Judgement.
Engels, Friedrich, 81, 119
Enlightenment, viii, 64–65, 67–72, 74–75, 91, 97, 106–107, 112, 117, 123–124, 126, 137, 143, 145–146
eschatology, viii, xi, 20, 32, 37–38, 40, 45, 55–57, 59, 90, 113, 115, 133, 166, 172
   eschaton, 108, 113
   realized eschatology, 171–172
Europe, vii, ix, 44, 56, 61, 64, 67–74, 82–83, 90, 94, 98, 105, 107, 111, 114, 116, 119–120, 123, 132, 140, 151–152, 154, 166
   European culture, 97, 100
   European literature, 70, 108
   European philosophy (thought), 75, 100, 122, 142, 154
Eurocentrism, 130
European Union (EU), 120
Eusebius of Caesarea, 40–43, 51–52, 97, 205
Exodus (motif), 1, 4–5, 18, 73
   Book of Exodus, 4, 10, 25
Ezekiel, 20, 26, 31

Fascism, 110, 174, 176
Fichte, Johann Gottlieb, 70–71, 76, 85–88, 101n36, 103n76, 108–110, 115
First Gulf War, 133
First World War, 176, 192
France, 83, 108, 111, 160
Franciscans (radical), 80
Frank, Manfred, 86–87
Freemasonry, 64
Freud, Sigmund, 119, 162, 190
Fukuyama, Francis, 119
fundamentalism (religious extremism), 122, 126, 151, 181, 203

Gadamer, Hans-Georg, xii, 105–107, 125
Germany, xi, 64, 69, 108; Prussia, 107, 110–112; Weimar, 193; West Germany, 116, 193
ghost (spectre), 117, 119–123, 142, 145–146, 183, 190–191. *See also* hauntology.
Girard, René, 10, 128–129
globalatinazation, 143
Goethe, Johann Wolfgang, 71
Görres, Joseph, 110
Gottfried of Auxerre, 56
Gray, John, viii, 201n95, 204
Gross, Benjamin, 22–23, 37
Guantánamo Bay, 153

Habermas, Jürgen, 152
hauntology, 13. *See also* ghost (spectre).
Hegel, G.W.F., viii, 66–67, 75–76, 81, 85, 87, 93, 98–99, 101n30, 104n116, 115, 136, 138–140, 143, 145, 182, 184–185, 189, 205
Heidegger, Martin, 107, 114, 125–128, 142, 145, 155
heresy, 39, 49
  heretics, 36, 57
hermeneutics, xii, 46, 69, 127, 130–133, 135, 204
  hermeneutic paradigm, 157;
  hermeneutic philosophy, 107, 125, 131, 193
Herodotus, 3
Heschel, Abraham, viii, xi, 3–4, 6, 11–13, 16, 28, 32, 124
historiography, 39–40, 163
Hitler, Adolf, vii, 111–112
Hoffmann, E.T.A., 64
Hölderlin, Friedrich, 67, 71, 75–77, 81, 85–86, 88, 101n30, 101n35, 101n36, 103n76
homosexuality, 162
Horkheimer, Max, vii
Hosea, 26

Howden, Roger, 45
human rights, 120, 186

idealism (German), xiii, 70, 76, 84–87, 107–109, 136, 141, 142, 190
identity politics, 154, 162, 171. *See also* multiculturalism.
ideology, vii–viii, 36, 105, 108, 111–113, 115–117, 120–121, 123, 162, 187, 192
  critique of ideology, xii, 107
  end of ideology, xii, 108, 116, 124
imperialism, 130, 133
Iraq invasion, 152–153
Isaiah, 5, 26, 122, 124
  Book of Isaiah, 2, 14, 18, 20–21, 23, 28–30, 58
  Deutero-Isaiah, 21, 30–31, 141
  Proto-Isaiah, 8–9, 11, 13, 18, 30
  Trito-Isaiah, 30
Islam, 44, 145
Israel (modern state), 151, 161
Israel (kingdom of antiquity), 8, 18, 40
Israel (theological notion), viii, 4–6, 8–9, 19–21, 25–27, 30–32, 54, 58, 139, 157
  'New Israel', 41, 97

Jacobin Terror, 84, 195
Jacobi, Friedrich Heinrich, 86–87, 109
Jameson, Fredric, 142, 164, 191
Jansenism, 194
Jena, 70–71, 77, 81, 83, 85–86, 91–93, 97, 110
Jeremiah, 6–7, 20, 26
Jerusalem, 7, 18, 20–21, 26, 30–32, 41, 44
Jesuits, 64
Jesus of Nazareth, ix, 1–2, 17, 22–24, 29, 34n42, 38–41, 48, 55, 97, 128, 140, 145–146, 155–157, 166, 169, 183. *See also* Christ.
Joachim of Fiore, viii, xi, 35–38, 43–47, 49–61, 67, 73, 80–82, 94, 96–97, 100, 113–115, 124, 129, 136, 138, 140–141, 146, 184–185, 190, 203, 205
  intellectus spiritualis, 46, 52, 58, 60
  Florenisan Order, 44
  on biblical interpretation, 45–47, 60
  on the *status* (age) of the spirit, xi, 47, 49–50, 53, 56–57, 59–60, 138, 146, 203, 205
  on the Trinity, 35–37, 46, 49–51, 94
Joel, 2, 31, 47–48, 51, 137
Judah (kingdom of antiquity), 7–8, 18
Judaism, ix, 2, 4, 18, 29, 32, 38, 40–41, 54, 56, 58, 61, 89, 97–99, 139–141, 145, 163, 166, 169, 173, 179, 183–184, 190, 204–205

Hellenic Judaism, 157, 161, 183
rabbinic Judaism, 1, 4, 22–23, 38, 49, 51, 54–55, 89, 146, 156, 166, 172
Second Temple Judaism, 4, 22, 55
justice, viii, xiii, 5, 7–16, 20, 22–24, 26–32, 47, 53, 55, 58, 60, 88, 118, 121, 124, 144–147, 158, 164, 167–168, 174–178, 183, 187, 189, 191, 195–198, 204–206
and righteousness, 7, 11–13, 191

Kabbalah, 56
Kant, Immanuel, 71, 75, 77–78, 84–86, 88, 95, 97–99, 110, 138, 142–145, 196
Kaufmann, Yehezkel, viii, xi, 3–4, 16, 32, 72
Kierkegaard, Søren, 81, 111
Kirsch, Adam, 201n95
Kristeva, Julia, 162

Lacan, Jacques, 179–181, 184
Last Judgement, 35, 37. *See also* End of Days.
law, 87, 97, 139–140, 144, 160, 170, 173–181, 188, 193, 195–198
and grace, xiii, 156–157, 173, 179, 182, 184, 195–196
and desire, 180
biblical (divine, revealed) law, 4, 12–13, 57–58, 156–157
Jewish law (*halakha*), 166, 173, 175, 179, 181, 183
'hyperbolic' (obscene) law, 181, 183
international law, 120, 152, 177
'law of faith' ('spirit'), 176–178
laws of nature (cosmic law), 57, 84, 115
'law of works', 176, 180; Roman law, 173, 183
rule of law, 174, 196. *See also* antinomianism.
Leibniz, Gottfried Wilhelm, 108
Leibowitz, Yeshayahu, 179
Levinas, Emmanuel, 17, 140, 144, 178–179, 181, 200n80
Lessing, Gotthold, 81, 115
liberalism: economic (market), 119, 121, 124, 156, 162; political, 153, 155, 185, 192–193, 195
Lilla, Mark, 93, 154–155
linguistic turn, 135
Locke, John, 108
Löwith, Karl, vii–x, xiii, 114–116, 121–122, 148n24, 192–193, 195, 204
Meaning in History, vii, x, 114, 121, 192
Lukács, Georg, vii, 111–112
Luke–Acts, 2, 39, 48
Luther, Martin, 68, 75, 82

Lutheran orthodoxy, 108
Lyotard, Jean-François, 162

Machiavelli, Niccolò, 113
Mähl, Hans-Joachim, 74, 81
Maimonides (Moshe ben Maimon), 17, 57–59, 61
Maoism, 195. *See also* Mao Zedong.
Marion, Jean-Luc, 144
Marty, Eric, 162–163
Marx, Karl, viii, 113, 115, 118–122, 143, 145, 160, 162, 164, 192
Marxism, vii, 111, 114, 118–119, 121–122, 160, 164, 173, 192
materialism (historical, dialectical), 111, 121–122, 160, 168, 185–186.
materiality (material existence), ix, 25, 45, 51, 97, 120, 160–161, 163–164, 171, 178, 181, 187, 190. *See also* embodiment.
mathematics, 158
May 1968, 159
Mendelssohn, Moses, 71
Mendenhall, George, 15
Messiah, ix, 2, 16, 23–24, 38, 54–55, 57–58, 146, 166–168, 172. *See also* messianic figure.
messianism, x, xii, 16–24, 38, 54, 59, 83, 88–91, 107, 109, 121–122, 142, 144–146, 154–155, 160–161, 164–169, 175–170, 179, 184, 188
apocalyptic messianism, xiii, 17, 22–24, 38, 54, 59, 158, 160, 165–166, 168, 172 (*see also* apocalypticism).
Christian messianism, viii, 156, 166
Jewish messianism, viii, 2, 16, 23–24, 56, 59, 156, 158, 166
messianic age (era, times), 22, 48, 55, 57–59, 61, 167
messianic event, 1, 16, 23–24, 144, 147, 156, 159, 167, 171, 184 (*see also* redemption).
messianic figure, 20, 23, 28, 36, 38, 54–55, 141, 157, 169 (*see also* Messiah)
messianic time, 171–172
and messianicity, 144–145, 167
restorative messianism, xiii, 22–24, 158, 165–166, 168, 172
Micah, 11, 26–28
Milbank, John, 151, 165, 185–187, 189, 204
militarism, 8–9, 174
millenarianism (chiliasm), viii, 43, 80, 113
modernity (modern era), viii, xiii, 10, 12, 36, 107, 111, 113, 123, 126, 134–137, 151, 173, 180, 192, 205
modern philosophy, 115, 125, 127, 136, 164

modern project, 115
Mohammed, 75
monotheism, 4, 30, 184
Montaigne, Michel, 77
Montanism, 49
Montesquieu, Charles, 111
multiculturalism, 154. *See also* identity politics.
Müntzer, Thomas, 80
Napoleon, 64, 110
Napoleonic wars, 64, 107, 110
nationalism, 109, 117
Nazism (National Socialism), 99, 111–114, 116, 153, 161–162, 171, 176, 193.
  Third Reich, 114–115
Neo-Babylonian Empire, 18, 21
New York, 152, 173
Newton, Isaac, 108
Nietzsche, Friedrich, 10, 33n9, 105, 110–111, 125, 128, 131
nihilism, 108, 131–132, 167
Novalis (Friedrich von Hardenberg), xi, 66–78, 80–88, 90–96, 98–99, 101n36, 107, 109–113, 117–118, 123–125, 129–130, 136–137, 166
  Christendom or Europe, 67–74, 76, 79, 84, 90, 92–94, 98, 117

Ohlsson, Anders, 108–109
oil crisis, 127
Orosius, Paul, viii

Paris Commune, 160, 167, 194
parousia (Second Coming of Christ), xi, 24, 38–40, 43, 55, 171–172
particularism (particularity), ix, 100, 145–146, 154, 156, 161, 163, 170–172, 181, 183, 187–189, 204
Pascal, Blaise, 108
Patočka, Jan, 144
patriarchy, 132
Paul, 38, 75, 77, 82, 94, 153, 155–163, 168–176, 179–183, 188
Pauline epistles, 38, 155, 169–171, 174; 1 Corinthians; 169; Galatians, 155, 169; Romans, 155, 157, 175
Pharisees, 22–23
phenomenology, 88, 144, 155, 193
philosophy of history, vii, xi–xiii, 2, 37, 65–67, 89, 99, 125, 132, 146, 193
pietism, 80, 108
Plato, 144
Platonism, 161
pneumatic motif. *See* spirit.

political theology, xiii, 8, 12–13, 41–43, 53, 92–93, 99, 195, 204–205
Popper, Karl, vii
positivism (legal), 193
postmodernism, 126, 135, 152, 186, 193, 197
postpolitical situation (postpolitics), 153, 168
poststructuralism, 163
progress(ion), viii, 29, 35–36, 47, 50, 53, 59, 64, 79, 94, 96, 113, 116, 129, 139–141, 174, 176–177, 193
prophetism, viii, x, xii–xiii, 3–18, 22, 31, 36–37, 39, 45, 47, 72–74, 88, 107, 115, 117–118, 121, 124, 191, 195, 198, 205–206
  prophetic literature, x–xi, 3–4, 6–7, 9–10, 14–15, 17–19, 22–30, 32, 36, 47, 54, 57, 59, 66, 137, 189, 191, 205
  prophetic promise, 1–2, 14, 16, 30
Protestantism, 3–4, 11, 68–69, 80–82, 92–94, 96–97, 99, 106, 138, 157
Proudhon, Pierre-Joseph, viii
providence, viii, 40, 42–43, 51–52, 65–66, 115–116
psychoanalysis, 180–181
  big Other, 180–183
  superego, 180–183
psychoanalytical philosophy, 173, 179, 181

Qumran literature (Dead See Scrolls), 18

Radical Orthodoxy, 185
Ralph of Coggeshall, 45
Rancière, Jacques, 188
Ratzinger, Joseph, 151
realism (theological), 186
realized eschatology, *see* eschatology
realpolitik, 173, 179
redemption, viii–ix, 1, 15–16, 18–20, 22–24, 30–31, 35–37, 39, 44–45, 47–48, 54–55, 58–59, 73–74, 80, 89–90, 94, 97, 113, 115, 121, 124, 130–133, 137–138, 141, 146, 156–158, 166–168, 171–172, 179, 183, 191, 197. *See also* messianic event.
Reformation, 68–69, 74, 80, 82, 84, 93, 97, 114, 123
refugees, 159
Renaissance, 135
Reinhold, Karl Leonard, 70, 84–86
relativism: cultural, 154, 156, 186; legal, 193
religion of the spirit (higher religion), xi–xii, 61, 66–67, 74–77, 81–83, 89–92, 94–96, 98, 107, 109, 129, 131, 133, 136–137, 141–142, 204
Revelation of John, 39, 43, 43, 51–52

revolution, 44, 84, 116, 155, 156, 159–160, 187
  Cultural revolution, 117, 163, 167, 194
  French revolution, 68, 74, 83–84, 90–93, 159, 166, 194
  October Revolution, 159
  revolutionary event, 198, 194–195, 197
  revolutionary movements, viii, 70
  revolutionary impulse (force), 168, 172, 187
  revolutionary project, 187–188
  revolutionary subject, 178, 194
Richard the Lionheart, 45, 47
Ricœur, Paul, 144
Riedl, Mattias, 53, 59
Roman Empire (antiquity), 36, 39–40, 42–43, 156; Holy Roman Empire, 52, 110
Romanticism, viii, x–xii, 61, 64–100, 105, 107–114, 123–125, 129–133, 136–137, 141, 146, 166, 168, 184, 190, 192, 203
  Romantic philosophy, 74, 76, 83, 85–89, 109, 129;
  romanticizing, 72, 93
Rosicrucians, 64
Rousseau, Jean-Jacques, 152, 160
Rushdie, Salman, 122
Rushdie Affair, 203

Safranski, Rüdiger, 70, 109–110, 116
Saladin, 44–45
Schelling, F.W.J., vii, xi, 66–67, 71, 75–76, 81–83, 87–88, 90–91, 93–96, 99–100, 103n76, 107, 109–111, 115, 125, 129, 136–137, 141, 201n93, 205
Schiller, Friedrich, 64, 110
Schlegel, August Wilhelm, 71
Schlegel, Caroline, 71
Schlegel, Friedrich, 67, 71, 74–77, 81, 85–86, 101n36, 108–109
Schleiermacher, Friedrich, xi, 67, 71, 77–80–81, 83, 87–88, 90–96, 98–99, 107, 109, 129, 137, 203
  On Religion, 67, 77–79, 83, 87, 90, 92–93, 99
Schmitt, Carl, 112–115, 152–153, 173–175, 192–195, 197, 205
  neo-Schmittian philosophy, xiii
  on the state of exception (emergency), 173–175
Schneerson, Menachem Mendel, 165
Schoenberg, Arnold, 159
Scholem, Gershom, viii, 16–18, 24, 158, 165
Schopenhauer, Arthur, 110–111
Second Coming of Christ. *See* parusia.
Second World War, vii–viii, 111

secularization (secular culture), ix, xi, 65–66, 73, 97, 100, 108, 113, 115, 131, 133, 140, 166, 173, 190, 195, 203
Seleucid Empire, 14
September 11 attacks, 151–152, 173
Shakespeare, William, 118
Sicily (medieval kingdom), 44
social democracy, 193
socialism, 111
Spinoza, Baruch, 108, 162
spirit, xiii, 2, 9, 24–31, 35, 41, 45–54, 56–57, 59–61, 66, 69, 75–76, 80–81, 83–84, 93, 96, 110, 117, 122, 129, 133–134, 137–138–140, 142–143, 146–147, 170, 172, 182, 184, 188–191, 195, 205
  absolute spirit, 93, 182
  and letter, xiii, 60, 68, 96, 129–130, 140, 195
  decent (outpouring) of the spirit, 2, 30–31, 47–48, 51–52, 56, 59–60, 80, 137–138
  doctrine of the Holy Spirit, 24, 49, 128
  spiritual perfection, 36–37, 53, 59, 114
  world-spirit (*Weltgeist*), 79, 99
spiritualization, 22, 96, 130, 161
state of exception (emergency). *See* Carl Schmitt.
supersessionism, 185, 203. *See also* anti-Jewish stereotypes.
Szondi, Peter, 89

Talmudic literature, 22–23, 54
Taubes, Jacob, viii, 155, 173
temporality, 89, 125, 131–132
Tertullian, 39–40
theocracy, 12, 204
theodicy, 65
theology of history, ix, xi, 1–3, 7, 23–24, 32, 36–38, 41–45, 49, 51, 59, 65, 67, 73, 80, 89, 114–115, 125, 166, 190, 193, 203–204
theopolitics, xiii, 8, 13–15, 53, 92, 94, 96, 99, 204–206
Thermidor coup, 194
Thucydides, 3, 38
Tieck, Ludwig, 71
Tingsten, Herbert, vii
totalitarianism, vii–viii, xi, 35, 105–108, 112–114, 116, 119, 121, 131, 192, 197, 205. *See also* ideology.
Trías, Eugenio, xii, 105, 107, 123, 125, 133–137, 140–142, 147
Trotsky, Leon, 162
Trotskyism, 164

United States, 112, 114, 152

universalism (universality), viii, 31–32, 39–40, 94, 96–97–98, 100, 109, 130, 133, 141–146, 152–153–154, 156–157, 162, 170, 173, 181–183, 185–189, 203–205

utopianism, vii–viii, xi–xii, 36, 59, 83, 90–91, 105–107, 113–114, 116–117, 121, 123–124, 131, 133, 137, 146, 166, 191–192, 203–204

Vattimo, Gianni, xii, 105, 107–108, 122, 125–133, 135–137, 140–142, 147, 185, 190, 193, 204

Veit (Schlegel), Dorothea, 71, 81

Vico, Giambattista, viii

violence: 'divine'/'pure'/'revolutionary' versus 'mythological'. *See* Walter Benjamin.

Voegelin, Eric, vii, 112–115

Voltaire, viii, 65–67, 115

voluntarism, 160

von Arnim, Achim, 110

'War on Terror', 151, 173, 176

Weber, Max, 106, 143

Weil, Simone, 164

Weimar, 70–71

Weimar Republic, 153, 192

Winter, Cécile, 161

xenophobia, 154

Zedong, Mao, 117, 163. *See also* Maoism.

Zionism, 205

Žižek, Slavoj, xii –xiii, 152–153, 155, 179–190, 193–194, 197–198, 200n80, 201n93, 201n95

Zvi, Sabbatai, 165

MAKING SENSE OF HISTORY
Studies in Historical Cultures
General Editor: Stefan Berger
Founding Editor: Jörn Rüsen

Bridging the gap between historical theory and the study of historical memory, this series crosses the boundaries between both academic disciplines and cultural, social, political and historical contexts. In an age of rapid globalization, which tends to manifest itself on an economic and political level, locating the cultural practices involved in generating its underlying historical sense is an increasingly urgent task.

Volume 1
Western Historical Thinking: An Intercultural Debate
   Edited by Jörn Rüsen

Volume 2
Identities: Time, Difference, and Boundaries
   Edited by Heidrun Friese

Volume 3
Narration, Identity, and Historical Consciousness
   Edited by Jürgen Straub

Volume 4
Thinking Utopia: Steps into Other Worlds
   Edited by Jörn Rüsen, Michael Fehr, and Thomas W. Rieger

Volume 5
History: Narration, Interpretation, Orientation
   Jörn Rüsen

Volume 6
The Dynamics of German Industry: Germany's Path toward the New Economy and the American Challenge
   Werner Abelshauser

Volume 7
Meaning and Representation in History
   Edited by Jörn Rüsen

Volume 8
Remapping Knowledge: Intercultural Studies for a Global Age
   Mihai I. Spariosu

Volume 9
Cultures of Technology and the Quest for Innovation
   Edited by Helga Nowotny

Volume 10
Time and History: The Variety of Cultures
   Edited by Jörn Rüsen

Volume 11
Narrating the Nation: Representations in History, Media and the Arts
   Edited by Stefan Berger, Linas Eriksonas, and Andrew Mycock

Volume 12
Historical Memory in Africa: Dealing with the Past, Reaching for the Future in an Intercultural Context
   Edited by Mamadou Diawara, Bernard Lategan, and Jörn Rüsen

Volume 13
New Dangerous Liaisons: Discourses on Europe and Love in the Twentieth Century
   Edited by Luisa Passerini, Liliana Ellena, and Alexander C.T. Geppert

Volume 14
Dark Traces of the Past: Psychoanalysis and Historical Thinking
   Edited by Jürgen Straub and Jörn Rüsen

Volume 15
A Lover's Quarrel with the Past: Romance, Representation, Reading
   Ranjan Ghosh

Volume 16

The Holocaust and Historical Methodology
  Edited by Dan Stone

Volume 17

What is History For? Johann Gustav Droysen and the Functions of Historiography
  Arthur Alfaix Assis

Volume 18

Vanished History: The Holocaust in Czech and Slovak Historical Culture
  Tomas Sniegon

Volume 19

Jewish Histories of the Holocaust: New Transnational Approaches
  Edited by Norman J.W. Goda

Volume 20

Helmut Kohl's Quest for Normality: His Representation of the German Nation and Himself
  Christian Wicke

Volume 21

Marking Evil: Holocaust Memory in the Global Age
  Edited by Amos Goldberg and Haim Hazan

Volume 22

The Rhythm of Eternity: The German Youth Movement and the Experience of the Past, 1900–1933
  Robbert-Jan Adriaansen

Volume 23

Viktor Frankl's Search for Meaning: An Emblematic 20th-Century Life
  Timothy Pytell

Volume 24

Designing Worlds: National Design Histories in an Age of Globalization
  Edited by Kjetil Fallan and Grace Lees-Maffei

Volume 25

Doing Conceptual History in Africa
  Edited by Axel Fleisch and Rhiannon Stephens

Volume 26

Divining History: Prophetism, Messianism and the Development of the Spirit
  Jayne Svenungsson

www.ingramcontent.com/pod-product-compliance
Lightning Source LLC
Chambersburg PA
CBHW072151100526
44589CB00015B/2186